Artificial Intelligence and Patents

An International Perspective on Patenting AI-Related Inventions

AIPPI Law Series

VOLUME 8

Series Editors

AIPPI

Introduction & Contents/Subjects

Books in this series are developed within the framework of the International Association for the Protection of Intellectual Property (AIPPI), a non-affiliated non-profit organization dedicated to the development and improvement of legal regimes for the protection of intellectual property at both national and international levels.

Objective & Readership

The aim is to publish innovative work appealing to practitioners, other users of IP systems and academics.

The titles in this series are listed at the back of this volume.

Artificial Intelligence and Patents

An International Perspective on Patenting AI-Related Inventions

Edited by

Jonathan P. Osha

Wolters Kluwer

Published by:
Kluwer Law International B.V.
PO Box 316
2400 AH Alphen aan den Rijn
The Netherlands
E-mail: lrs-sales@wolterskluwer.com
Website: www.wolterskluwer.com/en/solutions/kluwerlawinternational

Sold and distributed by:
Wolters Kluwer Legal & Regulatory U.S.
920 Links Avenue
Landisville, PA 17538
United States of America
E-mail: customer.service@wolterskluwer.com

ISBN: 978-94-035-2215-9

e-ISBN: 978-94-035-2223-4
Web PDF ISBN: 978-94-035-2231-9

AIPPI Law Series ISBN 98-888-8020-8

About the Editor

Jonathan P. Osha is the founding partner of Osha Bergman Watanabe & Burton LLP, an international IP firm with offices in the United States, France, Japan, China, and the UAE. Jonathan is a patent attorney and attorney at law with more than 33 years of experience in the field. His practice covers the full range of IP but he places special emphasis on assisting clients in building IP portfolios in the high-tech space. He holds an electrical engineering degree from Cornell University and a Juris Doctor degree from George Mason University School of Law. Jonathan is very active in IP associations, particularly relative to efforts toward international harmonization of laws and to laws and practices related to artificial intelligence (AI). He was a member of the Bureau of AIPPI from 2010 to 2020, serving as Reporter General for the last two years of that time. He remains an active member of the AIPPI-US group where he serves on the US steering committee and on the international IP Office Practice standing committee. He is a former member of the board of the American Intellectual Property Association (AIPLA), a member of the AIPLA harmonization committee, and currently chairs the AIPLA AI task force. At Intellectual Property Owners (IPO), Jonathan serves as co-vice chair of the Artificial Intelligence and New Emerging Technologies committee. Internationally, Jonathan chairs the Industry IP5 AI Task Force.

Outside the practice of law, Jonathan is the founder and president of Compudopt, Inc., a U.S. non-profit organization that provides computers, technical training, and broadband internet connections to children and families in underserved communities. To date, Compudopt has donated more than 65,000 free computers to children in need, provided almost 300,000 hours of technology training, and positively impacted more than 200,000 individuals.

About the Contributors

Ishraga Abutaha is an attorney at law at Abutaha Intellectual Property in Dubai with more than 25 years of IP experience. She holds an LLM Degree in Comparative Law concentrating on International Intellectual Property and is a certified federal court interpreter (English-Arabic). She has been appointed as an IP Expert by the UAE Federal Courts and Dubai Courts (First Instance and Court of Appeal) and has rendered expert opinions and oral expert testimony in more than 300 cases. She is also a member of the Sudanese Bar Association (Admitted Practicing Lawyer with full right of audience before all courts), the California State Bar Association (Foreign Attorney Registration), and the New York State Bar (Granted Motion to take bar Exam as Foreign Lawyer).

Seong Tahk Ahn is a Korean patent attorney with more than 25 years of experience in IP, and a partner at Lee & Ko IP in Seoul. He has been involved in patent prosecution, enforcement, opinion work, portfolio management, licensing and due diligence in a wide variety of technologies, including artificial intelligence (AI), telecommunication, business model, internet search, automation and biotechnology-electronics/IT fusion technology. He also served as an IP advisor for the Korea Trade Commission. In 2018, he updated the Korean Chapter of *Software Patents Worldwide* published by Wolters Kluwer. He also co-authored answers to AIPPI study questions related to AI and software on behalf of the AIPPI Korean Group in 2020 and 2021. Currently, he is the president of the AIPPI Korean Group, and a member of a standing committee on Patent and statutory committee on Membership in the AIPPI. He majored in electrical engineering and biology in Seoul National University and received an LLM degree in Georgetown University Law Center. He is also a member of the Illinois Bar.

Stefania Bergia (partner of Simmons & Simmons) is a patent and trademark attorney who assists clients, including on a pan-European level, on an extensive range of judicial and extra-judicial matters of IP law. She recently represented before the Unified Patent Court (UPC) a client for which she obtained the first two orders from the UPC Milan local division to preserve evidence of infringement. She then started two infringement actions before the UPC. Stefania received a Juris Doctor degree at the Catholic University of Milan and a PhD in IP Law at the University of Parma, where over the years has taught a course on 'Legislation and Patents'. She teaches postgraduate courses and is a lecturer for the annual 'Industrial Property – Patents' course organised by the Polytechnic University of Milan as well as for Just Legal Services' post-graduate courses on IP matters. She was also recently appointed as a trainer in the first online patent course ('Patent X') organised by Harvard University/ WIPO. Stefania is a member of the board of AIPPI Italia and heads the patent group of AIPPI Italia. She is a member, and deeply involved in the activities, of other main IP associations including AIPPI International and INTA.

Christophe Besnard is a registered French and European patent attorney with more than 20 years of experience in IP. He is also registered as European patent litigator before the Unitary Patent Court. Christophe focuses on patent practice, particularly strategic counselling, patent drafting, prosecution and litigation. Being based in the Paris office of the international IP firm Osha BWB, he advises non-European companies in European proceedings. He also handles international patent portfolios for established French companies, while helping young, innovative companies to define IP strategies aligned with their objectives. His practice covers a wide range of technologies, including computer implemented inventions. Christophe holds a Master's degree in Engineering and a LLM in Intellectual Property Law & Management.

Dr Hannah Ivy Brown is an Australian registered patent attorney and trade mark attorney, and a Principal of Davies Collison Cave Pty Ltd, an international specialist IP law firm, where she specializes in patents for high-tech inventions in ICT, (micro/ nano-)electronics and electrical engineering, physics, semiconductor science and technology and materials science. Previously, Hannah was a Research Professor at the Microelectronics Research Center at the New Jersey Institute of Technology, USA, a Resident Consultant at Bell Laboratories (Lucent Technologies) in Murray Hill, New Jersey, USA, a Visiting Fellow at the Australian National University, a Research Associate in the Materials Science & Engineering Department at North Carolina State University, USA, and a Research Associate in the School of Chemistry at La Trobe University, Australia. She has post-graduate degrees in physics and intellectual property law from the University of Melbourne and over 40 refereed technical publications. She is co-chair of AIPPI's standing committee on IT & Internet, and regularly represents Australia at AIPPI Congresses.

James Carlson is an attorney at law and patent attorney with Osha Bergman Watanabe & Burton LLP in the United States. James has a degree in electrical engineering from Georgia Institute of Technology and a juris doctor degree from University of Houston Law Center. James' practice focuses on patent prosecution and client counselling in the fields of computer software, gaming, data processing and artificial intelligence. He has extensive experience with handling subject matter eligibility issues at the US patent and trademark office and is a frequent speaker and author on these topics.

Héctor E. Chagoya-Cortes is Chemical Engineer and Attorney-at-law. After 24 years of practice when he prosecuted more than 10,000 patents across technology fields and representing a wide variety of applicants, he founded Mextrategy® in 2021. He has past experience in programming and in simulation of chemical processes, and currently focuses his practice on strategic consultancy for maximizing the impact and value of IP assets including patent drafting, patent portfolio management, patent transactions, and valuations. He is past President of LES Mexico, past International Vice-president of LES International, among other leadership positions in other professional associations. In AIPPI he represents the Mexican group in the Pharmaceutical Patents and Trade Secrets Committees and is part of the Information Technologies Committee and the Patents Committee within the Mexican group.

Peter Sungjin Chun is a registered Korean patent attorney with expertise in AI, software, computers, and communications. He is also a managing partner and a founder of MUHANN, and has been practising for more than 23 years. MUHANN is now one of the leading IP law firms in Korea. He also served as a research engineer for Samsung Electronics for several years. Mr Chun studied computer science and engineering at Seoul National University, and later attended graduate school. In 1992, during his time at university, he developed a speaker recognition system using neural networks. As part of his graduate studies, Mr Chun was involved in developing a machine translation system using AI. He is currently serving as the vice president of AIPPI Korea as well as the vice president of APAA Korea.

Anthony Curro is a senior intellectual property attorney at IBM with over 17 years of IP experience. He is a former examiner at the U.S. Patent and Trademark Office (USPTO) and is a member of the bars of New York, New Jersey, District of Columbia, and the USPTO. He has a bachelor's degree from Colgate University and a Juris Doctor degree from Tulane University Law School, where he was Managing Editor of the *Tulane Law Review*.

Pauline Debré is a lawyer at the Paris Bar. She heads the IP/TMT practice of Linklaters in Paris and has considerable experience in IP litigation and, specifically, patent litigation. She focuses on handling complex cross-border patent and trademark litigations, notably in the healthcare and telecommunications sectors. She assists major clients in all types of proceedings, including preliminary injunctions, seizures (saisie-contrefaçon), revocation and infringement actions, arbitration and mediation, often in a global context (parallel litigation in the US, pending oppositions before the EPO). Pauline also assists clients from various industries with negotiating and drafting contracts related to IP rights (JV agreements, R&D agreements, co-existence agreements) and on projects and corporate deals (acquisitions, carve out) where IP is a key asset. Pauline co-heads the Patent Commission of the French group of AIPPI as well as the Standing Committee on Patents and Standards. She is also a member of the Excom of APEB.

Antonio Di Bernardo is an Italian and European patent and trademark attorney who represents clients in trademark, patent and design matters. He is also a patent litigator qualified for representing clients before the Unitary Patent Court (UPC). He graduated in electronic engineering from the Polytechnic of Milan, where he also obtained a master's degree in IP management. Antonio is specialised in patents for software, telecommunications and physics and has a huge experience in SEPs (Standard Essential Patents) evaluation and litigation. Antonio has represented clients in hundreds of litigation matters and has been appointed as court technical expert in patent and software (computer forensics) litigations. He has also assisted public prosecutors with evaluations in the field of trademarks, designs, and patents. He is member of the professional associations AIPPI, EPI and LES and has been teaching 'Management of Licensing' for a couple of years in University 'La Statale' in Milan.

Jochen Ehlers is a German and European patent attorney and European trade mark and design attorney practicing with Eisenführ Speiser in Hamburg, Germany. Jochen mainly works on patent infringement cases and on the prosecution and defence of intellectual property. Jochen also has special experience in writing and defending national, European and international patent applications. He is the publisher and co-author of the 'Beck'scher Kommentar' on the European Patent Convention; Chairman of Special Committee Q176 of the International Association for the Protection of Intellectual Property (AIPPI) for drafting Implementing Regulations for the revised European Patent Convention 2000; and lecturer at the German Lawyers' Academy ('Strategic Deployment of Patents').

Tamara El-Shibib leads the patent practice in Gowling WLG's Dubai office and advises clients on the patentability of a range of innovations, including emerging tech areas such as Artificial intelligence (AI). She is committed to raising awareness of intellectual property and its role in driving innovation in the region and hosts a webinar series which aims to address the gaps and challenges in the innovation ecosystem in the GCC region. Tamara also works closely with R&D institutes and tech companies to carry out IP audits and implement strategies to support the identification, protection and commercialisation of their innovations. Tamara is a part-qualified UK attorney with a Graduate Diploma in Law from the University of Law, a Master's in Management of Intellectual Property Law and a Bachelor's of Science in Pharmacology. She worked previously for the Qatar Foundation, where she was involved in establishing an IP policy for the foundation and setting up the first Technology Transfer office.

Dr Kate Gaudry is a partner at Mughal Gaudry & Franklin PC, where she focuses her practice on data-driven, efficient and strategic patent prosecution. She particularly enjoys patent prosecution relating to artificial intelligence and/or computational-biology technologies. Kate believes that empirical research and community involvement are important to helping her clients and the patent community. She has authored over seventy publications and is an international speaker who shares results of generally applicable analyses. Her work was also pivotal in the shutting down of the USPTO's SAWS program, which secretly subjected select patent applications to increased examination scrutiny. Kate holds a JD from Harvard Law, a PhD in computational neurobiology from UCSD, and a BS in Physics from Fort Hays State University.

Dr Daniel Hill received his PhD from UC San Diego in computational neuroscience in 2010. He performed his post-doctoral research at the Technical University of Munich, studying synaptic integration in mouse motor cortex. Moving to industry in 2013, he served as a senior data scientist at Integral Ad Science, developing causal models of customer behaviour. He then joined Amazon in 2015 to work on personalization algorithms for both product recommendation and search. Currently, he works for Facebook Reality Labs in NYC as a research scientist.

Ben Husband is a chartered UK and European patent attorney with Carpmaels & Ransford LLP. Ben has a considerable practice in the MedTech field which covers a broad spectrum of mechanical and software technology. The ability to handle such a broad spectrum of work is supported by his electronics/software background and passion to understand how mechanical machines operate, especially in the automotive sector. Ben has a wealth of experience from handling a significant opposition portfolio across a number of different medical and electronics technology areas. Ben has a genuine interest in advising clients on protecting their software innovation, which includes several clients developing innovative AI solutions and often extends to areas that are at the fringes of patentability. Ben provides pragmatic advice when it comes to deciding whether patent protection is appropriate and on how the law and guidelines can be navigated when drafting and prosecuting applications for software-based inventions.

Dr Yusuke Ichikawa is a registered and qualified patent attorney (benrishi) at Anderson Mori & Tomotsune. He has been involved with various patent matters, conducting research, litigation and licensing, and is well-versed in international and domestic application and registration procedures as well as intermediate procedures. He is specialized in electronics technologies, including specifically technologies applicable to computer software, semiconductors, telecommunications and mechanical devices. He received his M. Eng. and Dr Eng. degrees in computer science from Waseda University, Tokyo. He is also a registered and qualified California lawyer.

Dr Mincheol Kim is a Korean patent attorney and a founder of GV IP Law Firm. As an IP strategist, he has extensive experience in patent disputes in major industries such as telecommunications, secondary batteries, and semiconductors, as well as cutting-edge computer technologies including machine learning and blockchain. Dr KIM studied networking and image processing at KAIST (Korea Advanced Institute of Science and Technology) and received his PhD degree in Intellectual Property Law from Peking University of Beijing.

Nevin Jacob Koshy is a partner and has been head of the patent and design department of United Trademark & Patent Services, a regional IP firm, since 2010. Prior to this position, he worked as a research scientist and an IP consultant for a number of reputable companies, including in a technology transfer department in the United Kingdom. He is a member of the Executive Board/Board of Directors of the United Arab Emirates (UAE) Chapter of the International Association for the Protection of Intellectual Property (AIPPI). He is actively involved in IP training sessions and is a sought-after speaker at regional and international conferences. Nevin has successfully overseen the prosecution of over 15,000 IP rights worldwide for his clients ranging from start-ups to Fortune 500 companies. He counsels clients on both contentious and non-contentious issues and often uses his negotiation skills to resolve the matter amicably.

Thomas Kretschmer is a European and Swiss patent attorney with Iprime Rentsch Kaelin AG in Zurich, Switzerland. He has extensive experience in the field of intellectual property protection in various areas of the ICT industry. His career as a patent attorney is based on many years of experience in IP departments of large software and computer companies. His particular technical specialties include modern technologies in the ICT environment, such as cryptography, IoT, blockchain and artificial intelligence. For many years he managed global patent portfolios of international companies. He holds a master's degree in Intellectual Property Law & Management (MIPLM), an LLM from the Centre d'Etudes Internationales de la Propriété Industrielle (CEIPI) and a postgraduate diploma in copyright law from King's College in London.

Alfred A. Macchione is an equity partner in the Intellectual Property Group of McCarthy Tétrault LLP in Toronto, Canada. He holds a Master's degree in Engineering and graduated from the McGill Faculty of Law in 1986 as an Elizabeth Torrance Gold Medalist. He is called to the Bars of Ontario and Québec and is a Registered Patent and Trademark Agent. Alfred is involved in all aspects of the clearance, acquisition, enforcement and exploitation of patents, trade marks, copyright, designs and other forms of intellectual property, with special emphasis on high technology. He has particular experience in the patenting of inventions in the fields of networked communications, business and financial services processes, software and other forms of computer technology. Alfred is a Past President of the AIPPI Canadian National Group and he is currently Chair of the international Standing Committee on IT and the Internet of AIPPI. Alfred is also a past Chair of the Computer Technology Committee of the Intellectual Property Institute of Canada (IPIC).

Sarmad Hasan Manto has almost twenty-five years of experience in the Middle East, Asia and Africa, Sarmad is the managing partner at Audiri Vox. He also acts as the global portfolio manager for a number of Middle Eastern companies. Sarmad's specialization includes trademark and patent prosecution, negotiations, anti-counterfeiting, litigation, due diligence, franchising, licensing, corporate and regulatory affairs. He has extensive experience in advising rights holders on portfolio development, management, franchising, licensing, data protection and enforcement strategies in the tobacco, information technology, electronics, telecommunication, cosmetics, luxury goods, pharmaceutical, foodstuff and auto industries. He also provides advice on a wide range of legal and compliance issues and is well-versed with the requirements and demands of the in-house and outside counsel aspects of the legal practice. His work includes, but is not limited to, drafting, prosecution and enforcement of Patent and Trademark applications, handling oppositions and enforcement actions, franchising and divestiture of IP rights, providing expert advice on data protection, entering negotiations and drafting a wide range of commercial contracts and rendering advice on compliance issues.

Stephen Middleton is a partner and patent attorney at Von Seidels and focuses on protecting computer-implemented inventions. Before joining Von Seidels, Stephen completed a master's degree in engineering within the University of Cape Town's Radar Remote Sensing Group, which included spending time in Antarctica as a technical assistant to South Africa's national space agency. Stephen honed his skills drafting patent specifications for an international payment organisation which focused on mobile banking and payment technologies. In addition to his patent practice, Stephen assists venture capitalists with IP due diligences and international clients with the formulation of IP strategies. He also has experience in data privacy and copyright matters.

Takashi Nakazaki has been ranked as one of the top lawyers in the data protection and information security field for the last several years. He was the author of publications focusing on GDPR in April 2018 and on the Metaverse in 2023. In addition, he regularly assists the Japanese government in data protection and cyber law areas including 'AI & Data Contracts Guidelines' and 'New legal issues surrounding content in the metaverse'. He leads the International Association of Privacy Professionals (IAPP) Tokyo as a co-founder and the technology and information practice group of Anderson Mori & Tomotsune. He holds a BA from the University of Tokyo and an LLM from Columbia University.

Dr Julian Potter is a chartered and European patent attorney, design attorney and trade mark attorney with WP Thompson in the U.K. Julian's practice encompasses all physics-based disciplines and reflects his high academic qualifications and technical abilities. Julian is also an experienced Higher Courts Litigator and has been involved in both Patents Court and Intellectual Property Enterprise Court (formerly Patents County Court) litigation covering a wide range of technologies. Whilst managing the UK patent department of a leading global cellular telecommunications company he gained wide experience of the commercial and strategic value of intellectual property on a global scale and regularly advises clients on the development, exploitation and enforcement of a global intellectual property portfolio. Julian is a member of AIPPI, FICPI, UNION, Institute of Physics and The Institute of Engineering and Technology. He is a Chartered Physicist and Chartered Scientist and his academic qualifications include a BSc, PhD and LLM. Julian is also a member of The International Technology Law Association, serving on its Board of Directors, and is a contributor to *Responsible AI*, a book published by the Association.

Dr Enrico Priori has an in-depth knowledge of the research world. Before joining the field of Industrial Property, Enrico prepared a PhD thesis in laser physics at the Politecnico of Milan and at the French Alternative Energies and Atomic Energy Commission (CEA Saclay). Enrico started his career as a Patent Attorney in 2003. After 10 years in a Parisian IP firm, Enrico joined Marks & Clerk France (now Atout PI Laplace – Groupe Vidon) in 2013, first as a team leader, in charge of training young engineers, then as a partner, before becoming Managing Partner in 2021. Very involved in the profession, Enrico is active in French Institute of Patent and Trade Mark Attorneys (CNCPI – Secretary of the Board) and in the International Association for the Protection of Intellectual Property (AIPPI – former member of the French group's Steering Committee).

Dr Sébastien Ragot is a European and Swiss patent attorney, also qualified in industrial property in France, with E. Blum & Co. in Zurich, Switzerland. He focuses on patent practice, particularly drafting and prosecuting patent applications and counselling clients in various areas of intellectual property including open source and software copyright. He has experience with opinions on infringement and validity of patents, litigation, oppositions and appeals before the European Patent Office. He attended the University of Marne-la-Vallée and completed his doctoral thesis at the École Centrale Paris, France (ECP), in the fields of materials science, solid-state physics and quantum simulations. He also holds a postgraduate degree in intellectual property from the CEIPI, France.

Ranveer Riyat joined the IP field after completing his MSc in Physics from Imperial College London. His postgraduate studies were diverse, covering an array of topics such as quantum systems, quantum optics, advanced particle physics, and nanotechnology in consumer electronic devices. During his research project, he honed his technical skills in geometric optics, nonlinear optics, high harmonic generation, and configuring PID controllers by building a frequency-doubled, phase-locked laser for the quantum entanglement of ultra-cold atoms. Ranveer had previously obtained a BSc (Hons) in Physics from the University of Warwick, where his research involved improving the identification of the Higgs to bb decay channel using state of the art machine learning techniques.

Ahmad Saleh is partner and head of Innovation, Patents & Industrial Property (3IP) at Al Tamimi & Company. He is a Canadian attorney and engineer with over 17 years of international and local experience in IP and commercial law and over 12 years of higher education studies in engineering, law and business management. Ahmad advises clients in the private and public sectors in a wide range of legal matters in the sphere of Research & Development and Innovation, from patent protection to technology transfer transactions and litigation. Ahmad holds a Bachelor degree in Computer Engineering and a Masters of Applied Sciences degree in Electrical Engineering from Ecole Polytechnique de Montreal, an LLB in Civil Law and a DESSS in common Law from the University of Montreal. Ahmad has completed executive education programs in General Management, Innovation & Technology and Artificial Intelligence for Business Strategies from MIT Sloan School of Management.

Anshul Sunil Saurastri is a Partner and Patent Attorney at Krishna & Saurastri Associates LLP. His practice areas include both contentious and non-contentious matters. Specifically, he is focused on patent, trademark and design prosecution, oppositions, revocations and appellate proceedings, infringement and invalidity opinions, litigation and arbitration matters, and due diligence and transactional issues. Prior to practicing law, he worked in a US-based investment firm and in research and development. Holding degrees in the sciences, engineering and law and training in legal, strategic and technical areas, he has amassed cross-functional expertise. Anshul holds a Master's in Engineering from the University of Pennsylvania, Philadelphia, a Bachelor's in Applied Sciences from Case Western Reserve University, Cleveland, and a Degree of Law from the Mumbai University. Anshul is registered to practice at the Bar Council of India and the Indian Patent & Trademark Office.

Dr Ian Schick is an accomplished intellectual property strategist and a pioneer in law practice innovation. Ian founded and is presently chairman of Ethan Nathaniel, Inc., a generative AI company focused on radically expanding the possibilities in IP portfolio development. Through AI and lean production principles, he is an innovator in enhancing routine writing tasks and workflows traditionally carried out by attorneys, which he studied first-hand during his decade of practice at boutique and global law firms. As a Stanford Law School CodeX Fellow, Ian leads the Machine-Generated Legal Documents project. He co-founded Specifio, the first commercially available patent application content generator, and Draft Builders, a platform providing on-demand drafting support for law firms through a network of vetted patent attorneys. Among other activities in the legal community, Ian serves as

Chair of the American Intellectual Property Law Association's Emerging Technologies Committee, helped found both the Practice Innovation and Artificial Intelligence Subcommittees, and is a member of the AI Task Force.

Alessandro Spina is a qualified European and Italian Patent Attorney and works as Legal Counsel with Whirlpool Corporation. He manages Whirlpool's IP portfolio, particularly in the EMEA region, as well as IP licensing, acquisition and litigation matters. As part of his in-house role, Alessandro also provides training and education on IP matters to Whirlpool colleagues, particularly but not exclusively to those working in R&D and Procurement areas.

Jeff Sun is an associate in McCarthy Tétrault LLP's national Intellectual Property Group in Canada. His practice is primarily focused on acquisition, commercialization, and enforcement of patent rights in the high tech space. Jeff leverages his technical expertise to prosecute Canadian patent applications and to assist electronics companies in settling their intellectual property rights disputes. Jeff is a registered patent agent in both Canada and the United States. Before entering the legal profession, Jeff conducted research related to neuromorphic computing, complementary metal-oxide semiconductor (CMOS), and nanoelectromechanical (NEM) relay technologies. Jeff received his B.S. in Electrical Engineering and Computer Sciences and Materials Science Engineering from the University of California, Berkeley in 2014, his MS in Electrical Engineering and Computer Sciences from the University of California, Berkeley in 2015, and his JD from the Peter A. Allard School of Law at the University of British Columbia in 2018.

Yeen C. Tham is counsel, regulatory compliance, with IBM in New York where she has worked in the IP field since joining IBM in 2007. Yeen has a wide variety of experience in IP from including drafting patent applications, providing IP guidance to research teams, handling IP transactions, and serving as legal strategist for artificial intelligence. She holds an undergraduate degree in computer engineering from University at Buffalo and a Juris Doctor degree from New York Law School.

Jochen Unland is a partner with Eisenführ Speiser Patentanwälte Rechtsanwälte PartGmbBin their Bremen office. He has special professional experience in drafting, prosecuting and enforcing German, European and international patent applications and patents for clients in Germany and worldwide, particularly Japanese clients. He is a co-author of the 'Beck'scherKommentar' on the European Patent Convention. Jochen holds a Master's degree in Physics ('Diplom-Physiker') from the Technical University of Clausthal and is registered as a German Patent Attorney and as a European Patent Attorney.

Dr Leron Vandsburger is an associate IP counsel at Thermo Fisher Scientific, Inc., where he supports the analytical instruments group. He regularly works with inventors to protect AI-ML enabled control, computer vision, and multi-modal data analysis and sample characterization technologies. Leron also serves in leadership positions at arts-focused legal-aid and music organizations. He has authored or co-authored numerous articles on technical subjects including materials science and plasma physics and legal subjects including access to IP protection for artists, AI-generated art and invention, and state-by-state differences in dead-naming at the USPTO.

Leron holds a JD from the University of Washington and a PhD in plasma sciences and nanotechnology and B. Eng. in Chemical Engineering from McGill University in Montreal, Canada.

Divyendu Verma is Managing Partner and Registered Patent & Trademark Attorney at DuxLegis Attorneys in India. In over 17 years of practice Divyendu has amassed broad experience in Intellectual Property strategic counselling, patent drafting, prosecution and litigation. He has handled and managed large IP portfolios for multiple national and international organizations involving drafting IP implementation frameworks and assisting clients to build their IP portfolio. Mr Verma appears regularly before various Indian Patent Offices and practices IP litigation in Bombay High Court, other lower courts and High Court of Delhi. Divyendu holds a Master's Degree in Computational Engineering, Double Bachelor's Degrees in Computer Engineering and Mathematics, and a Degree of Law from the University of Delhi. Divyendu is registered to practice at the Bar Council of India and the Indian Patent, Design & Trademark Office

Xiaowei Wei is a member of the PRC Patent Bar, working at Han Kun Law Offices in Beijing. She has extensive experience in patent prosecution, reexamination, counselling, invalidation and litigation for over 14 years. Ms. Wei has helped many well-known global companies to obtain nearly a thousand patents in China and has provided them with valuable advice for patent prosecution strategies in China. She has also helped a number of Chinese companies obtain patents in Europe, the United States and other countries. The technical fields in which Ms. Wei works include digital communications, computers, semiconductors, consumer electronics, signal processing, artificial intelligence, etc. She has a Master's Degree in Communication and Information Processing and a Bachelor's Degree in Electrical Engineering, both from Tsinghua University.

Lili Wu is a member of the PRC Bar and Patent Bar, working at Han Kun Law Offices in Beijing. She has focused her practice on providing whole-process patent portfolio management and patent enforcement since 1997. She has extensive experience in strategically managing patent portfolios for multinational clients to help clients increase the value of their IP assets. She has handled many patent invalidation and infringement cases before courts of different levels up to the Supreme People's Court. Several court cases that Ms. Wu has handled and led have been selected as typical cases by the Supreme People's Court. Her experience spans various technology industries including internet, telecommunications, semiconductor, information technology, automobile, medical device, manufacturing and green energy. Ms. Wu received an MS in Information Systems in 1997 from the Beijing Institute of Technology. She also received an LLM degree from Franklin Pierce Law Center in 2009.

Table of Contents

Foreword

Shoichi Okuyama, President of AIPPI

AIPPI is delighted to introduce another instalment in the AIPPI Law Series, entitled *Artificial Intelligence and Patents*. With the recent introduction of such chatbots as ChatGPT, artificial intelligence ('AI') is once again a focal point of technological and legal discussions. It is timely for us to be able to publish a book on patent law with respect to AI.

If the reader will allow me to divulge my old story, during my college years I briefly studied neural networks as part of graduation study. Toward the end of the 1970s, the first winter period of neural networks was about to end, and new ideas started to emerge. Soon after that, my personal interest moved to physical chemistry, and neural network studies eventually went into the second and long winter. Around 2012, significant developments appeared, mostly coming from Professor Geoffrey Hinton in Canada. It would be a fair statement that Professor Hinton's persistence and achievements led to the current explosion of AI technologies.

Now proper protection over technologies related to AI is important to elicit further developments and attract more investments. That is a challenge to practitioners, researchers, and policymakers. AIPPI hopes that this new book will give a global perspective on the patent protection of AI technologies.

Since its foundation in 1897, AIPPI – the International Association for the Protection of Intellectual Property – is the world's leading non-profit association dedicated to the development and improvement of laws for the protection of intellectual property. It is a politically neutral, non-profit organization based in Switzerland, with over 8,100 members worldwide from 131 countries across all continents. AIPPI members include lawyers, attorneys and agents working across all fields of intellectual property in corporate and private practice throughout the world, as well as academics, judges, government officials and other persons interested in intellectual property.

AIPPI promotes the protection of all types of intellectual property through comprehensive analysis of existing and proposed intellectual property laws and policies, and formulates proposals to harmonize intellectual property laws and their application.

AIPPI would like to cordially thank Jonathan P. Osha, the volume editor of this book, for his invaluable work and dedication in accomplishing such an enormous task.

Furthermore, AIPPI also expressly thanks the chapter contributors, all of whom are active AIPPI members, for their dedication and diligence, without which this impressive global law review would not have been possible.

Wolters Kluwer has been instrumental in the development of the AIPPI Law Series and the launch of this book. AIPPI very much appreciates the wonderful partnership with the publisher and acknowledges its ongoing support in this fruitful enterprise.

Shoichi Okuyama
President of AIPPI
February 2023

Acknowledgements

I would like to express my sincere gratitude to all the contributors who shared their expertise, their perspectives, and their valuable time to make this book a reality. We were indeed fortunate to have such a superb group of thought leaders on this cutting-edge topic from all over the world. Further, while I am hesitant to mention a specific contributor among this excellent group, I would be remiss not to express my special thanks to Dr Sébastien Ragot who took the labouring oar on not just one but three chapters.

I would also like to express my sincere thanks to Christine Robben, Simon Bellamy, and Steve Lambley of Wolters Kluwer for their support, patience, and guidance throughout this process.

I further wish to thank AIPPI, AIPPI President Dr Shoichi Okuyama, and all the members of the AIPPI Bureau for allowing me to undertake this extremely interesting endeavour. Special thanks go to Dr Ralph Nack, First Deputy Reporter General of AIPPI, for his active support and feedback on the chapter drafts without which this book would not have been possible. Sincere thanks also to Anne Marie Verschuur (former Reporter General) and Dr Ari Laakkonen (current Reporter General) for their continued support and encouragement throughout this process.

Finally, many thanks to my wife Talina Osha for her patience and support through many weekends and late nights working on this project.

Jonathan P. Osha

Chapter 1

Introduction

Jonathan P. Osha

§01.01 EMERGENCE OF AI

Artificial intelligence ('AI') and the AI sub-field of machine learning ('ML') are terms that originated in the fields of computer and data science but now form part of the common vernacular. AI has now found application in virtually every field. Some applications of AI have become part of our daily lives: virtual assistants, chatbots, search engines, online language translation and eCommerce all employ AI in various forms. Generative AI such as OpenAI's products ChatGPT (natural language generation), Jukebox (music generation) and DALL-E2 (image generation) have captured the public attention to an enormous degree and can, indeed, do amazing things. A myriad of other applications of AI are found in disparate fields that, while not as visible on a daily basis, impact on our lives in a wide variety of ways.

Artificial intelligence is not new; AI as a field of study dates back to a conference at Dartmouth College in 1956. Research and development in the field ebbed and flowed in the decades that followed. The surge in applications of AI we have witnessed in the last two decades comes not only from new technical developments in the field but also from the coincident availability of two very important things: vast quantities of raw data ('big data') and computing power sufficient to process it.[1] The ever-increasing numbers of sensors and devices driven by, among other things, the Internet of Things (IoT) generate enormous, dynamic data streams that can be mined by ML algorithms.[2] The fields of application are virtually limitless and touch

1. *See*, e.g., S. Bringsjord and N. Govindarajulu, 'Artificial Intelligence', *Stanford Encyclopedia of Philosophy*, 12 Jul. 2018 (available at: https://plato.stanford.edu/entries/artificial-intelligence/#-ExplGrowAI); R. Anyoha, 'The History of Artificial Intelligence', *Harvard University Blog, Special Edition on Artificial Intelligence*, 28 Aug. 2017 (available at: https://sitn.hms.harvard.edu/flash/2017/history-artificial-intelligence/).
2. A. Bifet and J. Read, 'Ubiquitous Artificial Intelligence and Dynamic Data Streams', *DEBS '18: The 12th ACM International Conference on Distributed and Event-based Systems*, 25–28 Jun.

almost all industries. All of this is to say we have only begun to see the potential impact of AI.

With this rapidly increasing impact comes not only exciting new technical capabilities but also new challenges for intellectual property ('IP') law. Are current laws fit for purpose or is something new or different needed? This is not a new question; one need only look back to the early days of digital music, computer software and 3D printing to find similar discussions of whether existing IP law is suited to emerging technologies. For the most part, the answer in the past has been 'yes', with perhaps a tweak here and there. Whether the same will be true of AI is, as yet, an open question.

§01.02 IMPACT OF AI ON IP LAW

AI has the potential to impact all areas of IP law. In its broadest sense IP refers to a right held by a human or legal person to certain intangible ('intellectual') property. The general categories of IP are patents, trademarks, copyrights, designs and trade secrets. AI raises interesting new questions in each of these categories.

Regarding trademarks and designs, AI provides a new ability to search intelligently for related images and thus is a powerful tool to search for prior art and detect instances of infringement. However, AI also is widely used in eCommerce to steer customers toward products the AI 'thinks' the customer might want. Some worry that AI 'bots' will become so intuitive about what customers want that the connection between the brand and the product, and hence the strength of the associated trademarks, will be weakened overall.

AI in the context of copyright also raises a host of issues. AI is already being used in amazing ways to generate music, artistic works, news casts and many other types of works that would typically be protectable by copyright. But in most of the world copyright requires a human author. So, are AI-generated works in the public domain from day one, unprotected and free for all to copy? If an AI system uses copyright-protected works as training data does this constitute infringement? Are the resulting works derivative works that are themselves infringing? Who is responsible for the infringement if it exists?

Trade secrets take on an increasingly important role in protection of AI-related innovations. This is due both to the difficulty of protecting some aspects of AI with patents and to the lack of a system for protecting data in most countries. Those who develop AI and applications of AI may prefer to keep their technology secret rather than risk pursuing patent coverage (and the associated disclosure requirements) to an uncertain end. Similarly, most companies will consider their proprietary data to be a trade secret. However, if AI is driving a trend toward increased use of trade secrets, what does this say about the future of collaboration and innovation on a larger scale?

These are but a few examples of the potential issues raised by AI in these fields of IP. Each of these topics could be the subject of a book in their own right. This volume of the AIPPI Law Series, however, focuses on AI and *patents*. The issues raised by AI in the patent context are numerous and some scratch at the very foundation of the

---

2018, Hamilton, New Zealand (available online at: https://www.researchgate.net/publication/325892515_Ubiquitous_Artificial_Intelligence_and_Dynamic_Data_Streams).

patent system. For example, can an AI system be an inventor? If it can, is the result patentable? If it is, who is the owner of the patent? How do we adequately describe an AI system in a written patent application, given that the behaviour of AI may depend to a large extent on the data with which it was trained or the data input for inference purposes? Must that data be disclosed explicitly? More broadly, is AI just another tool like a word processor or a paint brush, or is it really a game-changer that will require changes to patent law and practice? These and other considerations will be examined in this book from the perspectives of numerous different national and regional patent systems.

While policy considerations are discussed throughout this book, equally important is the question of how applicants can best protect AI-related inventions under existing patent law. Thus, this book provides not only an important treatment of the theoretical topics but also provides concrete examples and guidance for best practices in the major jurisdictions around the world.

§01.03 WHAT IS AN AI-RELATED INVENTION?

Because AI has in recent years become ubiquitous in perhaps an unprecedented fashion,[3] it has also become a 'buzz word' that is often used imprecisely, for instance in marketing campaigns.[4] This blurring of meaning complicates discussions of AI because two different people will often use the same term to mean different things or, conversely, different terms to mean the same thing. This is particularly problematic in the patent law context. Virtually every IP organization and all the major patent offices have held discussions and presentations on the subject of AI and patents. Many patent offices have issued requests for public comment on AI-related issues and some have issued specific guidelines for AI-related inventions. A common issue that runs through all of these activities is a lack of common terminology. This simple issue of terminology has, at times, frustrated efforts to have meaningful discussions on the merits of substantive issues relating to AI and IP.

Consider an example from a recent conference on AI and Patents. A first person volunteered, 'AI inventions are not patentable – only humans can invent.' A second person responded, 'Of course AI inventions are patentable – they are just like any other computer software.' These two people sound like they disagree, but in fact they do not. They simply have a different understanding of 'AI inventions'. The first person considers 'AI inventions' to mean inventions (allegedly) made *by* AI without human input or direction and thus concludes that, without a human inventor, such an invention should not be patentable. The second person considers 'AI inventions' to mean *the AI itself* (the combination of algorithms and hardware that make AI function) and concludes that these inventions are, in essence, no different from any other computer-implemented invention ('CII'). Neither position is incorrect, yet the result of the exchange – and many others like it – is confusion. The patent offices also use a variety of terms in different and inconsistent ways. This simple issue of

3. *See*, e.g., B. Ane, 'AI Is Ubiquitous in our Everyday Lives', *Int J Recent Sci Res.* 10(11), 35959–35961 (2019).
4. *See*, e.g., J. Wallis, 'AI – Game Changer, or Just the Latest Marketing Buzzword?', *AI Business*, 3 Oct. 2018.

terminology has, to a remarkable degree, hampered the ability to have coherent policy discussions on these issues.

§01.04 CONSIDERING ALL THE ISSUES

Another factor that has hampered understanding of the issues surrounding AI and patents is the predominance of the question of inventive AI. Dr Stephen Thaler filed a patent application naming as the inventor, 'DABUS, the invention was autonomously generated by an artificial intelligence'.[5] This patent application, which has been pursued in multiple jurisdictions but issued in the name of 'DABUS' only in South Africa, has dominated discussions of AI and patents. It is, indeed, very interesting to consider, from a philosophical perspective, the implications of inventive AI. Is it in society's best interests to allow patents to inventions made by machines? Who would own the rights to the patent? Who would have standing to sue in the event of infringement? Should AI entities have rights?

While these policy issues should be considered with a view toward a possible future when artificial general intelligence[6] is reached and sentient machines exist, more pertinent issues of AI and patents exist today yet often wilt in the shadow of this 'exotic' inquiry. For example, to meet the disclosure requirements for a patent claiming an application of AI in a specific field, how much detail about the training data and input data must be included in the patent specification? Does it matter if that data or similar data is publicly available? How are AI-related inventions best claimed (and disclosed) to ensure patent eligibility? Who, among many (human) people in an AI application development team, should be considered inventors? These and many other questions challenge practitioners *today* and will be discussed in the national and regional chapters of this book that follow.

§01.05 AI-RELATED INVENTION CATEGORY DEFINITIONS

In order both to minimize confusion from terminology and to delineate the various issues relating to AI and IP, this book introduces a set of 'AI category definitions' that will be used throughout all chapters.

Before introducing the AI category definitions, it is useful explain what they are not. First, they are not an attempt to define AI. AI is a moving target[7] that defies definition and, in any event, no definition of AI is necessary for the purposes of this book. Secondly, the category definitions are not an attempt to categorize *results* under substantive patent law. That is to say, the categories do not function such that, for example, inventions in Category 1 are patentable and inventions in Category 2 are

5. WIPO publication WO 2020/079499.
6. 'Strong artificial intelligence (AI), also known as artificial general intelligence (AGI) or general AI, is a theoretical form of AI used to describe a certain mindset of AI development. If researchers are able to develop Strong AI, the machine would require an intelligence equal to humans; it would have a self-aware consciousness that has the ability to solve problems, learn, and plan for the future.' IBM newsletter, available at: https://www.ibm.com/topics/strong-ai.
7. 'Intelligence is whatever machines haven't done yet', Tesler's Theorem (ca. 1970).

not. The laws of each jurisdiction must be applied to the inventions in each category and appropriate conclusions must be reached on a case-by-case basis.

What the category definitions do provide, as will be apparent from the following chapters, is a clear differentiation among the issues – legal, practical and policy – that arise for different types of AI-related inventions. They also create a standardized taxonomy that permits comparison and differentiation among AI-related inventions of different types.

For the purposes of this book, the generic term used is 'AI-related inventions'. Within this genus, five categories are defined. The categories refer to what is claimed, not what is disclosed in the specification of a patent application. Thus, different claims in a single patent application may fall in different categories. For example, a single patent application may disclose and separately claim both a new application of AI (Category 3) and an invention made using that new application (Category 4). It is also possible that a single claim could encompass more than one category. For example, a single claim may cover both an invention of AI (Category 1) and a particular implementation (Category 2). The categories therefore serve primarily to permit differentiation of the legal concepts, best practices, and policy issues that may arise.

[A] Category 1: Invention of AI

This category relates to the invention of new algorithms or models for the AI itself, independent of the data to which it is applied and independent of any particular use case. This is the 'core AI', which might be, for example a new type of deep neural network with improved capabilities over prior networks.

[B] Category 2: Invention of an AI Implementation

An invention of an AI implementation relates to the creation of a system or process of broad application using known AI technology plus additional elements, such as a particular arrangement of filters or a particular interface.

[C] Category 3: A New Application of AI

New applications of AI are by far the most commonly patented AI-related inventions. Artificial intelligence has found application in virtually every conceivable field. From AI applications that help farmers know when to plant and harvest crops to deep neural networks that allow self-driving cars to recognize stop signs and pedestrians, application of AI technology in new ways and in new fields is a vast and ever-increasing area of innovation.

Applications of AI in this category can be further broken down into two broad types: 'decision maker' and 'decision aid'. In a 'decision maker' application, AI causes something to happen: a car to stop, a website to show a product recommendation, a door to open when a face is recognized, etc. In a 'decision aid' application, AI may be used to perform an analysis that produces useful information for decision makers without actually effectuating a decision itself.

[D] Category 4: Inventions Made Using AI

Artificial Intelligence may be employed by a human innovator to help solve a particular problem or need. Through a combination of identification of the problem or need, selection of the AI technology to be used, and selection of proper training and input data, the result of application of AI may be, in and of itself, a patentable invention.

In the normal case the invention made using AI in the above scenario would be a solution to the problem or need being addressed. However, cases exist where an invention is produced that solves a different problem, i.e., is unrelated to the original goals of the human innovator. In this case, in might be argued that the invention was made 'accidentally' using AI.

[E] Category 5: Inventions Made by AI

Most (but not all) experts agree that AI is not currently capable of the conception required for invention and thus inventions currently are not made *by* AI but rather are made *using* AI (Category 4). However, it is conceivable that, in the future, AI will be able to, on its own and without direction by a human innovator, to identify problems and needs and make inventions that address them.

§01.06 APPLYING THE AI-RELATED INVENTION CATEGORY DEFINITIONS

Experts from multiple jurisdictions will consider various issues of IP law, practice and policy in the following chapters through the lens of these five categories. While it is up to each group of authors to draw conclusions for their own jurisdiction, some initial observations can be made. First, Categories 1–3 involve claims to AI, AI implementations and applications of AI. Thus, patent eligibility is likely to be an issue in some jurisdictions, with the issue being most profound for Category 1 and progressively less so for Categories 2 and 3. Secondly, Categories 4 and 5 involve claims to products or processes invented *using* (or, hypothetically *by*) AI. Thus, these claims may relate to any invention in any field and need not - and usually would not - recite AI at all. Hence, these categories illustrate the differences between inventions made *using or by* AI and inventions *of* AI. Lastly, Category 5 is the only category that addresses the issue of inventive AI. By separating this issue into its own category, while all of Categories 1–4 involve human inventorship, the issue of inventive AI can be addressed without overshadowing the other issues that exist for the other categories.

§01.07 CONCLUSION

AI is developing at a rapid pace and with that development comes a myriad of issues ranging from privacy and safety to ownership and IP. In the patent arena, there are both similarities and differences in how national and regional patent offices (and legislatures) are addressing this new technology. Sound policy starts, of course, with a sound understanding of the issues. Thus, to form a strong foundation upon which to base the discussions in this book, the next chapter provides a technical introduction to AI and ML. The subsequent national and regional chapters then consider how the laws and practices of each jurisdiction would apply to AI-related inventions in each of the five categories.

Chapter 2

What Is ~~Artificial Intelligence~~ Machine Learning?

Dr Daniel Hill

§02.01 INTRODUCTION

When I was asked to write an introduction on artificial intelligence ('AI') geared towards intellectual property professionals, I felt uncomfortable. Sure, there was some unease about dealing with lawyers. Their domain is a mystery to me. Over my career as a research scientist, I have had a few run-ins with the company legal team, usually whenever it was time to file for a patent. Typically, we would first meet to discuss my invention – a novel algorithm to addresses this or that problem. Then they would disappear for a couple weeks only to return with a disclosure that was for me incomprehensible. Was this legal-ese really describing what I worked on? Well, I thought, maybe the lawyers would also have trouble reading one of my conference papers. Our professions just speak two different languages.

However, what really made me uncomfortable was the notion of writing about 'artificial intelligence'. It had been a while since I had even heard those words. Professionally, nobody talks about artificial intelligence anymore. Researchers largely stopped using that phrase decades ago because in the public's imagination it conjures up images of sentient machines (or Hollywood's killer robots). That's not what we work on or what we are even particularly interested in. Now we almost exclusively use the phrase *machine learning* ('ML'). This is a much more benign phrase. I would define it as 'the study of algorithms that automatically identify patterns in data'. We are not creating thinking machines. We do not philosophize about whether they have a soul. We create software that learns to solve problems by ingesting data without us ever having to explicitly tell it what the solution looks like.

To be sure, machine learning is a sub-field of artificial intelligence. AI covers a few topics that ML does not, such as *knowledge bases* and *symbolic manipulation*. However, these topics are not the hot ones in the field today. There is also this notion of *General AI* which I concede does include, at least in theory, sentient machines. However, sentient machines are mostly a distraction. The work that is happening in ML these days is far more interesting. The advancements of the last decade are nothing short of amazing, due to revolutions in *deep learning* and *reinforcement learning* (both discussed below). These revolutions were largely enabled by the internet which has made datasets with millions or billions of records readily available. We now have algorithms that rival or exceed human skill on varied tasks from recognizing objects in images to playing games of Go. And these algorithms are not relegated to a few government supercomputers but are often available everywhere via our mobile devices. If the models are not running on the phone itself, they are running in the cloud and responding to our requests in real time.

Welcome to the exciting world of machine learning. In this chapter, I will give a general introduction to the landscape of ML. You will see the major problems we face and our general techniques for solving them. I will walk you through the typical process that researchers use for solving ML problems. I will introduce you to the people who do the work at each step in that process. Where applicable, I will describe when non-trivial innovation is required and what factors impact reproducibility. My hope is that after reading this chapter, we can move a little bit closer to speaking the same language.

Figure 1. Organization of artificial intelligence

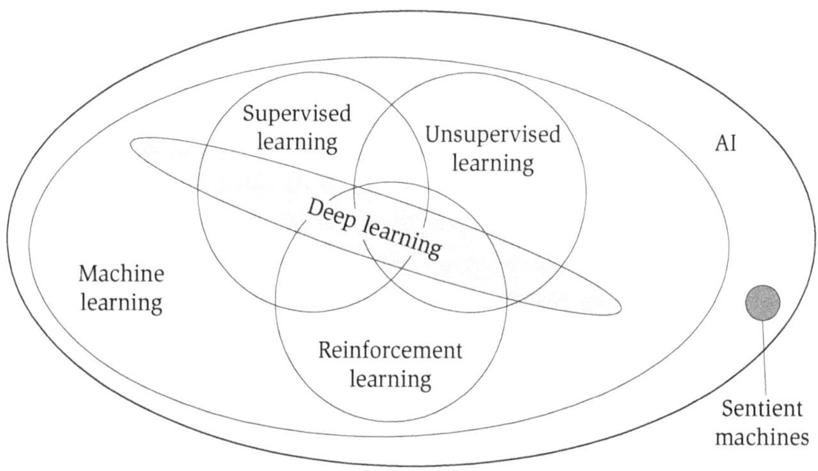

§02.02 TYPES OF MACHINE LEARNING ALGORITHMS

First, let's map out machine learning. It is traditionally divided into subcategories based on the type of data it uses. All machine learning algorithms operate on a *dataset*. A dataset is just a collection of *records* that contain information about individual observations. For example, a dataset for studying global warming might contain daily records of atmospheric CO_2 levels along with the location and time of the measurement. We often refer to the individual components of the record as *features*.

A dataset can be either *labelled* or *unlabelled*, indicating whether there is some value or outcome associated with each record. How much money was earned from this company's stock? Was this text from an e-mail message marked as spam? We divide machine learning into three broad categories based on whether we are given a label and how this label is used.

[A] Supervised Learning

When the label is present for each record, we are in the domain of *supervised learning*. Most machine learning falls under this category, where the goal is to predict the label for records we have never seen before based on their features. If the label is a number, such as CO_2 levels or return on investment, this is called a *regression*.

The most common type of regression is a *linear regression*, where the relationship between the values in the record and the label uses the equation for a line. Let's say we want to estimate how much money a new movie will make at the box office. For linear regression, this might look like:

Box office returns = A_1 * (Advertising budget) + A_2 * (# of A-list actors) + ...

This equation represents a simple *model* which describes how the record (features of the movie) relate to the label (box office returns). The symbols A_1 and A_2 are unknown parameters that need to be learned from data. The goal of supervised learning is to identify the values of the unknown parameters that best predict the box office returns.

If the label is instead a category, we are performing *classification*. For example, a task might be to label which breed of dog is present in a photo. When there are only two possible labels, such as true versus false, or good versus bad, this is called *binary classification*. The most common algorithm for binary classification is called (somewhat confusingly) *logistic regression*. The formula for logistic regression looks identical to linear regression except that there is a squashing function. It forces the predictions to lie between 0 and 1, so that they can be interpreted as probabilities. After we learn the unknown parameters, we can classify a record based on its probability of being in one class versus the other.

Figure 2. The logistic function

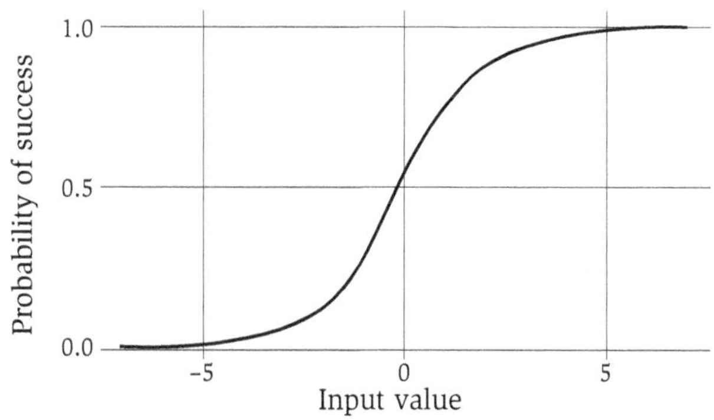

[B] Unsupervised Learning

When the dataset is unlabeled, we are working with unsupervised learning. Here the goal is not to make a prediction about the records, but to understand the underlying structure and patterns contained within the data. One way to extract patterns from a dataset is called *clustering*, where we divide the data into distinct clusters or groups. Records within a cluster should be more similar to each other than to records in different clusters. We might do this to identify different customer segments on an e-commerce website, or to identify distinct patterns in EEG recordings of brain activity. The canonical algorithm for clustering is called *k-means*. We identify the mean (centre) of *K* clusters, and then assign records to the closest centre.

Figure 3. Example of K-means clustering with K = 3. Membership of a data point (small marker) in a cluster (large marker) is indicated by shape

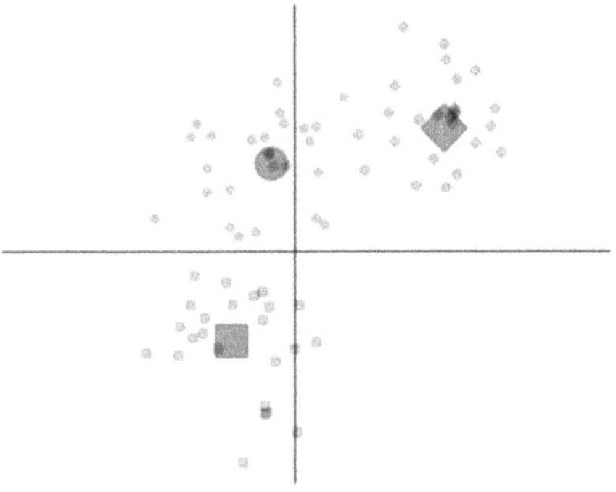

Unsupervised learning is also commonly used for *dimensionality reduction*. The *dimension* of a record is the number of features it contains. So, if a record contains a student's height measured monthly for a year, the record has a dimensionality of 12. In some applications, the dimensionality can be enormous. When working with text documents, we may have a feature for every word in the English language. With images, every pixel could be a feature. Reducing the dimensionality of a record lets us compress our data. It also makes it easier to visualize our data on two-dimensional paper. There are algorithms that essentially learn what combination of features contain the most information or variation in the dataset. We can then change the representation to contain fewer dimensions, while preserving most of the information of the original dataset.

[C] Reinforcement Learning

The last major category of machine learning is *reinforcement learning* ('RL'). In this case, the data is labelled … kind of. Imagine teaching a computer to win at chess. You could use a dataset where each record is the list of moves taken during a given chess match. The label could be which side won. However, it would be very difficult for the computer to learn how to play. A chess match consists of dozens or even hundreds of moves. The moves themselves are not labelled as good or bad, so which moves were important to win the game? This is called the credit-assignment problem.

RL is a specialized category of ML for dealing with this type of sequential decision-making problem, particularly when rewards (wins) might come at a delay. This category has received a lot of media attention lately because of new algorithms that are able to beat humans at our own games. AlphaGo from DeepMind famously beat the world Go champion – a milestone that was reached far earlier than researchers had anticipated. It is now routine to have computers learn how to beat human champions at videogames without ever directly telling the computer how to play.

Typically, these algorithms learn by doing. We don't show them a bunch of chess matches, we just have them play chess. Whether they win or lose, they learn something about how to play the game. One particular issue that arises in RL is the *exploration versus exploitation* dilemma. Since the computer only sees the outcome for moves that it actually makes, it must decide whether to try a new move – *explore* a new path – or use a move that has worked well in the past – exploit its knowledge. Finding the right balance between exploration and exploitation is the key to learning quickly.

§02.03 APPLICATIONS OF MACHINE LEARNING

Now that we have defined machine learning and a few of its major branches, let's look at some of its applications. The list below is far from exhaustive, but it should give a good overview about how the field is organized and what are the major areas of research and investment. As will be seen, ML is being used in broad and diverse domains. Where there's data, there's probably machine learning.

[A] Natural Language Processing

Natural Language Processing ('NLP') is the study of how to computationally process, understand, and generate text from human languages. People find languages intuitive to understand, yet it is difficult to explain to a computer how to deal with human text. Attempts to formalize language are never quite complete. It is impossible to account for all the ambiguities, inconsistencies, and exceptions in grammar and meaning. Modern approaches to NLP have largely given up on trying to formalize this mess and have instead addressed the problem with big data. We now have access to enormous, public corpuses such as Wikipedia that contain billions of words of text. Powerful machine learning algorithms can learn complex patterns in these texts, without creating any explicit set of rules.

A major output of these algorithms is called a *language model*, which estimates the probability of what word will come next given the sequence of words that have already been seen. One of the major applications of language models is *machine translation*. Tools such as Google Translate have made huge strides over the last decade by processing large parallel texts that give examples of the same document but written in different languages. By applying the language model, the translation software can choose the most probable word to come next based on the source text *and* the words that have been translated so far. Language models are also useful for human-computer interaction, such as automated question-answering systems and chat bots.

In addition to language modelling, NLP focuses on extracting semantic meaning from documents. Sentiment analysis is an application where we identify the emotional connotation of a message. Is the writer angry, happy, sarcastic? Companies assess their brand image by analysing the sentiment of tweets that people write about them. This is also applied in more serious applications such as identifying whether a person is feeling suicidal based on their social media posts.

A related field to NLP is speech recognition. Here the problem is to use measurements of sound waves to infer what phonemes were uttered by a human and convert them into text. Speech recognition faces all the challenges of NLP but also needs to address background noise, tracking or identifying the speaker, and interpreting a speaker's accent. However, combining speech recognition with NLP enables popular natural human-computer interfaces such as the Amazon Echo.

[B] Information Retrieval

Information retrieval ('IR') is synonymous with search engines. A search engine organizes a collection of documents (e.g., web pages, images, e-mails) and allows users to enter queries to find a subset of those documents. Typically, document retrieval occurs in two phases. First, there is a *matching* step where a subset of documents is retrieved that has some relevance to the user's query. Often, it is just the set of documents that contain all of the user's search terms. This is followed by a *ranking* step, where the relevant documents are scored and presented to the user in order of relevance. Originally, IR systems did not rely heavily on machine learning. The major focus was on how to organize documents so that the matching step could be performed in just a few milliseconds, even when searching through billions of documents. Ranking was often performed with simple heuristics. Then, in 1996, the founders of Google developed their PageRank algorithm which showed the value of using machine learning to rank documents. PageRank scores a web page by predicting how often a random web surfer would land on that page if they were randomly clicking on links. Pages that get more visits are ranked higher. Now, a modern commercial search engine may use hundreds or thousands of signals to rank items in real time. They even incorporate side information about the request such as the time of day, the user's GPS location or their browse history to identify the documents with the highest relevance.

[C] Recommender Systems

The internet has too much stuff. In 2020, YouTube reported that 300 hours of video were uploaded every minute. Amazon's catalogue contains hundreds of millions of products. Recommender systems help the user sift through all this stuff by highlighting the few items that may be of actual interest. This is similar to information retrieval, except the user has given no explicit query other than that they have shown up on the website. Recommender systems are usually *personalized*, which means the recommendations are made based on information about the user such as demographics or past behaviour. In *collaborative filtering*, a user is shown items that were enjoyed by other users who are the most similar to them. Another approach is predictive modelling where we infer what item the user is likely to interact with next. Then the recommender system helps that to happen by highlighting the item more prominently. Although it is not usually referred to as a recommender system, digital advertising uses the same type of algorithms to show 'the right ad, to the right person, at the right time'.

[D] Computer Vision

Humans intuitively understand the content of visual images, but as with natural language processing, it is difficult to explain to a computer how we do it. Early attempts at computer vision would identify lines and edges present in an image to infer what objects or 3-dimensional shapes they contained ('look for a couple ovals where the smaller one has two triangles on top, and maybe you have a cat'). Modern approaches use *neural networks* that are loosely inspired by the human visual system. We process visual information through a sequence of brain areas (retina → lateral geniculate nucleus → V1 →...) that extract progressively more complex, high-level information about the visual scene. We will discuss neural networks and deep learning more below, but these algorithms are organized into a sequence of layers that pool together more complicated visual features as they go deeper. These models now rival humans for accuracy in detecting objects in images, and their applications are ubiquitous. Facebook automatically labels friends in photos. Televised sports games annotate the movement on the field in real-time. Even hospitals conduct some diagnoses by first screening medical images through computer vision algorithms.

[E] Graphs

A graph is a collection of items, called *nodes* or *vertices*, connected to each other by *edges*. A prominent example of a graph is a social network. Here, the nodes are people, and an edge could represent a relationship such as 'A and B are friends'. If the edges are always mutual (think Facebook) this is called an *undirected graph*. Otherwise, it is a *directed graph* (think Twitter).

Figure 4. Examples of graphs

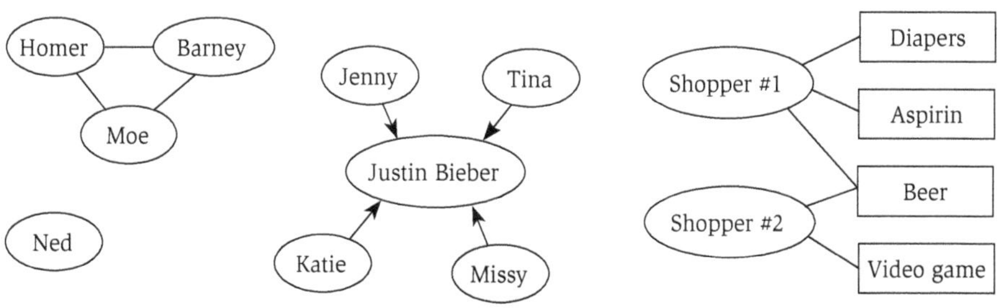

Undirected friendship graph

Directed followers graph

Bipartite purchase graph

Many big data problems boil down to an analysis of graphs. In social media, we try to predict which unconnected nodes are actually friends based on their overlapping connections in the social graph. A *bipartite graph* consists of two distinct types of nodes, and an edge can only connect nodes of different types. For example, on YouTube we can represent users and the videos that they have liked with a bipartite graph. Such a graph could be used to make recommendations by randomly hopping along the graph to find videos highly connected to ones already liked - an algorithm called *personalized PageRank*.

[F] Forecasting

Many datasets consist of a sequence of observations made over time. The observations may be a regularly spaced time-series, such as the daily closing value of a company's stock price. Or they may be irregularly spaced, such as a person's weight as measured whenever they visit the doctor's office. In either case, the goal of working with this data is to extract trends over time, and even to extrapolate to future time points. The applications for predicting the future are numerous - weather forecasting, supply chain logistics, credit scoring, etc. Machine learning methods for forecasting make the assumption that the past is correlated with the future, and then they identify these correlations from data.

[G] Generative Models

A generative model is one that learns to produce novel examples that look like they came out of its training dataset. This class of models has recently captured the public's imagination with its ability to synthesize realistic images and human-sounding text based on a prompt from the user. For example, ChatGPT by OpenAI is trained on massive internet text datasets. When a user enters a question ('What should I do on vacation in Thailand?'), out comes a short essay on the different historical sites one can visit and what cuisine to try. Another model from OpenAI called DALL-E generates images based on a caption entered by the user ('scuba-diving cat chases Abraham Lincoln'). Both types of models work by synthesizing their output little-by-little. ChatGPT merely predicts the next word, which then gets fed back into the model to predict the word after that. DALL-E starts with pure noise, and then repeatedly de-noises it until an image emerges. These models have the potential to improve productivity for artists, writers, and programmers alike. They may even compete with search engines as a more intuitive means to access information. While the results are often impressive, much research now focuses on getting these models under control. Generative language models have a tendency to make things up that just sound like something that could be true. Some models also create legal issues when they regurgitate material directly from their training data. In the case of image generation, they have even been known to sign the artist's name to their creation.

There are many other prominent applications of ML such as bioinformatics, fraud detection and robotics. However, now that we have seen some of the major problems addressed by machine learning, let's look at how machine learning is done.

§02.04 THE MACHINE LEARNING PROCESS

There is a general pattern to how machine learning projects evolve. Understanding this process will help illuminate how innovation and invention may enter into machine learning at each step. Typically, a project starts with the identification of some real-world or business problem that we need to pose as a machine learning problem. We then collect and clean data that will be used to model the problem. Next, we choose a model type that is appropriate for our data and objective. We then use our data to *train* the model and fill in its unknown *parameters*. After evaluating whether the model satisfies our objective, we finally deploy the model into the real world so that it can address the original business problem. I will now walk through each of these steps in more detail.

[A] Business Problem

Some companies such as AWS and MathWorks develop ML software and services as a product that is sold to customers. However, most companies use ML as a tool to solve a business problem. A project starts when someone identifies an opportunity to generate value from applying ML to data. Sometimes this is a new opportunity where ML has never been applied before but has good potential. Perhaps more often, the idea is to make an improvement on an existing system that already uses ML. Companies continuously iterate their systems as new data become available and as the tools in the field evolve.

One of the challenges at this stage is how to pose the business goal as a machine learning problem. Say that our goal is to speed up the screening of molecules as potential treatments for a disease. We can frame this as a machine learning task to build a binary classifier that predicts whether a molecule is a viable treatment based on its molecular structure. We are making a hypothesis that solving the machine learning classification problem will help with the real-world drug screening problem. Sometimes these hypotheses do not pan out. For example, in recommender systems it's typical to assume that we can make better recommendations if we more accurately predict how a user will behave. This can lead to a 'filter bubble' where the user tires of only seeing their own interests thrown back at them. The machine learning project thus becomes a research experiment to test whether our hypotheses are true.

[B] Data Collection

Once we define the goal, it is time to collect the data we will use to model our problem. Data is our most valuable resource! If the data is not rich enough to capture the patterns we seek to identify, no amount of sophisticated algorithms and modelling will save us. The most relevant data is usually found in-house. Websites log interactions with their users, and this provides behavioural data for their modelling needs. Hospitals archive medical records for the patient's lifetime which can be used decades later for modelling disease progression. This proprietary data is the most relevant for solving the problem, but unfortunately, this also leads to irreproducibility outside of the company. A machine learning model may only be successful because of the structure in the data it was applied to. The exact same model will operate differently when trained with a similar dataset but which contains different patterns. That is why for publishing machine learning research, it is increasingly required that authors must make their datasets public so that others can replicate their findings. (Note that it is also possible to share an ML model directly using an open format such as Open Neural Network Exchange. These artifacts can then be loaded in multiple different modelling frameworks.)

Fortunately, there are already many public datasets available. Governments (e.g., the US census) and non-profit organizations (e.g., the Wikipedia corpus) regularly post public data without any cost. Other datasets are published by academic researchers to help track progress in their fields. For example, the ImageNet dataset developed at Princeton contains tens of millions of categorized photos and is widely used to benchmark computer vision algorithms for image classification. Even companies will sometimes publish their datasets to promote innovation in research areas of interest. For example, Netflix sponsored the USD 1,000,000 Netflix Prize where they released anonymized video ratings to incentivize research into video recommendation. When relevant public data is available, it is also possible to take a hybrid approach where a model is first trained on a large, publicly available dataset and then fine-tuned on a smaller proprietary dataset. This combines the advantages of big data and relevancy.

Regardless of where the data comes from, the two main factors to consider in data collection are *volume* and *quality*. Volume refers to the amount of data collected. More is better. Low data volume will put constraints on the complexity of the model we can use. This will be discussed further below. The issue of data quality involves many factors, so let's discuss a few of these in turn.

First, the data should represent a random sample of all the data that could be collected. Think of a phone survey to find out how people will vote in an upcoming election. The survey is invalidated if people from only one demographic or political party are called. Any divergence from random sampling introduces bias, and the machine learning model will learn the wrong patterns. Sometimes we choose to intentionally collect biased data because of *imbalance* in the data. In digital advertising, the click rate on ads may be one in a thousand. In this case, it makes sense to over-represent clicks rather than collecting a dataset that is 99.9 % no-clicks. Even so, the biased sampling needs to be carefully accounted for during the modelling process.

A related problem to biased sampling is *domain mismatch* where we have collected data from a different domain from where we will apply our model. Perhaps we train a model on Wikipedia text but then it is applied to legal documents. The patterns in the two domains are different and the model may learn the wrong patterns. Domain mismatch can be particularly damaging for the issue of fairness. Some facial recognition algorithms perform well on white, male faces but perform poorly on black, female faces because they were not well represented in the training data. If these algorithms are then used by law enforcement to identify suspects, they potentially reinforce social injustice.

Even if the data is representative of the problem domain overall, there may be quality issues with the individual records. Real-world data is noisy. Recording instruments can be imprecise. Sometimes data just goes missing – a patient doesn't show up for their appointment or the network dropped a request. Due to this messiness, a significant step in data collection is that of *data cleaning*. Data can be smoothed or discretized to remove noise. If the data contains very large and unexpected deviations, called *outliers*, these should be removed. Many ML algorithms are overly sensitive to outliers as they provide data points that are difficult for the model to explain. For missing data, we can drop the records or impute reasonable values based on the rest of the data where the values are present. Imputation techniques can be quite sophisticated and may require their own machine learning models.

When working with big data, acquisition and cleaning require special systems. A company's logs and databases will not fit on a single machine, and access to the data needs to be regulated and controlled. Processing the data may require a cluster of computers to perform data transformations. Currently the most popular framework for this is Spark, developed at UC Berkeley, which allows a large dataset to be distributed across the memory of dozens or hundreds of machines.

Finally, the data collection process should also involve a good amount of manual inspection or visualization. The allows us to gain intuition into the data, which will help us make better decisions later about what features and machine learning model to use.

[C] Model Selection

We have already touched on models above with the discussion of linear and logistic regression. These two simple models are represented by equations that tell us how we can predict a label given a record, aside from some unknown *parameters* that we must learn from our data. A model is a way of declaring our assumptions about how the world works. We always need to make some assumptions, such as the past is representative of the future, or that similar inputs lead to similar outputs. Without assumptions, we could not generalize from the data we already have to the new data that we have not seen yet.

These assumptions help eliminate complexity from the problem by imposing constraints. They also have other impacts on the quality of our model, so tradeoffs need to be made. Before discussing the different kinds of models, it is helpful to understand what qualities a good model should have. Innovations in modelling generally come from improving one or more of these qualities, or from striking a better tradeoff between a multiple of them.

[1] Expressiveness

A model captures our assumptions about the world, but if those assumptions are wrong, the model will make poor predictions, no matter how much data we have. A model is sufficiently *expressive* if there exist values for the unknown parameters that can faithfully represent the patterns in our data. If the model is not expressive enough, we say it is *biased*. When a model is biased, our predictions have some offset from the ground truth, an error that just never goes away. In an unbiased model, we may sometimes predict the label too high or too low, but these mistakes will average out to zero. To avoid bias, we can add more unknown parameters to a model or increase its complexity. Much innovation in ML today is centred around matching the structure of the model to the structure of the data, as we will see in the section on deep learning.

[2] Data Efficiency

Expressive models make fewer assumptions about our data. While this helps us to avoid bias, it may require us to use even more data to make up for the fewer constraints. When data is limited, we may not learn good values for our unknown parameters. This leads to an increase in *variance*, which is the amount of random noise in our predictions due to not having learned the correct parameters. This is in contrast to *bias* which does not reduce with more data. Ultimately, we want to make a good *bias-variance tradeoff* to reduce our total error. A model should be expressive enough to capture the patterns in our data, but not so expressive that we need an excessive amount of data to reduce the variance.

Figure 5. The bias variance tradeoff shown by fitting the same data with different models

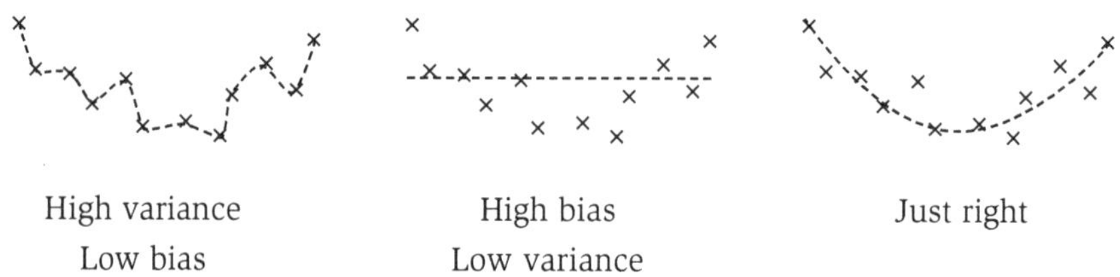

[3] Computational Efficiency

In addition to data efficiency we must consider computational efficiency. A low-bias and low-variance model is not worth much if it takes several years to process our data or it is too slow to use in real time on our website. The resources required for a model include both the processing time and the amount of computer memory required to work with the model. We shall see below that specialized hardware can enable certain models that are real resource hogs.

[4] Interpretability

Some models lend themselves to introspection. We can ask the model why it made a prediction and get a real answer. Other models are *black boxes,* where it is a mystery how decisions are made. The ability to explain a prediction is called *interpretability*. An interpretable model should tell us which feature of the record had the most influence on the prediction, or even how we should change the record to get a different outcome. There are critical domains where we are required to have an explanation for a prediction. In credit scoring, the USA has regulations stating a person has a right to know why they are rejected. Even when there are no regulations, it can still be helpful to understand why a decision was made. A user may want to know why they are getting a particularly annoying advertisement for the thousandth time. Generally, simpler and less expressive models lend themselves more to interpretability, but this is an active area of research.

Now that we have seen some factors to consider in model selection, let's look at a few of the major types of models.

[5] *Linear Models*

We have already seen the two major types of linear models: linear regression and logistic regression. Logistic regression is still considered to be a linear model even though the logistic function looks very non-linear. This is because the decisions made by a logistic regression can still be described with just a straight line. Data points on one side of the line will be labelled true, and on the other side they will be false. We can't do anything more complex than that. With respect to the model quality factors above, linear models have good data and computational efficiency because of their simple forms. Interpretability is also usually high because we can inspect which input features have the largest impact.

Figure 6. Linear vs. non-linear models

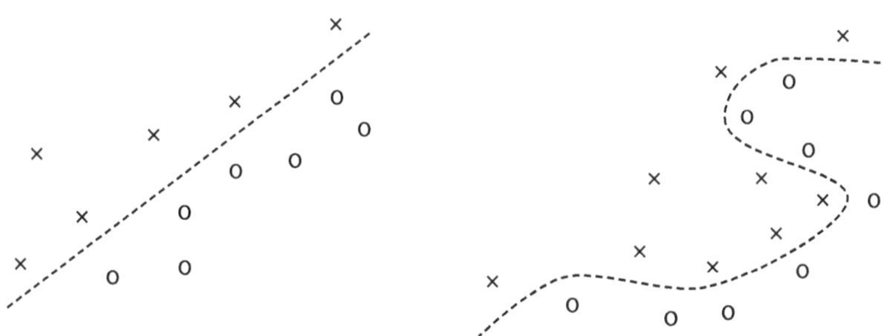

Linear decision boundary

Non-linear decision boundary

The simplicity comes at a price though, because these models are not very expressive. Typically, the world cannot be divided neatly by a single straight line. To get around this issue, we use the technique of *feature engineering.* We try to induce some non-linear behaviour in the model by giving it features that have themselves been transformed in a non-linear fashion. We can take individual features and warp them, say, by taking their square root or logarithm. We can also create a new feature that is the product of two individual features. Since linear models are efficient, we can cheaply add many new features to our model and not take too much of a performance hit. Either the linear model can learn to use them to help account for non-linearities, or it can ignore them by giving them zero weight.

Designing features that help linear models fit the data used to be a major part of the modelling process. It can take some creativity, and a lot of trial-and-error to create good new features. However, feature engineering has become a bit passé. Newer models have been popularized that are able to find non-linearities on their own without manual work.

[6] Decision Trees

A decision tree is a simple model where we make a decision by following the branches of a tree diagram. At each point, we make a decision about which branch to go down next, based on the values in our current record. When we get to a node where there are no more branches, called a leaf node, we have our decision. Tree models are computationally efficient. We are not performing complicated mathematical operations; we just check whether feature values are below or above a threshold. Decision trees are also very interpretable since they are easy to read off. What is most powerful about the decision tree, though, is that it introduces non-linearities. In the example tree below, we only get to the decision of 'duck' if it swims like a duck AND quacks like a duck. This type of AND operation is not generally possible in a linear model where we cannot automatically look for relationships between multiple features. The decision tree makes these non-linear decisions without any feature engineering.

Figure 7. Decision tree for animal classification

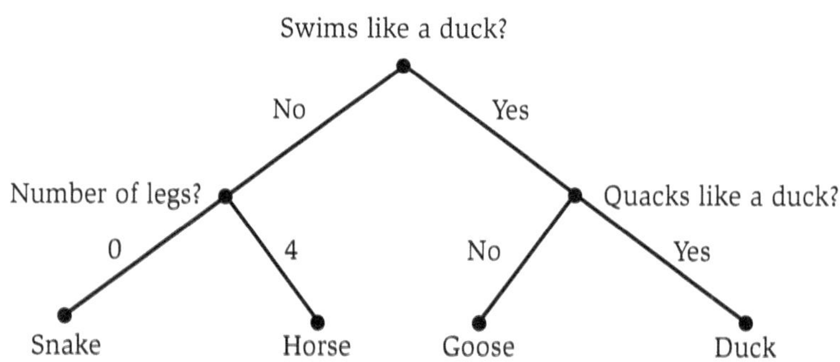

Nobody uses a solitary decision tree, however. A decision tree is fairly weak by itself, but becomes powerful when we use many of them together. There is a method called *ensemble learning* where we produce a more powerful learner from a set of weak learners. The one condition is that the weak learners should be different enough from each other that they add value. If they always make the same predictions, then it's not very useful to combine them. A *random forest* is a common way to generate a bunch of uncorrelated decision trees. To ensure each tree is different, we use random constraints when constructing each tree. At every branch, only a random subset of features and training data is allowed to be used. These trees are constructed efficiently since the work can be done in parallel, perhaps on different computers without any coordination.

One final type of decision tree ensemble is called *gradient boosting decision trees* ('GBDT'). The idea is similar to random forests, but the trees are generated in a sequence instead of in parallel. The next tree is built in such a way such that it partially makes up for weaknesses in the previous trees. Because of its high accuracy and computational efficiency, GBDTs are now one of the most widely deployed models in industry.

[7] *Deep Learning*

Over the last decade, tremendous excitement has surrounded the topic of *deep learning*. These models have blown the competition away on almost all machine learning leaderboards, sometimes producing performance that rivals or exceeds humans.

It is interesting to note that despite the recent popularity, deep learning has been around since the 1950s. Its origins are in *connectionist* models which built *artificial neural networks* ('ANN') inspired by the architecture of the human brain. Our brains consist of billions of neurons that receive and send signals to each other. A neuron by itself is not very computationally powerful, but with large enough numbers and the right patterns of connections between them, we get human intelligence. Similar to the brain, an artificial neural network is a computer model that consists of simple artificial neurons (also called units) that are connected together. Each neuron integrates the activity of its input units and then computes a signal to send to its output units. For their first 50 years, ANNs were more of scholarly interest than practical interest. They were slow, difficult to train, and ultimately did not perform that well. However, with the advancement of the internet, one of their major problems was solved by the availability of enormous datasets. Generally, there should be more records than unknown parameters in order to train successfully, and most useful neural networks have millions or even billions of unknown parameters. For example, a major breakthrough for NLP in 2013 was a model called *Word2Vec* which Google trained internally on a dataset of news articles containing a billion words. Data was no longer the bottleneck for training large ANN models.

It was around this time that ANNs went through a rebranding to deep learning, similar to how 'machine learning' is more common than 'artificial intelligence'. The similarity between ANNs and the human brain was always superficial. The size and architecture of ANNs, along with the way the neurons communicate and learn are all very different. In the 2010s a revolution was happening in machine learning with these models, and it seemed archaic to lump them together with an idea from the 1950s. The name 'deep learning' emphasizes that these ANNs are always organized into multiple layers. Each layer is a collection of units that receives outputs from a previous layer and sends signals on to the next one. The units in each layer are by themselves about as complex as a logistic regression, so models like logistic regression became known as *shallow learners*. If we stack several shallow learners, we get deep learning.

The power of deep learning is that it eliminates the need for feature engineering required by shallow learners. Each layer of the network applies a non-linear operation that essentially creates a new feature out of the inputs from the previous layer. As we go deeper in the network, each layer creates more complex features. With the right learning algorithm, the network will extract the right features for the task without the need for human feature engineering. In fact, it has become common practice to use one of a model's deeper layers as a feature generator. We can first encode the record using the network and extract its representation in that layer. This results in an *embedding vector* that we can use for other machine learning tasks. We could feed this embedding as an input into a shallow model, or we could use the embedding of two different records to measure how similar they are.

Figure 8. Feed-forward deep learning model

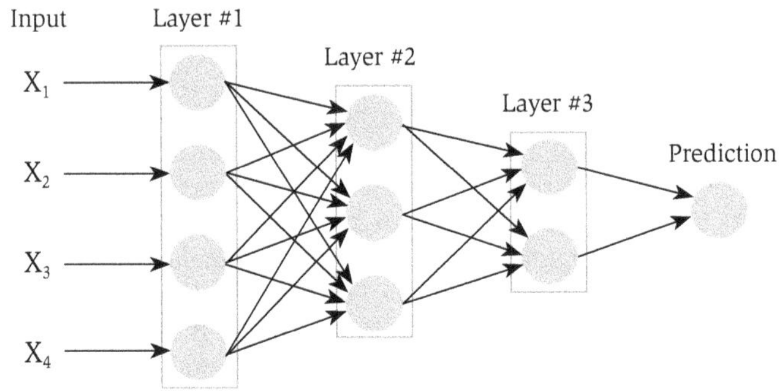

With deep learning, the focus of innovation has shifted away from feature engineering and on to network architecture. The feed-forward network illustrated above may work well for straightforward regression and classification problems, but in many specialized tasks, there are better choices. In NLP, we process human text that consists of sequences of words in sentences. These sequences can be of variable length. It would be difficult to represent sentences of all lengths as the input to a feed-forward network. Instead, we can use a *recurrent neural network* ('RNN') architecture that can process the text one word at a time. At each step, the RNN processes the next word in the sequence and updates its own internal state. The network is called recurrent because each step uses the same parameters – as if the layer keeps feeding back into itself. Conceptually we can *unfold* the network into an arbitrarily deep neural network.

Figure 9. Recurrent neural network model

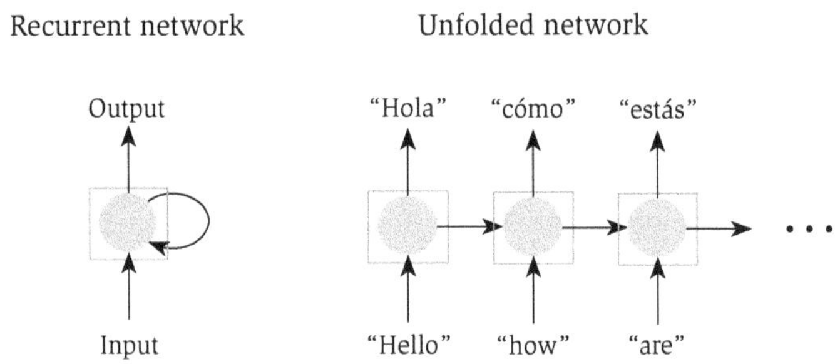

In computer vision, the most popular architecture is the *convolutional neural network* ('CNN'). This type of deep learning model takes inspiration from *receptive fields* of the human visual system. A receptive field is the relatively small region of the visual world that a neuron is responsive to. In the first layer of a CNN, units directly process small regions of pixels in an input image. In subsequent layers, each unit only receive inputs from a spatially localized set of units from the previous layer. Another trick is that each unit of a layer share all the same parameters, so that they apply the same calculation to their inputs. This reduces the total number of parameters a network must learn. Local receptive fields with parameter sharing make the network behave much like a mathematical convolution, hence the name.

Figure 10. Convolutional neural network model

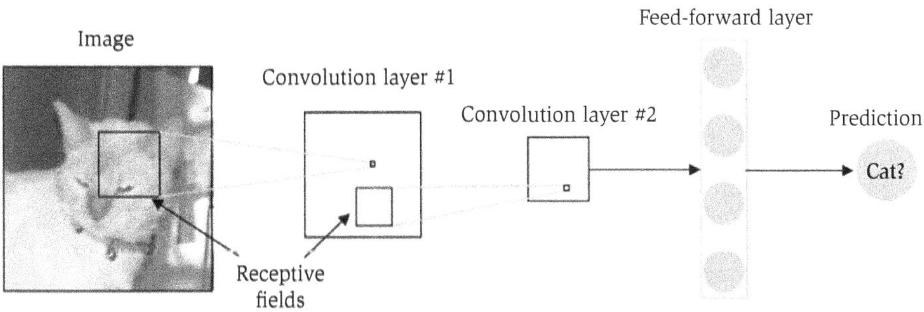

While deep learning and its specialized architectures have led to great leaps in performance, there are some drawbacks. For one, these models have become so complex that they are black boxes without any hope of interpretation. This is an issue in applications such as driverless cars where regulators would like to understand how the ML models make life-and-death decisions. Another issue is the growing divide between haves and have-nots for the resources needed to build state-of-the-art models. While data is generally more accessible these days, the largest datasets are often still proprietary. This enables the data owners to create the most complex models with the largest number of parameters. Those with access to less data cannot reproduce their results. Even when sufficient data is available, the computational resources to train these models may be out of reach. Deep learning requires massive computational power. Models often run on expensive, specialized hardware, such as GPUs (graphical processing units), that perform trillions of operations per second – a thousand-fold improvement over more standard CPUs (central processing units). If a model requires hundreds of GPUs, the computational cost is out of reach for most companies.

[D] Model Training

Once data is available and a model is selected, it's time to start learning the unknown parameters. This process is referred to as *training*. The first step in training is to define what makes one set of parameters better than another. This is expressed in terms of a *loss function*. Higher values of the loss indicate worse quality for the trained model, or larger errors. In a regression problem, the loss might be the average of the squared difference between the model's prediction and the actual value. Our goal is therefore to find the values of the parameters that *minimize* the loss.

While it is intuitive that the loss should capture our notion of how bad an error is, there are other considerations in choosing its form. Some loss functions make it easier to train our model. For example, the squared error is mathematically easier to work with than the absolute error even though they both indicate that big errors are bad. Sometimes we have multiple, competing objectives and the loss function must be designed to make tradeoffs between them. We can add *regularizers* to a loss function, discussed below, that induce side benefits to the model such as good generalization to new data.

[E] Optimization

After a loss function is chosen, we are ready to search for the model parameters that minimize it. This process is called *optimization*. The details of this step are highly dependent on the model being used. Some methods are as simple as putting the dataset into an equation and out pop the best parameters. There are exotic methods inspired by evolution that find better parameters by 'breeding' and 'mutating' the best parameters found so far. Random guessing even works well in some domains. However, the bread and butter for most machine learning optimization is *gradient descent*.

To understand gradient descent, think of the model parameters as coordinates on a topographical map where the loss function indicates the elevation. To minimize the loss function, we need to find the deepest valley on this map. A gradient is a concept from calculus that tells you which direction is downhill at a given position. If we are walking on the surface of the map, we can always reduce the loss function by taking a step downhill. This is what gradient descent does. We continually optimize the parameters by calculating the gradient and then updating the parameters with a step down the hill.

The major caveat about gradient descent is that it is liable to get stuck in a shallow valley. Once we hit the bottom of any dip in the loss function, there is no longer a downhill direction to follow. Therefore, gradient descent is only guaranteed to find a *local optimum* and not necessarily a *global* one. The procedure can stop when there is a much better solution somewhere out there.

Figure 11. Local and global minima in parameter optimization

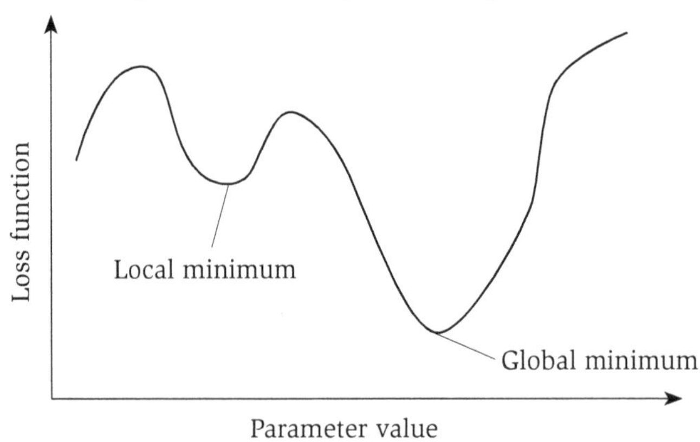

There are a lot of open choices when we use this method. Where do we start the walk? How big should our steps be? How do we know when it's time to stop walking?

Many tricks and techniques have been developed to answer these questions. Perhaps the most important innovation on gradient descent is *stochastic gradient descent.*

The gradient as described above is taken with respect to all of the training data at once, making it very expensive to calculate. In practice, we usually only calculate the gradient over a few random samples, called a *mini-batch.* Stochastic gradient descent calculates a noisy gradient from random samples. This means the step is sometimes taken in the wrong direction, but a local minimum still reliably be found if enough steps are taken. That is, the average heading is downhill. Today, virtually all deep learning models are trained using some variation of stochastic gradient descent. Fortunately, sophisticated tools are readily available such as TensorFlow from Google and PyTorch from Facebook that automatically calculate the gradients in a neural network. This lets ML practitioners focus on architecture instead of the mathematics.

One final consideration for optimization is called *generalization.* We minimize the loss function on our training data, but how well will we do on data we have not seen before? Can we generalize to new cases? Our model might get really good at memorizing the nuances of the training data, but if this goes too far, we start to *overfit* and perform worse on new data. We can diagnose this problem by calculating our loss not just on the training data, but also on holdout data, called the *test set.* If the loss on the training data is substantially lower than the loss on the test set, we have overfit. There are many tricks to fixing an overfit model. Often, they boil down to making the model simpler, with fewer free parameters. The handicapped model can no longer memorize random details of the training data. Alternatively, we can add a regularisation term to the loss function which penalizes large parameter values. This constrains the values of the parameters which acts similarly to reducing the number of free parameters.

[F] Deployment

The model is trained and the performance on the test set looks good. Now what? That depends on how the model is used. Sometimes the model is only being used for *decision support.* That is, the model generates predictions, but these are presented to a human who does the actual decision-making. This might happen in investment where projections of an asset's value are used as a factor in building a portfolio. In medical imaging, a computer vision algorithm may flag an X-ray for cancer but the doctor still makes the final diagnosis. In these cases, we can start using our model right away without much engineering effort. If the model's predictions are needed infrequently, the analysis could be run manually when needed. If reports must be generated more regularly, engineers could build an ETL (extract-transform-load) framework that automates refreshing the reports with new data. The expectation is that the time scale for reporting is slow. The calculations can be scheduled ahead of time, there will be some manual oversight, and there is tolerance to minor delays.

However, if instead the model is being used as a real-time *decision engine,* the work may have only just begun. For search engines and recommendations on websites, the model may need to generate millions of predictions per day with only a few milliseconds to respond to each request. In robotics, a controller model may be useless if it cannot keep up with the instantaneous physics of the robot's movements. Making predictions in real-time is referred to as *online inference.* Such systems need to be fast, reliable, and safe. Extra care is needed for monitoring so that faults are detected early. If there are large fluctuations in the number of requests, the system must be scalable so that it can provision more computational resources when demand is high.

Many of these challenges apply to any real-time information system, such as an online database or a telecommunications channel. However, some solutions are specific to machine learning. Model *compression* is a growing area of research where the computational complexity of the trained model is reduced *post hoc,* so that it performs inference faster. For example, we can throw away parameters that do not have a big impact, or even just round off the values of all parameters. If a model is compressed far enough, it may be able to run on a user's phone rather than on remote servers. We can also reduce the strain of online inference by identifying which parts of the inference can be pre-computed offline. If a model uses embedding vectors as described above, these embeddings could be stored in a database ahead of time and looked up for each request rather than calculated.

Despite the challenges of online inference, an advantage of these systems is that they close the loop on the machine learning process. We started this process by making a hypothesis about the model's impact on a business goal. When the machine learning model is making the decisions, it is also generating data about its own performance. This provides the most relevant possible training data for the next iteration of the machine learning process, leading to a virtuous cycle of continual improvement.

§02.05 ROLES IN MACHINE LEARNING

Now that we have seen the process used to develop machine learning solutions, let's meet the people who do the work. Labour is typically divided among several roles whose responsibilities emphasize different steps in the ML process. For each of these roles, I will describe their typical background and contribution. The exact titles vary from company-to-company, and any individual might find themselves fulfilling multiple roles. However, this list shows how different kinds of professionals contribute to innovation in machine learning.

[A] Research Scientist

Here we have the machine learning elite. These are the people driving innovation in machine learning models and finding new ways to learn patterns from data. They often have PhDs in computer science or another quantitative field, with the most highly sought after coming from universities such as Carnegie Mellon, Stanford, and Berkeley. Increasingly, these scientists are former professors, as industry competes to syphon off the top academic talent. Some of the top ML research scientists have even become celebrities in their own right. Yann LeCun (Facebook), Andrew Ng (formerly of Baidu), and Ian Goodfellow (Apple) each have over 100,000 followers on Twitter.

Given their academic backgrounds, research scientists are often eager to publish their work and give back to the scientific community. This can cause some tension with their companies as they need to strike a balance between publishing research and protecting intellectual property. However, it is a detriment to recruitment and retention if a company does not publish. Candidates go job-hunting at prestigious conferences such as the International Conference on Machine Learning ('ICML') and Neural Information Processing Systems (NeurIPS). If a research paper gets accepted there, it publicly demonstrates that interesting machine learning research is happening inside the company.

As for the research scientist's contribution to the machine learning process, they tend to advise in all steps of the process. However, their biggest impact is in the model selection and training steps. During their graduate work, they learned to invent machine learning methods that improve on the state-of-the-art or solve whole new problems. In industry, they apply these skills by creating new models to address the business problem at hand.

[B] Data Scientist

The data scientist's role is to organize, process, and extract insights from big data. Therefore, they make the biggest impact at the data collection and feature engineering stage. They also play a significant role in identifying opportunities to solve business problems with machine learning. When a data scientist does build a machine learning model, it tends to be for decision support rather than for decision engines. A word of warning – the line between data scientist and research scientist is blurry, and at some companies they mean the same thing. Applying for the right job is sometimes tricky.

Similar to research scientists, data scientists usually come with a PhD in a quantitative field. However, data scientists are more likely to come from a discipline other than computer science. Industry is eager to utilize the quantitative skills they acquired from academic research. I, myself, entered industry as a data scientist after a PhD in computational neuroscience. I found that the same skills I used to analyse spiking activity in the brain are also useful for understanding how customers interacted with websites. Industry pays better than the lab, too.

[C] Machine Learning Engineer

The deployment phase of the machine learning process involves very different skills from the prior steps. It requires hands-on, practical knowledge about how to build scalable and reliable information services. At this phase, the research scientist may actually hand off their machine learning model to machine learning engineers. This role is responsible for the *productionization* of the machine learning model. They are tasked to wrap the model inside a service that manages requests from users. The engineer must ensure good performance in terms of latency, throughput, availability, and load balancing. They may also need to build a data pipeline that periodicially *refreshes* the model with the latest data.

A machine learning engineer usually has a Master's degree in computer science. It is useful for them to also have a solid understanding of ML which will help them collaborate with researchers and data scientists.

[D] Product Manager

A product manager is the person who owns the vision for the project and manages its progress. Their impact on innovation is largest at the beginning of the project in the phase where we map a business problem onto a machine learning one. They are often the ones who had the original insight that there was an opportunity to create value by applying machine learning to the problem. After this initial phase, their role is to organize and motivate the other roles and see that their vision is realized. Typically, a product manager has an MBA, although I know many who are former research scientists.

§02.06 CONCLUSION

In this introductory chapter, I have given an overview of what machine learning is and what problems it can solve. I have discussed how machine learning projects are organized and what type of professionals do the work. I have also presented some of the most important terminology that machine learning practitioners use every day.

Still, I have barely scratched the surface on the innumerable algorithms and technologies available today, and our toolbox is ever expanding as investment in machine learning increases. Ten years ago, deep learning had not yet revolutionized the field and captured so much attention. I am afraid in ten more years this introduction will look rather quaint. The basic structure of machine learning however will remain the same as the practice of solving real-world problems by automatically learning patterns in data. And I hope in that future it will be a little bit easier to communicate with us machine learning practitioners.

Chapter 3
Australia

Dr Hannah Ivy Brown

§03.01 PATENTABILITY OF SOFTWARE AND COMPUTER-IMPLEMENTED INVENTIONS

The eligibility of an invention for patenting under Australian law is defined by the Patents Act 1990 (Cth) ('Patents Act'), wherein an invention is deemed to constitute patent-eligible subject matter only if 'the invention, so far as claimed in any claim, is a manner of manufacture within the meaning of Section 6 of the Statute of Monopolies',[1] where '*invention* means any manner of new manufacture the subject of letters patent and grant of privilege within Section 6 of the Statute of Monopolies, and includes an alleged invention'.[2]

The Statute of Monopolies of 1623 was the first English patent statute. The reference to a 400-year-old statute in current Australian law undoubtably will come as a surprise to those learning about this aspect of Australian law for the first time.

The leading authority for determining the meaning of the 'manner of manufacture' requirement remains the 'landmark' 1959 Australian High Court[3] decision, *National Research Development Corporation v. Commissioner of Patents* ('*NRDC*').[4] The High Court explained it as follows:

> The inquiry which the definition demands is an inquiry into the scope of the permissible subject matter of letters patent and grants of privilege protected by the section ... The word 'manufacture' finds a place in the present Act ... simply as the general title found in the Statute of Monopolies for the whole category under which all grants of patents which may be made in accordance with the developed principles of patent law are to be subsumed ... The right question

1. Patents Act 1990 (Cth), s. 18(1)(a).
2. Patents Act 1990 (Cth), Schedule 1 – Dictionary.
3. The High Court is Australia's highest legal authority.
4. *National Research Development Corp v. Commissioner of Patents* (1959) 102 CLR 252.

> is: 'is this a proper subject of letters patent according to the principles which have been developed for the application of s. 6 of the Statute of Monopolies?' [5]

It is thus left to the Courts to determine the boundaries of patent eligibility, but the High Court emphasized the importance of maintaining a flexible approach to the assessment of patent eligibility, stating:

> any attempt to state the ambit of s. 6 of the Statute of Monopolies by precisely defining 'manufacture' is bound to fail. The purpose of s. 6, it must be remembered, was to allow the use of the prerogative to encourage national development in a field which already, in 1623, was seen to be excitingly unpredictable. To attempt to place upon the idea the fetters of an exact verbal formula could never have been sound. It would be unsound to the point of folly to attempt to do so now, when science has made such advances that the concrete applications of the notion which were familiar in 1623 can be seen to provide only the more obvious, not to say the more primitive, illustrations of the broad sweep of the concept.[6]

The High Court then considered how the concept of 'manufacture' could be applied to a method or process:

> The point is that a process, to fall within the limits of patentability which the context of the Statute of Monopolies has supplied, must be one that offers some advantage which is material, in the sense that the process belongs to a useful art as distinct from a fine art - that its value to the country is in the field of economic endeavour.

The High Court ultimately held that the invention before it was a patentable method, observing that it provided 'a mode or manner of achieving an end result which is an artificially created state of affairs of utility in the field of economic endeavour', a phrase that became established as the touchstone for determining patent eligibility in Australia.

The expansive approach of *NRDC* was subsequently relied upon by the Federal Court in 1991[7] to establish that computer programs were not excluded from patent eligibility under Australian law, a decision that effectively opened the door for software patents in Australia. Subsequent Federal Court decisions held that a variety of computer-implemented inventions were patentable, including a computer program for the assembly of text in Chinese characters[8] and a smartcard system for consumer loyalty programs.[9]

In 2006, an attempt to patent an asset protection method involving purely financial and legal steps without the use of a computer was rejected by the Australian Full Federal Court in *Grant v. Commissioner of Patents*[10] on the basis that the

5. *Ibid.*, 269.
6. *Ibid.*, 271.
7. *International Business Machines Corporation v. Commissioner of Patents* (1991) 33 FCR 218.
8. *CCOM Pty Ltd v. Jiejing Pty Ltd* (1994) 51 FCR 260.
9. *Welcome Real-Time SA v. Catuity Inc* (2001) 113 FCR 110.
10. *Grant v. Commissioner of Patents* (2006) 154 FCR 62.

'artificially created state of affairs' of *NRDC* required 'a physical effect in the sense of a concrete effect or phenomenon or manifestation or transformation'. The Court contrasted the method before it with computer-implemented methods, noting that the latter were patent eligible because 'there was a component that was physically affected or a change in state or information in a part of a machine. These can all be regarded as physical effects.' Those comments were taken to indicate that any computer-implemented method would be patent eligible, and for the next few years that argument was relied upon to patent many computer-implemented business methods or schemes.

However, the tide turned in 2010, when the Australian Patent Office rejected a patent application for a scheme without computer implementation, and the applicant ambitiously attempted to force the Patent Office's hand by amending the claims to require that one of the steps used an 'electronically fillable checklist'. In a subsequent hearing,[11] the Patent Office took the position that the mere fact of computer implementation could not be sufficient to confer patent-eligibility to otherwise ineligible business, commercial or financial schemes (which *per se* have never been considered patentable in Australia). The Delegate of the Commissioner of Patents stated:

> the physical effect identified is in my view peripheral and subordinate to the substance of the claimed method ... There is no substantive effect produced through the operation of the computer which holds the 'electronically fillable checklist' and such an effect does not arise from a synergistic interaction in the operation of the method on the computer or other physical elements. Indeed the collection and presentation of information appears to have no physical consequence other than would arise in the computer with standard software in normal use. Computers and the internet are now as ubiquitous as paper and the postal service as means of collecting, displaying and disseminating information and their use as elements in a business scheme without something more, some substantial physical effect produced in the operation of the method, does not in my view and within the terms of NRDC result in an 'artificial state of affairs' any more than were those actions to be taken on paper and therefore in my view the invention claimed in claim 1 does not constitute a manner of manufacture.

Since then, there have been many Federal Court decisions confirming this view, and developing various criteria for assessing eligibility that show the influence of US and European jurisprudence.

In 2010, the Australian Patent Office handed down a decision[12] rejecting claims directed to 'a computer-implemented method for generating an index' by applying respective weightings to selected assets. On appeal to the Australian Federal Court,[13] the claimed method was held not to produce an 'artificially created state of affairs' because the result of working the method was considered to be only the index itself, which, in the words of the Court:

> is nothing more than a set of data ... If that were sufficient to satisfy the requirement of an artificially created state of affairs, any computer-implemented

11. *Invention Pathways Pty Ltd* (2010) 88 IPR 149.
12. *Research Affiliates, LLC* (2010) 90 IPR 607.
13. *Research Affiliates LLC v. Commissioner of Patents* (2013) 300 ALR 724.

> scheme would be patentable, merely by reason of the fact that it happens to be implemented by a computer.

Subsequent Federal Court decisions[14] and the subsequent *Aristocrat* decision of the Australian High Court[15] have confirmed this position. In one decision,[16] the Full Federal Court ('FFC') stated that 'the effect of [the applicant] Research Affiliates' submissions is that the mere implementation of any abstract idea or scheme in a well-known machine is sufficient to render that unpatentable subject matter patentable because it gives rise to an *"artificial effect"*. That approach is inconsistent with *NRDC* and is one of form not substance.'

The FFC said that the requirement for 'an artificially created state of affairs of economic significance was part of the High Court's reasoning [in *NRDC*], but did not represent a sufficient or exhaustive statement of the circumstances in which a claimed invention is patentable.'

The FFC said, '[i]n examining whether a claimed invention is properly the subject of letters patent, it is necessary to look not only at the integers of that claimed invention but also *at the substance of that invention*... It is a question of *understanding what has been the work of, the output of, and the result of, human ingenuity*.'

In another decision, the FFC said:[17]

> A claimed invention must be examined to ascertain whether it is in substance a scheme or plan or whether it can broadly be described as an improvement in computer technology. The basis for the analysis starts with the fact that a business method, or mere scheme, is not, per se, patentable. The fact that it is a scheme or business method does not exclude it from properly being the subject of letters patent, but it must be more than that. There must be more than an abstract idea; it must involve the creation of an artificial state of affairs where the computer is integral to the invention, rather than a mere tool in which the invention is performed. Where the claimed invention is to a computerised business method, the invention must lie in that computerisation. It is not a patentable invention simply to 'put' a business method 'into' a computer to implement the business method using the computer for its well-known and understood functions.
>
> It is not a question of stating precise guidelines but of deciding, in each case, whether the claimed invention, as a matter of substance not form, is properly the subject of a patent.[18]

---

14. *RPL Central Pty Ltd v. Commissioner of Patents* (2013) 121 IPR 378 ('*RPL Central*'); *Research Affiliates LLC v. Commissioner of Patents* (2014) 227 FCR 378; *Encompass Corporation Pty Ltd v. Infotrack Pty Ltd* (2019) 372 ALR 646; *Commissioner of Patents v. Rokt Pty Ltd* (2018) 277 FCR 267; *Repipe Pty Ltd v. Commissioner of Patents*, (2021) 164 IPR 1; *Aristocrat Technologies Australia Pty Ltd v. Commissioner of Patents*, (2020) 153 IPR 11; *Commissioner of Patents v. Aristocrat Technologies Australia Pty Ltd*, (2021) 286 FCR 572.
15. *Aristocrat v. Commissioner of Patents*, (2022) 168 IPR 1.
16. *Research Affiliates LLC v. Commissioner of Patents* (2014) 227 FCR 378.
17. *Commissioner of Patents v. RPL Central Pty Ltd*, (2015) 238 FCR 27, 49.
18. *Ibid.*, 49.

With a nod to the UK decisions *Aerotel Ltd v. Telco Holdings Ltd* and *Re Macrossan's Application*,[19] the Court stated that relevant considerations include whether the invention solves a technical problem and whether it makes a technical contribution.

It is now well-established that mere computer implementation is insufficient to transform an otherwise unpatentable scheme or abstract idea into patent-eligible subject matter.

One consideration is whether the computer is merely an intermediary or tool for performing the method while adding nothing of substance to the idea. However, if the claims and in particular the description indicate that the involvement of a computer is inextricably linked with the 'substance of the invention', or the invention can be seen as providing an improvement in computer technology, then the claims may be considered to constitute patent eligible subject matter in Australia.

In this writer's opinion, the primary problem is that the approach of Australian Courts (and consequently the Patent Office) to assessing the 'substance of the invention' has led to over-abstraction whereby claims are divided up to exclude from consideration any claim integers that are not themselves considered to represent part of the inventors' ingenuity. Thus, unless the computer implementation is itself at least part of the inventive step, it is ignored. What typically remains are only method steps, which in isolation are often characterized as nothing more than a 'scheme' or 'abstract idea', and are thus ineligible. This approach conflates the assessment of eligibility with assessments of novelty and inventive step[20] and, in this writer's opinion, is misguided.

At the time of writing (2023), the most recent decision on the eligibility of computer-implemented inventions is the High Court's *Aristocrat* decision, in which the Court was evenly split (3:3, in the absence of a seventh judge due to illness) on the question of whether claims directed to a computer-implemented gaming machine constituted eligible subject matter. Three of the judges considered that the invention was:

> no more than an unpatentable game operated by a wholly conventional computer, using technology which has not been adapted in any way to accommodate the exigencies of the game or in any other way.

It will be appreciated that this reflects the approach described above. In contrast, the other three judges argued that since a mechanical gaming machine must be eligible, it would be illogical to hold that an otherwise equivalent electronic gaming machine is somehow not eligible.

Because the Court was tied, the outcome of the appealed Full Federal Court decision stands, rejecting the claimed electronic gaming machine as ineligible, although happily the extremely restrictive test devised and applied by the Federal Court majority was rejected by all of the High Court judges. The divided High Court outcome also confirms a common view that the current state of Australian law on

19. *Aerotel Ltd v. Telco Holdings Ltd* [2006] EWCA Civ 1371; *Re Macrossan's Application* [2007] 1 All ER 225.
20. This approach is expressly rejected in AIPPI's 2017 Adopted Resolution on *Patentability of computer implemented inventions*.

the patent eligibility of computer-implemented inventions is manifestly unsatisfactory and that legislative reform is urgently needed.

For the sake of completeness, and as a caveat to the above, in the recent *D'Arcy v. Myriad* decision,[21] the High Court of Australia considered the boundaries of 'manner of manufacture' within the Patents Act, declaring that other factors to be taken into consideration include:

> (3) Whether patentability would be consistent with the purposes of the Act and, in particular:
> (3.1) whether the invention as claimed, if patentable under s. 18(1)(a), could give rise to a large new field of monopoly protection with potentially negative effects on innovation;
> (3.2) whether the invention as claimed, if patentable under s. 18(1)(a), could, because of the content of the claims, have a chilling effect on activities beyond those formally the subject of the exclusive rights granted to the patentee;
> (3.3) whether to accord patentability to the invention as claimed would involve the court in assessing important and conflicting public and private interests and purposes.[22]

It is conceivable that these three criteria could be considered applicable to some artificial intelligence ('AI')-related inventions (consider, for example, the recent proliferation of so-called 'deep fakes' and their potential to undermine public confidence), and consequently that an Australian court could consider that allowing a legal monopoly on an extremely powerful AI invention could, in some cases, be considered to be sufficiently contrary to the public interest as to deny patentability. However, this is speculative, and is not considered further in the remainder of this chapter.

§03.02 SPECIAL PROVISIONS RELATING TO PATENTABILITY OF INVENTIONS RELATING TO AI

There are no special provisions, guidelines or practices of any kind specifically directed to inventions relating to AI. The only Australian case law to date on AI-related inventions is confined to the legal question of whether an 'AI' can be an inventor for the purposes of the Patents Act. This is discussed in Section §03.06[B], *infra*.

§03.03 SUBJECT MATTER PATENTABILITY

The eligibility of some types of AI-related inventions for patent protection under Australian law is not entirely clear. As noted above, there is no relevant Australian case law on AI-related inventions, so one can only look to the case law on other types of computer-implemented inventions to imagine how the principles enunciated in those decisions might be applied to AI-related inventions.

---

21. *D'Arcy v. Myriad Genetics Inc. and Another* (2015) 258 CLR 334 ('Myriad').
22. *Ibid.*, 351.

The Australian case law on computer-implemented inventions highlights a vulnerability of inventions that can be (rightly or wrongly) considered to be, in substance, nothing more than a 'scheme' or 'abstract idea', whether computer-implemented or not. The difficulty this poses is that there are no definitions of these terms in the case law. The impression one has as a practitioner is that there will never be any such definitions but patent examiners and courts will simply 'know one when they see one'. Although the inventions considered to be schemes by Australian courts generally relate to business or finance, in the experience of this writer Australian patent examiners sometimes also reject inventions in other fields on the basis that they are, in the examiner's view, in substance nothing more than a 'scheme'.

Even if the claims are limited to a computing environment, if the computer implementation does not in itself add anything of substance to the invention beyond mere computer implementation *per se*, then the invention will not be considered eligible. If, on the other hand, there is some 'ingenuity in the way in which the computer is utilized',[23] then the invention is likely to be considered eligible. Ultimately, the answer will often hinge upon how the description and claims have been drafted.

[A] Category 1: Invention of AI; and Category 2: AI Implementation

The patent eligibility of an 'invention of AI' or an 'AI implementation'; that is, a new type of AI algorithm, AI model or AI configuration for a 'general-purpose' AI system (i.e., independent of any particular use case) will depend upon how it is described and claimed in the patent specification.

For example, if embodiments of the invention are described in general mathematical terms, and the described computer implementation is generic (meaning that it is a straightforward implementation of the mathematical method), then there is a significant risk that the invention would not be considered eligible for patent protection in Australia on the basis that it is effectively trying to claim a mathematical algorithm, abstract idea or 'scheme'. If, however, there is inventive merit in the specific implementation described in the patent specification, then that implementation, if claimed, should be eligible.

In contrast to the above, if the invention involves specific new (hardware and/or software) architectural and processing features that are technically advantageous, and if these features are described in significant and specific technical detail, then it should be possible to draft corresponding process and apparatus claims that would be considered patent-eligible, despite not being limited to any specific application. In particular, if the new features provide technical advantages such as overcoming a technical limitation of prior art AI systems (providing a 'technical solution' to a 'technical problem'), or providing a significant improvement in processing efficiency, then that should prevent the invention from being considered to be in substance nothing more than a generically implemented mathematical algorithm or scheme. The specification needs to make clear that the invention, in substance, constitutes an improvement in computer technology.

23. *RPL Central* at 104, citing *Research Affiliates*.

[B] Category 3: A New Application of AI

A novel and inventive application of AI would be considered patent-eligible in Australia, unless the application itself as claimed is considered to be in substance nothing more than a mere scheme or a business, commercial or gaming method, and there in no ingenuity in the computer implementation of the AI.

In cases where the AI is applied as a 'decision maker' to effect a physical action, then the invention should be eligible. In cases where AI is applied to simply provide information, rather than to effect a physical action, the eligibility is likely to depend upon how the information is used, the environment in which it is used, and whether the invention overcomes a technical problem or provides a technical advantage. For example, if the information is used in a subsequent technical process, then the invention may be considered eligible. Conversely, if the information is only used for business or financial purposes, then it is highly unlikely to be considered eligible.[24,25]

[C] Category 4: Inventions Made Using AI

The eligibility of an invention 'made using AI' (i.e., where the use of AI is not part of the invention), any patent protection will be unrelated to the use of AI, and subject to the usual considerations. Even if the invention is made 'accidentally' using the AI, this is akin to accidental discovery and application of that discovery to a practical problem is an invention.

[D] Category 5: Inventions Made by AI

In a hypothetical scenario wherein an AI system 'independently' identifies problems and constructs inventions that address those problems, the eligibility of such inventions for patent protection will be determined in the usual manner, i.e., whether those inventions satisfy the usual criteria for assessing the eligibility of any invention for patent protection. The circumstances of their creation are irrelevant, and if the invention does not require the use of AI for its implementation, then AI need not even be mentioned in the patent specification for the invention. A patent specification only needs to describe how to put an invention into effect, not the circumstances that led to its creation.

§03.04 INVENTIVE STEP

Inventive step for AI-related inventions will be assessed using well-established principles of Australian law. The Patents Act requires that:

> an invention is to be taken to involve an inventive step when compared with the prior art base unless the invention would have been obvious to a person skilled in the relevant art in the light of the common general knowledge as it

24. *Amplero, Inc.* [2018] APO 59.
25. *[24] 7.ai, Inc.* [2019] APO 50.

existed (whether in or out of the patent area) before the priority date of the relevant claim.[26]

The skilled person for the purposes of assessing inventive step can be a team of skilled persons, being 'those likely to have a practical interest in the subject matter of the invention. A variety of people may have that interest. There are those who might wish to make or construct the invention, those who may wish to compound the invention and those who may wish to use the invention.'[27]

Although the 'person skilled in the art' is a hypothetical construct, it would not include an AI, but may include a person using AI as a tool, if evidence can establish that AI tools are typically used in the relevant field when seeking to solve the problem described (in the patent specification) as being addressed by the invention, which highlights the importance of defining an appropriate problem or background setting.

With or without using AI tools, if the invention is described as addressing a particular problem, then obviousness can be assessed by posing the so-called 'reformulated Cripps question': 'would the notional [skilled addressee] at the relevant date, (in all the circumstances) ... directly be led as a matter of course to try [the claimed invention] ... in the expectation that it might well produce [a useful result]?'[28]

If the evidence establishes that the skilled person would typically use an AI tool to seek a solution to the problem addressed by the invention, then the assessment of obviousness will likely hinge on whether the type of AI tool used by such a person would almost certainly identify the invention and either indicate that it will or will be expected to provide a solution to the problem, or the skilled person themselves would expect that it would.

A caveat to this could be whether the invention is identified either as the only solution or as one of a practically small number of such solutions. For example, if an AI tool identified the invention along with, say, over 100 other such solutions or candidate solutions, it could be argued that the skilled person was not 'directly' led to that solution.

§03.05 ADEQUACY OF DISCLOSURE

The patent system is based on the *quid pro quo* principle that, in exchange for a limited-term monopoly, the patentee must describe the best-known implementation of their invention in sufficient detail so that others can take full advantage of the invention after the expiry of the patent, without the need for extensive experimentation or further invention.

Section 40 of the Patents Act states, *inter alia*:

(2) A complete specification must:
  (a) disclose the invention in a manner which is clear enough and complete enough for the invention to be performed by a person skilled in the relevant art; and

26. Patents Act 1990, s. 7(2), s. 7(3).
27. *Catnic Components Ltd v. Hill & Smith Ltd* (1982) RPC 183 at 242.
28. *AstraZeneca AB v. Apotex Pty Ltd* (2014) 226 FCR 324 at 451.

(aa) disclose the best method known to the applicant of performing the invention; and

...

(3) The claim or claims must be clear and succinct and supported by matter disclosed in the specification.

The requirement of s. 40(2)(a) is an enablement requirement, and s. 40(2)(aa) requires that the applicant disclose not just any working implementation of the invention, but the best implementation known to them at the date of filing the patent application.[29]

The requirement of s. 40(3) that the claims must be 'supported by matter disclosed in the specification' is there to ensure that the scope of the claims is commensurate with the detailed description so that the claims are fully enabled across the entire scope. This is a relatively recent change in Australian law and replaces the previous 'fair basis' test that only required the applicant to disclose and enable a single embodiment falling within the scope of the (potentially much broader) claims.

The requirements for adequacy of disclosure of AI-related inventions are the same as for any other type of invention. However, for AI-related inventions, this requirement could be challenging in circumstances where the implementation details are complex and/or the advantages of the invention require particular training data or particular features of the training data. Nevertheless, the requirement must be satisfied in order to obtain a valid patent, and whether the requirement is satisfied is a question of fact.

For example, if the patent specification describes results generated by an embodiment of the invention from a proprietary database, it is not necessary for full details of that specific database to be disclosed in the patent specification, provided that the specification teaches the reader what features of the input data are required in order to provide corresponding outputs, and how to obtain or otherwise generate suitable input data having those features.

Similarly, if there is something unconventional about the way that the AI is trained using the training data, then the relevant details of that training need to be fully disclosed.

Moreover, because the claims must be supported across their full scope, if the claims are very broad in scope relative to a specific embodiment or example, then it is important that as many embodiments and/or examples as possible are described in the patent specification in order to fully support the breadth of the claims. Failure to do so may require the scope of the claims to be narrowed by amendment during prosecution, and certainly prior to enforcement.

29. *Domestic Australia Pty Ltd v. Houghton Leisure Products Pty Ltd* (2018) FCA 1573; 135 IPR 403.

§03.06 INVENTORSHIP

[A] Inventorship in General

Inventorship under Australian law can arise from conception or reduction to practice, depending on the circumstances. Inventorship was discussed by Crennan J in *JMVB Enterprises Pty Ltd v. Camoflag Pty Ltd*:[30]

> '132 Rights in an invention are determined by objectively assessing contributions to the invention, rather than an assessment of the inventiveness of respective contributions. If the final concept of the invention would not have come about without a person's involvement, then that person has entitlement to the invention. One must have regard to the invention as a whole, as well as the component parts and the relationship between the participants.

As described by French J in *University of Western Australia v. Gray*:[31]

> A distinction between mere discovery and invention has long been made on the basis that it is only when a discovery is applied to a useful end that it comes within the concept of a manner of new manufacture: Lane-Fox v. Kensington and Knightsbridge Electric Lighting Co (1892) 29 RPC 413 at 416 (Lindley LJ). The dividing line is not clear. The High Court said in National Research Development Corporation 102 CLR 252 (at 264):
>
>> The truth is that the distinction between discovery and invention is not precise enough to be other than misleading in this area of discussion. There may indeed be a discovery without invention — either because the discovery is of some piece of abstract information without any suggestion of a practical application of it to a useful end, or because its application lies outside the realm of 'manufacture'.

Regarding multiple inventors, French J referred to *University of Southampton's Applications*:[32]

> Laddie J observed that an inventive concept frequently comes from a contribution of more than one mind with each putting the pieces together. Where it was impossible to distinguish the contributions of a number of individuals to a 'single inventive concept' they would all be inventors. This did not mean that those whose only contribution was to supply data for enabling disclosure thereby qualified as inventors.[33]

The identification of joint inventors was discussed by the Full Federal Court in *Polwood Pty Ltd v. Foxworth Pty Ltd*,[34] as follows:

30. *JMVB Enterprises Pty Ltd v. Camoflag Pty Ltd* (2005) 67 IPR 68.
31. *University of Western Australia v. Gray* (2009) FCAFC 116, 1421.
32. *University of Southampton's Applications* [2005] RPC 11.
33. *University of Western Australia v. Gray and Others* (No. 20) (2008) 246 ALR 603, 1435.
34. *Polwood Pty Ltd (ACN 010 708 146) and Others v. Foxworth Pty Ltd (ACN 010 516 855) and Others* (2008) 244 ALR 626.

> [33] The entitlement to the grant of a patent as the inventor is not determined by quantitative contribution. The role of joint inventors does not have to have been equal; it is qualitative rather than quantitative. It may involve joint contribution or independent contributions. The issue is whether the contribution was to the invention. What constitutes the invention can be determined from the particular patent specification which includes the claims. In some cases, evidence can assist. In some cases, the reduction of a concept to a working apparatus by a person may not be part of the invention, in other cases it may be. For example, the construction of an apparatus may involve no more than carrying out the instructions in the specification. This would not normally entitle that person to joint inventorship. On the other hand joint inventorship may arise where the invention is in the apparatus itself, or where the person constructing the apparatus contributed to a different or better working of it which is then described and claimed.
>
> [34] One criterion for inventorship may be to determine whether the person's contribution had a material effect on the final invention. It may be that an invention is made as part of a collaborative effort. In those circumstances, it would ordinarily follow that the collaborators are joint inventors of the product of the collaboration ...

In *University of Western Australia v. Gray*, French J noted, '[p]lainly there are no bright lines to be drawn between inventorship based on inventive concept and verification or reduction to practice.'[35]

The Full Court in *Polwood* held that inventorship is to be assessed in relation to the invention described in the patent application, not only that claimed:

> [35] To ascertain the inventor for the purposes of entitlement to the grant of the patent it is therefore necessary to determine the contributions to the invention described in the patent application. The claims may assist in that determination, bearing in mind that the claims may be to less than the totality of the invention. It may also be appropriate to investigate the contributions to the inventive steps giving rise to the invention.

[B] Determination of Inventorship for AI-Related Inventions

Inventorship for the first four categories of AI-related inventions would be determined using standard principles – thus, the person or persons whose contributions 'had a material effect on the invention'. Additionally, any other person who made a material contribution to reducing the invention to practice would also be considered to be an inventor if their contribution was beyond straightforward implementation that any person skilled in the art would make.

In the hypothetical fifth category case of an invention 'made by AI', although Australia was the first and to date the only country in which a court held[36] that an AI could be an inventor for the purposes of a patent, that decision was subsequently

35. *University of Western Australia v. Gray (No. 20)* (2008) FCA 498; BC200802595, 1441.
36. *Thaler v. Commissioner of Patents* [2021] FCA 879.

overturned,[37] and the Australian High Court refused an application for special leave to appeal the decision. With no avenues of appeal remaining, the final position (in the absence of legislative change) is that only human beings can be inventors under Australian law.

The patent application that gave rise to these decisions was initially rejected by the Deputy Commissioner of Patents on the basis that the applicant, Dr Stephen Thaler, had failed to properly name an inventor, as required by law, since the name provided was 'DABUS, The invention was autonomously generated by an artificial intelligence', which is not the name of a natural person.

In the initial decision (of a single Federal Court judge), the judge accepted the applicant's submission that there was no human inventor, and that the 'DABUS' artificial intelligence system was the sole inventor of the claimed invention. Consequently, the question before the Court was whether an artificial intelligence system or device could validly be named as an inventor for the purposes of the Patents Act.

Although the Patents Act does preclude an artificial intelligence system or device from being the *owner* of a patent, there is no definition of the word 'inventor' in the Patents Act, and the judge considered that 'an inventor is an agent noun; an agent can be a person or thing that invents … nothing in the Act dictates the contrary conclusion.'[38]

Noting also that the following object clause had recently been added to the Patents Act:

> The object of this Act is to provide a patent system in Australia that promotes economic wellbeing through technological innovation and the transfer and dissemination of technology. In doing so, the patent system balances over time the interests of producers, owners and users of technology and the public.[39]

The judge opined that: 'In my view it is consistent with the object of the Act to construe the term 'inventor' in a manner that promotes technological innovation and the publication and dissemination of such innovation by rewarding it, irrespective of whether the innovation is made by a human or not.'[40]

Regarding ownership of the claimed invention, His Honour stated:

> Dr. Thaler is the owner, programmer and operator of DABUS, the artificial intelligence system that made the invention … On established principles of property law, he is the owner of the invention. In that respect, the ownership of the work of the artificial intelligence system is analogous to ownership of the progeny of animals or the treatment of fruit or crops produced by the labour and expense of the occupier of the land (fructus industrialis), which are treated as chattels with separate existence to the land.[41]

37. *Commissioner of Patents v. Thaler* [2022] FCAFC 62.
38. *Ibid.*, 10.
39. Patents Act 1990, s. 2A.
40. *Thaler v. Commissioner of Patents* [2021] FCA 879, at 124.
41. *Ibid.*, 167.

In an appeal to the Full Court of the Australian Federal Court,[42] all five judges overturned the primary judge's decision, holding that:

> it is plain ... that the law relating to the entitlement of a person to the grant of a patent is premised upon an invention for the purposes of the Patents Act arising from the mind of a natural person or persons. Those who contribute to, or supply, the inventive concept are entitled to the grant. The grant of a patent for an invention rewards their ingenuity.[43]
>
> We respectfully disagree with the primary judge that ... a person ... may draw entitlement to the grant of a patent from an inventor who is not ... a natural person ... To so find overlooks the scheme of the Patents Act ... and fails to give s. 15(1) a natural reading. It also overlooks the history of the development of the law of patents to which one is directed by the term 'invention' in the chapeau to s. 15(1), defined in the Patents Act by reference to the Statute of Monopolies.[44]

Finally, the Court noted an urgent need to address issues concerning patents for inventions where an artificial intelligence is an or the inventor, including 'whether, as a matter of policy, a person who is an inventor should be redefined to include an artificial intelligence. If so, to whom should a patent be granted in respect of its output?'[45]

An application by Dr Thaler for special leave to appeal the Full Federal Court's decision to the High Court of Australia was rejected,[46] Their Honours stating simply that 'this is not the appropriate vehicle to consider the questions of principle sought to be agitated by the applicant'. Based on the High Court transcript, this may have largely been due to Their Honours' apparent skepticism that Dr Thaler was not, in fact and in law, the inventor, given that neither party was willing to challenge the 'agreed facts' that Dr Thaler was not the inventor.

In this writer's opinion, an AI, no matter how sophisticated, is nevertheless only a mathematical tool, and cannot 'invent' in the usual sense of the word. However, if no natural person had any conception of the invention, and if any reduction to practice did not involve human involvement or alternatively any ingenuity, then it is possible that a court may decide that any human involvement did not have the necessary character of either conception or reduction to practice.

As an AI does not have legal personality in Australia and cannot be named as an inventor,[47] the invention would not have an inventor. Under the Patents Act, entitlement to grant of a patent must derive from a human inventor,[48] and consequently under existing Australian law no legal person could have entitlement to grant, and therefore the invention would not be patentable.

42. *Commissioner of Patents v. Thaler* [2022] FCAFC 62.
43. *Ibid.*, 105.
44. *Ibid.*, 112.
45. *Ibid., 119.*
46. *Thaler v. Commissioner of Patents* (2022) HCATrans 199.
47. Ignoring the issue of how an AI could even have a 'name' and thus be identified in any case. An AI cannot be expected to be a fixed and stable entity, but rather one undergoing continuous improvement or development, arguably making it a different and continuously evolving entity over time.
48. Patents Act 1990 (Cth), s. 15.

Alternatively, it could be argued that the person or persons who configured the AI to identify problems and inventions that solve those problems are inventors, because without the contribution of that person or persons, the AI would not have identified the problem or the invention. Indeed, the AI would not even exist. Moreover, an AI of this hypothetical type is only a tool that uses a mathematical algorithm to process input data and generate outputs, albeit an unusually sophisticated and powerful one. Although the fact that a person who configured the AI to identify inventions did not 'conceive' of the problem or its solution is arguably philosophically problematic, to this writer it is not fundamentally different from other types of accidental discovery, such as accidental mixing of chemicals to produce an unexpected compound or structure, for example. Although even the recognition that the invention identified by the AI is a patentable invention could conceivably be provided by the AI itself (and thus be absent from the person's contribution – the AI could even conceivably draft and file a patent application without direct human involvement), it cannot be disputed that 'the person's contribution had a material effect on the final invention',[49] because the invention (indeed, arguably even the AI itself) would not exist without the contribution of that person. Similarly, because 'the final concept of the invention would not have come about without [that] ... person's involvement, then that person has entitlement to the invention.' [50]

It must be conceded that this latter interpretation is not without its difficulties. For example, while it might be intellectually straightforward to identify as an inventor a single person who configures an AI to identify problems and create inventions to solve them without the involvement of any other person, the situation may be considerably more challenging when, for example, one person configures the AI and a second person provides input data to the AI wherein, together, that input data and the AI configuration collectively lead to the identification of a problem and an invention that addresses that problem. On one view, both persons are inventors of the resulting invention. However, if the first person dies, then is the first person nevertheless an inventor of every invention that is subsequently identified by the AI in perpetuity? Additionally, what if the input provided by a second person is of a trivial or even arbitrary character totally unrelated to the resulting problem and invention? The answers to these questions will have to wait until the law in this area is more fully developed.

§03.07 AREAS FOR IMPROVEMENT

[A] Subject Matter Eligibility

As described above, there is a risk that some types of AI-related inventions could be considered to be nothing more than computer-implemented schemes or abstract ideas, and therefore ineligible for patent protection. This difficulty arises from the current approach (adopted by Australian courts and the Patent Office) of ignoring known claim integers when assessing eligibility, and the fact that there is no clear

49. *Polwood Pty Ltd (ACN 010 708 146) and Others v. Foxworth Pty Ltd (ACN 010 516 855) and Others* (2008) 244 ALR 626.
50. *JMVB Enterprises Pty Ltd v. Camoflag Pty Ltd* (2005) 67 IPR 68.

definition of what constitutes a 'scheme' or an 'abstract idea', although these terms and the prohibition on patenting such things comes from case law dating back to at least the nineteenth century, long before the advent of computer technology.

Australian courts do not appear to have questioned these traditional prohibitions at all, taking them as givens. Consequently, it is understandable that the courts would reject the proposition that simply using a computer to effect such ineligible schemes or abstract ideas would confer eligibility upon them (and thus circumvent these traditional prohibitions).

In the opinion of this writer, the philosophical basis of the prohibitions needs to be re-examined in the context of computer-implemented inventions and a global economy dominated by information technology. For example, the Full Federal Court briefly described the traditional prohibitions by quoting from a decision that is more than a century old:

> [y]ou cannot have a Patent for a mere scheme or plan – a plan for becoming rich; a plan for the better government of a State; a plan for the efficient conduct of business.[51]

However, there are fundamental differences between these types of prohibited 'schemes or plans' -- which have the character of philosophical thoughts, or 'mere intellectual information' -- and a computer software product or computer hardware programmed to execute specific data processing steps, whether as part of a business method, financial transaction or other application.

As observed by the High Court in 1938,[52] and cited with approval in both the *NRDC* and *Myriad* High Court decisions, 'a widening conception of a manner of new manufacture has been a characteristic of the growth of patent law'. However, it seems to this writer that the conception has narrowed over the past decade. The problem is not that the relevant cases are wrongly decided, but rather that the legal principles expressed in the decisions are so broad and unclear that they can be (and are) applied to sophisticated computer-implemented inventions that, in the opinion of this writer, should be eligible for patent protection.

Although the Full Federal Court warned[53] that 'care must be taken to consider the circumstances of the claimed invention' to avoid over-abstraction, they did not provide any guidance at all as to how this care is to be exercised, and in the experience of this practitioner, Australian patent examiners often over-abstract computer-implemented inventions and consequently allege that they are in substance nothing more than 'mere schemes'.

The result is legal uncertainty, which comes at the detriment to investment in innovation, and consequently innovation itself. A decision needs to be made as to what types of computer-implemented inventions should be patentable, and which should not, and this should be reflected by suitable amendments to the Patents Act. For example, although one might not like the limitations to patentability of computer-implemented inventions under the European Patent Convention, at least the assessment is highly predictable.

---

51. *Re Cooper's Application for a Patent* (1901) 19 RPC 53, 54.
52. *Maeder v. Busch* [1938] HCA 8; (1938) 59 CLR 684 (1 March 1938).
53. *RPL Central* FCAFC at 105.

The 'manner of manufacture' requirement from 1623 served Australia well up until at least 2010, but there is an argument that Australian courts are still applying criteria from at least a century ago to inventions of the information age, and in order to justify their decisions are formulating new assessment criteria that are so vague that they can easily be misapplied and thus do not provide legal certainty. The world economy is now driven by information technology and software-implemented processes. The difficulty of protecting computer-implemented processes makes it difficult for start-ups and individual inventors in particular to compete with *de facto* monopolies, who, due to their market power and considerable resources, do not require patent protection, and are largely free to copy the ideas of less powerful innovators.

It would be desirable for the Patents Act to be amended to at least clarify that certain types of invention are eligible for patent protection, including AI-related inventions. In particular, the approach of conflating eligibility with novelty and inventive step needs to stop. As our courts seem unable or unwilling to do so, legislative change is urgently needed.

[B] Inventorship

As described above, a hypothetical type of AI system that is capable of 'independently' identifying problems and inventions to address those problems challenges traditional notions of inventorship. In one view, such inventions would not have a human inventor, and consequently would not be patentable under current Australian law. This is not a desirable outcome, as the patent system provides an important role in fostering innovation by encouraging the public disclosure of inventions in exchange for a limited-term monopoly. It has been demonstrated that, where patent protection is not available, the owners of inventions tend to keep them secret, thereby depriving the public of detailed knowledge of inventions.

The main purpose of naming inventors in a patent application is to identify the source of rights to the corresponding invention so that the ownership of the invention can be determined and verified. Accordingly, under current Australian law, inventions 'made by AI' would not be patentable and this is not in the public interest. However, the situation could be remedied by amending the legislation so that a human inventor is not a necessary condition for grant of a patent. For example, where an AI system is considered to make a contribution to an invention such that if that contribution had been made by a human person it would be sufficient for that person to be named as an inventor, then the owner of that AI system could be deemed entitled to rights in the invention equivalent to those that the hypothetical human inventor would have had.

Conversely, if it remains the case that an AI system cannot be considered to be an inventor for the purposes of a patent, but a person who configures an AI to identify problems and create inventions is considered to be the (or an) inventor, then this could also create difficulties if the AI system is never publicly disclosed. For example, if the inventor dies, the inventor (or the inventor's heirs) could nevertheless be considered to own rights to inventions that are 'made' after the inventor's death, and indeed potentially in perpetuity. Accordingly, in such a scenario it might be appropriate to limit the use of such an AI system to create patentable inventions; for example, by requiring publication of the AI system (which may be by way of a published patent application for the AI system), or by only allowing patent applications to be filed within a fixed period from the date that the AI system was created (noting however, that this could create its own problems with defining that date, particularly where the AI system is continually improved over time).

§03.08 RECOMMENDATIONS FOR PATENT APPLICANTS

As described above in Section §03.05, *supra*, it is important that a patent specification for an AI-related invention describes at least one embodiment of the invention - the best embodiment known to the applicant - in substantial technical detail, including any required features of training data or the training process, in order to ensure that the invention is fully enabled. Additionally, if the claims are broader in scope than any one embodiment described in the patent specification, then it is important that as many embodiments as possible are described in the specification to enable the claims across their entire scope.

In addition to these standard requirements, in order to mitigate any risk that the AI -related invention might be considered to be in substance nothing more than a scheme, the patent specification should communicate any technical difficulties overcome, technical advances made, and the resulting (preferably technical) advantages of the invention. If appropriate to the specific invention under consideration, the specification should describe a problem addressed by the invention, where that problem is preferably not in a problematic 'non-technical' field such as commerce, finance, gaming, or operating a business.

§03.09 CONCLUSION

Although AI systems have been around for decades, a combination of the increasing amount of electronic information on essentially any subject being generated and the decreasing cost of high-power computing resources has led to their proliferation and increasing capabilities in recent times. It is in the public interest to ensure that patent protection is available for novel and inventive AI-related inventions to encourage innovation and investment in AI technologies, and public disclosure of such inventions.

As described above, the AI-related inventions currently available today are able to be patented under Australian law, subject to the qualifications described above. However, the prospect of AI systems that are able to 'independently' identify problems and create inventions to address those problems challenge traditional notions of invention. If it is accepted that there is no human inventor, then such inventions would not be patentable under current Australian law. However, the situation could be addressed by relatively minor amendments to the relevant legislation. It is time that such issues are considered and addressed so that our legal systems are ready for the inevitable challenges posed by AI technologies.

Chapter 4
Canada

Alfred A. Macchione & Jeff Sun

§04.01 PATENTABILITY OF SOFTWARE AND COMPUTER-IMPLEMENTED INVENTIONS

Under the Canadian patent statute (the 'Patent Act'), an invention is defined as 'any new and useful art, process, machine, manufacture or composition of matter, or any new and useful improvement in any art, process, machine, manufacture or composition of matter'.[1] In addition, the Patent Act excludes from patentability 'any mere scientific principle or abstract theorem'.[2] Accordingly, any subject matter for which patent protection is desired must fall within one of the recognized categories of an invention as defined in the Patent Act, and must not be a mere scientific principle or abstract theorem.

As in other jurisdictions, software and computer-implemented inventions may often be claimed in Canada as a machine-readable substrate (i.e., computer program product), apparatus, system, process, or computer-implemented method which falls within the patent-eligible categories of invention as defined in the Patent Act. However, propagated signal claims are not permissible in Canada as statutory subject matter in respect of software and computer-implemented inventions, or otherwise.[3] Numerous judicial decisions in Canada over the years have sought to provide guidance as to how to assess whether the subject matter recited in a claim meets the statutory requirements of patent-eligibility outlined above. It is fair to say that a reasoned, predictable and determinative legal solution to the problem of assessing patent-eligibility for computer-implemented inventions has thus far proven elusive under Canadian law and practice.

1. Patent Act (R.S.C., 1985, c. P-4), s2.
2. Patent Act (R.S.C., 1985, c. P-4), s27(8).
3. *Office Practice Regarding Signals*, published by the Canadian Intellectual Property Office on August 14, 2007.

The Canadian Federal Court of Appeal's decision in *Canada (Attorney General) v. Amazon.com*[4] provides some clarity in respect of computer-implemented inventions in terms of what types of inventions would be considered patent-eligible and what types would be excluded from eligibility. Generally, in the context of computer-implemented inventions, where hardware or physical computer elements are regarded as an 'essential element' of the claim under the long-established Canadian claim construction doctrine of purposive construction, then the claim is generally considered to be directed to patent-eligible subject matter. Likewise, if an essential claim element is directed to an aspect of the claim that produces a 'discernable effect or change', the claim is also to be considered as embodying patent-eligible subject matter.[5] The notion of a discernable effect or change is thought to at least embody a traditional test of subject matter patentability in Canada based on the recited subject matter producing a 'material' effect or change, namely a change in the character or condition of a material (i.e., 'physical') object. On the other hand, where no such elements of a given claim are found to be essential, the claimed subject matter would be held to be directed to non-statutory subject matter.

In *Choueifaty v. Attorney General of Canada*,[6] the Federal Court of Canada recently confirmed that there is a presumption of essentiality for every element recited in a claim. According to the court, a claim element will be found to be non-essential only if it would be obvious to a skilled person that varying the particular element would not affect the way the claimed invention works and if the particular element was clearly not intended by the inventor to be essential.[7] The Federal Court emphasized that both conditions must be satisfied to support a finding of non-essentiality for a claim element.

In response to the *Choueifaty* decision, the Canadian Intellectual Property Office ('CIPO') released updated examination practice guidelines[8] entitled *Patentable Subject-Matter under the Patent Act* to provide guidance to its examiners in applying an administrative test for patent eligibility. The new guidelines outline a three-step process for determining patentable subject matter, as follows. First, the 'essential elements' of a claim under consideration are to be identified using the Canadian patent interpretation doctrine of purposive construction mentioned above. Secondly, and as a seemingly added step to the test enunciated in the *Choueifaty* decision, the 'actual invention' recited by the claim must also be arrived at. The 'actual invention' may consist of a combination of elements that cooperate together to solve a stated problem and this analysis does not necessarily result in the inclusion of every essential element identified in the first step. Lastly, it is the 'actual invention' that must be examined in order to determine whether the claim falls within one of the recognized categories of patentable subject matter (i.e., whether the actual invention has physicality or can manifest a discernible effect or change), as well as whether the prohibition under Section 27(8) of the Patent Act is avoided.

---

4. *Canada (Attorney General) v. Amazon.com, Inc.*, 2011 FCA 328 ('*Amazon*').
5. *Amazon*, para. 66.
6. *Choueifaty v. Canada (Attorney General), 2020 FC 837* ('*Choueifaty*').
7. *Choueifaty*, paras 38–40.
8. *Patentable Subject-Matter under the Patent Act*, Canadian Intellectual Property Office, 3 Nov. 2020.

As such, this added determination around the concept of an 'actual invention' could very well permit a Canadian patent examiner to neglect or exclude routine or standard elements of computer hardware from the assessment that would be made in an invention otherwise meeting the physicality requirement under the essentiality determination described above. Adopting this approach is therefore expected to make it more difficult for typical software and computer implemented inventions to be recognized as patent eligible, unless the inventive concept pertains to an advance in hardware, enhances the efficiency of operation of such hardware, or produces a physical transformation.

Many have criticized the CIPO's insertion of an 'actual invention' concept in the foregoing administrative test as an arguable departure from the applicable case law in Canada in the area of subject matter eligibility. Some consider the CIPO's current policy in respect of patent-eligible subject matter to be a disguised version of the 'problem-solution' approach that had previously prevailed in its administrative assessment of the patentability of computer-related patent applications. However, this 'problem-solution' approach was rejected by the *Choueifaty* decision mentioned above.

The Intellectual Property Institute of Canada ('IPIC'), the largest IP professional organization in Canada, recently intervened in the Federal Court of Canada case of *Benjamin Moore & Co. v. Canada (AG)* [9] and proposed the following framework for assessing patent-eligible subject matter. First, the claims are to be construed under the previously mentioned doctrine of purposive construction. Secondly, the construed claim as a whole must be assessed as to whether it is directed only to a mere scientific principle or abstract theorem, or whether it comprises a practical application that merely employs a scientific principle or abstract theorem. Thirdly, if the construed claim comprises a practical application as foresaid, the construed claim is further assessed for the remaining patentability criteria under Canadian law, namely, statutory categories and judicial exclusions as well as novelty, obviousness, and utility. The Federal Court at first instance instructed the CIPO to adopt this test in its assessment of the appellant's patent applications that were under examination.[10]

The *Benjamin Moore* decision is currently under appeal, and it remains to be seen whether the IPIC's proposed framework will be adopted in respect of patent-eligible subject matter assessments for software and computer-implemented inventions. In the meantime, there remains some uncertainty under Canadian law in matters of patentable subject matter, with a dichotomy between the test for eligibility emerging from the Canadian courts and that currently applied by the CIPO in its examination practice.

§04.02 SPECIAL PROVISIONS RELATING TO PATENTABILITY OF INVENTIONS RELATING TO AI

Other than the Canadian Patent Office's examination practice guidelines entitled *Patentable Subject-Matter under the Patent Act* mentioned above which broadly cover computer-implemented inventions, Canada currently does not have any statutes,

9. *Benjamin Moore & Co. v. Canada (AG), 2022 FC 923* ('*Benjamin Moore*').
10. *Benjamin Moore*, para. 54.

regulations, procedures, or guidelines that provide provisions specifically directed to inventions relating to artificial intelligence ('AI').

§04.03 SUBJECT MATTER PATENTABILITY

AI technologies will presumably always require the use of a computer system in order to operate. Meeting the essential element or actual invention test under Canadian law and practice will therefore require special attention to be paid as to the manner in which the claims of a computer-implemented AI invention are drafted within the prescriptions of the Canadian examination practice guidelines discussed above. This is next discussed in greater detail with reference to the five Categories of AI-related inventions presented in the introduction to this book.

For inventions of AI itself (i.e., Category 1 inventions), care should be exercised to ensure that the claims are not drafted too broadly or conceptually, such that they may be construed as a mere scientific principle or abstract theorem. Typically, the enunciation of a practical application into the claim language of a Category 1 AI invention will reduce the risk of an examiner or a court coming to a finding that the claim is directed to a mere scientific principle or abstract theorem.

Otherwise, it would be expected that the core AI inventions of Category 1 would have a good likelihood to meet the requirements of patent eligibility under either of the judicial or CIPO tests discussed above, due to such inventions being capable of characterization as advances to the field of computer science itself. For example, this would result where the Category 1 invention enhances the efficiency or speed of operation of existing neural network architectures or their underlying hardware platforms. Arguably, this class of invention would have a tendency to result in any hardware or structural components in the claim being regarded as 'essential' or as being comprised in the 'actual' invention for purposes of assessment as statutory subject matter. To further improve the prospects of patent eligibility under the statutory categories of patentable subject matter in Canada, an invention of new algorithms, structures or models for the AI itself should be claimed as a new type of neural network or a method implemented on, or in conjunction with, specialized computer hardware.

For inventions of an AI implementation (i.e., Category 2 inventions) that may involve improvements or enhancements to an underlying AI platform or machine going to the amelioration of its operating parameters, such inventions would be expected to receive a favourable subject matter eligibility treatment, based on the same rationale as applied under Canadian law and practice to the Category 1 inventions discussed above.

Turning to the category of inventions constituting new applications of AI (i.e., Category 3 inventions), the subject matter eligibility of these inventions would be expected to turn on whether the claims would recite sufficient physicality or other features that manifest a discernible effect or change so as to fall within the patent-eligible categories of the Canadian Patent Act as discussed above.

In this regard, the second type of Category 3 AI invention, namely that of a 'decision maker' application, may be more likely to meet the requirements of subject matter eligibility on the grounds that the application presumably would directly interact with its surrounding physical environment to produce a transformative change. On the other hand, in the case of a 'decision aid' application, the intercession of human input to formulate a final decision with the support of the AI platform in question would likely detract from subject matter eligibility under Canadian law. Under longstanding Canadian law and practice, inventions requiring 'professional skill and judgement' or those which may comprise 'mental steps' do not typically receive favourable treatment in meeting the requirements for subject matter patentability.

Moreover, the presence or requirement of a human decision maker in an otherwise new and non-obvious method or process will typically attract a challenge to eligibility on the basis that the invention fundamentally would lack reproducibility. In the latter instances, then, any human decision step in such a method or process should not be explicitly recited in the claim language. It could also arguably assist in enhancing the prospects of subject matter patentability for these types of Category 3 inventions if the useful information produced by the decision aid application and directed to a human decision maker would be explicitly recited in a step that outputs a report or displays the information on a physical peripheral, such as a computer display monitor.

In respect of inventions made using AI (i.e. Category 4 inventions), subject matter eligibility considerations for this category of invention are wholly divorced from the presence, support and involvement of AI in arriving at such inventions. This is because once the invention in this category is created with the use of AI, the invention will stand alone and be reproducible in its own right without any further involvement of an AI platform. For example, where AI is used to create a new golf club head structure in the field of sports equipment or a new airfoil shape in the field of aviation, those inventions can thereafter be created and manufactured from their physical specifications independently of the AI which was used to conceive them. As such, the subject matter eligibility of Category 4 AI inventions would be expected to turn on whether the claims would recite sufficient physicality or other features that manifest a discernible effect or change to fall within the patent-eligible categories of the Patent Act as previously discussed.

The distinction drawn between 'non-accidental' and 'accidental' Category 4 inventions could arguably affect the subject matter eligibility determination on the basis that a mere discovery may not amount to an 'invention' under Canadian law and practice.[11] This is because of such innovations lacking any measure of inventive ingenuity that would be inherent to meeting the core requirement of what constitutes an 'invention' *per se* under Section 2 of the Patent Act. The accidental type of Category 4 invention may also affect other areas of patentability such as inventiveness, a topic discussed further below.

For inventions made by AI (i.e., Category 5 inventions), we expect that strictly for purposes of subject matter eligibility, these inventions will receive the same assessment as the Category 4 inventions discussed above. Namely, the patent eligibility of these inventions will depend on meeting the physicality and discernable effect requirements according to Canadian law and practice. Once again, and regardless of whether they are autonomously conceived, the inventions of Category 5 will stand divorced from the presence, support and involvement of AI in arriving at such inventions.

11. *Apotex Inc. v. Wellcome Foundation Ltd.* (1998), 79 C.P.R. (3d) 193 at p. 221 (F.C.T.D.).

§04.04 INVENTIVE STEP

For inventions pertaining to AI *per se* (i.e., Category 1 inventions), inventions of an AI implementation (i.e., Category 2 inventions), and new applications of AI (i.e., Category 3 inventions), there need not be any special considerations in respect of inventive step or obviousness under Canadian patent law as these inventions are conceived according to expected practices and methodologies which prevail with all other inventions in any field. However, we expect that special considerations would prevail for inventions arrived at using AI (i.e., Category 4 inventions) and made by AI (i.e., Category 5 inventions), for the reasons explained below.

The inventive step or non-obviousness requirement in Canadian patent law is set forth as follows in the Patent Act:[12]

> The subject-matter defined by a claim in an application for a patent in Canada must be subject-matter that would not have been obvious on the claim date to a person skilled in the art or science to which it pertains, having regard to
> (a) information disclosed before the one-year period immediately preceding the filing date or, if the claim date is before that period, before the claim date by the applicant, or by a person who obtained knowledge, directly or indirectly, from the applicant in such a manner that the information became available to the public in Canada or elsewhere; and
> (b) information disclosed before the claim date by a person not mentioned in paragraph (a) in such a manner that the information became available to the public in Canada or elsewhere.

In *Apotex Inc. v. Sanofi-Synthelabo Canada Inc.*,[13] the Supreme Court of Canada confirmed and restated the following four-step approach to assessing obviousness in Canada: (1) identify the notional 'person skilled in the art' and identify the relevant common general knowledge of that person; (2) identify the inventive concept of the claim in question or if that cannot readily be done, construe it; (3) identify what, if any, differences exist between the matter cited as forming part of the 'state of the art' and the inventive concept of the claim or the claim as construed; (4) viewed without any knowledge of the alleged invention as claimed, consider whether those differences constitute steps which would have been obvious to the person skilled in the art or do they require any degree of invention.

For inventions that fall under Categories 1 to 3, then, the test would remain whether it would be obvious to a person skilled in the art, under the *Sanofi* framework, to arrive at the claimed subject matter based on publicly available information and the common general knowledge of such skilled person, including the type of AI engines and prevailing architectures that have been made available, the type of training datasets and training methodologies that are known to be used in particular applications, and the known applications of AI systems, to name some examples.

For inventions made using AI (i.e., Category 4 inventions), it is arguable that such inventions may in many circumstances be non-obvious for the application of an AI to solve a given problem or to try a multitude of options in order to determine

12. Patent Act (R.S.C., 1985, c. P-4), s28.3.
13. *Apotex Inc v. Sanofi-Synthelabo Canada Inc.*, [2008] 3 S.C.R. 265 ('*Sanofi*').

an optimal solution. One could assume that as AI technologies and methodologies become more and more prevalent across all technical fields, resorting to such technologies and methodologies would eventually come to reside within the common general knowledge of the skilled person, thereby influencing the inventiveness determination for such Category 4 inventions. It would be expected that the extent of human involvement in the making of a Category 4 invention, as well as the degree of ingenuity involved in the particular application of AI to resolution of the technical problem, will play important roles in the inventiveness analysis for these inventions. As alluded to above, there is also some doubt as to whether the 'accidental' type of Category 4 inventions can meet the inventiveness requirement, given that a mere discovery may not fundamentally constitute an act of true invention under Canadian law.

For inventions made by AI (i.e., Category 5 inventions), as stated below in the context of inventorship considerations, to the extent that AI may arguably be viewed as an inanimate construct which simply executes a series of pre-programmed or pre-ordained operations within an expected or determinable scope of activity, it may prove problematic to establish that such operations would meet the standards for inventiveness under Canadian law. For example, it may very well be that an innovation which is entirely and autonomously machine-derived may not meet a basic requirement that invention under Canadian law requires a modicum of ingenuity, a scintilla of inventiveness – something a machine may not be capable of harbouring or exhibiting. There is also no law in Canada that would support, at the present time, that the knowledge and skill of a human inventor be used as a proxy in order to assess whether a machine-derived invention possesses the requisite degree of inventiveness for purposes of patentability. Likewise, there is no law in Canada that would mandate a comparable AI to be substituted in the stead of the notional skilled person for the purposes of assessing the inventive step requirement.

§04.05 ADEQUACY OF DISCLOSURE

In Canada, the statutory requirements of proper disclosure in respect of patent applications and patents are set out in the Patent Act as follows: [14]

> The specification of an invention must:
> (a) correctly and fully describe the invention and its operation or use as contemplated by the inventor;
> (b) set out clearly the various steps in a process, or the method of constructing, making, compounding or using a machine, manufacture or composition of matter, in such full, clear, concise and exact terms as to enable any person skilled in the art or science to which it pertains, or with which it is most closely connected, to make, construct, compound or use it;
> (c) in the case of a machine, explain the principle of the machine and the best mode in which the inventor has contemplated the application of that principle; and

14. Patent Act (R.S.C., 1985, c. P-4), s.27(3).

(d) in the case of a process, explain the necessary sequence, if any, of the various steps, so as to distinguish the invention from other inventions.

There is also longstanding Canadian jurisprudence requiring the description to provide a clear and complete disclosure of the invention such that the person skilled in the art can unambiguously identify what has been invented and that such person is enabled to practise this invention.[15]

It is generally understood that an AI system is typically built based on a particular AI or machine learning platform, then trained using a data set to carry out one or more tasks and, lastly, deployed to carry out the task(s) for which it is trained. For inventions of AI (i.e., Category 1 inventions), inventions of an AI implementation (i.e., Category 2 inventions), adequacy of disclosure is not expected to be an issue in Canada since the inventive establishment of a new AI system or the AI implementation will follow the expected approaches to inventive activity in the fields of computer-related technology. The actual architectures, structures or algorithms deployed in the Category 1 and 2 inventions will be described in the disclosure of a patent application following the same legal rules and established drafting practices as for all other computer-implemented inventions.

In the case of new applications of AI (i.e., Category 3 inventions), it is expected that where a training protocol and the use of specific training data lead to particular configuration of resultant parameters in an AI machine, then it will likely be sufficient for purposes of adequate disclosure, enablement and reproducibility to describe in detail the configuration of the resultant parameters instead of having to disclose the details of the training protocol and training data used to arrive at the new application of AI in question. However, where it will not be possible to disclose a particular configuration of resultant parameters for a specifically trained AI machine, the requirements of adequate disclosure, enablement and reproducibility would likely mandate an explicit detailing of the approach and steps of the training protocol (e.g., how various categories of training data are curated and labelled in the case of supervised learning) that was used to create the new application of AI, as well as the training data itself. It is expected that a disclosure of only the general type of data used will not meet the disclosure requirements under Canadian law, since this would not ensure enablement and reproducibility without undue experimentation or guesswork.

At least in the case of inventions categorized as 'machines', Canadian law also requires that patent applicants meet a 'best mode' requirement[16] in the disclosure of patent applications, with the risk that a description only of the general type of training data used may not meet this particular requirement. Moreover, unlike other jurisdictions, Canada does not allow any documents to be incorporated by reference into the description of a patent.[17] While it may be permissible to refer to a publicly

15. *Pioneer Hi-Bred Ltd. v. Canada* (Commissioner of Patents) [(1989), 25 C.P.R. (3rd), 257 (S.C.C.)] at p268; *Apotex Inc. v. Wellcome Foundation Ltd.*, 2002 SCC 77 at para 70; *Electrolytic Zinc Process Co. v. French's Complex Ore Reduction Co.*, [1930] S.C.R. 462 at para 22.
16. Patent Act (R.S.C., 1985, c. P-4), s27(3)(c).
17. Patent Rules (SOR/2019-251), s57(1).

available document such as a public dataset in the description[18] (without incorporating by reference the contents of the document), one must guard against the possibility that a public dataset may evolve and change over time, thereby potentially impacting questions of enablement and reproducibility. Applicants are therefore well-advised to err on the side of fully disclosing the training data itself, rather than simply making reference to the training data, to maximize the likelihood of meeting the various disclosure requirements discussed above.

The fact that a dataset is proprietary is not expected to absolve the patent applicant from the disclosure requirements above. It goes without saying, however, that the use or disclosure of a proprietary dataset may expose the patent holder to risks of liability in other areas of intellectual property law such as involving allegations of copyright infringement or the misuse or misappropriation of trade secrets and confidential information.

As an example of the foregoing, Category 3 inventions may include inventions known as 'black box' innovations in the AI community, for which the question of adequacy of disclosure could be problematic in Canada since the AI cannot necessarily reproduce, predict or know the details as to how the innovation operates. For example, a hypothetical human image identification system may be developed using AI that has been trained with images containing humans that have been recognized as such ahead of time. Internally, the AI system generates the necessary decision-making processes, based on the training images, to enable the image identification system to identify humans in images that are not the training images. The manner in which the system constructs and implements its decision-making processes may warrant patent protection. However, internal aspects of the system trained to such a task are sometimes not easily understood or discoverable by its human creators. In other words, the creators themselves do not know how the AI system does what it has been trained to do. Consequently, this lack of transparency or understanding may be problematic for those seeking patent protection for such black box innovations with respect to satisfying the adequacy of disclosure requirement. If the black box AI machine is itself commercially available, the disclosure of its sourcing coupled to a disclosure of the specific training methodology and associated dataset would be expected to meet the prevailing disclosure requirements under Canadian law and practice. If the black box AI machine is not commercially available, then it is doubtful whether the applicant can enable an invention by simply referencing the machine that the skilled person could not access.

In some circumstances, the issue of adequacy of disclosure is important when considering whether a particular application or use case of the invention has been established at the time of the patent application to meet the utility requirements under Canadian patent law. If an AI invention does not have a 'demonstrated utility' as the concept is understood under Canadian law, then it must be 'soundly predicted' from what the human inventor knows to demonstrably work.[19] Demonstrated utility requires that the invention as claimed must have been proven to work in practice as of the actual filing date of the application. For instance, where the abovementioned Category 3 invention for identifying humans from images has been shown to have

18. Patent Rules (SOR/2019-251), s57(2).

19. *Apotex Inc v. Wellcome Foundation Ltd*, 2002 SCC 77, [2002] 4 SCR 153 ('*Apotex*').

demonstrable utility, it may be possible to more broadly claim the subject matter in question merely 'predictively' as extending to the identification of animals even where the latter extension of the technology has no demonstrated utility. Under the disclosure principle of sound prediction in Canada, a 'factual basis' for the predicted subject matter of the claims must be provided, followed by a description of a 'sound and articulable line of reasoning' from which the extended scope of the invention, as claimed, can be inferred from the factual basis. As such, in describing the factual basis, the starting algorithm, the training data, and any other inputs used in building the AI technology for identifying humans would all be disclosed, followed by a sound and articulable line of reasoning to indicate how this disclosed factual basis can be applied to achieve the desired extended application for identifying animals. The sound prediction doctrine over the years has mainly found application in the pharmaceutical and chemical arts, but it is expected to find increasing application in AI inventions.

As previously mentioned, for inventions made using AI (i.e., Category 4 inventions) or by AI (i.e., Category 5 inventions), once the inventions in these categories are created with the use of AI, the inventions will stand alone and be reproducible in their own right without any further involvement of an AI platform. As such, these inventions themselves will be described in the patent specification according to the traditional requirements for adequate disclosure and enablement.

§04.06 INVENTORSHIP

[A] Inventorship in General

The Canadian Patent Act and Patent Rules[20] do not include a definition of 'inventor', nor do they set out any specific rules for determining inventorship. Instead, the Canadian courts have had to infer relevant principles from various sections of the Patent Act and Patent Rules in order to assess and adjudicate questions in connection with inventorship. The prevailing view in Canada is that inventorship is determined on the basis of the invention as claimed, as opposed to the invention as disclosed. An inventor is joined to a patent application where such person has contributed to the invention of at least one claim in the application.

As discussed above, an invention is defined in Section 2 of the Patent Act in the following manner:

> invention means any new and useful art, process, machine, manufacture or composition of matter, or any new and useful improvement in any art, process, machine, manufacture or composition of matter.

Section 27(1) of the Patent Act sets out the overriding principle that a patent for an invention may only be granted to an inventor or to the inventor's legal representative:

> The Commissioner shall grant a patent for an invention to the inventor or the inventor's legal representative if an application for the patent in Canada is filed in accordance with this Act and all other requirements for the issuance of a patent under this Act are met.

20. Patent Rules (SOR/2019-251).

In the Supreme Court of Canada's decision in *Apotex*, it was held that 'the inventor is the person or persons who conceived of the "new and useful" art, process, machine, manufacture or composition of matter, or any "new and useful" improvement thereto ...'.[21] and who reduced such subject matter to a definite and practical shape.[22] Presumably, Mr Justice Binnie in the foregoing citation was referring to natural persons when he sought to attribute the status of inventor to 'person or persons' who are responsible for conceiving the inventive concept. However, his statement was made in the context of determining whether all inventors were properly named in the patent application at issue, where it was ultimately held that those who engage in mere verification of an inventor's discovery do not themselves merit recognition as inventors under Canadian law.[23] For this reason, the reference in the *Apotex* decision to inventors being 'persons' may not stand as binding authority, but the reasoning would nevertheless presumably be persuasive as *obiter dictum* at the very least.

Other judicial authority in Canada suggests that an inventor under the Canadian patent statute is to be confined to a natural person. In the Federal Court decision of *Sarnoff Corp. v. Canada (Attorney General)*,[24] Mr Justice Hughes opined as follows:

> In Canada, the language of the jurisprudence assumes that an 'inventor' is a natural person as opposed to a juridical person such as a corporation... I note that some European applications for patents are filed naming corporate entities as the inventor. Not so in Canada...

The opinion was provided in the context of a patent application that had been deemed abandoned by the Canadian Patent Office on account of the payment of maintenance fees having been advanced by a new representative of the applicant for which some uncertainty existed as to whether the new representative had been duly recognized by the Patent Office. It was ultimately decided in *Sarnoff* that the patent application at issue would not be deemed abandoned where the maintenance fees in question were timely and correctly paid, but by a representative of the applicant who may not have formally recorded its status as such. It was in this context that the court opined to the effect that an inventor must be a natural person, such that the finding on this may be treated as being *obiter dictum* and therefore not binding authority.

Nonetheless, the *Apotex* and *Sarnoff* decisions strongly suggest that an inventor under Canadian patent law is to be confined to a natural person and cannot be extended to encompass inanimate entities such as corporations and, presumably, AI entities.

[B] Determination of Inventorship for AI-Related Inventions

At the present time, there is no specific legislative or jurisprudential authority in Canada on the question of inventorship in respect of inventions that result from the application of AI technology. Likewise, no official administrative policy in the area of AI technology has been adopted by the Canadian Patent Office as of this writing.

21. *Apotex*, para. 96.
22. *Apotex*, para. 97.
23. *Weatherford Canada Ltd. v. Corlac Inc.* (2010), 84 C.P.R. (4th) 237 (F.C.).
24. *Sarnoff Corp. v. Canada (Attorney General), 2008 FC 712.*

Accordingly, inventorship with respect to inventions of AI (i.e., Category 1 inventions) and inventions of an AI implementation (i.e., Category 2 inventions) will likely be addressed the same way as inventorship with respect to all other types of inventions. That is, individuals who contribute to the conception of the AI technology and its reduction to a definite and practical shape may be considered inventors according to the judicial test for inventorship under Canadian law.[25]

Also for new applications of AI (i.e., Category 3 inventions) and inventions made using AI (i.e., Category 4 inventions), inventorship will be attributed to the human inventor under the current framework (e.g., depending on the circumstances, all or any of: the person who has the idea of using AI for its intended purpose, the person who selects an AI technology and configures it to suit the intended purpose, the person who selects the data to be used to train the AI, the person who selects the input data fed to the trained AI system, or even the person who simply selects one optimal solution from a large number of potential solutions produced by the AI).

Inventions made by AI (i.e., Category 5 inventions) raise a different question because, at least hypothetically, there is no human inventor. While this has not yet been addressed by the Canadian courts, in the meantime, one might look to the general principles applicable to inventorship discussed above and other related provisions to anticipate how the Canadian courts may address the issue.

For example, one may apply the traditional test of inventorship set out in *Apotex* to ask: (i) whether the AI that begot the invention can be regarded as a 'person' under the judicially recognized test for inventorship; and (ii) whether the AI may be regarded as having engaged in acts of conceiving and of reducing the invention to a definite and practical shape. In this regard, an AI entity may not meet the presumed inventorship requirement of being a person. It could also be argued that the AI entity has not so conceived and reduced the invention on the basis that AI represents an inanimate construct which simply executes a series of pre-programmed or pre-ordained operations within an expected or determinable scope of activity, and thus does not meet the requirement of engaging in any act of conception of the invention or its reduction to a definite and practical shape. As previously addressed, an innovation for which an inventive contribution was autonomously machine-derived may not meet a basic requirement that an invention under Canadian law requires a modicum of ingenuity, a scintilla of inventiveness, namely characteristics that cannot be exemplified by a machine.

It should be noted that the terms 'applicant' and 'legal representative' are explicitly defined in the Patent Act[26] as follows:

- *applicant* includes an inventor and the legal representatives of an applicant or inventor;
- *legal representatives* includes heirs, executors, administrators of the estate, liquidators of the succession, guardians, curators, tutors, transferees and all other persons claiming through applicants for patents and patentees of inventions or through holders of certificates of supplementary protection

25. *Apotex*, paras 96–97.
26. Patent Act (R.S.C., 1985, c. P-4), s2.

It is noted that both statutory definitions above are stated in inclusive language, which would not in and of themselves entirely shut the door on the consideration of machine entities being recognized as inventors. However, the Canadian Patent Rules make it a requirement in a patent application to name each inventor of the subject matter of the application, and to state either that they are the applicants or that the applicants, if they are not the inventors, are legally entitled to apply for and be granted a patent:[27]

> (1) The application must indicate the name and postal address of each inventor of the subject-matter of the invention for which an exclusive privilege or property is claimed.
>
> (2) The application must contain a statement to the effect that either (a) the applicant is or, if there are joint applicants, the applicants are entitled to apply for a patent, or (b) the applicant is the sole inventor of the subject-matter of the invention for which an exclusive privilege or property is claimed or, if there are joint applicants, the applicants are all inventors and the sole inventors of that subject-matter.

Thus, under Canadian law and practice, taking all of the above-mentioned provisions of the Patent Act and Patent Rules into account, the chain of title in respect of a patent application begins with the inventor or inventors, and the legal entitlement of any other party to the resulting patent grant must flow from the inventor or inventors.

Section 49(1) of the Patent Act provides for the transferability of an application in the following terms:

> A patent, an application for a patent, and the right or interest in an invention are transferable, in whole or in part.

Given the foregoing framework of invention and inventorship under Canadian law, even if it could be accommodated under the language of the current Patent Act and Patent Rules that an AI entity could be regarded as an inventor, there would be no legitimate legal basis on which to have that entity assume and hold the originating ownership of the underlying invention as currently required by Section 54 of the Canadian Patent Rules discussed above. It is trite to say that a machine cannot hold legal title under the prevailing personal property laws of general application in Canada. Furthermore, there is no legal mechanism under Canadian law to support any transfer of the originating interest in the invention or patent application from such an AI entity to another owner.

Accordingly, it is expected that inventions made by AI (i.e., Category 5 inventions) will not be recognized under Canada's current framework of invention and inventorship. Even if an AI entity could somehow assume and assert an originating interest in an invention or patent application in Canada, there remains the hurdle that such an interest would not be further assignable. The AI entity, having none of the attributes of legal personality, would not have the requisite capacity to enter into a contract with an assignee to transfer whatever interest of the AI entity could claim

27. Patent Rules (SOR/2019-251, s54.

to possess. Amendments to the Patent Act and the Patent Rules will likely have to be introduced to accommodate Category 5 inventions.

§04.07 AREAS FOR FURTHER DEVELOPMENT

As described above, there remains some uncertainty under Canadian law in matters of patentable subject matter for computer-related inventions in general. Canada also currently does not have any statutes, regulations, procedures, or guidelines that provide provisions specifically directed to inventions relating to AI. Accordingly, Canadian patent practice can benefit from additional clarification from both the Canadian courts and the CIPO to address issues relating to the patent eligibility of inventions relating to AI.

For inventive step, the current analysis framework set forth in *Sanofi* is expected to be sufficient for inventions pertaining to AI (i.e., Category 1 inventions), inventions of an AI implementation (i.e., Category 2 inventions), and new applications of AI (i.e., Category 3 inventions). However, inventions arrived at using AI (i.e., Category 4 inventions) and inventions made by AI (i.e., Category 5 inventions) can benefit from additional clarification from the Canadian courts. For example, it is unclear under the current framework whether the 'accidental' type of Category 4 inventions can meet the inventiveness requirements. Another open question is whether the knowledge and skill of a human inventor, or a comparable AI, should be used as a proxy in order to assess whether a machine-derived invention possesses the requisite degree of inventiveness for purposes of patentability.

Regarding adequacy of disclosure, further developments in Canadian case law will help address the question of how Category 3 inventions might be able to meet the disclosure requirements in situations where the skilled person cannot easily reproduce, predict or know the details as to how the innovation operates. The longstanding doctrine of sound prediction, which has mainly found application in the pharmaceutical and chemical arts over the years, is expected to be expanded for application in AI inventions in the near future.

Finally, the issue of inventorship for new applications of AI (i.e., Category 3 inventions) and inventions made using AI (i.e., Category 4 inventions) is expected to benefit from additional clarification with regard to when inventorship should be attributed to the human inventor under the current framework. For Category 5 inventions, amendments to the Patent Act and the Patent Rules will likely have to be introduced if such inventions are to be patentable.

§04.08 RECOMMENDATIONS FOR PATENT APPLICANTS

Due to Canada's lack of statutes, regulations, procedures, or guidelines that provide provisions specifically directed to inventions relating to AI and the current state of flux regarding Canadian law on subject matter eligibility, extra care should be exercised when preparing applications relating to AI. Since different categories of AI inventions can attract different types of legal issues as discussed above, applicants are strongly encouraged to work with Canadian patent professionals who are well-versed in both the applicable law and with AI technology to minimize their risks of encountering some of the potential legal issues.

For example, for inventions of AI (i.e., Category 1 inventions), care should be exercised to ensure that the claims are not drafted too broadly or conceptually, such that they may be construed, by a Canadian examiner during prosecution or an adverse party after patent grant, as a mere scientific principle or abstract theorem. The enunciation of a practical application into the claim language of a Category 1 AI invention will also help reduce the risk of an examiner or a court coming to a finding that the claim is directed to a mere scientific principle of abstract theorem under prevailing Canadian law.

As another example, for new applications of AI (i.e., Category 3 inventions), it will be especially important to meet the as yet unproven requirements of an adequate disclosure. Details such as the training protocol, the training data, and other inputs used in building the AI technology for the new application should ideally all be disclosed in the specification of any application relating to such inventions in order to best support the claimed subject matter. In situations where not all new applications or use cases possess demonstrable utility at the time of filing a patent application (e.g., for a Category 3 invention), the foregoing descriptive elements should be tied together to form a factual basis for which a sound and articulable line of reasoning can be applied to achieve the desired new applications or use cases under the Canadian doctrine of sound prediction.

As yet a further example, it will be prudent in the case of new applications of AI (i.e., Category 3 inventions) and inventions made using AI (i.e., Category 4 inventions) to adopt a disciplined practice of keeping detailed records of the specific inventive activity regarding each human contributor to these inventions. Depending on the circumstances, this may include duly documenting the person or persons who, for example, possessed the idea of using AI for its intended purpose, who elected a particular AI technology or configured it to suit the intended purpose, who selected and vetted the data that was used to train the AI, who selected the input data fed to the trained AI system, or who evaluated and selected an optimal solution from a large number of potential solutions produced by the AI. Such record keeping can prove useful for the patent holder in defending against what can be expected to be increasing challenges to the validity and enforceability of AI inventions based on questions of inventorship and inventive contribution.

§04.09 CONCLUSION

In Canada, AI-related inventions are currently subject to the same requirements as all other types of inventions and can be granted patent protection as long as they meet the requirements of patentability. With the possible emergence of more advanced AI systems that are capable of independently identifying and addressing problems, it is expected that there will be new substantive challenges when considering whether specific AI-related inventions meet the statutory requirements under the current framework. As such, further developments in Canadian patent law are expected to help clarify the Canadian legal position on issues related to patentability, inventorship, and adequacy of disclosure for such inventions.

Chapter 5

China

Lili Wu & Xiaowei Wei

§05.01 PATENTABILITY OF SOFTWARE AND COMPUTER-IMPLEMENTED INVENTIONS

Software-implemented inventions or computer-implemented inventions ('CII') have been patentable in China for the last 20 years. As China's economy has developed, CII patent applicants have invested heavily in obtaining CII patents and a considerable number of applications are filed and granted each year.[1] This trend is especially pronounced with broader implementations of new technologies such as artificial intelligence ('AI'), blockchain, cloud computing, big data analysis, the Internet of Things, and 5G.

Like other jurisdictions, Chinese authorities, including the China National Intellectual Property Administration ('CNIPA') and the courts, have formulated revised rules regarding standards for examining CII patents and patent applications as well as regarding claim construction and infringement comparison in patent infringement litigations.

The scope of patentable subject matter is relatively broad for CII patents in China. The *Guidelines for Patent Examination*[2] (the 'Examination Guidelines'),

1. «2019知识产权主要数据发布：主要指标稳中有进 知识产权质量效益持续提升» [Primary intellectual property data announced for 2019: main indicators are stable, the quality and efficiency of intellectual property continue to improve] China Nat'l Intell. Prop. Admin., 1 Jan. 2020, *available at* http://www.cnipa.gov.cn/zscqgz/1145388.htm (Chinese). This states that 60% of top-ten patentees have primarily CII patent portfolios, including Huawei, Oppo, Lenovo, Tencent, ZTE, and Vivo.
2. «专利审查指南» [Guidelines for Patent Examination] (*as amended by* China Nat'l Intell. Prop. Admin., Ann. No. 343; promulgated 31 Dec. 2019, effective 1 Feb. 2020).

following a 2017 revision,[3] allow for claims on 'computer-readable storage media'. As a result, CII patents can now contain patent claims including the following:

- A method for XXX, comprising steps A, B, and C;
- An apparatus for XXX, comprising one or more processors; and one or more memories having instructions stored thereon to cause the apparatus, upon execution of the instructions by the one or more processors, to: perform steps A, B, and C;
- An apparatus for XXX, comprising a module for performing a step A, a module for performing a step B and a module for performing a step C; and
- A computer-readable storage medium comprising instructions stored thereon to cause an apparatus, upon execution of the instructions by one or more processors of the apparatus, to: perform steps A, B, and C.

The latest development, in *Draft Amendment to Guidelines for Patent Examination (Draft for Soliciting Public Comments)*[4] (the 'Draft Amendment to Examination Guidelines 2021') published by the CNIPA on 3 August 2021, states that a 'computer program product' is to become a patentable category of claimed subject matter in China. As a result, not only a computer program product carried on a physical medium such as a disc, but also a computer program distributed on the internet, etc., would also be covered by such claims. We expect that the new Examination Guidelines could come into effect in 2023. For patentable subject matter in general, a claim can be patentable so long as it is not 'rules and methods for mental activities' and it defines a technical solution which, as a whole, solves a technical problem, utilizes a technical means, and has a technical effect.

The requirements regarding novelty/inventiveness and adequate disclosure for CII patents are, in general, similar to other types of patents, with one exception. Specifically, a non-technical feature (a feature of an abstract algorithm or a feature of a business rule) will not be considered to have a technical contribution in an inventiveness assessment if the non-technical feature does not have a mutually supportive and interactive functional relationship with the technical feature.

§05.02 SPECIAL PROVISIONS RELATING TO PATENTABILITY OF INVENTIONS RELATING TO AI

CNIPA recently added a new Section 6 in Part II, Chapter 9 of the Examination Guidelines regarding AI and other algorithm-related inventions which came into effect on 1 February 2020.[5] The background to the addition of the new Section 6 is that

3. «知识产权局关于修改«专利审查指南» 的决定» [Decision of the State Intellectual Property Office on Amending the Guidelines for Patent Examination] (St. Intell. Prop. Off., Decree No. 74; promulgated 28 Feb. 2017, effective 1 Apr. 2017).
4. «专利审查指南修改草案 (征求意见稿)» [Draft Amendment to Guidelines for Patent Examination (Draft for Soliciting Public Comments)] (Int. Property Admin.; promulgated 3 Aug. 2021).
5. «关于修改«专利审查指南» 的公告 (第343号)» [Announcement on Amending the Guidelines for Patent Examination (No. 343)] (China Nat'l Int. Property Admin.; promulgated 31 Dec. 2019, effective 1 Feb. 2020).

patents and patent applications involving features of algorithms, for example those related to AI, 'internet + ' and big data, or features of business rules and methods, have been increasing and inventors have been demanding that patent examination practice should keep pace with the times. This new section of the Examination Guidelines thus provides specific rules for examination of such patents and patent applications, informs the public how such patent applications should be examined, and offers guidance on how to draft patent applications for such types of inventions.

Algorithm-related inventions are specifically discussed in the new Section 6 of the Examination Guidelines, which provides examples of AI-related algorithms. The new Section 6, in particular, addresses issues of patentable subject matter, novelty/inventiveness, and drafting requirements for descriptions and claims regarding algorithms, and offers and analyses examples of AI algorithm-related inventions.

In the Draft Amendment to Examination Guidelines 2021, a computer program is to become a patentable category, the rules for examining patentability and inventiveness of CII patent applications are set forth in more detail, and more examples are added to explain the rules.

AI-related patent applications are generally subject to the patent examination rules applicable to CII patents, because they are considered a subset of CII-related patent applications. However, CNIPA provides examination rules specifically for AI and other algorithm-related inventions because abstract algorithms, such as pure AI algorithms without any technical application or technical implementation, are considered *per se* to constitute legally non-patentable subject matter, i.e., 'rules and methods for mental activities'. The details of 'technical' requirements for patentable AI-related inventions will be discussed in the following parts.

§05.03 SUBJECT MATTER PATENTABILITY

The *Patent Law of the People's Republic of China*[6] (the 'Patent Law') governs the patentable subject matter of AI-related inventions, with Articles 25.1(2) and 2.2 providing threshold tests for patentability. The first test concerns whether the subject matter is non-patentable (Article 25.1(2)), the second test (Article 2.2) determines whether the subject matter constitutes an 'invention' under the Patent Law. To be patentable, an AI-related invention must pass both tests.

Article 25 of the Patent Law specifies certain subject matter that is non-patentable, including 'rules and methods for mental activities' at Article 25.1(2). An AI-related invention may be considered a rule or method for mental activities if it is not applied to a technical field or implemented by technical means.

In practice, it is relatively simple to determine whether an AI-related invention falls within the ambit of Article 25.1(2). A claimed solution is not patentable subject matter under Article 25.1(2) if it contains only purely algorithmic features and no technical features. It is relatively easy to satisfy this first test, because even a small technical feature will usually suffice to distinguish the claimed solution from a purely

6. «中华人民共和国专利法» [Patent Law of the People's Republic of China] (*as amended by* Standing Comm. Nat'l People's Cong., Pres. Order No. 8; promulgated 27 Dec. 2008, effective 1 Oct. 2009).

abstract algorithm. Thus, if a claimed solution contains at least one technical feature, it will pass the Article 25.1(2) test and proceed to the second test under Article 2.2.

Article 2.2 defines inventions for purposes of the Patent Law as 'new technical solutions proposed for a product, a process or the improvement thereof'. In other words, to be considered an invention, Article 2.2 requires a solution to be claimed that is, as a whole, 'technical'.

According to the new Section 6, a solution defined in a claim is considered a technical solution under Article 2.2 if the claim recites a technical mechanism that utilizes the laws of nature to solve a technical problem, thereby achieving a technical effect in conformity with the laws of nature.

The test under Article 2.2 is relatively difficult to pass because it is possible that even if a solution involves a 'technical feature' (for example, a general-purpose computer or the internet), the solution as a whole may actually lie in an abstract algorithm or purely artificial rule, and such a solution cannot pass the Article 2.2 test even if it can pass the Article 25.1(2) test.

In the Draft Amendment to Examination Guidelines 2021, it is specifically provided that a claim on an algorithm-related invention can be deemed as reciting a technical solution and thus can pass the Article 2.2 test if:[7]

(i) The data processed by the algorithm is the data with definite technical meaning in the technical field. The execution of the algorithm can directly reflect the process of solving a technical problem by using natural laws, and obtaining technical effects;
(ii) There is a specific technical correlation between the algorithm and the internal structure of the computer system, which can solve the technical problem of how to improve the hardware operation efficiency or execution effect, thereby obtaining the technical effect of improving the internal performance of the computer system that complies with natural laws; or
(iii) The solution targets big data in specific application fields, and uses algorithm tools to mine the inherent correlation in the data which complies with laws of nature, thereby solving the technical problem of how to improve the reliability or accuracy of big data analysis in specific application fields, and obtain corresponding technical effects.

The following is a list showing whether the five categories of AI-related inventions can pass the two tests for patentability under Articles 25.1(2) and 2.2.

7. «专利审查指南修改草案（征求意见稿）» [Draft Amendment to Guidelines for Patent Examination (Draft for Soliciting Public Comments)] (Int. Property Admin.; promulgated 3 Aug. 2021), Part II, Ch. 9, Sec. 6.1.2.

Category	Patentable subject matter	Test of 'rules and methods for mental activities' (Article 25.1(2))	Test of three technical elements (Article 2.2)
1. Invention of AI	Not patentable	A new AI algorithm or AI model invention *per se* cannot pass the Article 25.1(2) test because it is an invention for establishing a mathematical model, which is based on an abstract algorithm and contains no technical features. If the solution is intended to pass the Article 25.1(2) test, at least one technical feature will be necessary.	An invention of a new AI algorithm or AI model *per se* cannot pass the Article 2.2 test because it does not contain any technical means, does not solve any technical problem of a particular technical field, and does not render any technical effect. If such an invention is intended for patent protection, it will be necessary to have a technical means, e.g. a specific technical application or a specific technical implementation, which, when considered with the algorithmic features, is deemed to solve a technical problem and achieve a technical effect.
2. Invention of an AI implementation	Potentially patentable	An invention of an AI implementation can pass the patentability tests if the claimed solution includes implementation of AI in association with computer internal hardware or software structure to improve the internal performance of the computer system that complies with laws of nature.	An invention of an AI implementation can pass the patentability tests if the AI implementation is technical. For example, if the implementation is in terms of a special arrangement or operation of the components of a computer or in terms of a special hardware circuit or a software structure, the implementation element of the claimed solution, when considered with other elements as a whole, is deemed to solve a technical problem, utilize technical means, and render a technical effect. In contrast, if the AI implementation is merely an abstract data processing algorithm or a pure training algorithm in relation to general data, the solution as a whole would still be considered an abstract algorithm rather than a technical solution.

Category	Patentable subject matter	Test of 'rules and methods for mental activities' (Article 25.1(2))	Test of three technical elements (Article 2.2)
3. A new application of AI	Potentially patentable	A new application of AI can pass the patentability tests if the claimed solution recites a specific technical application of the AI algorithm, or the use of AI reveals inherent correlation in the data which complies with laws of nature.	A new application of AI can pass the patentability tests if the new application is a particular technical application or at least involves a technical attribute. For example, if an AI algorithm is used in the application of image processing, agriculture, automatic industrial controls or the like, the algorithm, when considered with the technical features as a whole, could be deemed to solve a technical problem of the particular technical field, utilize technical means, and render a technical effect. Alternatively, if a correlation in the data that is revealed by the use of AI is an inherent correlation and complies with natural laws, this is also considered 'technical'. In contrast, if an AI algorithm were used to predict the movements of a stock market index, which is neither technical nor follows any law of nature but rather is purely financial, the solution as a whole would be non-patentable.
4. Inventions made using AI	Potentially patentable	The criteria are the same as those for Categories 1–3.	The criteria are the same as those for Categories 1–3.
5. Inventions made by AI	Potentially patentable	The criteria are the same as those for Categories 1–3 but note that the AI cannot listed as an inventor.	The criteria are the same as those for Categories 1–3 but note that the AI cannot listed as an inventor.

For both Categories 4 and 5 it may be worth mentioning that, unlike Categories 1–3, what is being claimed is the result of the use of AI, not the AI itself or the application of the AI. Thus, for Category 4, what is claimed is whatever was invented by the human using AI as a tool. For Category 5, the theoretical case of an invention being made by AI itself, what is claimed is whatever was purportedly invented by the AI. Thus, the claim may be for something completely unrelated to AI or software. For example, if a person uses AI as a tool to invent a new hammer, and she/he claims the hammer, then clearly the claim is subject-matter eligible. The means by which the invention was made is not relevant to subject matter eligibility.

Below, we present examples to illustrate the subject matter patentability of AI-related inventions falling under Category 1, Category 2, and Category 3.

[A] Category 1

A solution relating to a pure AI algorithm is not patentable subject matter under Article 25.1(2) if it is independent of any application scenario in a particular technical field (e.g., image processing or robot control) and does not contain any technical feature for implementing the AI algorithm (e.g., in terms of a special arrangement or operation of the components of a computer or in terms of a special hardware circuit). An example of such a solution is presented in Example 1:

> [Example 1] A method for processing data with a model, comprising:
>
> receiving, at a first layer of the model, a first input data, the first layer including a first weight;
>
> determining a first state based on the first input data;
>
> determining a first output data based on the first state;
>
> receiving, at a second layer of the model, a second input data, the second layer including a second weight;
>
> determining a second state based on the second input data, the second weight and the first state;
>
> determining a second output data based on the second state.

The solution in Example 1 as above does not relate to any specific application field. In the solution, the first and second input data, the first and second weight, the first and second states, and the first and second output data are all abstract general data. The process is a series of steps of an abstract mathematical process, and the result thereof is outputs of respective layers without any technical meaning. This solution is an abstract method for processing data with a mathematical process without any technical features, namely none of its object, process, nor result relates to any connection with a specific application field. Therefore, this solution is not patentable subject matter as it constitutes 'rules and methods for mental activities' stipulated in Article 25.1(2) of the Patent Law.

If a new model of an AI algorithm is intended to be patentable, one method is to impart the claimed AI algorithm with a technical meaning so that the solution is connected to a specific technical field. For example, if the data to be processed by the invention is defined with a technical meaning (e.g., image data) instead of general or abstract data, such a solution is not considered 'rules and methods for mental activities' but a solution that is 'technical.'

Example 2[8] is an example which relates to a new convolutional neural network ('CNN') model used to identify images of any size rather than to identify images of a fixed size. The claimed solution in Example 2 is:

8. Examination Guidelines, Part II, Ch. 9, Sec. 6.2, Ex. 2.

[Example 2] A method for training a convolutional neural network (CNN) model, characterized in comprising:

acquiring initial model parameters of a CNN model to be trained, the initial model parameters including initial convolution kernels and initial bias matrices of respective convolutional layers, and initial weight matrices and initial bias vectors of fully connected layers;

obtaining a plurality of training images;

on respective convolutional layers, implementing convolution and max pooling operations on each training image by using the initial convolution kernels and the initial bias matrices of respective convolutional layers to obtain first feature images of each training image on respective convolutional layers;

implementing horizontal pooling operations on the first feature images of each training image on at least one convolutional layer to obtain second feature images of each training image on respective convolutional layers;

determining feature vectors of each training image based on the second feature images of each training image on respective convolutional layers;

processing each feature vector based on the initial weight matrices and the initial bias vectors to obtain category probability vectors of each training image;

calculating category errors based on the category probability vectors and initial categories of each training image;

adjusting model parameters of the CNN model to be trained based on the category errors;

proceeding to adjust the model parameters based on the adjusted model parameters and the plurality of training images until the number of iterations reaches a preset number;

taking the model parameters obtained when the number of iterations reaches the preset number as the model parameters of the trained CNN model.

The claimed solution relates to a method for training a CNN model, in which the data to be processed is image data. The claimed training method recites how to process the image data in respective steps. Therefore, technical features are involved in the solution and thus the solution passes the Article 25.1(2) test. Further, the technical problem solved by this solution is to overcome the defect that the CNN model can only identify images of a fixed size. This solution utilizes the technical means of differently processing and training images in different convolutional layers, which is in conformity with the laws of nature, and achieves the technical effect that the trained CNN model can identify images of any size. Therefore, this solution is patentable subject matter as it constitutes a technical solution as stipulated in Article 2.2.

However, if, in Example 2, the data to be processed is recited as general 'data' instead of 'image data', the claimed solution would constitute 'rules and methods for mental activities' because the improvement relates to the abstract algorithm itself and does not relate to any technical field.

Further, the claimed solution would not be rendered patentable simply by tying the preamble of the claimed solution to a technical field while all the other features still relate to an abstract algorithm or abstract data. For example, if the preamble in Example 2 is changed into 'a method for training a convolutional neural network (CNN) model used in an information classification system' and the data to be processed is described as abstract 'data' instead of data having technical meaning such as image data, the solution would not be patentable because the claimed solution has not closely connected to a technical field but is, in essence, an abstract algorithm.

[B] Category 2

Whether a solution with specific implementation using known AI technology plus additional elements is patentable depends on whether the implementation is a substantive technical implementation. If the implementation is a substantive technical implementation in terms of a special arrangement or operation of the components of a computer or in terms of special hardware circuitry or software structures to improve the internal performance of the computer system that complies with laws of nature, the technical implementation in connection with the AI algorithm, as a whole, may be considered as constituting a technical solution. In contrast, if the AI implementation is merely a trivial technical element (e.g., a general mentioning of a general-purpose computer or the internet) or merely another abstract data processing algorithm or a pure training algorithm in relation to general data, the solution as a whole is still considered an abstract algorithm instead of a technical solution. An example of technical implementation of an AI algorithm is shown in Example 3:[9]

> [Example 3] A method comprising:
>
> when an amount of training data changes, calculating the time consumption with respect to the data after the change based respectively on at least two preset candidate training schemes;
>
> selecting, from the at least two preset candidate training schemes, a training scheme with the smallest time consumption as an optimal training scheme for the data after the change, at least two preset candidate training schemes including at least a one-processor scheme and a multiple-processor scheme based on parallel data processing; and
>
> training the data after the change according to the optimal training scheme.

This solution does not lie in improvement of a training algorithm of machine learning *per se* but relates to improvement of a technical implementation of the training algorithm. The various training schemes are closely related to the special operations of the components of the computer (the one-processor scheme versus the multiple-processor scheme). In addition, a technical effect of decreasing the time consumption of the training is derived by the close interaction between the data training method and the operations of the processor(s), leading to improvement in the internal performance of the computer implementing the training algorithm. Thus, the solution is a technical solution and is therefore patentable.

9. Example 26 in 'Typical patent application analysis in new fields and new industries', CNIPA, Intellectual Property Publishing House, January 2020.

In contrast, the following Example 4[10] presents an example where an additional element for implementing an AI algorithm is not technical and thus the solution is not patentable.

> [Example 4] A method for establishing a mathematical model, characterized in comprising:
>
> training an initial feature extraction model to obtain a target feature extraction model based on feature values in training samples for a first classification task and feature values in training samples for at least one second classification task, wherein the second classification task is another classification task related to the first classification task;
>
> processing the feature values in every training sample for the first classification task respectively to obtain extracted feature values corresponding to every training sample based on the target feature extraction model;
>
> forming extracted training samples by the extracted feature values and tag values corresponding to every training sample to train an initial classification model and thus obtain a target classification model; and
>
> forming the mathematical model of the first classification task by the target classification model and the target feature extraction model.

The solution in the above Example 4 does not relate to any specific application field. In addition, the improved implementation of the mathematical model relates to enrichment of abstract training data instead of any technical means. In the solution, the feature values, the extracted feature values, the tag values of the training samples, the target classification model, and the target feature extraction model all relate to abstract general data. The process of training the mathematical model by using relevant data of the training samples is a series of steps of an abstract mathematical process, resulting in a mathematical model for abstract general classification. This solution is an abstract method for modelling without technical features and none of its processing object, process, or result relates to any combination with a specific application field. Therefore, although this solution involves an improved implementation of the mathematical model, since the improved implementation is not technical, this solution is not patentable subject matter as it constitutes 'rules and methods for mental activities' stipulated in Article 25.1(2).

The 'technical effect' is one of the critical factors of the Article 2.2 test. Usually, improving the internal performance of a computer system is considered a 'technical effect'. However, such an advantageous effect is not considered a 'technical effect' if the improvement of the performance of a computer system is based merely on the optimization of an abstract algorithm *per se* without utilizing the inherent nature of the computer system (e.g., particular hardware components, particular operations specific to the computer system), even if the computer system can thereby operate with a higher efficiency. Only if the improvement of the internal performance of a computer system takes advantage of the interaction between the algorithm and the inherent nature of the computer system would such an advantageous effect be considered a 'technical effect'.

10. Examination Guidelines, Part II, Ch. 9, Sec. 6.2, Ex. 1.

Examples 3 and 4 discussed above are also examples exemplifying the rule of whether improving the performance of a computer system can be considered a 'technical effect'. In Example 3, because the higher training speed is derived by the interaction between the training algorithms and the different operations of the components of the computer system (i.e., the one-processor scheme versus the multiple-processor scheme), it is considered a 'technical effect'. On the other hand, in Example 4, since the higher accuracy of establishing the model is achieved by the enrichment of the abstract training data without interaction with the inherent nature of the computer system, it is not considered a 'technical effect'.

[C] Category 3

Many AI-related inventions are created and filed in China under Category 3, 'A new application of AI'. According to a WIPO report, China leads in patent applications in distributed AI, planning and scheduling, predictive analytics, and robotics.[11] Whether an AI algorithm embedded in a specific application scenario can be patentable depends on whether the specific application scenario is a technical application or at least involves a technical attribute. More specifically, if the specific application is a technical application in a specific technical field or at least has a technical attribute, the solution is considered 'technical'. In contrast, if the specific application scenario does not involve any technical attributes but, for example, only involves a purely financial scenario, the solution is still not considered a technical solution. Example 5.1[12] describes patentable subject matter in which AI is applied in robotics:

> [Example 5.1] A method for detecting a fall state of a humanoid robot based on information from a plurality of sensors, characterized in comprising:
>
> (1) establishing a sensor information fusion model of a hierarchical structure by fusing posture sensor information, Zero Moment Point (ZMP) sensor information and robot walking phase information;
>
> (2) determining stabilities in the anterior-posterior direction and the left-right direction of the humanoid robot with an anterior-posterior fuzzy decision system and a left-right fuzzy decision system, specifically comprising:
>
> 2.1 determining a walking phase of the humanoid robot based on contact situations between support feet of the humanoid robot and the ground and offline gait planning;
> 2.2 implementing fuzzification of ZMP position information by a fuzzy reasoning algorithm;
> 2.3 implementing fuzzification of a pitch angle or a roll angle of the humanoid robot by the fuzzy reasoning algorithm;
> 2.4 determining an output membership function;
> 2.5 determining a fuzzy reasoning rule based on steps 2.1–2.4;
> 2.6 implementing defuzzification.

11. World Intell. Prop. Org., *WIPO Technology Trends 2019 – Artificial Intelligence*, at p. 97, figs. 5.12 and 5.14, *available at* https://www.wipo.int/about-ip/en/artificial_intelligence.
12. Examination Guidelines, Part II, Ch. 9, Sec. 6.2, Ex. 7.

The claimed solution in this example relates to a method for detecting a fall state of a humanoid robot based on a plurality of sensors, which involves technical features. Therefore, it satisfies the first test regarding Article 25.1(2). Further, the solution solves the technical problem of how to determine the stable state of the humanoid robot and how to accurately predict the possible fall directions of the humanoid robot, utilizes technical means of determining the stable state of the humanoid robot by fuzzy algorithms, and achieves the technical effect of effectively improving the stable state of the humanoid robot and increasing the accuracy and reliability of determining possible fall directions of the humanoid robot. Thus, the solution satisfies the second test regarding Article 2.2.

In the Draft Amendment to Examination Guidelines 2021, an interesting example (Example 5.2 below)[13] is provided to show that use of algorithm tools to mine inherent correlations in data that comply with laws of nature is considered 'technical', even if the application does not pertain to a typical 'technical' field.

> [Example 5.2]: A method for analysing the propensity of using e-coupons, which is characterized by comprising:
>
> categorizing an e-coupon based on information of the e-coupon to obtain e-coupon types;
>
> obtaining user sample data based on the application scenarios of the e-coupons;
>
> extracting user behaviour characteristics from the user sample data based on user behaviours, the user behaviours comprising: browsing web pages, searching keywords, adding to favourites, adding to cart, purchasing and using e-coupons;
>
> training the recognition model of e-coupon using propensity for different types of e-coupons with the user sample data as training samples and the user behaviour characteristics as attribute labels; and
>
> predicting using probability of the e-coupons by the trained recognition model of e-coupon using propensity, obtaining the using propensity of the user for different types of e-coupons.

The solution in Example 5.2 is considered to fall within patentable subject matter because the method mines the internal correlation between user behaviour characteristics (long browsing time, large searching times, frequent use of e-coupons, etc.) and the propensity to use e-coupons. This internal correlation is considered as complying with natural laws.

On the other hand, an AI algorithm used in a non-technical application such as a business method may still be considered 'non-technical' because a purely financial or business application scenario cannot remedy the lack of technical attributes of the algorithm. Example 6[14] presents an example in which algorithms are used for analysing an economic sentiment index.

> [Example 6] A method for analysing an economic sentiment index based on electricity consumption characteristics of an area, characterized in comprising:

13. Draft Amendment to Examination Guidelines, Part II, Chapter 9, Section 6.2, Example 6.
14. Examination Guidelines, Part II, Ch. 9, Sec. 6.2, Ex. 6.

> selecting initial indicators of an economic sentiment index of the area to be detected according to economic data and electricity consumption data of an area to be detected, the initial indicators comprising an economic indicator and an electricity consumption indicator;
>
> determining an economic sentiment indicator system of the area to be detected by a clustering analysis method and a time difference relevant analysis method implemented by a computer, the economic sentiment indicator system comprising a leading indicator, a consistent indicator and a lagging indicator;
>
> acquiring the economic sentiment index of the area to be detected by a synthetic index calculation method, according to the economic sentiment indicator system of the area to be detected.

This solution relates to a method for analysing and calculating the economic sentiment index implemented by a computer, and the data processed are economic indicators and electricity consumption indicators. The problem to be solved by this solution is to judge an economic trend, which is not a technical problem, and the means employed by this solution is to analyse economic conditions based on the economic data and the electricity consumption data, which is an economic management means in conformity with the laws of economics rather than a technical means in conformity with the laws of nature. This solution can ultimately derive the economic sentiment index for evaluating the economic conditions, which is not a technical effect. Therefore, this solution is not a technical solution.

As described in the above, if an AI algorithm were used to predict the movements of a stock market index, which is not technical but purely financial, the solution as a whole would generally be non-patentable. Nevertheless, a solution would still be patentable if the AI algorithm solves a particular technical problem, such as synchronizing data on two computers in predicting the movements of a stock market index, because the application scenario has a technical attribute despite the coexisting financial attribute.

In view of this, there may be a question. The correlation between user behaviour and the propensity to use e-coupons and the correlation between historical price data and future price data both seem to be related to human behaviour. Why is the former one considered to comply with natural laws, while the latter one is considered to be with economic laws?

The issue involved here is a complex question about human attributes. In fact, humans have both biological and social attributes. Those behaviours and rules that follow the biological attributes of humans can generally be considered as having technical attributes and belong to natural laws while those behaviours and rules that follow the social attributes of humans can generally be considered as having economic attributes and belong to human-made rules.

More specifically, specific behaviour characteristics involving a single individual (such as specific interaction behaviours between a user and applications, like click actions, browsing time, and search times) can be considered as having biological properties and comply with natural laws.

On the other hand, statistical characteristics involving human groups (such as the result of a large population of human actions, like price changes, and buying and selling volumes) are generally considered as having social properties and belong to the field of economics or sociology.

Because the data correlation mined in Example 5.2 involves the correlation related to the specific behaviour of an individual user (such as browsing the web, searching keywords, adding to favourites, adding to the shopping cart, purchasing, and using e-coupons), the correlation can be considered as an internal correlation that complies with natural laws. On the contrary, because the data correlation mined in Example 6 involves the correlation between historical prices and future prices as statistical data derived from group behaviours, the correlation is considered as not complying with natural laws but economic laws.

[D] Category 4 and Category 5

Turning now to inventions in Category 4 and Category 5, i.e., 'inventions made using AI' and 'inventions made by AI', whether AI was used as a tool or even contributed to the main inventive concept would not necessarily be reflected in the claims or description because they describe the claimed invention, not how it was invented. Therefore, whether AI was used as a tool or even contributed to the main inventive concept will not be a factor to decide the eligibility of the claimed solution. The tests for patentability do not change, regardless of how the invention was created, and such solutions are patentable if what is claimed can pass the two tests under Articles 25.1(2) and 2.2.

§05.04 INVENTIVE STEP

[A] Inventiveness Assessment of AI-Related Inventions (Categories 1–3)

The requirements regarding inventiveness of AI-related inventions are, in general, similar to other types of patent applications. In China, a 'three-step approach' is applied to assess inventiveness, which is similar to the 'problem-solution' approach applied by the European Patent Office. The three-step approach comprises:[15]

- Step 1: identifying the closest prior art reference;
- Step 2: identifying a distinguishing feature from the closest prior art reference and the technical problem that is to be actually solved by the invention based on the distinguishing feature; and
- Step 3: judging whether the invention is obvious to a person of ordinary skill in the art based on the distinguishing feature and the technical problem that is to be actually solved by the invention.

Note that Step 2 involves identifying the 'technical' problem that is to be actually solved by the invention based on the distinguishing feature. On the other hand, since AI-related inventions may involve features that are considered not technical but are abstract algorithmic features or financial or business-related features, a rule specific to AI and other algorithm-related inventions is needed to address circumstances where the problem to be solved is not a 'technical' problem.

15. Examination Guidelines, Part II, Ch. 4, Sec. 3.2.1.1.

More specifically, the inventiveness assessment rule specific to AI and other algorithm-related inventions is that, when determining inventiveness of a claimed solution which includes both technical features and algorithmic features, the technical features and algorithmic features will be considered as a whole for solving a technical problem and for obtaining the corresponding technical effect if they *have a mutually supportive and interactive functional relationship*. On the other hand, an algorithmic feature (which is considered a non-technical feature) will not be considered to have a technical contribution in the inventiveness assessment if the non-technical feature does not have a mutually supportive and interactive functional relationship with a technical feature.

For an AI-related invention, if a claim clearly recites that an AI algorithm is used in a particular technical field or technical application or is implemented by improved technical means, it is considered that the algorithmic features and the technical features have a mutually supportive and interactive functional relationship, and thus algorithmic features and the technical features will be considered as a whole when inventiveness is evaluated. In contrast, if an algorithmic feature is not combined with a particular technical field or technical application and is not implemented by improved technical means but is a stand-alone algorithmic feature, the feature will not be considered to render a solution inventive because it fails to solve any technical problem and thus does not have any technical contribution.

In the Draft Amendment to Examination Guidelines 2021, the following solutions are exemplified as those with inventiveness. Again, we can see that non-technical features can contribute to inventiveness only when they cooperate closely with technical features:[16]

1. ***Problems improved by the algorithm in specific technical fields:*** if the algorithm features are applied to specific technical fields and can solve specific technical problems, the contribution of the algorithm features to the technical solution shall be considered during the inventive step examination.

2. ***Combining the algorithm with the internal structure of the computer system to jointly improve the internal performance of the computer system:*** if there is a specific technical correlation between the algorithm features and the internal structure of the computer system, which achieves the improvement of the internal performance of the computer system, the contribution of the algorithm features to the technical solution shall be considered during the inventive step examination.

3. ***Technical features that help improve business rules and methods:*** if the implementation of business rules and method features requires adjustment or improvement in technical means, the contribution of the business rules and method features to the technical solution shall be considered during the inventive step examination.

4. ***Taking the improvement of user experience as an auxiliary factor:*** if there are improvements of user experience brought or produced by technical features, or brought or produced by the technical features, algorithm or business rule

16. Draft Amendment to Examination Guidelines, Part II, Chapter 9, Section 6.1.3.

and method features jointly, it should be considered during the inventive step examination.

We will again refer to Example 5.1, above, to discuss the standard for evaluating the inventiveness of AI-related inventions in China.

When evaluating the inventiveness of Example 5.1, we assume that a prior art D1 discloses step (1) of this solution, and this solution differs from D1 in the fuzzy decision method involving the specific algorithms in step (2).

The solution defined in Example 5.1 effectively improves the stable state of the humanoid robot, and the accuracy and reliability of determining possible fall directions of the humanoid robot. In particular, the solution takes the posture information, the ZMP position information, and the walking phase information as input parameters and outputs information for determining the stable state of the humanoid robot by fuzzy algorithms and thereby provides a basis for issuing an accurate posture adjustment command. In the solution, although the distinguishing features are algorithmic, the algorithmic features have a mutually supportive and interactive functional relationship with the technical features. As compared with D1, the technical problem actually solved by this solution can be defined as how to determine the stable state of the humanoid robot and how to accurately predict the possible fall directions of the humanoid robot. Neither the above fuzzy decision algorithm nor the application thereof to determine the stable state of the humanoid robot is disclosed by any other reference document or belongs to common knowledge in the art. There is no teaching for those skilled in the art to improve D1 to obtain the claimed invention, so the claimed technical solution is not obvious as compared with the closest prior art and thus possesses inventiveness.

From the above analysis and reasoning, we can tell that, in China, importance is attached to the mutual relationships and interactions between technical features and non-technical features. Technical effects usually derive from such mutual relationships and interactions between the features.

Example 7[17] is another contrary example used to explain why an AI-related invention might lack inventiveness.

[Example 7] A method for visualizing evolution of dynamic views, characterized in comprising:

step 1), determining by a computing device an emotional subordination degree and an emotion classification of information in a set of collected information, wherein the emotional subordination degree of the information represents a possibility that the information belongs to the emotion classification;

step 2), determining the emotion classification as positive, neutral or negative, wherein: the emotion classification is determined as positive if a resulting value 'r' of dividing the number 'p' of likes by the number 'r' of dislikes is larger than a threshold value 'a', the emotion classification is determined as negative if the resulting value 'r' is less than a threshold value 'b', and the emotion classification is determined as neutral if $b \leq r \leq a$, wherein $a > b$;

step 3), automatically establishing a geometric layout of an emotion visualization graph of the set of collected information based on the emotion classification of

17. Examination Guidelines, Part II, Ch. 9, Sec. 6.2, Ex. 10.

> the information, wherein a horizontal axis represents the time of the information being produced, and a vertical axis represents the amount of information belonging to respective emotion classifications;
>
> step 4), rendering by the computing device the established geometric layout based on the emotional subordination degree of the information, wherein the information on respective emotion classification layers is rendered according to the gradient colours corresponding to the information.

When discussing the inventiveness evaluation of this example, we assume that a prior art D1 discloses a visualization analysis method based on emotions, wherein time is represented by a horizontal axis, and a width of each colour stripe at a different time represents a metric of an emotion at that time, and different emotions are represented by different colour stripes.

The solution of this patent application differs from D1 in the specific rule for emotion classification defined in step 2). As can be seen from the recitations in the patent application, even if the rule for emotion classification is different between the patent application and D1, the technical means for rendering corresponding data of the patent application is the same as that for D1 without any change or improvement to be adapted to the new rule. In other words, the above rule for emotion classification and the specific means of visualization, which is a technical feature, do not have a mutually supportive and interactive functional relationship. As compared with D1, the solution of this patent application merely proposes a new rule for emotion classification, and does not actually solve any technical problem or make any technical contribution to the prior art. Therefore, the technical solution as claimed does not possess inventiveness as compared with D1.

In Example 7, although the patent application has a distinguishing feature compared to D1, the distinguishing feature is considered to solve no technical problem and have no technical contribution, and thus the solution does not have inventiveness over D1. This is so because the distinguishing feature of emotion classification is not a technical feature but a purely algorithmic feature, and the pure algorithm feature, i.e., non-technical feature does not interact with the technical feature in respect of visualization.

[B] Inventiveness Assessment of AI-Related Inventions (Categories 4–5)

AI-related inventions under Category 4 and Category 5 are inventions that have been made by a human using AI as a tool or, hypothetically, made partially or fully by AI. This manner of creating inventions is different from conventional ways of creating inventions in that AI may undertake a huge number of simulation experiments within a reasonable timeframe, which would have been difficult for human beings. Therefore, it is possible that the machines running AI do a majority or all of the work in creating an invention.

When assessing the inventiveness of an invention, the current examination rules in China regarding inventiveness do not consider whether the invention was made, for example, incidentally or on purpose, by serendipity, or by conducting a huge number of difficult experiments. In addition, patent applicants or inventors are not required to disclose how an invention was created.

Therefore, as long as a person of ordinary skill in the art, who is a natural person instead of an AI robot, would not easily conceive of the invention starting from the prior art, the invention is considered to have an inventive step. In other words, whether an invention was made by a human being with or without the aid of AI does not affect the application of the existing rules of inventiveness assessment.

Similarly, current law does not provide any special standard for a person of ordinary skill in the art for inventions that are partially or fully created by AI, and therefore persons of ordinary skill in the art remain natural persons, and this definition is the same for other types of inventions.

§05.05 ADEQUACY OF DISCLOSURE

The adequacy of disclosure requirement for AI-related inventions is largely similar to the general requirement. Specifically, Article 26.3 of the Patent Law[18] provides that '[t]he written description shall contain a clear and comprehensive description of the invention or utility model so that a person of ordinary skill in the art can carry it out'. No matter what technical field the patent application is in, the above-mentioned requirement should be met.

For example, if the improvement lies in a new structure of an AI model, the new structure should be described in detail. If the improvement lies in the processing of the input and output data of the AI model, the input and output data, as well as the method for obtaining the data, should be described in detail. If the improvement lies in a new training method, the training method and the training data should be described in detail. Experimental data may be necessary if the invention is based on a new finding of an inherent correlation between two factors (e.g., input and output data of the algorithm) and the technical effect is difficult to predict (e.g., a new diagnostic system including input of some physical parameters and output of a diagnosis).

If the invention is to use a known AI algorithm in a specific application scenario, the AI algorithm may be described as 'black box' if the structure of the known AI algorithm is not to be modified, but the input and output data should still be described and the technical effect of applying the AI algorithm to the specific application scenario should be mentioned. Note that in many cases, although the improvement lies mainly in one aspect, other aspects need also to be modified adaptively. In such cases, the other aspects should also be described so that a person of ordinary skill in the art would have no difficulty in implementing the whole invention.

The Examination Guidelines provide some requirements for adequacy of disclosure in consideration of the nature of AI and other algorithm-related inventions.

For example, for an algorithm-related invention, the written description should describe how the technical features and the algorithmic features, which have a mutually supportive and interactive functional relationship with the technical features, interact and thereby produce advantageous effects. For example, when an algorithmic feature is involved, a specific technical field should be described in connection with the abstract algorithm, and definitions of input parameters and output result(s) of

18. Patent Law of China, Article 26.3.

the algorithm should be correspondingly associated with specific technical data in the specific technical field.

Further, the description should clearly and objectively describe advantageous effects of the invention as compared with the prior art, for example, improvement of quality, accuracy or efficiency, improvement of the internal performance of a system, and so on. The description can also describe experience improvements from the perspective of users. Meanwhile, it should also be described how user experience improvements are created or derived by the technical features in connection with the algorithmic features that have a mutually supportive and interactive functional relationship with the technical features.[19]

Although the Examination Guidelines do not specifically address the issue of training (e.g., how an AI model should be trained and/or the input data fed to the trained model), we can deduce such a requirement from the general requirement provided in Article 26.4 and the nature of AI algorithms.

As is well known for AI algorithms, training is an important part of building an AI model. Parameters and intermediate data of AI algorithms are usually not decided by human beings but through training, and thus are difficult to predict or describe in a logical way.

On the other hand, many known training algorithms (e.g., the famous Gradient Descent algorithm) have been proposed and widely used, and some AI-related inventions involve improvements of training methods while some do not. If an AI-related invention involves an improvement of the training method, or the modification of other aspects of the AI model makes it necessary to modify the training method adaptively, the training method and the training data should be recited in the description to meet the adequate disclosure requirement. Otherwise, if an AI-related invention does not involve any improvement of the training method, and a person of ordinary skill in the art could readily understand that a well-known training method can be used without modifications, the training method can be described briefly without details.

§05.06 INVENTORSHIP

[A] Inventorship in General

According Rule 13 of *Rules for the Implementation of the Patent Law of the People's Republic of China*[20] (the 'Implementing Rules'), '[a]n inventor or creator referred to in the Patent Law means any person who makes creative contributions to the substantive features of an invention-creation. Any person who, during the course of accomplishing the invention-creation, is responsible only for organizational work, or who only offers facilities for making use of material and technical means, or who only takes part in other auxiliary functions, shall not be considered as an inventor or creator.'

19. Examination Guidelines, Part II, Chapter 9, Sec 6.3.
20. «中华人民共和国专利法实施细则» [Rules for the Implementation of the Patent Law of the People's Republic of China] (as amended by St. Council Decree No. 569; promulgated 9 Jan. 2010, effective 1 Feb. 2010).

The essence of the Patent Law provides that a person will be considered an 'inventor' so long as the person has made creative contributions to any feature defined in the claims.

'Person' cited in Rule 13 refers to natural persons, which is also supported by the Examination Guidelines. In particular, the Examination Guidelines require that an inventor must be a natural person and be identified in the request form when filing a new patent application. An entity or group is not eligible to be named as the 'inventor'. When the name of the individual needs to be changed, a certificate provided by the local public security bureau must be provided. When an applicant requests to add an inventor or delete an inventor, signed declarations by all other inventors are needed.[21]

[B] Determination of Inventorship for AI-Related Inventions

As explained regarding Rule 13 of the Implementing Rules, 'inventor' or 'creator' as mentioned in the Patent Law means any person who has made creative contributions to the substantive features of the invention-creation. Therefore, in general, if a person makes creative contributions to at least one feature of a claim, he or she will be named as an inventor. Under this principle, we will discuss whether a person is considered an inventor in each of the five categories.

As to Category 1, 'invention of AI', a person who creates a new algorithm or model for AI itself will be named as an inventor.

As to Category 2, 'invention of an AI implementation', a person who invents additional elements for the AI implementation will be named as an inventor.

As to Category 3, 'a new application of AI', and Category 4, 'inventions made using AI', the same rule of 'creative contributions to the substantive features of the invention' will be applied to determine whether a person is eligible to be an inventor. For example, a person who merely has the idea to use a general AI technology for a certain purpose may not be eligible as an inventor because it is too general and does not contribute to the substantive features of the invention. However, a person who selects a particular AI technology and configures it to suit the intended purpose, a person who selects the particular data to be used to train the AI, a person who conceives of the data processing method for obtaining the input data, and a person who recognizes the value of and selects one optimal solution from a large number of potential solutions produced by the AI are each eligible to be named as inventors where the substantive features of the invention(s) include the person's contributions.

As to Category 5, 'inventions made by AI', a machine is not eligible to be an inventor, and the person, entity, or group owning the machine is also not eligible to be an inventor on the basis of such ownership.

§05.07 AREAS FOR IMPROVEMENT

The current allowable AI-related inventions need to be closely tied to 'technical' characteristics, such as technical effect, technical contribution, or non-technical

21. Examination Guidelines, Part I, Chapter 1, Sections 4.1.2, 6.7.2.1, and 6.7.2.3.

features' interactional relationship with technical features. It is then very difficult for pure algorithm inventions in Category 1 and improvements in AI implementation in Category 2 to be allowed because the improvements are not regarded as having 'technical' characteristics as discussed above. However, some entities do have great ideas for innovations in these categories, particularly in Category 2. These types of innovations have broad application and thus can therefore be applied in many scenarios. The policy reason for refusing to grant the patent rights to the innovations in Categories 1 and 2 might be a concern to avoid monopolies in fundamental research. But taking very strict requirements on the inventions in Category 1 and Category 2 will, of course, hurt the interests of the entities or inventors who are doing fundamental research. In the long run, how to encourage these entities or inventions in the patent law aspect would provide an area for authorities to make improvements.

Another concern that AI-related inventions have to face is the difficulty of getting evidence of infringement, because features of AI-related inventions are inherently hidden from being easily detected from outside or from reverse engineering. Besides, patent litigation plaintiffs in China must carry all the burden of proof of providing evidence to prove the infringement. Therefore, how to efficiently help patentees to get evidence with reasonable efforts is another area for authorities to make improvements in the future.

Technologies develop very quickly but the CNIPA does not discuss Category 4 and Category 5 of AI-involved inventions. We expect the CNIPA will provide guidance on how to handle these types of inventions in due course.

§05.08 RECOMMENDATIONS FOR PATENT APPLICANTS

As discussed above, China is friendly in general to AI-related inventions. Applicants usually can get patents for AI-related inventions if the applications are well drafted to help examiners easily understand the 'technical' characteristic. The following are some recommended approaches for applicants when drafting AI-related inventions.

[A] Technical Aspects of the AI-Related Invention Should Be Emphasized

As AI can be applied in many areas, business elements such as finance, trading and media distribution may also be involved in addition to traditional industries such as manufacturing, power transmission, medical devices, or automobiles. CNIPA looks into 'technical' aspects of the solution more than commercial aspects. Therefore, when drafting business method-related applications involving AI technologies, it is recommended to describe in the embodiments the technical aspects of features and associations/interactions between the algorithmic features, the business features and the technical features.

For example, for an invention related to display of advertisements which may automatically provide advertisements based on user browser histories, the effects or advantages include associating displayed content data with user browser history data and increasing the value of the advertisements by displaying appropriate advertisements to targeted users. When describing the embodiment for this invention, in order to render the solution more 'technical', it is advisable to describe the solution in 'more technical' context, such as how the browser history data is acquired by an application and how the browser history data is stored in a database. In addition, in order to comply with adequacy of disclosure, how the content of the advertisements is selected based on the browser history data (e.g., by an AI algorithm) should also be described in detail. If the processing and/or analysing of the browser history data and the advertisement data utilizes, for example, image processing, such processes may also add to the technical attributes of the solution. The advantage of increasing the value of the advertisements or selling more products is generally not regarded as 'technical' and therefore should, at most, be described after describing the technical advantages of associating displayed content data with user browser history data.

[B] Describe the Relationships Between Features Without Leaving Any Feature Isolated

When assessing inventiveness, CNIPA looks not only at technical features of AI-related inventions but also the algorithmic feature and the technical feature as a whole if they have a 'mutually supportive and interactive functional relationship'.

Therefore it is recommended that when drafting embodiments, the specific technical field to which the invention is used be clearly indicated and the associations/ interactions between algorithmic features and technical features be described in detail. For example, the input data and output data having technical meanings should be defined clearly, and what technical effect and how this technical effect can be achieved through the interactions between the technical data and the algorithm is better described with reference to the particular technical field or technical application.

[C] Describe in Detail the Features in which the Improvement Lies and Include the Necessary Description of the Interfaces Between the Improvement and the Prior Art

As mentioned in the above, it is recommended that the features in which the improvement lies (e.g., the structure of the model, the pre-processing or post-processing of the data, the training method, or the correlation between data) be described in detail to meet the requirement of adequate disclosure.

In addition, we suggest further describing the interfaces between the improvement and the prior art. For example, although a known AI algorithm can be described as a 'black box' and the main innovation may lie in a novel application of the known AI algorithm to a particular technical field, it may also be necessary to describe the input and output data of the technical field or necessary pre-processing and/or post-processing method with respect to the known AI algorithm.

[D] Describe the Improvement of the User Experience in Conjunction with Technical Features

When using the effect of user experience improvement to reinforce inventiveness arguments, it is necessary to describe what specific technical means or what combination of technical means and non-technical means contribute to the user experience improvement. Therefore, we suggest describing, in the description, how user experience can be improved as a result of the technical means and in a technical way. This may help in inventiveness arguments.

§05.09 CONCLUSION

AI-related inventions continue to become more valuable for patent holders in China, with more and more new implementations launched by using AI technologies. The amendments of the Examination Guidelines in February 2020 sent a signal to the public indicating the willingness of China to provide strong protection of AI-related inventions. This might be a good time for applicants to file and get AI-related patents in China.

Chapter 6

European Patent Office

Jochen Ehlers, Ben Husband, Thomas Kretschmer, Dr Julian Potter, Dr Sébastien Ragot & Jochen Unland

§06.01 PATENTABILITY OF SOFTWARE AND COMPUTER-IMPLEMENTED INVENTIONS

As in other jurisdictions, the question of what subject matter is patentable at the European Patent Office ('EPO') is exercising the minds of intellectual property ('IP') players, particularly with regard to software and computer-implemented inventions.

[A] Legal Provisions, Excluded Subject Matter, and Technical Character

Patentable inventions are defined by Article 52(1) of the European Patent Convention ('EPC'), which reads:

> European patents shall be granted for any inventions, in all fields of technology, provided that they are new, involve an inventive step and are susceptible of industrial application.

Article 52(1) EPC explicitly sets out three patentability conditions related to novelty, inventive step, and industrial application, which are further defined in Articles 54, 56, and 57 EPC.

The EPC does not define what is meant by 'invention'. However, Article 52(2) EPC provides a non-exhaustive list of examples of subject matter that are not regarded as inventions within the meaning of Article 52(1), namely:

(a) discoveries, scientific theories and mathematical methods;
(b) aesthetic creations;
(c) schemes, rules and methods for performing mental acts, playing games or doing business, and programs for computers;
(d) presentations of information.

These examples all relate to abstract or intellectual matters, which do not aim for any direct technical result. Such matters are sometimes referred to as 'non-inventions' or 'abstract subject matter'.

Importantly, Article 52(3) EPC points out that abstract subject matter as listed in Article 52(2) EPC is excluded from patentability 'only to the extent to which a European patent application or European patent relates to such subject-matter or activities as such'. The subject matter excluded by Article 52(2) EPC is an exception to the general rule defined by Article 52(1) EPC and should accordingly be construed narrowly.

The interplay between Articles 52(1), 52(2), and 52(3) EPC implicitly gives rise to a fourth patentability condition. Namely, the fact that abstract subject matter is only excluded 'as such' means, *a contrario*, that an invention involving non-abstract subject matter may constitute patentable subject matter even if the invention additionally contains abstract subject matter.

At the EPO, the 'technical character' is the fundamental concept that distinguishes a patentable invention from excluded subject matter such as that listed in Article 52(2) EPC. Thus, even though the technical character of a claimed invention is not positively defined by the EPC, it is an implicit requirement for the presence of an 'invention' within the meaning of Article 52(1) EPC.

Accordingly, an important issue is to distinguish between abstract ideas, considered not patentable, and subject matter having technical character, considered patentable in the sense of the EPC. This distinction is at the heart of debates concerning the patentability of software and computer-implemented inventions ('CIIs').

Over the years, the EPO has established a special legal framework for the examination of software and CIIs, i.e., the so-called 'two-hurdle approach', which is discussed *infra* in detail. A particularity of this approach is that the technical contribution and inventive step are jointly assessed, with the important proviso that only the so-called 'technical features' can contribute to this inventive step while non-technical features are disregarded.

[B] Technical Features vs. Non-technical Features

The distinction between technical and non-technical features is thus pivotal, not only for patent eligibility but also for the inventive step assessment. This distinction is often tricky, hence the need of definitions provided by the Guidelines for Examination in the EPO[1] (hereafter the 'Guidelines').

To start with, Section F-IV 2.1 of the Guidelines provides that, as a general rule, the claims must be drafted in terms of the 'technical features of the invention'.[2] That being said, the Guidelines acknowledge that it is 'legitimate to have a mix of technical and non-technical features appearing in a claim, as is often the case with computer-implemented inventions'.[3]

Technical features are structural or functional features that contribute to the technical character of the invention, starting with inherently technical features such

1. *Guidelines for Examination in the European Patent Office*; Mar. 2023 edition.
2. *See also* Guidelines F-IV 6.5.
3. Guidelines, G-VII, 5.4.

as a central processing unit or a memory circuit. By contrast, the term 'non-technical features' refers to features which, on their own, would be considered 'non-inventions' under Article 52(2) EPC.[4]

Importantly, however, a distinction is made between purely non-technical features and features which, when taken in isolation, are non-technical but do, in the context of the invention, contribute to producing a technical effect serving a technical purpose, thereby contributing to the technical character of the invention.[5] This distinction is consistent with the narrow interpretation of the subject matter excluded by Article 52(2) EPC: the terminology 'as such' used in Article 52(3) EPC is a bar to a broad interpretation of what is excluded.[6]

As a result, an abstract feature such as an algorithm or a computational model may indirectly contribute to the technical character but 'only to the extent that it serves a technical purpose of the method'.[7]

Features that do contribute to the technical character, even indirectly, are regarded as technical features by the EPO. However, speaking of technical features versus non-technical features can sometimes be misleading when dealing with a feature that is non-technical 'as such' (i.e., when taken in isolation), but actually does contribute to the technical character in the context of the invention. Thus, it is often more appropriate to refer to features that do contribute to the technical character of the claimed invention, as opposed to features that do not, particularly when dealing with mathematical method steps relating to machine learning ('ML').

For completeness, the clarity requirements set out in Article 84 EPC must be interpreted as meaning not only that a claim must be comprehensible from a technical point of view, but also that it must indicate all the essential features of the claimed invention. The concept of 'essential features' as defined by the Guidelines again points to the technical character requirements:

> Essential features of a claim are those necessary for achieving a technical effect underlying the solution of the technical problem with which the application is concerned (the problem usually being derived from the description).[8]

To summarize: a claim must be drafted in terms of technical features or, more precisely, in terms of features that do contribute to the technical character of the claimed invention at least indirectly. A mix of technical and non-technical features is acceptable so long as the claimed features recite all essential features which, as a whole, define a technical solution to a technical problem.[9]

4. *Ibid.*, G-II 2.
5. *Ibid.*, B-VIII 2.2 and G-VII 5.4.
6. Guidelines2Day: Computer-implemented inventions in Guidelines 2021, available at: https://e-courses.epo.org/pluginfile.php/75122/mod_label/intro/PL92-2021_GL2day_CII.pdf.
7. *See* G 1/19, T 1227/05 (Circuit simulation I/INFINEON, point 3.1), and T 1784/06 (Classification method/COMPTEL), point 3.1.1.
8. Guidelines F-IV 4.5.2.
9. *Ibid.*, F-IV 2.1, 4.5.2, 4.10, 6.5, and G-VII, 5.2.

[C] Two-Hurdle Approach and COMVIK Criterion

According to the Guidelines[10] and the case law of the EPO,[11] whether a patent can be obtained for software or CIIs is to be determined in accordance with a two-fold assessment, known as the two-hurdle approach.[12] This approach is rooted in Articles 52(2), 52(3), 54(2) EPC, and 56 EPC. Article 52(2) EPC provides a non-exhaustive list of abstract subject matter or activities considered non-inventions, whereas Article 56 EPC requires an invention in the sense of Article 52 EPC to involve an inventive step, in view of the state of the art as defined in Article 54(2) EPC. The Boards of Appeal ('BoAs') further rely on an interpretation of the term 'technical' in Rules 42(1), 43(1)(a) and (b) EPC to require that a patentable claim should specify a 'technical solution to a technical problem'.[12]

As set out in Section G-II 2 of the Guidelines: 'The first hurdle, also referred to as the patent eligibility hurdle, requires that the claimed subject-matter as a whole must not fall under the "non-inventions" defined in Article 52(2) and (3).' So, a patent claim that includes at least one technical feature avoids exclusion under Article 52(2) EPC and, as a result, overcomes the first hurdle. For instance, a 'computer-implemented method', i.e., a method performed by a computer, would immediately pass the first test because a computer has technical character *per se*. Similarly, a 'method of training a machine learning model' can be made patent eligible simply by claiming it as a 'computer-implemented method of training a machine learning model'.

The second hurdle is where inventive step is assessed. It is the trickiest, inasmuch as only the claimed features considered to contribute to the technical character participate in the inventive step assessment while purely non-technical features are disregarded. That is, the assessment of the inventive step takes account of only those features that make a technical contribution, according to a principle set out in the EPO decision T 641/00 ('COMVIK').[13] Namely:

> An invention consisting of a mixture of technical and non-technical features and having technical character as a whole is to be assessed with respect to the requirement of inventive step by taking account of all those features which contribute to said technical character whereas features making no such contribution cannot support the presence of inventive step.

This principle is known as the COMVIK approach or COMVIK criterion. In T 1543/06 the Board stated that the principle expressed in T 641/00 may also be reformulated as follows: 'an invention which as a whole falls outside the exclusion zone of Article 52(2) EPC (i.e., is technical in character) cannot rely on excluded subject matter alone, even if novel and non-obvious (in the colloquial sense of the word), for it to be considered to meet the requirement of inventive step'.[14]

10. *Ibid.*, G-II 2.
11. *See* G 1/19, discussed *infra*.
12. *See* W. Chandler, *Patentability of computer-implemented inventions (CIIs): state of play and developments*, OJ EPO, Supplementary publication, p. 73, May 2015.
13. EPO decision T 641/00 ('COMVIK'); *see also* opinion G1/08 and decision G 1/19.
14. T 1543/06, Reasons 2.5.

To summarize: the inventive step examination performed by the EPO is agnostic to purely non-technical features. Rather, it is an assessment of the non-obviousness of the sole features that contribute to the technical character, if only indirectly.

The COMVIK approach was confirmed in a number of BoA decisions, starting with decision T 258/03 ('Hitachi'), the opinion G 3/08 ('Programs for computers') of the Enlarged Board of Appeal ('EBA'), and the EBA decision G 1/19 ('Pedestrian simulation'). The EBA noted that the BoAs in general were *quite comfortable* with the COMVIK approach (G 3/08, Reasons, points 10.13.2). Furthermore, the EBA in G 1/19 affirmed 'the COMVIK approach has long been the prevailing method for the assessment of computer-implemented inventions and the Enlarged Board has deemed it a "practicable system" for this purpose'.[15]

Apart from endorsing the COMVIK approach, decision G 1/19 confirmed the EPO practice in terms of CII patentability. As such, this decision is regarded as maintaining the stability of CII patentability in Europe. Findings of this decision were implemented in the 2022 version of the Guidelines, which notably mention new worked-out examples of mathematical steps making a technical contribution, as discussed *infra*. Also, decision G 1/19 clarified that the term 'technical' must remain open to further development as technology evolves, which is the reason why this term is not explicitly defined, as such, in the EPC, the Guidelines, or the BoA decisions.

A practical consequence of the two-hurdle assessment and the COMVIK approach is that the technical contribution of an invention is properly examined as part of the inventive step assessment. An invention that is essentially non-technical, such as a business method, cannot be rendered patentable by merely specifying that it is implemented by a 'computer', as it would not pass the second hurdle, i.e., the inventive step test. Indeed, all that is left after discarding the business method features in that case is a 'computer', the use of which is not inventive.

The above remarks illustrate how essential is the distinction between features contributing to the technical character and features that do not. Clearly, it is difficult to achieve a uniform application of the provisions of the Guidelines relating to this distinction, especially as the 'granularity' of such features is not precisely defined. In that respect, some practitioners have reported punctilious debates, pushing analyses down to the word level, at the risk of disregarding interactions between the claimed features. Practitioners have also lamented hurried interpretations of the claimed subject matter by EPO examiners, who would quickly reject patent claims having both technical and non-technical features. That said, there is little doubt that a uniform application of such provisions will eventually prevail. And it is fair to acknowledge that the EPO practice as to CIIs has now reached a certain stability.

§06.02 SPECIAL PROVISIONS RELATING TO PATENTABILITY OF INVENTIONS RELATING TO AI

The patentability of artificial intelligence ('AI')-related inventions directed to specialized hardware (e.g., neuromorphic devices) is not an issue; such inventions have technical character and are in principle patentable, just like any other physical machine. More uncertain, however, is the patentability of AI-related innovations implemented in

15. G 1/19 at D. II. B. 61.

software running on conventional computer hardware.[16] The reason stems from the fact that mathematical methods, including algorithms, and computer programs, are as such not regarded as inventions,[17] as discussed in Section §06.01, *supra*.

[A] Explicit Provisions Relating to Patentability of AI

Neither the EPC nor its Implementing Regulations[18] explicitly refer to AI or ML, although the EPC includes provisions regarding programs for computers and mathematical methods, as discussed in Section §06.01. However, Section G-II, 3.3.1 of the Guidelines explicitly addresses AI and ML. This section further highlights that the guidance provided in Section G-II, 3.3 ('Mathematical methods') generally applies to computational models and algorithms related to AI and ML. Finally, Section G-II, 3.3 points to Section G-II, 3.6, which concerns programs for computers; this section is also relevant to AI and ML.

In general, Section G-II, 3.3.1 of the Guidelines make a distinction between, on the one hand, the abstract mathematical nature of AI-related computational models and algorithms and, on the other hand, the technical purpose, use, or technical character that may be sought in a claim involving such computational models and algorithms. But while the Guidelines optimistically note that '[a]rtificial intelligence and machine learning find applications in various fields of technology',[19] they also express reservations about the technical character of such subject matter or activities.

To start with, Section G-II, 3.3.1 defines AI and ML as being 'based on computational models and algorithms for classification, clustering, regression and dimensionality reduction, such as neural networks, genetic algorithms, support vector machines, k-means, kernel regression and discriminant analysis'.[20] In addition, this section notes that such computational models and algorithms 'are per se of an abstract mathematical nature, irrespective of whether they can be 'trained' based on 'training data', whereby such concepts are, as such, excluded from patentability, by virtue of Articles 52(2) and 52(3) EPC.

In a more nuanced way, Section G-II, 3.3.1 further points out:

> Terms such as 'support vector machine', 'reasoning engine' or 'neural network' may, depending on the context, merely refer to abstract models or algorithms and thus do not, on their own, necessarily imply the use of a technical means, something that has to be taken into account when examining whether the claimed subject-matter has a technical character as a whole (Article 52(1), (2) and (3)).

Section G-II, 3.3.1 of the Guidelines then moves on to discuss the technical character of examples of AI-related concepts. Technical character can be acknowledged in some cases. For example,

---

16. AI is here considered to at least include ML.
17. Article 52(2) and 52(3) EPC.
18. Implementing Regulations to the Convention on the Grant of European Patents, last amended 13 Oct. 2022.
19. Guidelines, Section G-II, 3.3.1.
20. *Ibid.*

> the use of a neural network in a heart monitoring apparatus for the purpose of identifying irregular heartbeats makes a technical contribution.

Similarly,

> the classification of digital images, videos, audio or speech signals based on low-level features (e.g. edges or pixel attributes for images) are further typical technical applications of classification algorithms.

For completeness, Section G-II, 3.3.1 notes that

> where a classification method serves a technical purpose, the steps of generating the training dataset and training the classifier may also contribute to the technical character of the invention if they support achieving that technical purpose. [21]

The last example echoes decision T 1286/09, where the gist of the invention consisted 'essentially in increasing the diversity of exemplar images used to train a semantic classifier by systematically altering an exemplar colour image to generate an expanded set of images with the same salient characteristics as the initial exemplar image'.[22]

However, the technical purpose of an invention is not always apparent from the claimed features. In that case, the underlying algorithm will not enter into the examination for inventive step. For example,

> Classifying text documents solely in respect of their textual content is however not regarded to be per se a technical purpose but a linguistic one.[23]

Closely related,

> Classifying abstract data records or even 'telecommunication network data records' without any indication of a technical use being made of the resulting classification is also not per se a technical purpose, even if the classification algorithm may be considered to have valuable mathematical properties such as robustness.[24]

The distinction between a technical purpose and non-technical purpose will be better understood in the light of Section G-II, 3.3, which concerns mathematical methods.

[B] Provisions Relating to Mathematical Methods

Section G-II, 3.3.1 of the Guidelines mentions that further examples of technical purposes for which AI and ML could be used may be found under Section G-II, 3.3 ('Mathematical methods'). As a result, Section G-II, 3.3 is relevant to AI and ML too.

Importantly, Section G-II, 3.3 points out (emphasis added):

> A mathematical method may contribute to the technical character of an invention, i.e. contribute to producing a technical effect that serves a technical

21. *Ibid.*
22. T 1286/09, Reasons 2.2.
23. T 1358/09.
24. T 1784/06.

> purpose, by *its application to a field of technology* and/or by being *adapted to a specific technical implementation*.[25]

First, the above passage defines a contribution to the technical character as being a contribution to the production of a technical effect that serves a technical purpose. Secondly, it provides two sufficient conditions for a mathematical method to contribute to the technical character: (i) either it is applied to a field of technology and/or (ii) it is adapted to a specific technical implementation. In practice, the EPO relies on these conditions to appreciate the patentability of AI-related inventions involving ML models run on conventional hardware.[26]

Section G-II, 3.3 otherwise sets out a number of principles to keep in mind when assessing the contribution made by a mathematical method to the technical character of an invention. In particular, 'it must be taken into account whether the method, in the context of the invention, produces a technical effect serving a technical purpose'. That said, 'a generic purpose such as "controlling a technical system" is not sufficient to confer a technical character to the mathematical method. The technical purpose must be a specific one.'[27]

Furthermore, the Guidelines explain:

> the mere fact that a mathematical method may serve a technical purpose is not sufficient, either. The claim is to be functionally limited to the technical purpose, either explicitly or implicitly. This can be achieved by establishing a sufficient link between the technical purpose and the mathematical method steps, for example, by specifying how the input and the output of the sequence of mathematical steps relate to the technical purpose so that the mathematical method is causally linked to a technical effect.[28]

This causal link must be sufficient. In particular, 'defining the nature of the data input to a mathematical method does not necessarily imply that the mathematical method contributes to the technical character of the invention.' [29]

By contrast, if the 'steps of a mathematical method are used to derive or predict the physical state of an existing real object from measurements of physical properties, as in the case of indirect measurements, those steps make a technical contribution regardless of what use is made of the results.'[30] The concept of indirect measurements is considered in G 1/19, which explains:

> The calculation of the physical state of an object (e.g. its temperature) is typically part of a measurement method. It is generally acknowledged that measurements have technical character since they are based on an interaction with physical reality at the outset of the measurement method. Measurements are often carried out using indirect measurements, for example, the measurement of

25. Guidelines, G-II, 3.3.
26. Guidelines2Day: Computer-implemented inventions in Guidelines 2021, available at: https://e-courses.epo.org/pluginfile.php/75122/mod_label/intro/PL92-2021_GL2day_CII.pdf.
27. Guidelines, G-II, 3.3.
28. *Ibid.*
29. *Ibid.*, referencing decisions T 2035/11, T 1029/06, and T 1161/04.
30. *Ibid.*

> a specific physical entity at a specific location by means of measurements of another physical entity and/or measurements at another location (see e.g. T 91/10, Reasons, point 5.2.1; T 1148/00, Reasons, point 9). Even though such indirect measurements may involve significant computing efforts, they are still related to physical reality and thus of a technical nature, regardless of what use is made of the results.[31]

The above principles are clearly relevant to AI and ML. Section G-II, 3.3 of the Guidelines further provides examples of technical contributions of a mathematical method:

- controlling a specific technical system or process, e.g. an X-ray apparatus or a steel cooling process;
- determining from measurements a required number of passes of a compaction machine to achieve a desired material density;
- digital audio, image or video enhancement or analysis, e.g. de-noising, detecting persons in a digital image, estimating the quality of a transmitted digital audio signal;
- separation of sources in speech signals; speech recognition, e.g. mapping a speech input to a text output;
- encoding data for reliable and/or efficient transmission or storage (and corresponding decoding), e.g. error-correction coding of data for transmission over a noisy channel, compression of audio, image, video or sensor data;
- encrypting/decrypting or signing electronic communications; generating keys in an RSA cryptographic system;
- optimising load distribution in a computer network;
- determining the energy expenditure of a subject by processing data obtained from physiological sensors; deriving the body temperature of a subject from data obtained from an ear temperature detector;
- providing a genotype estimate based on an analysis of DNA samples, as well as providing a confidence interval for this estimate so as to quantify its reliability;
- providing a medical diagnosis by an automated system processing physiological measurements.

All such examples may potentially benefit from ML algorithms. Of course, the examples above are for illustrative purposes and must be interpreted with caution; each particular case has to be assessed on the merits.

Apart from its purpose, a mathematical method may also contribute to the technical character of the invention because it is adapted to a particular technical implementation. For instance,

> a mathematical method may also contribute to the technical character of the invention independently of any technical application when the claim is directed to a specific technical implementation of the mathematical method and the mathematical method is particularly adapted for that implementation in that

31. G 1/19, para. 99.

> its design is motivated by technical considerations of the internal functioning of the computer system or network.[32]

For example, this may happen if 'the mathematical method is designed to exploit particular technical properties of the technical system on which it is implemented to bring about a technical effect such as efficient use of computer storage capacity or network bandwidth'.[33]

Section G-II, 3.3 further provides examples of acceptable technical implementations, including:

> assigning the execution of data-intensive training steps of a machine-learning algorithm to a graphical processing unit (GPU) and preparatory steps to a standard central processing unit (CPU) to take advantage of the parallel architecture of the computing platform. In that case, the claim should be directed to the implementation of the steps on the GPU and CPU for this mathematical method to contribute to the technical character.[34]

To summarize, a mathematical method may contribute to the technical character of an invention (i.e., contribute to producing a technical effect that serves a technical purpose) if:

- *The claim targets a technical application (first criterion).* The technical purpose must be specific, and the claim must be functionally limited to that technical purpose, either explicitly or implicitly, such that the mathematical method is causally linked to a technical effect. In practice, the claim must specify (explicitly or implicitly) how the output of the mathematical method is used, except where, e.g., the mathematical method is used to derive or predict the physical state of an existing real object from measurements of physical properties;[35] and/or
- *The claim is directed to a specific technical implementation (second criterion) of the mathematical method.* For example, the mathematical method is designed to exploit particular technical properties of a technical system. In practice, this means that the mathematical method is specifically adapted to exploit the hardware or is designed based on technical considerations relating to, e.g., the internal functioning of the hardware.

[C] Provisions Relating to Computer Programs

For completeness, it is necessary to comment on provisions concerning computer programs as these are also relevant to the patentability of inventions relating to AI, given that the underlying computational models are mostly implemented in software running on conventional computer platforms.

32. Guidelines, G-II, 3.3, referencing decisions T 1358/09 and G 1/19.
33. *Ibid.*
34. *Ibid.*
35. Guidelines, G-II, 3.3.

According to Section G-II, 3.6 of the Guidelines, 'a computer program must produce a "further technical effect" when run on a computer' in order to be acknowledged as a technical character (and thus not be excluded from patentability).[36]

The concept of 'further technical effect' is defined as:

> a technical effect going beyond the 'normal' physical interactions between the program (software) and the computer (hardware) on which it is run. The normal physical effects of the execution of a program, e.g. the circulation of electrical currents in the computer, are not in themselves sufficient to confer technical character to a computer program.[37]

A question this statement raises is whether computer programming always involves 'technical considerations', given that such considerations may possibly confer technical character on the claimed subject matter. In the opinion G 3/08, the EBA noted:

> In T 1173/97 the Board concentrated on the effect of carrying out an algorithm on a computer, noting that there were always technical effects, which led the Board [...] to formulate its requirement for a 'further' technical effect. Only if a computer program, when run, produced further technical effects, was the program to be considered to have a technical character. In the same way, it would appear that the fact that fundamentally the formulation of every computer program requires technical considerations in the sense that the programmer has to construct a procedure that a machine can carry out, is not enough to guarantee that the program has a technical character (or that it constitutes 'technical means' as that expression is used in e.g. T 258/03, Hitachi). By analogy one would say that this is only guaranteed if writing the program requires 'further technical considerations'.[38]

So, in practice, no technical character will be acknowledged from the mere fact that the computer program has been designed such that it can be automatically performed by a computer. Rather, 'further technical considerations' are required, which are typically related to the technical considerations of the internal functioning of the computer, going beyond merely finding a computer algorithm to perform a task are needed. There, an important proviso is that such considerations have to be reflected in claimed features that cause a further technical effect. There is no requirement that the 'further technical effect' has to be new or surprising – to the contrary, the effect may be known in the prior art.[39] While, by means of a formal amendment, e.g., by introducing some hardware interaction, the first hurdle of patent eligibility may be taken, the more important second hurdle is whether or not the features contributing to the (further) technical effect support the presence of an inventive step.

Examples of further technical effects that confer technical character to a computer program are the control of a technical process or of the internal functioning of the computer itself or its interfaces. In practice, however, computer program [product]

36. *Ibid.*, 3.6.
37. *Ibid.*, referencing decisions T 1173/97 and G 3/08.
38. G 3/08.
39. *See* EPO decisions T 931/95, T 1461/12, and T 556/154.

claims mostly refer back to a corresponding method claim, such that it is sufficient to focus the patentability assessment on the method claim.

To conclude this section: two essential criteria to assess the technical character of an AI/ML invention (in particular an AI/ML computational model) are 1) whether a corresponding method claim targets a specific technical application and/or 2) whether the method is adapted to a specific technical implementation, provided there is a sufficient link between the technical purpose and the mathematical method steps. A third criterion can be taken into consideration for claims directed to a computer program [product], which is the presence of a further technical effect or closely related further technical considerations. In all cases, the claimed features must produce a technical effect serving a technical purpose, and the technical aspects must be reflected in the claim.

§06.03 SUBJECT MATTER PATENTABILITY

At the EPO, an invention must make a technical contribution to be patentable, as discussed *supra* in Section §06.01. Over the years, the assessment of whether claimed subject matter constitutes an invention according to Article 52 EPC has shifted from the so-called 'technical contribution' approach[40] to a two-fold assessment of subject matter patentability, where the technical contribution of the invention is properly examined as part of the inventive step assessment.[41]

As also explained in Section §06.01, the first hurdle of this two-fold assessment requires a patent claim to include at least one technical feature to avoid exclusion under Article 52(2) EPC. This condition is easily met in practice as it is sufficient for a claim to mention even a single technical feature (e.g., a computer or processor); something that applies to any invention in at least Categories 1 to 3 below.

However, given that only the claimed features considered technical participate in the assessment of the inventive step (second hurdle, see discussion *supra* in Section §06.01), it is worth investigating which types of features may potentially be acknowledged as having technical character. Stated another way, the question of what subject matter is eligible for patent protection is intimately linked to the inventive step assessment.

In particular, the computational model underlying an AI-related invention may be acknowledged as having technical character if it satisfies either of the two major criteria identified in Section §06.02 for mathematical methods. That is, the claim targets a technical application (first criterion) and/or is directed to a specific technical implementation (second criterion), provided there is 'a sufficient link between the technical purpose and the mathematical method steps'.[42]

---

40. *See*, e.g., EPO decisions T 208/84, T 26/86, T 115/85, and T 6/83.
41. *See*, e.g., EPO decisions T 258/03, T 424/03, and G 1/19.
42. Guidelines, Section G-II, 3.3.

[A] Category 1

The preceding remarks apply in particular to 'core' AI inventions (Category 1), for example inventions directed to a new type of neural network (e.g., a transformer), where the core innovation may essentially boil down to a new computational model or algorithm.

An invention in Category 1 can easily pass the first hurdle provided the claim mentions at least one technical feature, e.g., a processor, a computer, or any form of computing means. Then, it remains to assess whether the computational model or algorithm underlying the core AI invention may be acknowledged as having technical character in view of the two criteria identified in Section §06.02 for mathematical methods.

However, as follows from the discussion in Section §06.02, a core AI invention is unlikely to be restricted to a specific technical application (first criterion), given that the core model or algorithm is usually agnostic to specific applications; it may have multiple potential applications. If a claim to such an invention is silent on any processing means (or other hardware component), it will likely be regarded as a non-invention and challenged based on Article 52(2) EPC.

A core AI invention that does not serve any specific technical purpose will likely not be acknowledged as having any form of technical character beyond the mere presence of a computer or processing means, if any. An example of this would be a claim directed to a new type of transformer network for predicting the next words in a sentence.

A core AI invention that is adapted to and claimed as a specific technical implementation would, under the category definitions of this book, be regarded as an invention in Category 2, discussion of which follows.

[B] Category 2

A new AI implementation may, for example, concern the creation of a new system or process of broad application using known AI technology plus additional elements, e.g., a particular arrangement of filters or a particular interface.

The remarks made above with respect to inventions in Category 1 apply to Category 2 as well. To start with, inventions in Category 2 will easily pass the first hurdle, as the corresponding claim will likely mention at least one technical feature, e.g., a computer or a processor. In addition, the additional elements involved in the new AI implementation may contribute to the technical character of the invention. Consider the example of an AI system that dynamically interacts with its environment to learn, as opposed to ML methods that passively learn thanks to training data fed by human users.[43] Here the additional components required for the AI system to interact with its environment may have technical character in the sense of the EPC.

Irrespective of the additional elements that an invention in Category 2 may involve, the core computational model itself may be acknowledged to indirectly contribute to the technical character if it satisfies either of the two criteria identified

43. According to certain interpretations, in contrast to passive ML methods, AI could further involve an entity that dynamically interacts with its environment to learn.

in Section §06.02, i.e., the claim targets a specific technical application (first criterion) and/or implies a specific technical implementation (second criterion). This, however, assumes there is a sufficient link between the technical purpose and the mathematical method steps as explained *supra*.

By definition, a new AI implementation has broad application and primarily concerns a new implementation. Therefore, it will likely not be directed to a specific technical application. However, the model or algorithm underlying the new AI implementation may be acknowledged to contribute to the technical character of the invention if it satisfies the second criterion, as discussed in Section §06.02, *supra*, i.e., if it is adapted to 'a specific technical implementation', provided that the model or algorithm is specifically adapted to exploit the hardware or is designed based on technical considerations relating to the internal functioning of the hardware.[44]

An example from the Guidelines is an invention 'assigning the execution of data-intensive training steps of a machine-learning algorithm to a graphical processing unit (GPU) and preparatory steps to a standard central processing unit (CPU) to take advantage of the parallel architecture of the computing platform.'[45] Note, however, that the claim should be directed to the GPU/CPU implementation for the corresponding method steps to be considered as contributing to the technical character.

Another example can be extrapolated from the teaching of decision T 2330/13, where the Board considered that 'features supporting parallel processing contribute to the technical character of the claim'.[46] This example would be a method directed to the execution of an ensemble model of decision trees, which leverages vector processing to 'walk', and thus execute, the trees in parallel for inferencing purposes. In this example, the method is designed based on technical considerations relating to the functioning of the vector processor.

[C] Category 3

Just like inventions in Category 2, inventions in Category 3 will be typically technical enough to pass the first hurdle, if only because the corresponding claim will likely mention at least one feature that is inherently technical such as a processor or another hardware component. In addition, inventions in Category 3 target a specific application by definition. This specific application will be considered to contribute to the technical character if the claim is restricted to that application. For example, 'the use of a neural network in a heart monitoring apparatus for the purpose of identifying irregular heartbeats makes a technical contribution'.[47] Furthermore, the underlying model or algorithm may also contribute to the technical character of the invention if it is adapted to a particular technical implementation, as discussed *supra*. In that case, the invention would fall into both Categories 2 and 3.

In principle, the model or algorithm underlying an invention in Category 3 may possibly exploit a specific hardware implementation (such as vector processing) or be designed based on technical considerations relating to the internal functioning of

44. Guidelines, G-II, 3.3; *see also* T 1358/09 and G 1/19.
45. Guidelines, G-II, 3.3.
46. T 2330/13; *see also* T 1321/11.
47. Guidelines, Section G-II, 3.3.1.

the computer. However, since the computational model is, by definition, not novel for inventions in Category 3, a question that arises is whether there is a sufficient link between the underlying mathematical method and the technical purpose of the claimed invention. Indeed, the underlying computational model will often be agnostic to the technical purpose of its outputs in that case.

Of course, if the new application of AI (Category 3) neither serves a specific technical purpose nor requires a specific technical implementation, then the underlying computational model will not be regarded as contributing to the technical character. This issue is illustrated in EPO decision T 755/18, where the Board held that 'if neither the output of a machine-learning computer program nor the outputs' accuracy contribute to a technical effect, an improvement of the machine achieved automatically through supervised learning to generate a more accurate output is not in itself a technical effect'.[48]

However, the catchwords of decision T 755/18 must be interpreted cautiously, inasmuch as the technical character of a computer program may, in principle, also derive from other features of the program, not necessarily related to its inputs or outputs.[49] In particular, the design of the underlying method may be 'motivated by technical considerations of the internal functioning of the computer system'.[50]

[D] Category 4

The result of an application of AI may be, in and of itself, a patentable invention (Category 4), just like a new aircraft designed using computer-aided design ('CAD') is a potentially patentable invention. For AI-related inventions in Category 4, what is claimed is the *result* of the use of AI, not the use of AI itself. That result could possibly be an invention in Category 1, 2, or 3, as discussed above, or anything else from, for example, a mechanical device to a new industrial process to a new drug. The AI used during the invention process need not appear in the claim, or even the patent disclosure, at all.

Accordingly, the technical character and thus the patentability of the resulting invention will be assessed based on whatever is claimed, regardless of the tool used to arrive at the invention, just like parts or products designed by CAD. It will, in fact, be irrelevant that this invention was obtained using AI.

[E] Category 5

According to the current case law, it is not possible to name an AI entity as inventor. Doing so does not permit issuance of a patent to an invention in Category 5. The invention will not even be prosecuted in that case, as discussed *infra*, such that the question of subject matter patentability would not even be assessed by the EPO in that case.

---

48. T 755/18, catchwords and reasons 3.2.
49. *See also* Report of the Swiss AIPPI group on the '*Inventorship of Inventions made using Artificial Intelligence (Q 272)*'; Sic! 10|2020.
50. Guidelines, G-II, 3.3; *see also* T 2330/13, T 1358/09, and G 1/19.

However, assuming for sake of argument that an AI entity can invent, an invention 'made' by an AI entity (either alone or, for example, as a co-inventor with a human) may possibly be prosecuted without naming the AI entity as inventor.[51] In that case, the same conclusion as reached for Category 4 holds for inventions in Category 5.

As the technical contribution of the invention is properly examined as part of the inventive step assessment, the question of which subject matter is susceptible to patent protection is intimately linked to the inventive step, as discussed in the next section.

§06.04 INVENTIVE STEP

While the first hurdle of the two-fold assessment made by the EPO is easily overcome, the second hurdle (the inventive step) is based on the principle set out in decision T 641/00[52] (the COMVIK approach), whereby only the claimed features considered technical participate in the assessment of the inventive step, while non-technical features are disregarded, as discussed in Section §06.01.

This approach requires identifying all the novel technical features of a claim, including features that indirectly contribute to the technical character of the invention (see Sections §06.01 and §06.02), and then assessing the inventive step of the sole features considered to contribute to the technical character. In practice, the assessment of the technical character of the claimed features is deferred to the inventive step examination: only the technical character of the novel features is assessed. The question to answer then is whether the residual differences identified with respect to the prior art make a technical contribution that is non-obvious.[53]

Features that appear to be non-technical when taken in isolation may nonetheless contribute to the technical character of a claimed invention if, in the context of that invention, they contribute to produce a technical effect serving a technical purpose. According to the EBA decision G 2/21, the relevant standard for the reliance on the purported technical effect when assessing whether or not the claimed subject matter involved an inventive step under Article 56 EPC concerns the question of what the skilled person, with common general knowledge in mind, would understand at the filing date from the application as originally filed as the technical teaching of the claimed invention. The technical effect relied upon, even at a later stage, needs to be encompassed by that technical teaching. Specifically, the EBA found that:

> A patent applicant or proprietor may rely upon a technical effect for inventive step if the skilled person, having the common general knowledge in mind, and based on the application as originally filed, would derive said effect as being encompassed by the technical teaching and embodied by the same originally disclosed invention.

51. These assertions are controversial, *see*, e.g., the Report of the Swiss AIPPI group on the '*Inventorship of Inventions made using Artificial Intelligence (Q 272)*'; Sic! 10|2020.
52. EPO decision T 641/00 ('COMVIK').
53. Guidelines, G-VII, 5.4.

As with other types of CIIs, a challenge with AI-related inventions is to identify all technical features or, more precisely, the features that contribute to the technical character, beyond the mere presence and operation of general computerized means. The novel aspects of the claimed invention, whether arising from the computational model or other claimed features, must have sufficient bearing on technical character to achieve inventive step.[54]

[A] Category 1

The challenge is particularly thorny for core AI inventions (Category 1) that boil down to reciting a new ML algorithm or a new computational model, such as a model based on a new neural network architecture. Assuming that such an invention clears the first hurdle (e.g., the underlying method is claimed as being implemented by a computer), the question to be answered next is whether the invention makes a non-obvious contribution to the prior art.

If the sole residual novelty revolves around the underlying algorithm or model, a fundamental question is whether this algorithm or model serves a technical purpose. Indeed, as noted by the BoA in decision T 1784/06, 'where an intrinsically non-technical solution (mathematical algorithm) seeks to derive a technical character from the problem solved, the problem must be technical. Otherwise, the solution remains non-technical and does not enter into the examination for an inventive step.'[55] That is, the algorithm would not enter into the examination for inventive step because 'the general idea of performing an algorithm by means of a computer program product is a commonplace way of running an algorithm automatically.'[56]

One may want to assess whether the underlying computational model or algorithm can be considered to indirectly contribute to the technical character of the invention in view of the two criteria discussed in Section §06.02. However, as discussed therein, an independent claim directed to a core AI invention in Category 1 is unlikely to be restricted to a specific technical application (first criterion), given the numerous potential applications that the core AI invention may have. Conversely, a core AI invention claim that requires a specific technical implementation can be regarded as a new AI implementation (Category 2) as discussed below.

A residual novel feature that neither serves a specific technical purpose nor requires a specific technical implementation (e.g., a new type of transformer network for predicting the next words of sentences) will likely not be acknowledged as having any form of technical character, such that the corresponding claim will likely be rejected for lack of inventive step, Article 56 EPC.

A typical pitfall concerns computational efficiency, especially for inventions in Category 1. Arguing that the claimed mathematical method is algorithmically more efficient may prove useless. Or, as recited in the Guidelines:

> If the mathematical method does not serve a technical purpose and the claimed technical implementation does not go beyond a generic technical

54. Guidelines, G-II, 3.3 and 3.3.1.
55. T 1784/06, Reasons 10.1 and 11.5.
56. *Ibid.*, Reasons 3.2.

> implementation, the mathematical method does not contribute to the technical character of the invention. In such a case, it is not sufficient that the mathematical method is algorithmically more efficient than prior-art mathematical methods to establish a technical effect.[57]

Conversely, if the patent owner manages to demonstrate that the mathematical method contributes to producing a technical effect, then the computational efficiency of the steps concerned will be taken into account in the inventive step assessment. Namely,

> if it is established that the mathematical method produces a technical effect due to having been applied to a field of technology and/or adapted to a specific technical implementation, the computational efficiency of the steps affecting that established technical effect is to be taken into account when assessing inventive step.[58]

[B] Category 2

A key criterion for a new AI implementation (Category 2) to be considered inventive (in the sense of EPO decision T 641/00) is the level of technical interactions, i.e., the degree of impact of the residual novel features on the technical character.

Because new AI implementations would typically involve additional technical elements as compared with inventions in Category 1, inventions in Category 2 may potentially involve more technical interactions, which may favourably participate in the inventive step assessment.

Moreover, the underlying method may be acknowledged to contribute to the technical character of the invention if it is adapted to *a specific technical implementation*, as discussed *supra* in Sections §06.02 and §06.03.[59] In turn, the adaptation of the method to that specific implementation may be acknowledged as having an inventive step if it is non-obvious in view of the prior art, Article 56 EPC. One example of this would be the implementation of ML steps on a GPU and a CPU, as discussed in Section §06.03. Another example is provided by decision T 1286/09, where the gist of the invention consisted essentially in increasing the diversity of exemplar images used to train a semantic classifier by systematically altering an exemplar colour image to generate an expanded set of images with the same salient characteristics as the initial exemplar image.

Conversely, if the mathematical method does not contribute to the technical character, the inventive step assessment will focus on the sole technical implementation of an algorithm, which is usually not considered to be inventive, as illustrated above with decision T 1784/06. As another example, in decision T 1358/09, the Board concluded that the technical contribution lacked inventive step because the 'only implementation features specified in the claim are references to the method being "computerized" and the text documents being "digitally represented in a computer"'.[60]

---

57. Guidelines G-II 3.3 and 3.6.
58. Guidelines G-II 3.3; *see also* T 1358/09 and G 1/19.
59. *Ibid.*
60. T 1358/09, Reasons, 5.7.

In general, the outcome of the inventive step assessment will largely depend on the extent to which abstract features (e.g., the underlying ML computational model) are tied to technical features, starting with hardware components of the physical machine running the model. For that reason, the inventive step will typically be easier to defend for new AI implementations (Category 2) than core AI inventions (Category 1) in practice.

[C] Category 3

In principle, a claim directed to a new application of known AI technology (Category 3) may possibly be novel because: (i) a known ML feature is used for the first time in an application that is not novel *per se*; and/or (ii) the application itself is novel. The latter case disposes the claim favourably toward inventive step, assuming that the application has technical character and is recited so as to have a limiting effect on the claim.

The former case, however, is less likely to succeed. Indeed, applying known AI technology (Category 3) to a known application may likely be perceived by EPO examiners as being a common design option for the skilled person. In particular, where the residual novelty boils down to using an ML model, or ML-related concepts, the residual novel feature has little chance of fulfilling an inventive step analysis. This is illustrated, for example, by decision T 1191/19 where the Board held, 'the mere application of a known machine learning technique to problems in a particular field is a general trend in technology and cannot be inventive as such.'

The same conclusion holds, *a fortiori*, where the sole residual novel feature is the use of an ML model in place of another mathematical function.[61] Just like the mere automation of functions previously performed by human operators, substituting a given mathematical function or procedure for a known AI technology will likely be perceived to be in line with the general trend in technology and thus not considered inventive. The fact that an ML algorithm can theoretically learn any mathematical function will, in typical cases, prompt the skilled person to replace a known mathematical function with a trained ML model, in an obvious manner.

A recurrent issue with inventions in Category 3 is the difficulty to demonstrate technical advantages of the underlying ML model. In particular, the lack of disclosure of the training of the ML model may affect the ability to demonstrate a technical effect and, in turn, an inventive step. This is illustrated by the decision in T 161/18, which stated:

> Since in the present case the claimed method differs from the prior art only by an artificial neural network, the training of which is not disclosed in detail, the use of the artificial neural network does not lead to a specific technical effect which could establish an inventive step.[62]

In particular, it can be difficult to demonstrate the superiority of the ML model over a previous mathematical function. For instance, in decision T 2803/18, the Board noted that it was,

61. *See*, e.g., decisions T 0161/18, T 2803/18, and T 1191/19.
62. T 161/18, catchword (machine translation).

> not convinced by the respondent's argument that the accuracy of the estimation would be increased. The accuracy would depend on many factors (size of training sets, number and type of elements/variables constituting the representative vectors, etc.), none of which are defined in claim 1, so that the results obtained by the claimed method are not necessarily more accurate than the results obtained by the regression analysis, the resulting mathematical model and the threshold criteria applied in D2. The patent in suit does also not support such an alleged benefit by comparative data.[63]

Section G-VII, 5.4.2.5 of the Guidelines provides another example, which is inspired by decision T 1968/08. In this example, the difference between the method of claim 1 and D1 concerns the use of a neuro-fuzzy controller combining a neural network and fuzzy logic rules. The Guidelines acknowledge the technical character of this difference, inasmuch as it contributes to the control of the coating process claimed; the output of the mathematical method is directly used in the control of a specific technical process. However, in the view of the Guidelines, 'the mere fact that the parameters are calculated using a combination of results of a neural network analysis and fuzzy logic - without any details on specific adaptation to the thermal spray coating process - cannot credibly ensure any technical effect beyond a different adjustment of the process parameters'. Thus, in the absence of such evidence, the objective technical problem that arises is to provide an alternative solution to the problem of adjusting the process parameters which control the thermal spray coating process which is already solved in D1. Now, a second prior-art document D2 is assumed to disclose a combination of a neural network and fuzzy logic rules providing a neuro-fuzzy controller in the technical field of control engineering, which leads the Guidelines to conclude to a lack of inventive step in this example.

The examples above show that additional efforts are required to obtain a patent for a Category 3 invention. Tying ML-related features with inherently technical features, whether concerning the technical application and/or a specific technical implementation, will certainly be useful, as discussed in Section G-II of the Guidelines and in Section §06.03, *supra*.

An important thing to keep in mind is the tension between inventive step and sufficiency of disclosure: the more inventive step arguments are made on the basis of alleged technical effects resulting from the underlying computational model, the more the description must support such allegations, as also discussed in the next section.

[D] Categories 4 and 5

At the EPO, the person of ordinary skill in the art is determined according to the objective technical problem solved by the invention, i.e., the problem solved by the residual, novel technical features of the invention.[64] Where the result of application of AI is, in and of itself, a patentable invention having technical character, the inventive step of the resulting invention will likely be assessed regardless of the AI tool used to arrive at the invention, normally by using the problem-solution approach.

63. T 2803/18, Reasons, 4.2.
64. Guidelines G-VII 3.

The same conclusion holds for inventions claimed to be made by an AI entity (Category 5). This assumes that the AI entity is not named as inventor since otherwise the patent application would not reach the stage of inventive step examination.

But, again, all such scenarios will have to be assessed on a case-by-case basis.

§06.05 ADEQUACY OF DISCLOSURE

The concept of adequacy of disclosure is referred to as 'sufficiency of disclosure' under the EPC. The requirements of sufficiency of disclosure are formulated in a technologically neutral manner:

> The European patent application shall disclose the invention in a manner sufficiently clear and complete for it to be carried out by a person skilled in the Article.[65]

Therefore, the criteria governing the sufficiency of disclosure are the same as for any other type of invention. In particular, 'the description must notably disclose any feature essential for carrying out the invention in sufficient detail to render it apparent to the skilled person how to put the invention into practice, without undue burden and without needing inventive skills'.[66]

Emphasis must be put on what is actually useful to the skilled person in order to be able to carry out the invention. Indeed, 'since the application is addressed to the person skilled in the art, it is neither necessary nor desirable that details of well-known ancillary features are given, but the description must disclose any feature essential for carrying out the invention in sufficient detail to render it apparent to the skilled person how to put the invention into practice'.[67]

The Guidelines further provide that a limited amount of trial and error may be permissible, notably in an unexplored field, something that may perhaps be applicable to certain areas of AI.

In general, for the requirements of Article 83 EPC, Rule 42(1)(c) and Rule 42(1)(e) EPC to be fully satisfied, 'it is necessary that the invention is described not only in terms of its structure but also in terms of its function, unless the functions of the various parts are immediately apparent. Indeed, in some technical fields (e.g., computers), a clear description of function may be much more appropriate than an over-detailed description of structure.'[68]

[A] Categories 1 and 2

For core AI inventions and new AI implementations (Categories 1 and 2), pseudo-code or short excerpts from programs and flow diagrams will certainly be useful, though not mandatory.[69] Obviously, the AI system itself must be sufficiently described. In principle, it should be sufficient to provide a high-level, functional description of the

65. Art. 83 EPC.
66. Guidelines F-III, 1.
67. *Ibid.*
68. *Ibid.*
69. *See* Guidelines, F-II, 4.12.

various components involved (algorithms, modules, units, etc.), how they interact, and how they allow new technical effects to be achieved, without having to add pseudo-code or program excerpts. Obviously, the ins and outs of the underlying computational model or algorithm, and its interactions with the hardware, must be carefully described in detail. Also, if the underlying model or algorithm is adapted to a specific technical implementation this should be explained in detail.

Regard must be had to the facts and evidence of the particular case, remembering that the person of ordinary skill in the art is typically a computer or data scientist or a software engineer who is possessed of average knowledge and ability.

[B] Category 3

High-level flow diagrams will likely be useful to describe new applications of AI (Category 3), although are not mandatory. The AI system itself must be sufficiently described, especially where the novelty of the claimed invention comes down to using this AI system. As this is unlikely to be acknowledged as having an inventive step (see Section §06.04, *supra*), particular care should be taken in describing how the computational model 'interacts' with the technical application, as noted in the previous sections (see Sections §06.02, §06.03, and §06.04, *supra*). This notably requires a sufficient description of the computational model, the training algorithm, and the training dataset, as further discussed below.

EPO decision T 161/18 ruled that a description merely referring to a general training algorithm and general types of training data is insufficient. In particular:

> Regarding the training of the neural network according to the invention, the present application only discloses that the input data should cover a wide range of patients of different age, gender, constitution type, health condition and the like, so that there is no specialization of the network [...]. However, the application does not disclose which input data are suitable for training the artificial neural network [...], or at least one data set suitable for solving the present technical problem. Therefore, the training of the artificial neural network cannot be reworked by the person skilled in the art, and therefore the person skilled in the art cannot carry out the invention. Thus, the present invention [...] is not sufficiently disclosed, since the training according to the invention cannot be carried out in the absence of a corresponding disclosure.[70]

And, conversely, the lack of technical disclosure may negatively affect the inventive step.[71]

More generally, the tension between inventive step and sufficiency of disclosure must be kept in mind. Excessive inventive step arguments as to the underlying computational model (e.g., an ANN) may lead the EPO to find an insufficiency of disclosure, should such arguments not be supported by the description.

Thus, where a known ML algorithm is used for training the computational model, then at least the training data must be described sufficiently precisely, together

70. T 161/18, reasons 2.2 (machine translation).
71. *Ibid.*, catchword; *see also* Section §06.04, *supra*.

with the technical goal to be achieved, to allow the skilled person to train the AI system, perform the invention, and obtain its technical advantages.

Technically speaking, a minimal description of the training dataset includes a precise description of the data structure (e.g., examples formed as pairs of input data and associated labels, together with the types of input data and labels, such as images and class labels). The description should address desired properties of the training dataset (e.g., typical number of examples needed to suitably train the model and statistical properties of the training data). An explanation as to the evaluation of the trained model through a validation dataset would be welcome, too. For example, decision T 1191/19 took issue with the absence of any example set of training data and validation data, which were required as input to the claimed learning scheme, and thus concluded a lack of sufficiency of disclosure.

In general, some indications as to the type and architecture (or topology) of the computational model is needed (also for inventions in Category 1 or 2). For an ANN, for example, one needs to know the type of ANN (e.g., a recurrent neural network), the number and types of layers, and the number of nodes (the layer width). For completeness, applicants would be well-advised to indicate the type of objective function used to train the model, as this impacts on the goal to be achieved, if only indirectly. Providing an adequate level of description of such aspects will be useful to defend both the sufficiency of disclosure and inventive step, and provide support to amend the claims, if necessary. Additional information may address the types of activation functions (especially where activation function parameters are learned). Finally, quantization, if any, should be discussed, as it affects the performance of the execution of the model and has technical consequences.

In practice, it may well be impossible or cumbersome to explicitly list the parameters learned by the computational model upon training it. For example, an ANN may well involve a very large number of synaptic weights. Instead, it may be sufficient to precisely describe the computational model, how it is trained, as well as a suitable training dataset, as discussed above.

Obviously, it would be quite unreasonable for Patent Offices to require an explicit disclosure of actual data used to train the AI system, given the very large number of examples that are often necessary to suitably train a model. This is anyway not necessary where the type and structure of the training data are sufficiently described, also considering the ongoing democratization of AI and the ubiquity of data in times of an all-pervasive internet. Likewise, the actual data used to fit a curve or an analytical function are usually not requested.

True, the actual training datasets are often proprietary data, which are not available to the public. However, numerous databanks exist and are available, which can often be used to train computational models that fall under the terms of a given claim. The description may also provide guidance on how to aggregate, preprocess, and curate training data, how such data should be structured to form suitable training examples, as well as desired properties of such data, as discussed earlier. For example, the description may indicate a general data structure, e.g., {image → class label}, where the labels correspond to a 'defective sample' or an 'acceptable sample'. The drawings may possibly include typical examples of images used to train the model, should such images support black and white rendering.[72] The description may also indicate one or more sources of adequate training data, such as by way of a URL pointing to an online file containing examples.

In that respect, it is worth remembering that it is not necessary, under the EPC, to disclose the 'best' embodiment of the invention. Rather, the description can merely give examples or describe alternative embodiments or variations extending over the area protected by the claims. Clearly, the precise type and structure of training data used will not be pivotal in all cases, especially where the invention is directed to a core AI innovation, inasmuch as the resulting AI system may well be compatible with a broad range of data. For example, a new ML pipeline may be architected to automatically select a suitable feature extractor based on the input data type, prior to feeding extracted features (i.e., vectors) into a given ANN, making the model fairly independent of the type of input data. In that case, a precise description of the various possible types of input data may be superfluous. Conversely, a reasonably sufficient description of the training data may be needed for inventions concerning a new application of a known ML algorithm (Category 3), as discussed above.

[C] Categories 4 and 5

Finally, an invention made using AI (Category 4), or made by an AI entity (Category 5), must be sufficiently described based on what is claimed, irrespective of the AI tools used to arrive at the invention. As noted *supra*, a claim to an invention in Category 4 and 5 may be completely unrelated to AI or CIIs; the claim could be directed to anything in any field. The duty to 'disclose any feature essential for carrying out the invention in sufficient detail to render it apparent to the skilled person how to put the invention into practice, without undue burden and without needing inventive skills'[73] attaches to the claimed invention, not to the manner in which the invention was made. Thus, for example, a Category 4 invention may involve a human inventor using a sophisticated AI system to design a wing of an airplane. If that wing is what is claimed, then the disclosure duty is to describe how to put the wing into practice, not to describe how to design a wing using AI. Notably, apart from the inventorship issues for an invention in Category 5 (discussed in the next section), there would be no duty to even mention that AI was used as part of the inventive process.

As a final remark, clarity is a requirement set out in Article 84 EPC,[74] which is distinct from, albeit related to, the requirement of sufficiency of disclosure, Article 83 EPC. An ambiguity in a claim may possibly trigger an objection under Article 84 and/or Article 83, as illustrated in decision T 2574/16. An objection under Article 83 is in order where an unclear feature affects the whole scope of the claim, such that it is impossible to carry out at all the invention defined therein.

72. Guidelines A-IX, 1.2.
73. Guidelines F-III, 1; Art. 83 EPC.
74. Art. 84 EPC ('The claims shall define the matter for which protection is sought. They shall be clear and concise and be supported by the description.').

§06.06 INVENTORSHIP

[A] Inventorship in General

According to Article 62 EPC an inventor has a right to be mentioned as such. In addition, the inventor must be designated in the application (Article 81 EPC). In practice, however, the EPO does not investigate inventorship, which is not regarded as a patentability criterion; this is considered a matter of national law.

Besides, the EPC does not provide an explicit definition of inventorship. That being said, inventors are usually perceived as human beings who have sufficiently contributed to an invention, with inventive inputs, such that their respective contributions reflect in at least one claim of the corresponding patent application. And beyond European national laws, the patent law of other jurisdictions (starting with the US) also influences the European practice, as patent applications that are concurrently prosecuted in other countries must comply with foreign inventorship provisions.

A person who has contributed to the overall disclosure may also be considered an inventor if this contribution impacts the interpretation of the meaning and/or the scope of a claim. This follows from the fact that claims must be supported by the description (Article 84 EPC) and are interpreted with the help of the description, in accordance with Article 69(1) EPC and its Protocol on Interpretation. Thus, an inventor is a person who contributes to one or more of the claimed features, as interpreted in view of the description.

[B] Determination of Inventorship for AI-Related Inventions

The above rules apply in straightforward fashion to AI-related inventions in Categories 1–3, where a human inventor (or inventors) conceives of an invention relating to core AI, an AI implementation, or an application of AI. The rules similarly apply to AI-related inventions in Category 4 (inventions made using AI), despite the fact that human contributions may be less tangible in that case.

However, for AI-related inventions in Category 5, i.e., those claimed to have been made by an AI entity, additional scrutiny is required. The Legal Board of Appeal of the EPO confirmed the decisions of the Receiving Section to refuse patent applications in which an AI system called DABUS was designated as inventor in the application forms.[75] The applications had been refused on the grounds that they do not meet the EPC requirement that an inventor designated in the application has to be a human being, not a machine. Such decisions were largely expected, especially since the publication of an academic study on AI inventorship commissioned by the EPO,[76] and are consistent with similar court decisions in most jurisdictions.

As a result, one understands that an invention involving AI is only eligible for patent protection if it sufficiently involves one or more human beings in the invention

75. EPO decisions J 8/20 and J 9/20.

76. *See* http://documents.epo.org/projects/babylon/eponet.nsf/0/3918F57B010A3540C125841900280653/$File/Concept_of_Inventorship_in_Inventions_involving_AI_Activity_en.pdf.

development process,[77] where such human beings (and only those) are named as inventors. The rationale of the above decisions would also exclude patent protection in a case of AI being named a co-inventor with one or more humans.

Various types of human interventions or acts may potentially be acknowledged as contributing to inventorship, provided that such contributions include inventive inputs that are sufficiently reflected in at least one of the patent claims. Decisive for legal inventorship, and hence patent protection overall, are the occurrence and extent of such contributions. Whether or not these contributions are sufficient to be acknowledged, inventorship has to be assessed on a case-by-case basis.

What are the possible types of human contributions to AI-related inventions? To start with, software engineers are involved in the design of the AI algorithms and the programming of the AI system. Users of the AI system typically have to select a type of computational model (e.g., ANN, support vector machine, decision tree), set hyperparameters of the AI system, as well as, for example, parameters determining the type of feature extraction, dimensionality reduction, training algorithm, and objective function, even if default settings may often be available for each type of computational model. Importantly, users further have to obtain and select suitable training data, and often pre-process such data (e.g., to clean, prune, aggregate, normalize, and reformat the data), before feeding them to the AI system for training purposes. Thus, an AI system may notably be designed, programmed, and parameterized by humans. In addition, an AI system may access training data prepared by humans and process such data according to parameters set by humans, with a view to learning its internal parameters (e.g., synaptic weights), in order to achieve a desired output or goal, also set by humans. For completeness, human beings may eventually have to select subsets of outputs produced by the AI system, possibly refine, or otherwise modify such outputs, and/or feed such outputs to another algorithm (not necessarily AI), for further processing. So, there are many areas where human users may potentially contribute to an AI-related invention.

Of course, the more automation, the less potential human contributions. In practice, however, human contributions may be restricted to any subset of the above tasks. For example, inventorship may already be acknowledged for a human being who selects a given AI technology and configures it to suit the intended purpose of the invention.

Where a human being merely selects data used to train the AI algorithm, a key aspect to consider is the extent to which this selection impacts the training of the AI system and consequently the invention. Indeed, this selection may be obvious in some cases (e.g., dictated by the problem to be solved). Besides, different data selections may possibly lead to a similar trained model, also falling under the terms of the claims. In other cases, selecting a particular training dataset to train the AI may be pivotal, in particular where this basically amounts to identifying key variables of the function to be trained. A similar remark can be made with respect to input data fed to the trained AI algorithm for inference purposes. However, since the latter case relates to the utilization of the AI system after it has been trained (in a supervised setting), it is less likely to involve inventive contributions from human

77. Report of the Swiss AIPPI group on the '*Inventorship of Inventions made using Artificial Intelligence (Q 272)*', Sic! 10|2020.

users in practice as data used for inferences are normally imposed by the problem to be solved by the AI system, i.e., such data must be of a similar type as the input data part of the training examples.

Selecting a particular output from a large number of outputs produced by the AI and recognizing it to be a patentable invention may again potentially be acknowledged as contributing to inventorship, provided that the selection performed has a sufficient impact on the resulting invention; a parallel can be made with selection inventions in other fields. Actually, recognizing even a single AI output to be a patentable invention may already contribute to inventorship, remembering that an invention is a technical solution to a technical problem.[78]

What about the inventorship of human beings who design and program the AI code used in the invention? Two cases can notably be examined. In the first case, the AI code is developed independently of (i.e., before) the invention, whereas, in the second case, the AI code is specifically developed for the purpose of the invention.

The first case evokes computer programs used to create copyrightable material: the authors of the corresponding software are typically not regarded as authors of the works subsequently created by persons using such software, provided that the creative influence of such authors has no steering impact on the final output. For example, the authors of a digital audio workstation (software) are normally not regarded as the authors of a musical work (e.g., a song) created with this workstation. Similarly, the authors of CAD software are normally not regarded as inventors of an object (e.g., a part, a device, an apparatus, or a machine) created with this software. Thus, the authors of an AI code (the 'AI authors') that is subsequently used to make an invention will likely not qualify as inventors of the invention subsequently made independently of these authors.

However, in the second case, the AI authors of the program code that is specifically developed for making the invention may qualify as inventors, because of the impact the AI code may have on the resulting invention. This may in particular be the case where the AI authors design a code and parameterize an ML model with the specific goal of developing an invention.

Further situations may occur wherein, for example, the AI authors may happen to be actively involved in the development of the invention, which may be the case when they are essentially users of their own AI code, and thus inventively contribute to an invention.

In all cases, a sufficient causal link must exist between the human contributions made during the inventive process and the definition of the resulting invention, as with any other type of invention.

To conclude this section, AI-related inventions discussed herein (in particular ML) remain computer-implemented inventions. As such, they can be compared to various other computerized techniques that have emerged in the last decades, such as CAD, graphics and image editors, and digital audio workstations. Now, as far as IP protection is concerned, there is no reason to consider AI-related inventions as fundamentally different from inventions related to other computerized techniques. And since European patent law generally attempts to provide protection requirements in a technologically neutral way, the criteria applied for the appreciation of

78. *Ibid.*

inventorship should be agnostic to the technical field(s) of the invention. Accordingly, the inventorship requirements for inventions made using AI should be the same as with any other type of invention. That being said, it is acknowledged that AI favours ever less apparent, tangible human involvement in the inventive process (just like other computerized techniques). Thus, the threshold of human involvement required for patent law protection may further evolve in the future.

§06.07 AREAS FOR IMPROVEMENT

Difficulties stemming from the definition of technical features and technical character.

While the EPO's approach has now reached some stability, it is still the subject of criticism, mostly due to the lack of definition of what is 'technical', the difficulties in the differentiation between the technical and non-technical features, and the possible impact of the non-technical features on the technical character.

State of the art limited to technical disclosures (or not).

Beyond the technical character of an invention, the above distinctions may also impact the definition of the 'state of the art' for the purposes of assessing the inventive step of the invention. In that respect, contradictions were noted between decisions of the Boards of Appeal of the EPO, namely decisions T 172/03 ('Ricoh') and T 2101/12 ('Vasco'). A question debated was whether Article 54(2) EPC excludes non-technical disclosures from the prior art. In decision T 2101/12 the Board considered that the interpretation of Article 54(2) EPC given in EPO decision T 172/03 was incorrect. In other words, Article 54(2) EPC itself contains no limitation according to which a non-technical process may not be considered state of the art.

Consideration of sui generis rights for CIIs.

Patent practitioners and other stakeholders in AI had the opportunity to meet at a conference organized by the EPO ('Patenting Artificial Intelligence', Munich, May 2018). The following conclusion was drawn by the EPO: patents are still regarded as a fit IP to encourage innovation in the area of AI and ML.[79] However, the patent prosecution delays and the twenty-year lifetime of patents were put into question in view of the rapid evolution of AI technology. Similarly, the eighteen-month secrecy period until the publication of a patent application could perhaps be shortened, as it may lead to unnecessary parallel research and development. The debates raised questions as to the need for a *sui generis* right for AI-related inventions and, more generally, for CIIs. Intermediate IP rights, between mere copyrights and patents, would certainly be useful for applicants active in the field of information technology.

§06.08 RECOMMENDATIONS FOR PATENT APPLICANTS

Given that the EPO relies on the inventiveness of the sole technical features, the same recommendations hold as with other types of CIIs. So, how can applicants improve their chances of success?

---

79. *See* http://documents.epo.org/projects/babylon/acad.nsf/0/D9F20464038C0753C125829E-0031B814/$FILE/summary_conference_artificial_intelligence_en.pdf.

Obviously, they should make sure that all the relevant technical features are clearly and convincingly explained in the patent application, with emphasis put on their contributions to the technical character. In particular, the computational models, and their operation, should be explained in detail, inasmuch as these may indirectly contribute to the technical character of the invention. In all cases, applicants should endeavour to describe and claim the invention in terms of technical features actually involved, rather than merely describe what the invention achieves in terms of result. Needless to say, this requires a good understanding of the invention, hence the need for skilled patent drafters.

A claim must include all the essential features, i.e., the minimal set of features that interact to make something work, in principle. At least some of these features should be technical, i.e., contribute to the technical character, if only indirectly. The problem itself should at least be derivable from the description. In addition, the technical character of both the claimed features and the problem solved should be addressed in the description. The patent drafter may seek to rephrase non-technical problems solved as technical problems, if possible. The same holds for the advantages of the invention.

Applicants should also consider describing differences with or improvements to standard computer operations, including an explanation of the technical benefits, such as why less memory is needed, why less power is used, or why an ML model is more efficient than a standard algorithm in the context of the invention.

In addition, the application should make sure that features, which might appear non-technical at first sight, sufficiently impact on and are possibly interlinked with the other technical features claimed (whether structural or functional) and thus directly or indirectly contribute to the technical character of the claim. More generally, all the claimed features should be sufficiently linked to each other. This may, for instance, lead to operable connections between the claimed features, which tend to enhance the ability to confer technical character.

As an example, instead of claiming a mere step of iteratively training an ANN, a computer-implemented invention may recite steps of sequentially loading training examples in a main memory of a computer system and executing a training algorithm by processing means of the system to iteratively learn ANN parameters (i.e., the synaptic weights) based on the sequentially loaded training examples. The assumed context is that the training examples have too large a memory footprint to be all loaded in the main memory for training purposes. As naïve as it is, the above example interlinks the processing means, the main memory, the loaded training examples, the training algorithm, and the resulting ANN parameters.

A key point is whether the underlying model or algorithm is applied to a field of technology (technical application) and/or adapted to a specific technical implementation, as discussed *supra*. Thus, applicants are encouraged to describe all interactions, or links, between the underlying model or algorithm and the technical application, and/or any adaptation to a specific technical implementation.

More generally, applicants should describe the technical purpose, or technical use being made, of the model/algorithm, in particular its inputs and outputs. Not all purposes or uses will be regarded as being intrinsically technical. For example, certain purposes or uses may be considered by the EPO to be essentially related to business or administrative aspects.

Applicants should keep in mind that non-technical subject matter will likely be identified as such by the examiner and, thus, create some 'prejudice' against the invention. Applicants may thus consider remaining silent on some of the non-technical aspects, especially those relating to business or administrative methods. However, mathematical aspects of the ANN models may have technical implications and should therefore be sufficiently described, as noted earlier. Ideally, the description should describe the computational models as such (e.g., network architecture, activation functions, learning algorithm, objective function), how they interact with other features claimed (e.g., technical data used as inputs/outputs), and more generally, how they impact on the technical character and the technical advantages of the invention.

Where a standard ML algorithm is used, the training data should be adequately described (e.g., at least in terms of data structure and properties), together with the technical goal to be achieved by the training (i.e., the objective function optimized), to meet the requirements of sufficiency of disclosure, as discussed earlier in detail.

For AI inventions relating to supervised learning, applicants should consider having claims directed to each of the training and inference phases. The inference phase is typically what applicants want to primarily protect, as an infringement of this phase is more likely to be detected. In practice, however, the training phase will often involve more inventive considerations than the inferencing phase. Also, method claims should ideally be complemented by claims directed to a computerized system and computer program products.

For completeness, all the necessary technical bases should be provided in the priority application. In that respect, all of the above recommendations already apply to priority applications. In this way, a European counterpart of the priority application can adequately claim the priority of the initial application. Although claims can be amended during the European prosecution, any amendment must be 'directly and unambiguously' derivable from the application as filed under the EPC, which often means verbatim or almost verbatim. This is particularly important as the EPO is very strict when it comes to assessing added subject matter.

Finally, some practitioners noticed that CII-related patent claims that are EPO-proof will generally perform well in other jurisdictions. The reverse is less true, due to the two-hurdle approach set by the EPO, whereby only those features that contribute to the technical character participate in the inventive step assessment.

§06.09 CONCLUSION

Beyond the areas of AI, ML, and cognitive computing, many leading-edge technologies imply ever more abstract human inputs, calling for a convincing representation of the technical character of such solutions. This has serious consequences on how applicants must draft their patent applications and, indeed, on the subject matter for which applicants will be able to secure patent rights in Europe. Stakes are even higher with the advent of Unitary Patents in Europe. Such questions are not only relevant to European IP professionals, but also to all IP professionals preparing priority applications worldwide. They are also relevant to inventors, hence the need for guidance as to which information to effectively put into an invention disclosure to maximize the chance for an invention to be considered technical and therefore patentable by the EPO.

Chapter 7

France

Christophe Besnard, Pauline Debré, Dr Enrico Priori & Dr Sébastien Ragot

§07.01 PATENTABILITY OF SOFTWARE AND COMPUTER-IMPLEMENTED INVENTIONS

France is a contracting state of the EPC. The validity of European patents validated in France is independently assessed by national courts under French law, which refers[1] to Article 138 of the European Patent Convention ('EPC').[2] Accordingly, the law applicable to the validity of such patents is the EPC.

French courts, however, are not bound by the case law of the Boards of Appeal ('BoAs') of the EPO. While they are generally influenced by and, to a certain extent, inclined to follow such case law, they do not systematically adopt the same approach as the BoAs, in particular for what concerns the patentability of computer-implemented inventions ('CIIs').

National patents and patent applications in France are subject to French intellectual property ('IP') law. The patentability requirements are essentially identical to the corresponding EPC provisions. The validity of national patents and European patents are thus subject to similar conditions.

The patentability conditions of software and CIIs derive from Article L. 611-10 of the French IP Code ('CPI')[3] for French national patents and patent applications, and from Article 52 EPC[4] for European patents validated in France.

Paragraph 2 of Article L. 611-10 CPI, which is similar to Article 52(2) EPC, states:

1. Code de la propriété intellectuelle ('CPI'), Art. L. 614-12.
2. European Patent Convention ('EPC'), Art. 138.
3. Art. L. 611-10 CPI.
4. Art. 52 EPC.

> (2) The following in particular shall not be regarded as inventions within the meaning of paragraph 1:
> (a) discoveries, scientific theories and mathematical methods;
> (b) aesthetic creations;
> (c) schemes, rules and methods for performing mental acts, playing games or doing business, and programs for computers;
> (d) presentations of information.

However, paragraph 3 of Article L. 611-10 CPI, which is similar to EPC Article 52(3), states:

> (3) Paragraph 2 shall exclude the patentability of the subject-matter or activities referred to therein only to the extent to which the patent application or patent relates to such subject-matter or activities as such.

Thus, French patent law, like the EPC, excludes from the field of patentability certain subject matter or activities, including mathematical methods and computer programs, when taken 'as such'. What these exclusions have in common, when considered 'as such', is that they refer to abstract or intellectual matters. The interpretation *a contrario* of the foregoing provisions and the general understanding that an invention is a technical solution to a technical problem have led the French courts to consider that CIIs are eligible for patent protection, i.e., are *not* excluded from the field of patentability, only if the claimed subject matter, taken as a whole, has a 'technical character'.

In addition to the technical character requirement, French patent law and the EPC set out additional patentability conditions in terms of novelty, inventive step and industrial application, as in other jurisdictions. Patentability conditions under French patent law are further discussed in the guidelines (hereafter the 'INPI Guidelines'[5]) of the National Institute of Industrial Property ('INPI'), i.e., the intellectual property office in France.

Until 2020, the INPI implemented only a soft examination. Unlike the EPO, the French patent office could not refuse a patent application for lack of inventive step. This has facilitated the granting of patents in France, including those directed to CIIs and artificial intelligence ('AI'). That said, the INPI's former approach to determining whether an invention has sufficient technical character for it to be patentable was stricter than EPO's 'first hurdle', which in essence requires merely that a claim include at least one technical feature.[6] Basically, the INPI used to assess whether the gist of the invention is a technical invention or not, similar to the earlier 'contribution approach' of the EPO. Conveniently enough, this assessment was independent of the prior art and allowed the INPI to 'filter' CII inventions, notwithstanding the lack of inventive step assessment.

---

5. *Grant of patents and utility certificates: Guidelines for patent and utility certificate applications*, available at: https://www.inpi.fr/sites/default/files/guidelines_for_patent_examination.pdf.
6. *See Guidelines for Examination in the European Patent Office* ('EPO Guidelines'), Mar. 2023 edition, Sec. G-II 2 ('The first hurdle, also referred to as the patent eligibility hurdle, requires that the claimed subject-matter as a whole must not fall under the "non-inventions" defined in Art. 52(2) and (3)').

So, the French practice has had to cope with the duality between the lack of examination of inventive step by the INPI and the adjudication processes of the French courts. Depending on requests and allegations of the parties and the case at hand, the courts have to potentially assess all patentability requirements, including those related to technical character and inventive step.

An important legal reform, the so-called PACTE Law,[7] gave rise to the entry into force of various measures, which apply to patent applications filed on or after 23 May 2020. It notably introduced an opposition procedure (similar to the EPO's) and an examination for inventive step by the INPI. As a result, the INPI can now refuse patent applications on the ground of lack of inventive step. Thus, the INPI may now, in principle, also reject non-technical inventions on this ground.

The INPI Guidelines have been updated and are now closely aligned with the EPO Guidelines. In particular, the updated INPI Guidelines provide for an assessment of inventive step based on the 'problem-solution' approach of the EPO, which is also routinely applied by the French courts.

While not bound by the case law of the BoAs of the EPO, the French courts are influenced by it. In the field of CIIs, the EPO case law gradually evolved from the 'technical contribution approach'[8] adopted in the mid-1980s with the landmark decision T 208/84 (Vicom), to the 'further technical effect approach' with the landmark decision T 1173/97 (IBM), to the 'any hardware approach'[9] adopted in the mid-2000s with the landmark decision T 258/03 (Hitachi). The 'any hardware approach' is still in force today at the EPO.

The 'any hardware approach' results in a low patent-eligibility hurdle, which is easily overcome by the presence of at least one technical feature in the claimed subject matter. No comparison of the invention with the prior art is performed at this stage and the required technical feature may even be trivial. For instance, in the case of CIIs, referring to a computer, a processor, or any hardware, in the claim is enough.

French courts have often applied the 'technical contribution approach'[10] and the 'further technical effect approach'[11] to assess the technical character of CIIs. The 'any hardware approach' was rarely applied until 2019.

An early, albeit isolated, example of application of the 'any hardware approach' is provided in the decision *Infomil v. Atos*.[12] The first instance court held that the fact that the claimed CII (namely a device, a process and a computer system) was meant to implement a business method did not preclude the patentability of the CII, even though the patent was eventually invalidated due to a lack of inventive step.

7. Le plan d'action pour la croissance et la transformation des entreprises ('PACTE'), Law No. 2019-486 of 22 May 2019.
8. *See* decisions T 208/84 (Vicom), T 26/86, T 38/86 and T 121/85.
9. The 'any hardware approach' was gradually developed through landmark decisions T 931/95, T 641/00, T 258/03, and T 0424/03.
10. TGI Paris, 7 June 2013, *Starsight v. Numéricable*, No. 10/08326; TGI Paris, 11 Jul. 2019, *Koninklijke Philips NV v. SAS HTC France Corporation & HTC Corporation*, No. 16/02073.
11. TGI Paris, 18 June 2015, *Orange v. Free SAS and SAS Freebox*, No. 14/05735; TGI Paris, 18 Nov. 2016, *Xaga v. Ewala*, No. 13/11351.
12. TGI Paris, 20 Nov. 2007, *Infomil v. Atos*, No. 01/11641.

More recently, two (2019) decisions from the Paris Court of Appeal, the *Thales*[13] and *Bull*[14] decisions, have shown signs of adhesion to the 'any hardware approach'. The INPI appealed both decisions to the French Supreme Court. The Supreme Court hinted at the acceptance of the 'any hardware approach' in the second case[15], while its decision in the first case[16] did not reveal any incompatibility with this approach. The fact that the Supreme Court did not invalidate the legal approach chosen by the Court of Appeal in the second case can be perceived as implicitly endorsing the 'any hardware approach'.

Further guidance is expected from the French courts. This could be sooner rather than later, as the *Thales* case is now going back to the Court of Appeal.

However, whether the INPI will align its practice with the EPO's 'any hardware approach' is uncertain, as this approach is at odds with the INPI Guidelines. For instance, according to the INPI Guidelines, 'the mere fact of automating the mathematical method by generic computer-based means shall not result in conferring a technical character to such a method'.[17] The INPI Guidelines further provide several examples of inventions involving abstract methods implemented by 'generic computer-based means', which are considered not patentable.

§07.02 SPECIAL PROVISIONS RELATING TO PATENTABILITY OF INVENTIONS RELATING TO AI

Specific provisions related to AI and machine learning are provided in the section of the INPI Guidelines dedicated to mathematical methods.[18] According to the INPI Guidelines, 'artificial intelligence, to the extent that it is based on computational models, is considered by definition to be a computer-implemented mathematical method which, when claimed as such, does not constitute an invention'.[19]

However, the INPI Guidelines provide that a 'mathematical method shall not be regarded as such if it serves a technical purpose, i.e., if it presents a technical solution to a technical problem. To this end, the subject matter claimed must be limited to that technical purpose and a sufficiently strong link must be established between that technical purpose and the steps of the mathematical method.'[20]

The INPI Guidelines further provide several examples of inventions involving mathematical methods that are considered patentable and, conversely, not patentable. For example, a 'process ... for generating mathematical function values by using iterative interpolation processes' is considered not patentable. By contrast, a 'method for analysing audio signals or digital images/videos, such as a method for cancelling out noise or for detecting people in a digital image', is regarded as patentable.

13. Cour d'appel de Paris, 21 May 2019, *Thales v. Directeur Général de l'INPI*, No. 18/19669.
14. Cour d'appel de Paris, 22 Nov. 2019, *SAS Bull v. Directeur Général de l'INPI*, No. 18/21161.
15. Cass. com., 11 Jan. 2023, No. 10041 F, Pourvoi No. Z 20-10.935.
16. Cass. com., 11 Jan. 2023, No. 29 F-D, Pourvoi No. M 19-19.567.
17. INPI Guidelines, Section C, Chapter VII, 1.3.
18. *Ibid.*
19. *Ibid.*, Sec. 1.3.2.
20. *Ibid.*, Sec. 1.3.

Moreover, the INPI Guidelines indicate that 'if the claim relates to a specific technical implementation of the mathematical method, designed on the basis of technical considerations relating to the internal functioning of a computer, it shall be regarded as technical (for example: a method for optimizing memory by means of an algorithm)'.

It is understood that the INPI Guidelines notably delineate two patentability criteria, which relate to: (i) the technical application; and (ii) the technical implementation of the mathematical method, just like the EPO Guidelines.

A claim directed to new algorithms or models for the AI itself, regardless of the data to which it is applied and any particular use case, may thus be regarded by the INPI as a mathematical method 'as such', deprived of technical character. Such a claim may accordingly not qualify for patent protection.

Regarding AI specifically, the INPI Guidelines further state that the use of expressions such as: 'support vector machine (SVM)', 'genetic algorithm', 'artificial neural network (ANN)' or 'automatic/deep learning' is not sufficient in and of itself to confer a technical character to the claimed subject matter.[21]

The INPI Guidelines nevertheless make a distinction between the abstract mathematical nature of the AI computational models or algorithms and applications of AI to a field of technology. Just like an invention involving a mathematical model, an AI-related invention may qualify for patent protection if it serves a technical purpose, i.e., if it provides a technical solution to a technical problem.

To this end, the claimed subject matter must be limited to that technical purpose and there must be a sufficiently strong link between that technical purpose and the AI technology. The contribution to the technical character 'may be made, in particular, by introducing a technical solution to a technical problem by non-generic technical means or by processing measured technical data'.[22]

The INPI Guidelines provide examples of AI applications that are considered to be of a technical nature in different fields:

> Computer vision:
>
> Computer vision, for the recognition, processing and/or classification of images and/or videos. The following, for example, are considered to be of a technical nature:
>
> - the recognition of the environment of an autonomous vehicle based on data obtained via sensors;
> - the use of artificial intelligence to analyse digital images in order to recognise an incident such as a tumour in a series of images or to detect movement within a video sequence.
>
> Language processing:
>
> Speech recognition and/or human-machine dialogue. For example, the use of artificial intelligence is considered technical when it is used to enable a dedicated robot to analyse human speech, with speech data being acquired via audio sensors and converted into language data via speech recognition software

21. *Ibid.*, Sec. 1.3.2.
22. *Ibid.*

in order to determine and vary the robot's behaviour in terms of gestural and vocal output.

Process control and monitoring:

Robotics and/or monitoring/control processes. The following, for example, are considered to be of a technical nature:

- the real-time control of a drilling tool, based on physical properties measured in the drilling environment by training an ANN;
- the classification of Internet Protocol (IP) traffic between nodes using machine learning to improve traffic management on the IP network.

Predictive analysis:

the use of an ANN in a heart monitoring device to detect an irregular heartbeat was considered to be a technical contribution.

However, the INPI Guidelines also provide examples of non-technical inventions. For instance, a 'process using artificial intelligence to predict stock market prices' and a 'tool to extract business-related keywords from content in order to enable their identification and indexing by means of artificial intelligence' were found to be non-technical.[23]

§07.03 SUBJECT MATTER PATENTABILITY

Consideration will now be given to how the French patent law, as explained above, would likely be applied to the five categories of AI-related inventions described in the introduction to this book.

[A] Category 1

AI-related inventions in Category 1 are directed to the 'core AI', i.e., new algorithms or models for the AI itself, independent of the data to which it is applied and independent of any particular use case.

In view of the discussions *supra*, a claim directed in the abstract to a new algorithm or model having no particular technical purpose will be considered devoid of technical character by the INPI. The conclusion will remain unchanged even if such a claim recites that the underlying model/algorithm is run by conventional computing means, as discussed in Section §07.01, *supra*.

Whether French courts would acknowledge the technical character of such a claim is of little importance, given that they would likely deny any technical contribution to the prior art as part of the subsequent inventive step assessment, as further discussed *infra*.

23. *Ibid.*

[B] Category 2

AI-related inventions in Category 2 relate to an AI implementation, i.e., claim a system or process of broad application using known AI technology plus additional elements, such as a particular arrangement of filters or a particular interface.

Although the law would be applied on a case-by-case basis depending on what is actually claimed, an AI-implementation would likely be considered by the INPI to have technical character, provided that it involves technical features that are specific enough, as opposed to generic computing means. Moreover, the underlying computational model or algorithm may be acknowledged to contribute to the technical character if there is a sufficient link between the model or algorithm and the specific technical features (see Section §07.02, *supra*).

[C] Category 3

AI-related inventions in Category 3 are applications of AI to a particular use case, such as causing a car to stop at a stop sign, performing facial recognition, or identifying candidates for new pharmaceutical products. An AI-related invention in this category may be a 'decision-maker' application that causes a result to occur, or a 'decision aid' application that provides advice or a plurality of choices to a human user.

So, AI-related inventions in Category 3 may be acknowledged as having technical character if the application (or use case) itself is technical, provided that the use case is reflected in the claim, so as to limit the claim accordingly. Moreover, the underlying computational model or algorithm may be acknowledged to contribute to the technical character if it sufficiently links to this application (see Sections §07.01 and §07.02, *supra*).

[D] Categories 4 and 5

Unlike Categories 1–3, in Category 4 (invention made by a human using AI as a tool) and Category 5 (invention made by AI without human involvement), what is claimed is the output or result of use of AI, not the AI itself. Thus, what is claimed could be anything in any field. Accordingly, setting aside the inventorship issue with Category 5 cases (see *infra*), subject matter eligibility would be determined based on what is claimed and that analysis would be completely divorced from the AI with which the invention was made.

§07.04 INVENTIVE STEP

To date, French courts have not yet ruled on the patentability of an invention involving artificial intelligence. It is therefore difficult to predict what approach they will adopt and, in particular, how they will assess the technical contributions of AI-related inventions.

For instance, despite recent signs from the French Supreme Court, it is still too early to tell whether the French courts will definitely adopt the 'any hardware approach', on which the 'two-hurdle approach' of the EPO[24] hinges. As discussed *supra*, the first hurdle of this approach relates to patent eligibility and requires technical character. This first hurdle generally can be overcome by reciting a single technical feature in the claim. The second, and more difficult, hurdle is the inventive step assessment.

At the EPO, for the second hurdle, the inventive step of a CII or AI claim comprising a mix of technical and non-technical features is assessed using the 'COMVIK approach' which was first applied in decision T 641/00 in 2002[25]. According to this approach, a feature may support the presence of an inventive step if and only to the extent that it contributes to the technical character of the invention. The 'COMVIK approach' is regarded as a specific application of the problem-solution approach.

The following addresses how the INPI and French courts might apply the French patent law to the five categories of AI-related inventions, despite the lack of decisions by French courts regarding AI-related inventions and the lack of hindsight since the entry into force of the PACTE Law.

[A] Category 1

According to the INPI Guidelines, the INPI will likely deny technical character for core AI inventions (Category 1) that boil down to reciting a new machine learning algorithm or computational model, for example a model based on a new neural network architecture, such as a transformer network architecture, even if it involves 'generic computer-based means'. Thus, in principle, such an invention would not even be examined for inventive step.

Whether French courts will consider that such an invention clears the first hurdle of the two-step approach of the EPO (because the underlying method is implemented by a computer, which is technical *per se*) is unimportant, inasmuch as they will likely not acknowledge any non-obvious contribution to the prior art in that case, for reasons discussed in Sections §07.01 and §07.02, *supra*. That is to say, the sole inventive contribution (in a colloquial sense) in that case will typically be non-technical, such that the courts will likely conclude a lack of inventive step, as with any other type of CII.

[B] Category 2

A key criterion for new AI implementations (Category 2) to be considered inventive is the non-obviousness of those claimed features that are considered to contribute to the technical character.

Because new AI implementations typically involve non-conventional technical elements, compared with inventions in Category 1 (see Section §07.03, *supra*), inventions in Category 2 may potentially involve more technical features that will favourably participate in the inventive step assessment. In addition, the interactions between the underlying computational model or algorithm and such elements also

24. *See* Section §06.04 of the EPO chapter.
25. EPO decision T 641/00 ('COMVIK') of 26.09.2002.

may be regarded as contributing to the technical character, which will also favour inventive step (*see* EPO chapter, Section §06.04).

In particular, new AI implementations may exploit a specific technical implementation (going beyond 'generic computer-based means', e.g., GPU or vector processing means). Thus, the adaptation of the underlying method to that specific implementation may be acknowledged as an inventive step if it is non-obvious in view of the prior art.

[C] Category 3

In principle, a claim directed to a new application of known AI technology (Category 3) may possibly be novel because: (i) a known AI technology (e.g., a known computational model) is used for the first time in an application that is not novel *per se* (the combination, however, is novel); and/or (ii) the application itself is novel. As in the EPO, the latter case disposes the claim favourably toward inventive step, assuming that the application has technical character and is recited so as to have a limiting effect on the claim.

The former case, however, is less likely to succeed. Indeed, applying known AI technology to a known application may be perceived by the INPI or French courts as being a common design option for the skilled person, as it is in the EPO, even more so where the sole residual novel feature is the use of a machine learning model in place of another mathematical function. In other words, applying known AI technology to a known use case may be perceived to be in line with the general trend in technology and thus not considered inventive, much like automation.

[D] Categories 4 and 5

Where the result of application of AI by a human inventor (Category 4) is, in and of itself, a patentable invention having technical character, the inventive step of the resulting invention will likely be assessed regardless of the AI tool used to arrive at the invention, normally by using the problem-solution approach.

The same conclusion holds for inventions claimed to be made by an AI entity (Category 5). This, however, assumes that the corresponding patent application reaches the stage of inventive step examination, which is unlikely (see Section §07.06, *infra*), unless the patent application names human inventors only.

Of course, all such scenarios will have to be assessed on a case-by-case basis. And, again, further guidance is needed from the French courts.

§07.05 ADEQUACY OF DISCLOSURE

Beyond the requirements of technical character and inventive step, AI-related inventions may pose additional problems in terms of sufficiency of disclosure. Such issues are not explicitly addressed in the INPI Guidelines, at least not specifically with respect to AI-related inventions.

Article L. 612-5 CPI, which is similar to Article 83 EPC, provides that:

> The patent application shall disclose the invention in a manner sufficiently clear and complete for it to be carried out by a person skilled in the art.

The principles to be considered to determine whether an invention is sufficiently described in a patent application are outlined in the French case law. In particular:[26]

> the description is insufficient if it does not enable the person skilled in the art in the industry considered to carry out the invention with the help of his knowledge and by simple operations of execution;
>
> the person skilled in the art must find in the description the means to achieve without undue difficulty the intended result over the entire field covered by the invention.

The foregoing principles apply to any type of invention. The French patent law has no additional requirement for CII or AI-related inventions. It only provides, as an option, that:[27]

> The following may be included as an appendix at the end of the description:
>
> Short extracts of computer programs presented in the form of listings written in common programming languages, when they are necessary for the understanding of the invention.

That is, short extracts of computer programs (presented in the form of lists written in current programming languages) may be appended to the description, where necessary for the understanding of the invention. Pseudocode should, *a fortiori*, be accepted too. While short extracts of computer programs may perhaps be useful for core AI inventions and new AI implementations, they may well be superfluous where the 'core' AI technology is already known *per se*, as with inventions in Category 3. Instead, flow diagrams may be more appropriate in that case, following well-established practice. For inventions in Categories 4 and 5, sufficiency of disclosure would be based on what is claimed, regardless of the means by which the invention was made.

The following addresses, in more detail, how the requirements in terms of adequacy of disclosure might be applied with respect to each of the five categories of AI-related inventions.

[A] Categories 1 and 2

The requirements of sufficiency of disclosure should remain the same as for any other CII invention. Of particular importance would be the description of the underlying computational model or algorithm and how it interacts with the hardware. Interactions with the hardware may be particularly important for inventions in Category 2, inasmuch as these may determine whether the underlying computational model or algorithm contribute to the technical character or not.

26. TGI Paris, 15 Jun. 1999, *Tran Ngoc A. v. Rochepierre*, PIBD 2000, No. 692, III, p. 80 ; *see also* Cour d'appel de Paris, 25 Nov. 2014, *Tissue France v. Sipinco*, No. 13/13513.
27. Art. R. 612-13 CPI, paragraph 1; *see also* INPI Guidelines, Section C, Chapter II, 1.

[B] Category 3

Again, the lack of decisions by French courts regarding AI-related inventions makes it difficult to describe minimal requirements in terms of adequacy of disclosure. In the absence of better guidance, the reader may rely on explanations provided in the EPO chapter, which are assumed to remain generally valid for France.

For instance, one may expect French courts to require minimal indications as to the type and architecture (or topology) of the computational model involved, the training algorithm, the objective function used, and the training dataset, as discussed in detail in the EPO chapter.

In a supervised setting, the data used to train the underlying model may play an important role, given that inventions under Category 3 may be partly defined by the data that is used to train a machine learning system. Thus, care should be taken, in that case, to describe the training dataset in a relatively precise manner. At a minimum, the description should indicate the general data structure, as well as properties of the dataset. The description may also indicate how input data are obtained, in operation, for inferencing purposes.

[C] Categories 4 and 5

For inventions in Categories 4 and 5, the adequacy of disclosure depends entirely on what is claimed and is unrelated to the AI that was used to achieve the claimed invention.

§07.06 INVENTORSHIP

[A] Inventorship in General

While the French patent law refers to the 'inventor' on a number of occasions[28], it provides no detail about the criteria by which the concept of inventor is defined. Slightly more informative are the INPI Guidelines, which mention 'the inventor's contribution'[29] in the inventive step assessment.

According to legal doctrine,[30] inventorship can be assessed with regard to the features or means of the invention, the inventor being the person who invents these means. It follows that the mere fact of posing a problem or setting an objective to be achieved will not necessarily be considered an act of invention. While the extent of inventors' contributions may vary somewhat, case law generally conforms to legal doctrine.

Such a definition is consistent with the European practice, according to which inventors are usually perceived as human beings who have sufficiently contributed to the invention, with inventive inputs, such that their respective contributions

28. *See*, e.g., Art. L. 611-6, L 611-7 and L. 611-9 CPI.
29. INPI Guidelines, Section C, Chapter VII, 5.4.(a).
30. Paul Mathély, *Le nouveau droit français des brevets d'invention* (1992).

reflect in at least one claim of the corresponding patent application. This definition is further compatible with a number of potential contributions to AI-related inventions.

[B] Determination of Inventorship for AI-Related Inventions

[1] Categories 1–4

The French law is formulated in a technologically neutral manner. Therefore, as far as intellectual property protection is concerned, AI-related inventions do not fundamentally differ from other types of inventions. Consistent with this, there is no specific inventorship requirement applying to AI-related inventions.

All cases under Categories 1–4 of AI-related inventions involve human inventorship. As in other fields of technology, various types of human interventions or acts may potentially be acknowledged as inventorship, provided that such contributions include inventive inputs that are reflected in at least one of the patent claims. Decisive for legal inventorship, and hence patent protection overall, are the occurrence and extent of such contributions. Whether or not these contributions are sufficient to be acknowledged as inventorship has to be assessed on a case-by-case basis. From a legal standard perspective, no new issues are raised with respect to Category 1–4 AI-related inventions.

Inventions under Category 3, while raising no new legal standard issues, may raise new practical issues as to which persons should be properly named as inventor(s). Inventions under Category 3 may be partly defined by the training dataset, i.e., data that is used to train a machine learning system in a supervised setting. Therefore, a person involved in obtaining, selecting, and/or curating such training data, for example, may make an inventive contribution depending on the facts of the particular case (see EPO chapter, Section §06.06). Accordingly, we expect to see further guidance on how the law of inventorship applies to these new fact patterns in the future.

[2] Category 5

An invention under Category 5 – the hypothetical situation where an invention has been made by an AI system without human involvement or control – does raise a new issue of law. Neither the INPI nor the French courts have so far had the opportunity of deciding whether an AI entity can be designated as inventor or co-inventor in France.

However, Article R. 612-10 CPI refers to the name and surname of the inventor, suggesting that an inventor must be a natural person. Moreover, the INPI Guidelines provide that the 'identity of the inventor(s), natural person(s), must be indicated in the request at the time of filing',[31] leaving little doubt that the inventor must be a human being.

31. INPI Guidelines, Section B, Chapter II, 3 ('Request for grant'), Section 7 ('Inventors').

Therefore, inventorship would likely be denied to an AI entity in France, just like in the EPO.[32]

§07.07 AREAS FOR FURTHER DEVELOPMENT

As noted *supra*, the PACTE Law brought substantial changes to the IP landscape in France and gave rise to the entry into force of various measures applying to French patent applications filed on or after 23 May 2020. One of the objectives of the 'IP' section of the PACTE Law was to strengthen the trust and value given to French patents, hence the need to align with the practices of the major national and regional patent offices. However, achieving these objectives also requires reducing legal uncertainties for applicants, including in the field of CIIs.

In the long run, the recent developments in the French IP law should result in multiple convergences between the approaches of the INPI, the French courts, and the EPO, thereby providing improved legal certainty for patent owners.

Meanwhile, the more thorough examination of national patent applications that is now implemented by the INPI will likely result in a reduction of grant rates and/or longer times to grant; so far, the vast majority of applications received by the INPI were granted. Conversely, the granted patents should now be less prone to revocations by the French courts, especially where such patents have further passed the test of opposition in France.

§07.08 RECOMMENDATIONS FOR PATENT APPLICANTS

Instead of or in addition to a patent, applicants still have the possibility to request a utility certificate in France, which roughly corresponds to the utility model available in, for example, Germany or China. Interestingly, utility certificates extend to method claims in France. The PACTE Law has extended the duration of utility certificates to a maximum of ten years[33] from the filing date, versus six years before. Moreover, since 31 May 2020, a utility certificate can be transformed into a patent application;[34] the converse of which was already possible before the PACTE Law and remains possible.[35]

The main differences with patent applications are that no opposition procedure is provided for and that no search report is established for utility certificates, which are therefore subject to a limited examination. This certainly makes utility certificates attractive for AI-related inventions and, more generally, for CIIs and other inventions having short commercial lifespans. Thus, applicants may consider requesting a utility certificate to avoid a thorough examination by the INPI, something that may have benefits for CIIs and, in particular, AI-related inventions. Accordingly, utility certificates are tools that applicants should consider as part of their patent strategy.

32. 'DABUS' decision of the European Patent Office of 27 Jan. 2020, regarding patent applications EP 18 275 163 and EP 18 275 174.
33. Art. L 611-2 CPI.
34. Art. L 612-15, Art. R 612-53, and Art. R612-53 CPI.
35. Art. L 612-15 and Art. R 612-55 CPI.

§07.09 CONCLUSION

The recent revision of the French IP law further aligns the patent grant procedure with that of the EPO. Thus, the recommendations provided in the EPO chapter remain generally valid for France, all the more so if the French courts confirm the new direction taken in respect of CIIs.

Chapter 8
Germany

Jochen Ehlers & Jochen Unland

§08.01 PATENTABILITY OF SOFTWARE AND COMPUTER-IMPLEMENTED INVENTIONS

The limits and considerations as to the patentability of software and computer-implemented inventions according to German patent law are virtually identical to those applicable before the European Patent Office ('EPO'). Indeed, the wording of the respective provisions in German patent law and those in the European Patent Convention ('EPC') are largely identical.

Based on case law,[1] referring to the provisions of Sections 1, 3 and 4 of the Patent Act ('PatG'),[2] the approach to the patentability of computer-implemented inventions ('CII') now employed in Germany in general includes three steps:

In the first step, only those inventions are excluded that do not contain at least one technical feature, i.e., a feature that contributes to solving a technical objective. In the case of artificial intelligence ('AI') this step is always passed, as AI typically requires the use of a computer. A computer is a technical means.

In a second step, it is checked whether there is a particular technical problem that is solved by technical means. The subjective problem indicated in the application itself is not decisive but may be used for determining the objective technical problem. In the Guidelines for Examination of the German Patent Office ('Examination Guidelines'),[3] a solution by technical means could mean modifications to device components or a different or novel particular addressing thereof. Examples may

1. *See* Bundesgerichtshof ('BGH') Oct. 26 2010, X ZR 47/07 *Wiedergabe topografischer Informationen* and BGH Feb. 24 2011, X ZR 121/09 *Webseitenanzeige.*
2. Patent Act (PatG), last amended Aug. 30 2021, translation at: https://www.gesetze-im-internet.de/englisch_patg/englisch_patg.html.
3. Richtlinien für die Prüfung von Patentanmeldungen, Mar. 2022, translation at: https://www.dpma.de/docs/english/formulare/patent_eng/p2796_1.pdf.

include the development of a computer program being determined by technical factors outside the computer or the design of the computer program such that it takes into consideration technical factors of the computer. Specifically, for AI, the majority of cases will likely involve a technical problem that is tackled. It is thus anticipated that in many cases of AI applications the second step also will be passed.

In a third step, novelty and inventive step are examined. The only claimed features or aspects that will be considered are those that determine, or at least influence, the technical solution. Those features or aspects that do not participate in solving the technical objective will be disregarded.

Compared with the approach of the EPO, there is a significant overlap between the third step outlined above and the applicable case law of the EPO to disregard those features from the examination of inventive step that do not contribute to solving a technical objective (so-called 'non-technical features'). The first step listed above seems to comply with the examination under Article 53 EPC,[4] whereas the second step seems to be part of the examination of Article 56 EPC.[5]

There is a slight difference in the approaches of the EPO and the German Patent and Trademark Office ('GPTO'), however. In the approach of the EPO, the examiner first identifies those features that are *prima facie* of technical nature. Based on only such features, the closest prior art is determined, which is then used for identifying the delimiting features, leading to the identification of the objective technical problem. In consideration of the objective technical problem, then the identification of apparent non-technical features needs to be re-considered.

In contrast, according to the German approach, the problem solved by the present invention is considered without reference to the prior art. In particular, rather than labelling, *a priori*, certain features defined in a claim as being of non-technical nature and then focusing on the remaining technical features, in Germany the focus is put initially on the technical problem solved by the invention, with the determination of such technical problem being made more or less irrespective of the prior art. Once the technical problem is identified, the assessment as to novelty and the presence of the inventive step is made, where – similar in effect to the situation before the EPO – only those features are taken into consideration which contribute to or have influence on the claimed solution. Rather than differentiating between technical and non-technical features, in Germany only the contribution to or the influence on the provided solution is considered. This may possibly result in disregarding a feature which could be considered as being of technical nature in the approach of the EPO. On the other hand, in the case of a feature which may appear, by itself, as not being of technical nature, there is no negative bias to be overcome for possibly acknowledging such feature as 'technical' (i.e. contributing to the technical solution), in contrast to the practice before the EPO, where an apparently non-technical feature is disregarded until it can be shown that it indeed (despite its apparent non-technical nature) contributes to the technical solution. To put it differently, one may say that, according to the German approach, all features are considered as possibly contributing to the technical solution, whereas, according to the EPO, certain features are rather considered as likely not contributing.

---

4. European Patent Convention ('EPC'), Art. 53.
5. EPC, Art. 56.

In the vast majority of cases, as with the EPO, the exclusion from patentability of mathematical methods or programs for computers may be avoided by the embedding of the non-technical aspects into a technical environment. Drafting the claims such that technical means or steps are included, such as by defining that a method is carried out by a computer, may circumvent such exclusion from patentability.

As with the EPO, this merely shifts the issue to the assessment of the presence of an inventive step, where only technical features (i.e., features contributing to solving a technical objective of the claimed invention) are taken into consideration. This general consideration is applicable also for inventions relating to AI.

§08.02 SPECIAL PROVISIONS RELATING TO PATENTABILITY OF INVENTIONS RELATING TO AI

German patent law does not specifically address or target inventions relating to AI. To the extent that AI is involved in the subject matter of the invention, such subject matter may fall under one or more of the exclusions from patentability (e.g., mathematical methods, performing mental acts, and programs for computers) and would fall under the same scrutiny discussed above with respect to presence of an inventive step.

While currently not discussed in any of the official papers (let alone addressed in any court decision), it seems that the use of AI in the inventive process may lead to a different assessment when it comes to the skilled person's knowledge applicable to establish an inventive step. If AI would be in reach of the skilled person, one might (in the future) arrive at a point where solutions provided by available AI would also fall into expected results, i.e., would not justify an inventive step. While an AI machine itself probably will not be considered as the skilled person, the use of AI might become routine matter to the extent AI becomes available. This is discussed in more detail in Section §08.04, *infra*.

§08.03 SUBJECT MATTER PATENTABILITY

According to German patent law, 'patents shall be granted for any inventions, in all fields of technology, provided that they are new, involve an inventive step and are susceptible of industrial application'.[6] However, German patent law limits this broad approach in that certain subject matter is not to be regarded as an invention,[7] namely:

1. discoveries, scientific theories and mathematical methods;
2. aesthetic creations;
3. schemes, rules and methods for performing mental acts, playing games or doing business, and programs for computers;
4. presentations of information.

These exceptions apply 'only to the extent to which protection is being sought for the subject matter or activities referred to *as such*',[8] which means that, for example,

6. Sec. 1 (1) PatG.
7. Sec. 1 (3) PatG.
8. Sec. 1 (4) PatG.

the implementation of a mathematical method within a technical framework is not excluded from patentability.

While, with proper claim drafting, the above limitations rarely pose a problem in practice, these exclusions may serve as guidelines as to whether or not a problem solved by the invention is indeed of a technical nature.

Turning now to the categories of AI-related inventions as set out in the introduction to this book, we consider each as follows:

[A] Category 1

As before the EPO, the invention of new algorithms or models for the AI itself, independent of the data to which such AI is applied and independent of any particular use case, would be excluded from patentability as far as it may be considered a mathematical method, a mental act, and/or a computer program, devoid of any particular technical effect or purpose.

[B] Category 2

As far as the creation of a system or process of broad application using known AI technology in combination with additional elements, for example, a particular arrangement of filters or a particular interface, is concerned, in Germany (as before the EPO) this would be considered a provision of technical means. The subject matter including such technical features would fulfil the requirement of subject matter patentability (i.e., the first step of the German approach as discussed above).

[C] Category 3

The specific nature of a new application of AI may or may not be sufficient, in Germany (as before the EPO), for fulfilling the requirement of subject matter patentability. The specific outcome in this regard may rather easily be addressed by proper claim drafting, as the mere presence of one technical feature is sufficient.

[D] Category 4

As is the case before the EPO, in Germany the way in which an invention was made or conceived is not relevant for the issue of subject matter patentability. Therefore, subject matter patentability for inventions in Category 4 would depend on what is claimed. Here, what is claimed is the *result of the use of AI*, not the AI itself. Accordingly, the claimed invention could be anything from a mechanical device to a chemical compound to a manufacturing process. Subject matter patentability would depend on what is claimed, not on the manner by which the invention was made or conceived.

[E] Category 5

The above comments regarding Category 4 are also true for a scenario in which an invention is made, hypothetically, *by* AI. However, the question of subject matter patentability would not be reached because, before the GPTO, an application directed to an invention allegedly made by artificial intelligence would be objected to in view of the need for designating an inventor, whereas only a natural person may be an inventor. This is discussed in more detail in Section §08.06, *infra*.

§08.04 INVENTIVE STEP

The general approach taken in Germany on the determination of whether an inventive step is involved is independent of the particular nature of the subject matter of the invention. Thus, inventions falling under Categories 1 to 3 would be assessed for inventive step in the same manner as any other invention.

For Category 4, i.e., the invention being the result of an application of AI, the involvement of the AI, by itself, is of no further consequence. If, however, it could be shown, in a particular case, that the use of AI (either in general or of a particular AI) would fall within the routine of the skilled person and that such use, in view of the particular problem to be solved, would more or less necessarily lead to the claimed subject matter, this would indicate lack of inventive step, since the skilled person would arrive at the invention using their routine skills and tools.

For Category 5, where a claimed invention is made, hypothetically, by AI, it is not foreseen, currently, that anyone other than a natural person can be an inventor. Assuming such obstacle may be overcome, for example, by a change of law or practice, the situation would be comparable to that of Category 4.

§08.05 ADEQUACY OF DISCLOSURE

Similar to the situation before the EPO, adequacy of disclosure in Germany is to be considered in view of the skilled person's common general knowledge and the information provided in the application, i.e., the skilled reader needs to be put in a position where the implementation of the invention is possible.[9] Differing from the practice before the EPO, it is generally considered sufficient to provide enough information to put the skilled person in the position to implement one example falling under the scope of the claims,[10] whereas only in extreme cases is the lack of information as to a part of the scope of the claims considered a problem.[11]

For Category 1 and 2 AI-related inventions, complying with adequacy of disclosure is similar to complying with adequacy of disclosure for any other CII invention.

For Category 4 and 5 AI-related inventions, the duty to adequately disclose the invention is tied *to the claimed invention*, not to the method by which that invention

9. BGH Jul. 13 2010, Xa ZR 126/07 *Klammernahtgerät*.
10. BGH Jun. 16 2015, X ZR 67/13 *Übertragungspapier für Tintenstrahldrucker*.
11. BGH Jul. 19 1984, X ZB 18/83 *Acrylfasern*; BGH Feb. 25 2010, Xa TR 100/05 *Thermoplastische Zusammensetzung*.

was made. Accordingly, adequate disclosure for claims in these categories depends entirely on what is claimed, noting that the claims may not relate to AI or CIIs at all.

The same standards for adequacy of disclosure apply to Category 3 (applications of AI) inventions as well. However, certain practical issues may arise when attempting to meet this standard. Here, two aspects are of particular concern, namely, both the tool itself (i.e., the AI system used) and the details of setting up and/or using the tool must be disclosed in sufficient detail.

Typically, general references to an AI system that is well known to the skilled person should be enough for the first aspect.

The second aspect, which particularly concerns the training data used for enabling the generic AI system for the particular use case, may require more disclosure. Since, however, there is no need for a direct and unambiguous disclosure of the details of a practical implementation,[12] rather than disclosing the training data itself, it should be sufficient to provide information to the skilled person such that the skilled person would be able obtain their own training data by themselves, which then allows for achieving the objective of the invention. Thus, the outcome of a case in Germany comparable to that underlying the EPO decision T 161/18,[13] where the disclosure was found to be insufficient under Article 83 of the EPC due to lack of detail concerning the training data, would depend on the details of the situation. If there is, however, no information at all as to the nature of the training data, the disclosure would generally be considered insufficient.

The common general knowledge of the skilled person includes only publicly available information and thus does not necessarily include all information potentially available to an actual person in the field. An example of this is the case of standards specifications for CD-ROM, DVD and BluRay,[14] where information is made available to interested circles only subject to acceptance of a non-disclosure agreement. Thus, if a claimed application of AI requires use of a proprietary dataset that is not available to the public but is necessary for implementation, this would endanger the adequacy of disclosure unless there would be a publicly available replacement described in the application or present as part of the common general knowledge of the skilled person.

Assuming the basic tool (i.e., the 'core AI') is publicly available to the skilled person, the necessary level of further information (e.g., details as to training, input data) would depend on the particular details of each case, in view of the need to 'reproduce' the results of the invention. The issue of 'undue burden' would also change from case to case, in particular as some degree of experimentation is still acceptable.

§08.06 INVENTORSHIP

German law[15] provides that the inventor needs to be indicated by the applicant. However, there is no check performed by the GPTO as to the correctness of the

12. BGH Jul. 13 2010, Xa ZR 126/07 *Klammernahtgerät*.
13. T 0161/18 (*Äquivalenter Aortendruck*/ARC SEIBERSDORF) May 12 2020.
14. *See Guidelines for Examination in the European Patent Office*, G-IV, 7.6, available at https://www.epo.org/law-practice/legal-texts/html/guidelines/e/g_iv_7_6.htm.
15. *See* Sec. 37 PatG.

indication. The underlying regulations stipulate that the name, including first name and last name, of the inventor must be given, which is understood as limiting the status of the designated inventor to a natural person.[16]

Regarding AI-related inventions falling under Categories 1 to 4, there is no particular concern, since here indeed a natural person is involved. However, an invention falling under Category 5, where the invention was, hypothetically, made by an AI system without human involvement, raises new issues regarding inventorship.

In a decision relating to the alleged inventorship by the AI 'DABUS', the Federal Patent Court[17] decided that the application may be not be refused in view of a designation of inventor naming the owner of the AI as inventor, even though there was an additional statement on the provided form indicating that the designated inventor caused the AI to generate the invention.

The Federal Patent Court had to address a number of requests as to the indication of the inventor. In the Main Request, the designation of the inventor was directed just to the AI 'DABUS', whereas in the course of the first Auxiliary Request, it was requested to find that no natural person could be considered as an inventor in this case, so that there would be no need for the otherwise required designation of an inventor. The Federal Patent Court rejected these requests in view of the notion that the current law provides that only natural persons can be considered as inventor and that there can be no inventions without such human inventor.

A second Auxiliary Request, including an amendment to the description indicating that the AI generated the invention, was rejected as going beyond the content of the application as filed.

The Federal Patent Court allowed the third Auxiliary Request, since the corresponding 'designation of inventor' indicated a natural person as inventor. This finding, however, is to be understood as being based on consideration of a formalities issue, since the German law does not require a check in substance of the content of the form used for the designation of an inventor. In other words, the Federal Patent Court merely found that the filed 'designation of inventor' was formally proper, without ruling on whether the designated natural person was actually the inventor. In this context, the Federal Patent Court further found that the additional information included in the filed form (as to the inventor having caused the AI to generate the invention), while going beyond the information required by the applicable law, did not contravene the requirements for a proper 'designation of inventor'.

Furthermore, the Federal Patent Court pointed out that the question of whether the actual inventor is the AI or the AI's owner is a legal issue instead of a factual issue, so the provision[18] that parties shall make their statements on the factual circumstances fully and truthfully would not prevent the owner of the AI from indicating him or herself as the inventor.

An appeal against the decision is currently pending with the Federal Court of Justice.

16. Verordnung zum Verfahren in Patentsachen vor dem Deutschen Patent- und Markenamt (Patentverordnung -PatV) Sec. 7.
17. BPatG Nov. 11 2021, 11 W (pat) 5/21.
18. Sec. 124 PatG.

Beyond the above details, there are no fundamental differences between the practice as to inventorship in Germany and that before the EPO, so that further detail may be found in the chapter addressing the EPO.

§08.07 AREAS FOR IMPROVEMENT

The second step of the approach on the patentability of computer implemented invention, i.e., the check as to the solution, by technical means, of a particular technical problem, still brings about a certain 'grey area', where it is difficult to estimate, beforehand, whether the invention indeed solves a technical problem. This is somewhat comparable to the situation before the EPO.

In view of the short 'life cycle' and fast developments in the area of AI-related inventions, and considering the delays involved with substantive patent examination, *sui generis* rights having a shorter lifespan and perhaps a different regime as to publication and other aspects of protection may be worthy of consideration in the future. However, there seems to be no widespread desire or coordinated push to move in such direction at the moment.

§08.08 RECOMMENDATIONS FOR PATENT APPLICANTS

It is important not only to provide a disclosure of specific AI algorithms and program structure, but also to describe functionally how the AI algorithm works and what conceptual ideas are provided with certain functional modules within the software. Applicants should bear in mind that it would be best practice to protect the AI decision-making process and also the outcome thereof. Applicants should be advised early on to draft separate sections for these two different issues.

Likewise, it is important to establish particular application fields of the invention, in order to support the assertion that elements of the claim contribute to solving a technical object. Claim drafting should be done by technically skilled persons, knowledgeable in AI. Relevant sections of the disclosure and the claims should refer to, as appropriate: aspects of the algorithm, the structure of the software modules, the specific function of elements of the software, or the result that is or may be achieved by AI. The claim drafter should follow only one of these tasks at a time, in order to avoid unclear claims mixing different conceptual levels in a single claim.

For patenting purposes, it is not advisable to rely, without further disclosure, on any 'black box' effect. An invention must be based on a description that makes clear how any technically skilled reader could put the claimed invention into practice. The means that provide any alleged 'black box' effect should be clearly and unambiguously described. The same applies to machine learning, inference engines, and any effect provided by changing weights within neural networks.

Applicants may take advantage of guidance provided in the 'slide to unlock (Apple)' decision[19] of the German Federal Court of Justice:

> With the requirement to move an unlock image 'in accordance with the contact' along a predetermined indicated path on the screen ..., the patent in suit teaches

19. BGH, Urt. v. 25.8.2015 – X ZR 110/13 *Entsperrbild*.

> to visually indicate to the user the control movement for unlocking functions of the device, which he performs by executing a certain movement on the touch-sensitive screen, by the fact that an icon displayed on the screen in turn executes a corresponding (not necessarily identical) movement. The patent claim thus teaches to indicate optically to the user that he has given a command to the computer with the movement, which can cause the unlocking and actually causes it, if the movement of the user corresponds to the (minimum) requirements of the given (finger) movement. In other words, the control command inherent in the finger movement is intended to trigger not only the unlocking, but also an indication symbolizing the command and the progress of its execution. This is a technical solution to the technical problem of making the unlocking process visually recognizable to the user and thus increasing operating safety.
>
> However, the instruction to execute this display as movement of an unlock image along an indicated path on the screen concerns the content design of the information given by graphic means. The movement of the unlock image imitates the control movement of the user and thus makes the initiation and the progress (or the abort) of the unlocking effected by this particularly vivid. However, this only takes into account the human imagination …

This distinction is helpful at the GPTO. Different from EPO practice, the applicant may argue that a seemingly 'non-technical' feature (like 'sliding an image on a screen as user input') serves to solve a technical object ('making the unlocking process visually recognizable to the user and thus increasing operating safety'). Thus, an applicant of an AI-related invention should attempt to assign technical objects to claimed features.

§08.09 CONCLUSION

The practice of the GPTO with respect to AI-related inventions is, at a high level, no different from the practice at the EPO. However, as explained above, certain differences in approach do emerge in some respects. Overall, it is expected that the case law and practice at the GPTO will continue evolve in concert with that of the EPO.

Chapter 9

India

Anshul Sunil Saurastri & Divyendu Verma

§09.01 PATENTABILITY OF SOFTWARE AND COMPUTER-IMPLEMENTED INVENTIONS

In India, the protection and enforcement of patents is governed by the Patents Act, 1970, as amended most recently in 2005 (the 'Act'),[1] and the Patents Rules, 2003, as most recently amended in 2021 (the 'Rules').[2] The Controller General of Patents, Designs and Trademarks (the 'Controller') is the sole authority appointed under Act for administering the provisions thereunder including examination, opposition, grant and revocation of patents in India. The Office of the Controller ('IPO') is an agency under the Department for Promotion of Industry and Internal Trade, Ministry of Commerce & Industry, Government of India.

The Act defines what are and are not inventions. Patentability of an invention is determined based on a combined reading of Sections 2(1)(j) and 3 of the Act. Specifically, the most relevant legal provisions that govern patentability of software and computer-implemented inventions ('CRIs') are Sections 2(1)(j), 2(1)(ja), 3(k), 3(m), 3(n), and 3(o) of the Act.

Section 2(1)(j)[3] of the Act defines inventions to mean 'a new product or process involving an inventive step and capable of industrial application'. This definition has three facets, i.e., novelty, inventive step, and industrial applicability.

Section 2(1)(ja)[4] of the Act defines inventive step to mean 'a feature of an invention that involves technical advance as compared to the existing knowledge or having economic significance or both and that makes the invention not obvious to a person skilled in the art'.

1. The Patents Act, 1970 (No. 39 of 1970), Gazette of India, Part II, Sec. 1, 21 Sep. 1970.
2. The Patents Rules, 2003, Gazette of India, Part II, Sec. 3, 02 May 2003.
3. *Ibid.*, Sec. 2(1)(j).
4. *Ibid.*, Sec. 2(1)(ja).

Inventions in the fields of software and computers ('CRIs') are expressly excluded under sub-sections (k), (m), (n) and (o) of Section 3[5] of the Act, which define the following as *not* inventions:

> (k) a mathematical or business method or a computer programme per se or algorithms;
>
> (m) a mere scheme or rule or method of performing mental act or method of playing game;
>
> (n) a presentation of information; and
>
> (o) a topography of integrated circuits.

These exclusions were introduced into the Patent Act through an amendment in 2002, at which time the Joint Parliamentary Committee (Amendments) Act, 2002[6] explained:

> In the new proposed clause (k) the words 'per se' have been inserted. This change has been proposed because sometimes the computer programme may include certain other things, ancillary thereto or developed thereon. The intention here is not to reject them for grant of patent if they are inventions. However, the computer programmes as such are not intended to be granted patent. This amendment has been proposed to clarify the purpose.

This explanation was notable as it kept the door open for patentability of CRIs. Interestingly, in 2004, an amendment was proposed to Section 3(k) that changed the wording to read 'computer program *per se* other than its technical application to industry or a combination with hardware'. However, through a 2005 amendment, those amendments were disregarded and the language went back to the original position as presented in the 2002 amendment. Ever since, there has been no change in the language of the relevant legislative exclusions relating to CRIs.

In 2013, the IPO issued Draft Guidelines for Examination of Computer-Related Inventions (the 'Draft Guidelines'). The Draft Guidelines defined 'technical effect' under paragraph 3.15 to mean 'a solution to a technical problem, which the invention taken as a whole, tends to overcome' and illustrated this concept through examples such as higher speed, reduced hard disk access time, more economical use of memory, more efficient database search strategy, more efficient data compression techniques, improved user interface, better control of a robotic arm, or improved reception/transmission of a radio signal. The Draft Guidelines also defined 'technical advancement' under paragraph 3.16 as 'contribution to the state of art in any field of technology' and explained:

> It is important to divide between software, which has a technical outcome, and that which doesn't, while assessing technical advance of the invention. Technical advancement comes with technical effect, but all technical effects may or may not result in technical advancement.

This explanation essentially meant that to overcome the exclusions, an applicant was to prove 'technical effect' of the claimed invention, which could be explained through

5. *Ibid.*, Sec. 3.
6. Report of the Joint Committee, 19 Dec. 2001.

technical improvements, increased technical advantages, and/or reduced technical disadvantages. This can be easily shown if the claims are of a technical character, such that the invention when considered as a whole overcomes a technical problem by implementing a technical solution, and the solution involves a comparative 'technical advancement' over the state of the art. The Draft Guidelines essentially put in writing the common practice followed by examiners for determining eligibility with regard to consideration of inventive step.

In 2016, after much deliberation, the IPO issued the finalized Guidelines for Examination of Computer Related Invention (the 'Guidelines').[7] Interestingly, the definitions and concepts of 'technical effect' and 'technical advancement' were removed. Further, a three-step test was laid down to examine the eligibility of a CRI. While the Guidelines have been further revised (as discussed below), it is important to mention that in accordance with the guidance thereunder, to overcome exclusion from patentability, CRIs had to be claimed as computer programs in conjunction with novel hardware, and an applicant was required to show that the technical contribution lay in both the computer program and the hardware.

One year later, in 2017, the IPO issued Revised Guidelines for Examination of Computer Related Inventions[8] (the 'Revised Guidelines'). The Revised Guidelines included procedural recommendations and some illustrative examples. In the Revised Guidelines, CRIs were defined to comprise:

> inventions which involve the use of computers, computer networks or other programmable apparatus and include such inventions having one or more features of which are realized wholly or partially by means of a computer programme or programmes.

Most notably, the Revised Guidelines made it clear that to determine exclusion of CRIs, the focus should be on the underlying substance of the invention and not the claimed format. The Revised Guidelines acknowledged that CRIs are usually claimed in the form of an apparatus/system/device, a method/process, or a computer-readable medium/computer programmable product, but reinforced the idea that the substance of the claim must be judged by taking it as a whole and, if it does not fall in an excluded category, it should not be denied. The Revised Guidelines illustrated this by stating that the mere presence of a mathematical equation in a claim would not render it a mathematical method, nor would the mere usage of the terms, 'transaction', 'business', or 'finance' in a claim render the claimed invention a business method. Furthermore, mere presence of a mathematical formula in claims for inventions related to improved communication systems would not cause the claim to be considered a mathematical method. The Revised Guidelines also state that 'means plus function' claims that do not contain disclosure of structural features in the specification should not be allowed, as they are nothing but software or computer programs *per se*. Further, the Revised Guidelines indicate that claims directed to one or more of instructions, routines, sub-routines, computer readable media, storage media with instructions, databases and computer memory with instructions stored on a computer readable medium are treated as computer program products, which are specifically excluded.

7. Guidelines for Examination of Computer Related Inventions (CRIs), 19 Feb. 2016.
8. Revised Guidelines for Examination of Computer Related Inventions (CRIs), 2017.

However, recently, in *Ferid Allani v. Union of India & Ors.*[9] ('*Ferid*'), the Delhi High Court reiterated the principle laid down in the Draft Guidelines that CRIs are not barred from patentability but that such an investigation requires assessment of the 'technical effect' or 'technical contribution' of the underlying invention. This decision was passed by the Delhi High Court while exercising its writ jurisdiction under Article 226 of the Constitution of India[10] against a decision of the Intellectual Property Appellate Board ('IPAB') that had confirmed the IPO's decision to refuse the petitioner's patent application. Before the Delhi High Court, in *Ferid*, the petitioner had argued that 'the specification disclosed a technical effect and technical advancement, and that the claims did not relate to a mere software but a particular method of implementation'. Allowing the petition, the Delhi High Court in *Ferid* held:

> the bar on patenting is in respect of 'computer programs per se ...' and not all inventions based on computer programs. In today's digital world, when most inventions are based on computer programs, it would be retrograde to argue that all such inventions would not be patentable. Innovation in the field of artificial intelligence, blockchain technologies and other digital products would be based on computer programs, however the same would not become non- patentable inventions – simply for that reason. It is rare to see a product which is not based on a computer program. Whether they are cars and other automobiles, microwave ovens, washing machines, refrigerators, they all have some sort of computer programs in-built in them; thus, the effect that such programs produce including in digital and electronic products is crucial in determining the test of patentability.

In *Ferid*, the Court further held, referring to CRIs, that patent applications in these fields would have to be examined to see if they result in a 'technical contribution' and that '[i]f the invention demonstrates a "technical effect" or a "technical contribution" it is patentable even though it may be based on a computer program.'

On the back of the *Ferid* ruling, Patent Office jurisprudence may develop on this principle of 'technical effect', and presumably 'further technical effect', which was for instance discussed by the Technical Board of Appeal for the Examining Division of the European Patent Office ('EPO') in the landmark decision of T 1173/97 (Computer program product/IBM).[11] In T 1173/97, the Board of Appeal laid down, albeit in relation to Article 52(2) and (3) of the European Patent Convention that 'a computer program product is not excluded from patentability under Article 52(2) and (3) if, when it runs on a computer, it produces a further technical effect which goes beyond the normal physical interaction between the program (software) and computer (hardware)'. Although EPO decisions are not binding in India, they are generally considered and have persuasive value. Accordingly, we may see a similar approach being used by the IPO and higher courts in relation to the principle of 'further technical effect'.

9. *Ferid Allani v. Union of India & Ors.*, W.P.(C) 7/2014 & Cm Appl. 40736/2019, 12 Dec. 2019.
10. The Constitution of India, 1949, Art. 226.
11. EPO Board of Appeal T 1173/97, 1 Jul. 1998.

§09.02 SPECIAL PROVISIONS RELATING TO PATENTABILITY OF INVENTIONS RELATING TO AI

Presently, in India, there are no specific provisions governing artificial intelligence ('AI')-related subject matter. When faced with such applications, the IPO has been examining them as CRIs under the exclusion of Section 3(k) of the Act. In fact, an analysis of nearly 1,600 patent applications/patents revealed a consistency among examiners to object to AI-related inventions as algorithms or computer programs *per se*. A reading of the Revised Guidelines also suggests that AI-related inventions would be construed similarly, and which may pass the patent eligibility test only in their contextual setting of a machine, device, or manufacturing process. While such a criterion is not wholly erroneous given the current state of law, it would be helpful if specific guidelines are issued that would make examination more consistent and predictable.

In *Ferid*, the Court noted that '[i]nnovation in the field of artificial intelligence, blockchain technologies and other digital products would be based on computer programs; however, the same would not become non-patentable inventions simply for that reason'. This ruling essentially lays down that examiners cannot summarily reject inventions relating to AI under the computer programs *per se* ground, but rather imposes the obligation upon them to assess the presence of 'technical effect' or 'technical contribution' of the claimed subject matter. It is axiomatic that claims which comprise a technical means, or are implemented by use of a computer to solve a specific technical problem, would in most likelihood overcome the excluded category. For this, the disclosure in the detailed description is paramount, in that emphasis should be made on following the well-established problem-solution approach. This requires describing the objective technical problem and the implementation of the technical solution in a method or by a device using an AI model, and by stating its advantageous effects with reference to background art. This approach would highlight the technical effect and aid such arguments during prosecution. For example, for inventions relating to a machine-learning algorithm, it would be necessary to disclose the crux of the main algorithm, for instance, in the form of a pseudocode. For inventions relating to applications of AI, and hence likely involve training and self-learning, identifying the source and nature of the data would play an important role. Also, it would be advisable to establish a proper connection or interrelation of the modules with the source of data and the interacting AI system.

§09.03 SUBJECT MATTER PATENTABILITY

Before we assess subject matter patentability requirements in India, it is important to outline the classification criteria used by the IPO for patent applications directed to AI-related inventions. Based on a statistical review of the published data, it is observed that the IPO predominantly classifies such inventions into IPC class G06.[12] This class covers patents relating to:

12. IPCPUB v. 9.5, WIPO, available at: https://www.wipo.int/classifications/ipc/en/ITsupport/Version20180101/transformations/ipc/20180101/en/htm/G06.htm#G06.

simulators which are concerned with the mathematics of computing the existing or anticipated conditions within the real device or system;

simulators which demonstrate, by means involving computing, the function of apparatus or of a system, if no provision exists elsewhere; and

image data processing or generation.

A closer analysis suggests that a majority of patent applications filed at the IPO in this technical field are classified under the subclass G06N[13] which covers technical fields relating to 'computer systems based on specific computational models'. As per details publicly available at the time of writing this chapter, 80% of published patent applications filed at the IPO for AI-related inventions are classified under this subclass. There are two other subclasses, namely, G06F[14] and G06K,[15] that are prominently used by the IPO to categorize patent applications in this technical field. The subclass G06F generally covers AI inventions relating to 'electric digital data processing', and particularly, to 'processing or transporting of data and data processing equipment'. This implies an association of an electric digital data processor classifiable under group G06F 7/00 with one or more arrangements classifiable under groups G06F 1/00 - G06F 5/00 and G06F 9/00 - G06F 13/00. Subclass G06K covers AI inventions generally relating to 'recognition of data; presentation of data; record carriers; handling record carriers', and particularly relating to 'the marking, sensing, and conveying of record carriers; recognising characters or other data; presenting visually or otherwise the data recognised or the result of a computation'.

The parameters of the IPO's classification above provides a basis for hypothesizing the treatment of AI-related inventions during the substantive examination process as being similar, if not identical, to the framework used to examine CRIs. A cursory review of another dataset, i.e., 120 first examination reports ('FERs') issued by the IPO after substantially examining patent applications in this field, confirms this hypothesis. Specifically, there is a clear consistency at the IPO to object to AI-related inventions under Section 3(k), 3(m) and 3(n) of the Act, which excludes inventions relating to a 'mathematical or business method or a computer programme per se or algorithms, a mere scheme or rule, and a presentation of information respectively'.

Based on the IPC classifications used by the IPO, it can also be inferred that AI-related inventions are broadly viewed as mathematical models or advanced mathematical concepts, which are, unfortunately, not patentable subject matter under Section 3(k) of the Act. However, as discussed above, if such claims include a technical means or are implemented by using computers and/or are by running on a machine to solve a specific technical problem, then they may qualify.

AI-related inventions are often considered mixed-type inventions from a patentability perspective. These inventions include both eligible and ineligible features. For instance, a simple algorithm such as a neural network that is implemented as a computer program, which is not usually seen as a technical feature, would be excluded under Section 3(k). However, when this neural network is configured to operate like an artificial neural network or connectionist system, which emulates a biological

13. *Ibid.*, G06N.
14. *Ibid.*, G06F.
15. *Ibid.*, G06K.

neural network like animal brains, it would be treated differently. Another example would be a machine learning algorithm that is implemented on a computer system to perform image recognition. If the algorithm only involves processing images and does not improve the performance of the computer system, it may not be considered as a technical feature. However, if the algorithm improves the performance of the computer system, for instance by reducing processing time or increasing accuracy, it would be treated differently. In such instance, since the algorithm is applied to a technical problem, it can take on a technical character and consequently ought not to be rejected *per se* and instead require the examiner to proceed to an inquiry of inventiveness under the Revised Guidelines and the *Ferid* principle.

Subject matter patentability will now be considered for each of the five categories of AI-related inventions,

[A] Category 1: Invention of AI

As mentioned above, this category of inventions can be referred to as 'core AI' inventions. These inventions relate to a new kind of algorithm or mathematical or computer model that are of an abstract mathematical nature and, therefore, would face challenges to pass the patent eligibility test as both these categories of inventions fall under non-patentable subject matter. This poses a significant challenge for both the IPO in terms of examination and the applicant in obtaining allowance for AI algorithms as such. Under Section 3(k), these algorithms or mathematical models are not patentable; however, we cannot overlook the fact that they represent the core of AI inventions. Unless the Act is amended to alter the language under Section 3(k), to either remove or substitute the word 'algorithms', it may be difficult for this category of AI-related inventions to pass the hurdle of patent eligibility in India, and may lead to unintended downstream effects in research in this field.

However, all is not lost, and there may indeed be light at the end of the tunnel, under the *Ferid* principle, if such mathematical or computer models are presented in a way such that the underlying algorithm or mathematical model focuses on the technical character of the claimed invention. Of course, more concrete steps such as specific examination guidelines and properly fleshed out judicial decisions would improve predictability in this area. However, until such measures are taken, one may expect the IPO to refer to the practice of the EPO for guidance.[16] We understand that the EPO has recently updated its Guidelines for Examination,[17] which provide that 'AI and machine-learning algorithms should serve a technical purpose in order to be

16. The IPO may rely on the EPO to some extent while examining patent applications in India. One such instance is when the IPO may refer to the EPO Guidelines or case law for guidance on specific patentability issues, such as whether an invention involves an inventive step or is non-obvious. Additionally, the IPO and the EPO constantly cooperate and exchange information on matters related to patent law and examination procedures. However, it is important to note that the IPO is an independent organization that makes its own decisions on patentability and examination, and its reliance on the EPO may vary depending on the specific case or situation.
17. EPO, Guidelines for Examination in the European Patent Office, March 2023.

patentable'. It is our view that the patentability of core AI inventions may be dealt with somewhat similarly by the IPO.

The challenges do not end here, in that claiming core AI inventions can be very tricky. More often than not, the obvious choice is to draft method claims broadly so as to cover and protect the essential parts of the main algorithm or mathematical model of the proposed invention. However, the requirement of demonstrating a technical character in the claims may lead to challenges in drafting them where the emphasis is on the arrangements of the claim elements being adapted to a specific technical implementation. It may be useful to claim such algorithms or mathematical/computational models in the form of system/computing platform claims elaborating the components of the computing platform involved in executing the essential parts of the algorithms or mathematical/computational models. For completeness, the system claims could be followed by a group of claims directed to a method of performing essential steps of the algorithms or mathematical/computational models. However, in the current scenario, obtaining allowance of such method claims may be difficult.

[B] Category 2: Invention of an AI Implementation

As defined in this book, and invention of an AI implementation is the creation of a system or process of broad application using known AI technology plus additional elements, such as a particular arrangement of filters or a particular interface. Thus, by definition, a new AI implementation has broad application and primarily concerns a new implementation as opposed to being directed to a specific technical application. Accordingly, the comments and concerns expresses above with respect to Category 1 inventions apply here as well. However, the model or algorithm underlying the new AI implementation may be acknowledged to contribute to the technical character of the invention if it is a specific technical implementation, i.e., the model or algorithm is specifically adapted to exploit the hardware or is designed based on technical considerations relating to the internal functioning of the hardware.

Under this category, the invention of an AI implementation refers to the creation of a new and innovative way of using AI to solve a problem or perform a specific task. This category of invention may involve developing new algorithms, machine learning models, or neural networks, or improving upon existing AI technologies. Inventions under this category are potentially patentable. The subject matter patentability is determined based on whether inventive step is present, i.e., are the added elements sufficient for the existence of inventive step. One such example of invention under this category is a new deep learning algorithm that can more accurately identify and classify different types of cancer cells in medical images. Another example is a neural network model that can generate highly realistic images of human faces or other objects.

[C] Category 3: A New Application of AI

This category of inventions is the most common amongst AI-related patent applications in India. At the present time, AI has touched virtually every possible field of activity and its influence continues to grow. While it may be advantageous to use AI across industries, patent protection for such industry-agnostic inventions is extremely challenging. Examples of new applications are endless; they may include, for example, applying AI to more accurately identify and classify different types of cancer cells in medical images; a neural network model that can generate highly realistic images of human faces or other objects; or control of a self-driving car. Considering the self-driving car example, such an application would involve combining sensors and software to control, navigate, and drive the vehicle without the need for a human driver. Unlike prior static software control systems, the AI system, if properly trained, can analyse multiple inputs from the different sensors fitted into the car which are continuously feeding the data as inputs to the system. The simplest way to understand the application of AI here is in the manner in which the system is comparing the data generated from various sensors with historical data. Due to self-learning or machine learning aspects of AI, the AI subsystems are able to predict 'correctly' the next action item after receiving inputs from sensors to stop the car because the sensor senses a 'stop sign' or 'pedestrian', or to change to a different driving style as it receives inputs from the sensors which indicate rain and consequently slippery road conditions.

Such inventions can be said quite clearly to be technical because the auto-driving car is a technical car, i.e., a technical device. The contribution of AI components and self-learning algorithms contribute to the overall technical nature of such an autonomous vehicle because such contributions involve improvement of the efficiency of the car which in turn enhances the handling or driving of the car. Since these contributions provide a technical character to the invention, the invention can be determined as patentable provided it satisfies the requirements of novelty, inventive step and industrial applicability.

It is important to understand that the patentability of AI-related inventions may look difficult at the outset. However, claiming them in a technical context may solve the problem relating to their patentability. In the context of an autonomous vehicle or, for example, an application of AI in healthcare, the invention might be claimed as a device/apparatus embedded in a larger claim, defined as functional features which solve the stated technical problem.

Let us consider another example, where a group of claims are directed to a system and another group of claims are directed to a method for identifying whether an object, such as an executable file, is associated with a cyber-attack using artificial neural network techniques. This is a classic example, whereby a known artificial neural network technique is used to identify whether one or more executable files are associated with a cyber-attack. Such identification is performed with the help of intelligence-driven subsystems that are used to identify multiple indicators in communication packets containing the executable file(s). Apart from this, there are subsystems which are used to inspect and evaluate any communication protocol having any anomalies or other suspicious content. These techniques are well known in the prior art; however, when one deploys these techniques over large datasets to observe patterns, then such sub-systems start predicting suspicious content which can be used to achieve the object of the exemplary invention described above. In the technical field of AI, such inventions can also be classified as deep-learning models/ techniques. Other examples of such learning models include identification of spam e-mails in an inbox, or categorization of emails with the labels of, for example, 'primary', 'social', 'promotion' as accomplished by Google on its Gmail platform.

Under this category of inventions, to overcome the hurdles of patentability, it is essential to embed the AI component/tool into the technical implementation of the claimed subject matter. Therefore, the technical characteristic must directly contribute to the resolution of a technical problem with the help of embedded AI components/tools such as deep learning models/methods. Such deep learning models/methods must be implemented via a specific hardware architecture.

It is important to remember that the generic implementation of such invention by simply using a computer likely will not suffice for eligibility. Therefore, it is useful to assimilate the AI implementation in the proposed architecture of the claimed invention. In other words, the underlying applications of the AI component/tool implemented with the proposed system helps in determining the patentability of the claimed subject matter.

It is also equally necessary to understand how to claim such complex inventions. In our view, the best approach might be to recite the essential features of the invention in the claims directed to the structure of the system. Such claims should include the AI component/tool such as the artificial neural network which is configured to perform the essential part of the invention. Therefore, system component(s) claimed in conjunction with the AI component should be able to showcase the technical characteristic as well as direct contribution to the resolution of a technical problem. A group of claims directed to a method may also follow, wherein the essential steps of the invention can be recited, such that each step is tied in with the system components which are required to perform the steps of the method. While claiming such arrangements, method steps must inherently include the step performed by the AI component. Needless to say, all other supplementary steps can be covered through other method claims.

[D] Category 4: Inventions Made Using AI

This category of invention is developed by a human using an AI tool to solve a technical problem in any field. Inventions made using AI are potentially patentable provided they meet the standard patentability requirements. More importantly, the subject matter eligibility of such inventions is determined based on what is claimed. Further, if an invention is created unintentionally or accidently using AI, it can still be considered an invention, similar to a situation where someone accidentally discovers something and then applies that discovery to solve a practical problem. Furthermore, it is important to note that IPO does not allow 'use' claims, so any claims made must be directed towards a system or method instead.

[E] Category 5: Inventions Made by AI

This category of inventions includes those that are self-developed by AI tools without any or limited external input. When faced with a problem, an AI system, just like a human inventor, may be capable of devising useful solutions. Such category of inventions can be considered as autonomous inventions where the human contribution is next to nothing. From the patentability perspective, inventions made by AI are unlikely to be patentable as per the present Patent Law in India because of the inventorship issue. If the inventorship issue is addressed and therefore a claim to an invention made, hypothetically, by AI can be considered for subject matter patentability, as in Category 4, the decision would depend entirely on what is claimed and not on the method by which the invention was made.

§09.04 INVENTIVE STEP

The foregoing definition of inventive step under Section 2(1)(ja) of the Act requires the fulfilment of few aspects, namely, the existence of a feature or features that involve a comparative technical advancement from prior public knowledge, or economic significance, and which is non-obvious to a person skilled in the art.

The examination of inventive step has been largely developed on judicial expositions in the famous cases of *Bishwanath Prasad Radhey Shyam v. Hindustan Metal Industries Ltd*[18] and *F. Hoffmann La Roche v. Cipla Ltd.*[19]

In *Bishwanath Prasad*, the Supreme Court held:

> obviousness has to be strictly and objectively judged, and that the definition suggested by Salmond L.J in *Rado v. John Tye & Son Ltd.* is apposite i.e. 'whether the alleged discovery lies so much out of the track of what was known before as not naturally to suggest itself to a person thinking on the subject, it must not be the obvious or natural suggestion of what was previously known.'

In *La Roche*, a two-member bench of the Delhi High Court, after referring to *Bishwanath Prasad* and other famous European and American case law, laid down a five-step test for assessing obviousness or lack of inventive step, where the following inquiries are to be conducted:

1. to identify an ordinary person skilled in the art;
2. to identify the inventive concept embodied in the patent;
3. to impute to a normal skilled but unimaginative ordinary person skilled in the art what was common general knowledge in the art at the priority date;
4. to identify the differences, if any, between the matter cited and the alleged invention and ascertain whether the differences are ordinary application of law or involve various different steps requiring multiple, theoretical, and practical applications; and
5. to decide whether those differences, viewed in the knowledge of alleged invention, constituted steps which would have been obvious to the ordinary person skilled in the art and rule out a hindsight approach.

In arriving at the test, the Court also held that 'whether an invention involves "novelty" and "inventive step" or is "obvious" is a mixed question of law and fact, depending on the facts and circumstances of each case. Though no absolute or uniform formula can be laid down to ascertain obviousness however certain broad criteria have been laid down in various decisions'. The Court also identified the ordinary person skilled in the art as 'a person who practices in the field of endeavour,

18. *Biswanath Prasad Radhey Shyam v. Hindustan Metal Industries Ltd.*, (AIR 1982 SC 1444), 13 Dec. 1978.
19. *F. Hoffmann-La Roche Ltd v. Cipla Ltd.*, Mumbai Central, CS (OS) No.89/2008 and C.C. 52/2008, 7 Sep. 2012.

belongs to the same industry as the invention, possesses average knowledge and ability and is aware of what was common general knowledge at the relevant date'.

There is no denying that an accurate identification of the 'ordinary person skilled in the art' is where most of the debate lies in discussions focused on assessment of inventive step in respect of AI-related inventions. It is also rarely disputed that human ingenuity and creativity may be supplanted by exceptional AI-related inventions, if it has not been already. Therefore, this first step, which forms the basis of an inventive step inquiry under Indian law, as reinforced in *La Roche*, becomes an extremely challenging task. It is also equally important to appreciate the complexities in identifying and imputing to such person the common knowledge, i.e., the tools, platforms and ever-increasing knowledge source that is courtesy of AI. Consequently, the difficulty increases in assessing obviousness accurately and in ruling out a hindsight approach. Nonetheless, these challenges can be overcome by an appropriate identification of the person skilled in the art, recognizing that such person should be able to correctly understand the AI and its nuances in the field to which the claims are directed.

Therefore, it may be necessary to make an additional assessment, through the eyes of the person skilled in the art, of whether the claimed invention would have been obvious when an AI-driven system or an algorithm is trained with the data from the relevant technical field of the invention. If the answer to additional assessment is in the affirmative, the invention in question would not pass the hurdle of inventive step. In view of this, additional consideration is required in the assessment of inventive step in view of AI-related inventions.

Regarding inventions listed under Categories 1, 2 and 3, the Act and Rules provide no specific guidance. Thus, the general test as prescribed in *La Roche* is used to apply the test of inventive step. Further, as discussed under the subject matter patentability section of this chapter, since the AI itself, including a mathematical/computational model or an AI tool/component, does not meet the patent eligibility requirement, it shall not go through an inventive step determination. For AI-related inventions, the test of inventive step, in the present circumstances, may not be much different, if at all, to that applied while assessing conventional inventions or computer related inventions, provided that step 1 of *La Roche* is determined accurately. In other words, it can be said that if AI-related inventions under Categories 1, 2 and 3, pass the test prescribed in *La Roche* under steps 2, 3, 4 and 5, then it could be said that the inventive step requirement is met.

Turning now to inventions made using AI, or by AI, as discussed in Categories 4 and 5, the Act and Rules again provide no specific guidance. Moreover, there is no data available in terms of IPO examination reports or decisions, which further reduces accuracy of an inventive step assessment. In our view, the question of inventive step as it relates to inventions made by or using AI presents a conundrum. Since inventive step is a mixed question of law and fact, and its assessment must be objective, the facts and the law of inventorship must be accurate and crystal clear. In the current scenario, this is impossible. Also, drawing the line between what is public knowledge and what is not, to conduct analysis of comparative technical advancement, is rather complicated. Having said so, it may also be stated, for good measure, that it is risky to apply a different standard for assessing inventive step. In addition to presenting other legal challenges, any changes in the level of proof will have a direct impact on research and development in the field and therefore this approach is fraught with risks. Since we know that the IPO examines general AI-related inventions such as CRIs, going forward it would be interesting to see how the IPO differentiates such inventions made by or using AI, from other AI-related inventions and generally from CRIs. Probably, when faced with examining such an invention, the IPO might realize the pressing need for creating and issuing guidelines directed to AI-related inventions.

In any case, we feel that the IPO might be tempted to come up with two different standards for assessing the presence of inventive step. But much before that, we find that it is necessary for the IPO to develop a mechanism for differentiating AI-related inventions with non-AI inventions to reduce uncertainty. In any case, the existence of two different standards for inventive step test might create counterproductive results. In our considered view, this is surely a Catch 22 situation for the IPO.

§09.05 ADEQUACY OF DISCLOSURE

The Act does not have any special provisions with respect to disclosure or enablement requirements of AI-related inventions. The general consensus is that patent applications directed to such inventions are required to meet the threshold for claim support and enablement in accordance with Section 10(4)[20] of the Act:

> Section 10 – Content of Specification:
>
> ...
>
> (4) Every complete specification shall –
> (a) fully and particularly describe the invention and its operation or use and the method by which it is to be performed;
> (b) disclose the best method of performing the invention which is known to the applicant and for which he is entitled to claim protection; and
> (c) end with a claim or claims defining the scope of the invention for which protection is claimed;
> (d) be accompanied by an abstract to provide technical information on the invention

These provisions are further supplemented by the Manual for Patent Office Practice and Procedure[21] ('the Manual'), version 3.0 published by the IPO on 26 November 2019. Specifically, the Manual states, *inter alia*,

> 05.06.09 Detailed Description of Invention:
>
> a) Description of an invention is required to be furnished in sufficient detail so as to give a complete picture of the invention and follows the Summary of invention. The nature of improvements or modifications effected with respect to the prior art should be clearly and sufficiently described. It may include examples/drawings or both for clearly describing and ascertaining the nature of invention. Examples must be included in the description, especially in the case of chemical related inventions.

20. Act, Sec. 10.
21. IPO, Manual for Patent Office Practice and Procedure, v. 3.0, 2019.

> b) Disclosure of invention in a complete specification must be such that a person of average skill and average knowledge in India should be able to perform the invention based on what is disclosed in the specification.

Further, the Manual explains that the Act requires the 'Best Method' to be disclosed in the complete specification:

> 05.06.12 Best Method:
>
> The Act specifically requires that the complete specification must describe the best method of performing the invention known to the applicant, including the one, which he may have acquired during the period of provisional protection prior to the date of filing the complete specification.

Under the foregoing standards, the claimed subject matter must be fully and particularly disclosed in the specification. Additionally, the specification must clearly and sufficiently disclose the specific means of performing the invention so that the ordinary person skilled in the art can arrive at the invention by reading the written description. It is also required that the specification be clearly and unambiguously written, without any room for confusion or obscurity.

These principles were reiterated in *Ram Narain Kher v. Ambassador Industries New Delhi*[22] by the Delhi High Court where it ruled that '[i]t is incumbent under Section 10(4) of the Act to fully and particularly describe the invention and its operation or use and the method by which it is to be performed and disclose the best method of performing the invention which is known to the applicant and for which he is entitled to claim protection ending with a claim or claims defining the scope of the invention for which protection is claimed'.

In a separate ruling in *Press Metal Corporation limited v. Noshir Sorabji Pochkhanawalla*,[23] the Bombay High Court held that 'the invention is described in an obscure and ambiguous language and on this ground, the patent is liable to be refused.'

Therefore, it is apparent that an invention is to be determined to be adequately disclosed if the specification contains a sufficient, clear and unambiguous written description, which includes the best method of performing the invention, examples for support, and in such manner that a person of average skill and average knowledge in India is able to perform the claimed invention without undue experimentation.

Presently, there is no clarity on the specific level of disclosure required for AI components such as a neural network or core algorithm, machine learning, or deep learning module in order to meet these requirements. Until further clarity is forthcoming, similar principles are to be applied when evaluating the disclosure requirements for AI-related inventions. Further, it is important to note that the adequacy of disclosure for AI-related inventions would depend largely on the scope of the claims as filed. Therefore, the specification must disclose how to use and perform the AI-related invention in as much detail as possible to meet the sufficiency of disclosure requirement.

---

22. *Ram Narain Kher v. Ambassador Industries New Delhi*, AIR 1976 Del 87, 28 May 1975.
23. *Press Metal Corporation limited v. Noshir Sorabji Pochkhanawalla*, 1982 PTC 259 (Bom), 16 Apr. 1982.

Specifically, for inventions under Category 1, where the claimed subject matter of the patent application is directed to a neural network structure or a related invention thereof, it is advisable to disclose particular algorithms behind the working of such neural networks.

For inventions under Category 2, the disclosure requirement would be similar to any other CRIs. The patent specification must provide a comprehensive description of the invention that enables a person of average skill and average knowledge in India to create and use the claimed invention without undue experimentation. The patent specification should contain a clear explanation of the AI algorithm or implementation, highlighting any unique characteristics or components that distinguish it from the prior art. Special emphasis should be given to any technical integration between the algorithm used and the particular implementation employed.

For inventions under Category 3, if the claimed subject matter of the patent application is directed to a machine learning or learning model/computational model, it is advisable to disclose the complete process including data correlation, and how the input data is accepted and then processed and the final properties of the output data. It is important to note that the deep machine learning has capabilities of learning from supervised and unsupervised data which is not necessarily structured. In such an unstructured or unlabelled environment, it is important to provide enough varieties and sufficiently detailed examples of dataset types in the patent specification. When claiming an AI-enabled algorithm's application to a particular type of data, it is advisable to disclose all possible categories of dataset types to which the algorithm may be applied, thereby enabling the genus of all dataset types.

Regarding inventions under Category 4, where a human uses AI as a tool to invent something, the general principles of adequacy of disclosure requirements which apply to inventions in any technical field ought to apply, since AI is not being claimed, but rather that 'something' invented using AI as a tool by human intervention is. As such, ideally the adequacy of disclosure requirements for such inventions ought to be guided by the type or nature of the invention generated using AI as a tool. However, given the lack of established case law or regulation regarding the extent and depth of disclosure requirements with regard to AI-related inventions or AI-generated inventions, and given that the general principles of sufficiency of disclosure which apply to CRIs are often applied to AI-related inventions, it is currently advisable to disclose the calculation process of the mathematical/training model and the specific manner in which the calculation process/program interacts with the AI component and also any corresponding hardware interaction.

As regards inventions under Category 5, where the AI machine on its own and without direction or involvement by a human inventor produces the invention, what is claimed would be the 'something' that was invented, not the AI itself. Therefore, the comments above with respect to Category 4 inventions apply equally here. Of course, as explained in the next section, unless the laws of inventorship are changed, a Category 5 invention would not be considered patentable due to non-human inventorship.

Also, under each of the foregoing categories of inventions, there may be issues that need consideration under the plausibility requirement. Generally, the assessment of plausibility is a factual assessment based on the information provided in the patent specification and the category and level of common general knowledge available to the person of average skill and average knowledge in India. As mentioned above, paragraph 05.03.12 of the Manual states that the Act requires the 'Best Method' to be disclosed in the complete specification and the claims must be clear. In practice, the IPO may object based on plausibility issues by requesting clarifications of the subject matter and the proposed solution to the technical problem.

Further, with the nature and complexity involved in technical implementation of the foregoing categories of inventions, the IPO may object as to credibility of an AI system as being sufficiently trained to carry out a particular task, or the ability of an AI model trained on generic datasets to credibly perform all applications stated in the specification. In our view, tying the training of AI to the technical effect will be one of the major challenges faced by those drafting patent applications in this area.

§09.06 INVENTORSHIP

[A] Inventorship in General

Under Indian law, the expression 'inventor' is not expressly defined in statute. It is a well-accepted principle of law that the determination of inventorship is a question of fact which must be tried by the appropriate authority.

Section 6[24] of the Act provides that the following persons can make a patent application, either alone or jointly:

a person claiming to be the true and first inventor;

an assignee of the person claiming to be the true and first inventor;

legal representative of any deceased person who immediately before his death was entitled to make an application.

Section 2(1)(y)[25] of the Act defines a true and first inventor to 'not include either the first importer of an invention into India, or a person to whom an invention is first communicated from outside India.' The expression 'person' is defined in an enumerative manner under Section 2(1)(s)[26] of the Act as 'includes the government', which must also be read in conjunction with the corresponding definition under the General Clauses Act, 1897, in that a person '*shall* include any company or association or body of individuals, whether incorporated or not'. It is settled law that when the word 'includes' is used in a definition, it should not be read restrictively, but extensively beyond just its natural import.

However, in *V.B Mohammed Ibrahim v. Alfred Schafranek & Ors.*,[27] the Karnataka High Court, while deciding on a legal entity's claim of inventorship, held that 'a firm cannot be said to have a capacity to invent. It cannot be called an inventor although there may be no objection to its being registered as a patentee either on assignment or jointly with the true and first inventor'. This principle was also reiterated in the

24. Act, Sec. 6.
25. *Ibid.*, Sec. 2(1)(y).
26. *Ibid.*, Sec. 2(1)(s).
27. *V.B. Mohammed Ibrahim v. Alfred Schafraneck And Ors.*, AIR 1960 Kant 173, 4 Jun. 1958.

ruling of *Shining Industries v. Sri Krishna Industries*,[28] where the Allahabad High Court acknowledged that an invention was to be assigned by the employee, or partner of a firm to the firm. In light of these rulings, it has been well accepted in practice that a person claiming to be a true and first inventor must be a natural person. However, a person claiming to be an assignee may be a legal person.

Further, while on the topic of determining inventorship, the language found in Section 28(1)[29] of the Act also deserves to be reproduced:

> (1) If the Controller is satisfied, upon a request or claim made in accordance with the provisions of this section, –
> (a) that the person in respect of or by whom the request or claim is made is the inventor of an invention in respect of which application for a patent has been made, or of a substantial part of that invention; and
> (b) that the application for the patent is a direct consequence of his being the inventor, the Controller shall, subject to the provisions of this section, cause him to be mentioned as inventor in any patent granted in pursuance of the application in the complete specification and in the register of patents:
>
> Provided that the mention of any person as inventor under this section shall not confer or derogate from any rights under the patent.

This provision can be invoked by unnamed inventors to be mentioned in a patent.

Also, in *V.B. Mohammed Ibrahim*, the Court further held that a person can claim inventorship only when 'he contributed any part of his ingenuity or skill or technical knowledge towards the invention' and that a person merely providing financial support cannot be treated as an inventor. While this decision provided some clarity, the Court understandably did not delve into the finer nuances of inventorship such as linkage of inventive contribution to claims, and so on. This issue was to some extent discussed in a ruling of the Controller in an opposition matter of *National Institute of Virology v. Mrs. Vandana S. Bhide*.[30] Relying on dictionaries and legal reference books, the Controller carved out the difference between an inventor and a hired hand, namely,

> to be named as an inventor, he must have made some intellectual contribution in achieving the final results of research work leading to a patent. A person who has not contributed intellectually in the development of an invention is not entitled to be included as an inventor. A person who provides ideas to produce the 'germ of the invention' need not himself/herself carry out the experiments, construct the apparatus with his/her own hands or make the drawings himself/herself. The person may take help of others. Such persons who have helped in conducting experiments, constructing apparatus or making the drawings or models without providing any intellectual inputs are not entitled to be named as inventors.

---

28. *Shining Industries and Anr. v. Shri Krishna Industries*, AIR 1975 All 231, 3 May 1974.
29. Act, Sec. 28.
30. *National Institute of Virology v. Mrs. Vandana S. Bhide*, IPO decision in 581 /BOM/ 1999.

The Controller concluded that a person can be called an inventor only if he has introduced a new idea which actually made the invention feasible. In the same ruling, the Controller also linked claims to inventorship by noting that the inventor is the deviser of what is being claimed and that co-inventorship should be restricted to those that make key contribution for devising the invention.

In light of the above, the principles of being named as an inventor are plainly clear; a person desirous of being named as an inventor must contribute at least substantially to the invention and a causal link must be demonstrated by direct association of his contribution to the claimed subject matter. In this background, it is axiomatic that a formulaic approach cannot be applied to determine inventorship, but that any analysis must be a factual determination subject to the aforesaid principles.

[B] Determination of Inventorship for AI-Related Inventions

With regard to determining inventorship of inventions falling under Categories 1, 2 and 4, the general principles for determining inventorship ought to apply since humans are the sole inventors. The general principles would also apply to inventions in Category 3. However, in Category 3, there may be challenging fact issues associated with determining inventorship with respect to the humans who contribute to training and operating the AI tool and perhaps the ruling in *National Institute of Virology* would be a guiding factor.

As to Category 5 inventions, it is worthwhile to first and foremost state that a wide debate is necessary to assess whether the framework of laws that currently govern patents is adequately prepared to recognize and permit this category of inventions to undergo the test of patentability. We have already seen one such patent application. DABUS (Device for the Autonomous Bootstrapping of Unified Sentience) is an artificial intelligence system developed by Dr Stephen Thaler that has been named as the inventor on several patent applications in various countries around the world. The DABUS invention has undergone a certain level of scrutiny in major jurisdiction around the world. Specifically, in United States, the USPTO has rejected two patent applications for which DABUS was listed as the inventor. The USPTO stated that current patent laws only allow natural persons to be listed as inventors. Similarly, the EPO in 2021 rejected two patent applications for which DABUS was listed as the inventor. The EPO stated that the inventor must be a natural person and that an AI system cannot be considered a person under the European Patent Convention. The same approach was also followed by United Kingdom; the UK Intellectual Property Office ('UKIPO') ruled in 2021 that DABUS cannot be listed as an inventor on a patent application. The UKIPO stated that the inventor must be a natural person and that an AI system cannot be considered a person under UK patent law. In February 2021, the Australian Patent Office ('APO') ruled that DABUS cannot be listed as an inventor on a patent application. The APO stated that the inventor must be a natural person, and that an AI system cannot be considered a person under Australian patent law.

However, the German Federal Patent Court in July 2021 on a similar case provided some clarification in dealing with a scenario where the AI machine is listed as inventor. Like the other jurisdictions, the German Federal Patent Court ruled that an AI system cannot be listed as an inventor on a patent application because inventorship requires a creative contribution from a natural person. That is, the German Court stated that an AI system, even if it can create something new and inventive, cannot be considered a natural person capable of making a creative contribution to the invention. The Court further stated that in cases where an AI system is used to create an invention, the natural person who programmed or otherwise directed the AI system should be listed as the inventor.

On 25 January 2022, the Japan Patent Office ('JPO') provided 'Manga Patent Examination Guidelines for the Artificial Intelligence (AI)/Internet of Things (IoT) fields'[31] on its web page with a section titled 'The JPO Key Features'. The JPO in 'Patent Examination Case Examples pertinent to AI-related technologies'[32] has clearly provided that the inventor listed on a patent application must be a natural person who made a creative contribution to the invention. The guidelines also state that if an AI system was used in the invention process, the role of the human inventor must be clearly identified. The guidelines provide examples of situations where a human inventor may be credited, such as where a person selects the data used by the AI system, or where a person designs the algorithm used by the AI system. Therefore, it seems that patent offices in various countries are largely in agreement that an AI system cannot be listed as an inventor on a patent application. However, the debate around AI inventors is far from over, and it will likely be revisited as AI technology continues to advance.

To summarize, there are limitations in the current law to recognizing AI as inventors, while at the same time, it may not be entirely appropriate to ignore the contribution of AI and solely attribute inventorship to a human. The other aspects which may also require wider debate include those that govern ownership of such inventions, and/or assignments thereof from the true and first inventor.

§09.07 AREAS FOR FURTHER DEVELOPMENT

The current patent policy may need to be revisited in order to make room for the widespread use of AI in research and development.

First and foremost, the law needs to be revised to the extent that it addresses the issues connected with inventorship of AI-related inventions. Subject to the nature of changes, if any, there may arise a need to address the associated issues of assignment and transfer of ownership of AI-related inventions. This would also help remove uncertainty in meeting the proof of right requirements of the Act.

Furthermore, the IPO could seek to clarify the patent eligibility treatment with respect to inventions under Categories 4 and 5 vis-à-vis those in 1, 2 and 3. It would also be helpful if the IPO could decide whether it should apply a different criterion for examination of AI-related inventions under Categories 1, 2 and 3, when compared with other CRIs. Next, the IPO must invite stakeholders to debate on how the well-recognized standard of judging obviousness based on the knowledge

31. JPO, Examination Guidelines in Manga: AI/IoT Edition, Oct. 2021, available at: https://www.jpo.go.jp/e/system/laws/rule/guideline/patent/comic_ai_iot_e.html.
32. JPO, Patent Examination Case Examples pertinent to AI-related technologies, available at: https://www.jpo.go.jp/e/system/laws/rule/guideline/patent/ai_jirei_e.html.

of 'ordinary person skilled in the art' should be applied, and how the prior art is determined, particularly in relation to inventions under Categories 4 and 5.

Another area of improvement would be to address disclosure requirements by exemplification, for instance, the extent of disclosure required in the written description in relation to input datasets/training data.

At the outset, these areas identified for improvement may seem like a long list, but addressing these would help open the gates for patenting AI-related inventions.

§09.08 RECOMMENDATIONS FOR PATENT APPLICANTS

First, claim-drafting techniques for CRIs can be adopted for AI-related inventions falling under Categories 1, 2 and 3 by placing emphasis on embedding technical characteristics in the claims.

Also, care must be taken to ensure that the specification has characterized the AI-related invention in the form of providing an improvement to a CRI (e.g., providing an efficiency or other performance metric in the computer running the AI-related invention, as compared to a computer running previously known solutions).

When preparing a patent application it is also important to ensure that the patent specification sufficiently discloses the technical solutions of the AI-related invention. Special emphasis could be made by highlighting how the use of AI tools/components demonstrates technical characteristics in the invention. In this regard, it would be advisable to prepare the patent specification in a manner such that the AI-related tools/components are disclosed in context of their application and thereby demonstrating the technical characteristics in the invention.

One must also remember that the patent specification must support the technical function of the new AI/machine learning related features of the invention and the contribution made by these AI/machine learning related features in the technical applications of the claimed subject matter.

Finally, it would be prudent, in appropriate applications, to include parameter ranges for input as well as output datasets (if available) of AI-enabled hardware or tools or machine learning/deep learning algorithms in order to bring out the presence of an inventive step.

§09.09 CONCLUSION

As per the recently published report on AI by the World Intellectual Property Organisation[33] in 2019, India is recognized as an emerging jurisdiction for patent filings in the field of AI and is top ranked among all countries for publications in computer vision and natural language processing. Also, with a relatively young population, large consumer base, huge number of scientists and researchers, and great emphasis on education in computer science and mathematics, India is poised to see a major thrust in this field. Further, if the above explanations hold good, one may conclude that it is possible to obtain allowance of patents at the IPO for inventions relating

33. Francis Gurry, *WIPO Technology Trends 2019 Artificial Intelligence* 2019, available at: https://www.wipo.int/publications/en/details.jsp?id=4386.

to AI falling at least under foregoing Categories 1 to 4, perhaps, subject to minor amendments in the Act and Rules. Accordingly, in the near future, we predict greater attempts at patent protection for industrial applications of AI in India, both by foreign and domestic entities. India's strengths in AI might be unlocked within the next few years and it may be safe to say that India has the potential to be categorized among the most important jurisdictions for protection and commercialization of AI-related inventions. This is all only going to be possible if lawmakers and administrators wake up and 'smell the coffee', and suitably address the associated challenges. Of course, the burden is not only on the legislators, but also on all stakeholders to continuously voice their unique concerns, and make themselves heard at the national and international stage to set the stage for the patenting of AI-related inventions in India.

Chapter 10

Italy

Stefania Bergia, Antonio Di Bernardo & Alessandro Spina

§10.01 PATENTABILITY OF SOFTWARE AND COMPUTER-IMPLEMENTED INVENTIONS

The Italian rules on patentability of software and computer-implemented inventions ('CIIs') essentially mirror those of the European Patent Convention ('EPC'). Specifically, Article 45 of the Italian Industrial Property Code ('IIPC') provides generally, 'patents shall be granted for any inventions, in all fields of technology, provided that they are new, involve an inventive step and are susceptible of industrial application'. Article 45 IIPC also follows Article 52 EPC in listing subject matter that cannot constitute patentable subject matter. Among these are:

(a) discoveries, scientific theories and mathematical methods;
(b) schemes, rules and methods for performing mental acts, playing games or doing business, and programs for computers;
(c) presentations of information.

The law specifies, however, that this exclusion applies only to the extent to which the subject matter is claimed *as such*. Generally, the provision of technical means in the claims is sufficient to avoid an objection of patent eligibility, but not necessarily one of lack of inventive step, as will be discussed in more detail below.

§10.02 SPECIAL PROVISIONS RELATING TO PATENTABILITY OF INVENTIONS RELATING TO AI

The IIPC does not contain special provisions relating to patentability of artificial intelligence ('AI')-related inventions. Consequently, the inventions in question must meet the same validity requirements as any other patentable invention.

The Italian Patent and Trademark Office ('IPTO') does not provide guidelines for examining AI-related inventions. However, as of 1 July 2008,[1] patent applications for inventions filed in Italy without a foreign priority claim are subjected to a prior art search by the European Patent Office ('EPO'), which issues a search report and a written opinion. The agreement between the IPTO and the EPO sets out the procedures for carrying out prior art searches and search reports. In addition, the parties agreed on special rules for the application of the Guidelines for Examination in the European Patent Office ('Guidelines').[2] The Guidelines provide, *inter alia*:

> There are four basic requirements for patentability:
> (i) there must be an 'invention', belonging to any field of technology (see G-II);
> (ii) the invention must be 'susceptible of industrial application' (see G-III);
> (iii) the invention must be 'new' (see G-IV to VI); and
> (iv) the invention must involve an 'inventive step' (see G-VII).
>
> A technical character is an implicit requisite for the presence of an 'invention' within the meaning of Art. 52(1) (requirement (i) above, see G-II, 1 and 2 for further details).

In the first step, the IPTO will examine whether the invention has to be excluded because it is a pure mathematical method or a method relating to business. Since AI is generally implemented in a computer device or network, technical means are usually present in the claims. Hence, this type of objection is seldom raised.

In the second step, the IPTO will examine novelty and inventive step of the claimed AI-related invention. In examining inventive step, only the features having a technical character, i.e., providing a technical effect, are considered, whereas features having a non-technical character, such as related to business issues, presentation of information and the like, will not be considered.

§10.03 SUBJECT MATTER PATENTABILITY

As already mentioned above, Article 45 IIPC mirrors Article 52 EPC in providing a list of subject matter that is excluded from patent eligibility. However, these exceptions apply only as far as the patent claims these activities 'as such'. Therefore, eligibility objections can typically be overcome by proper claim drafting, such as by including technical features like computer processors.

Coming to the five different AI related inventions categories, the following considerations apply.

[A] Category 1: Invention of AI

According to Italian practice,[3] a new AI algorithm independent from the data to which it is applied, such as a new neural network, would not be considered to be patentable as it is a pure mathematical method with no technical character.

---

1. D.M. 27.06.2008.
2. Guidelines, G.I.1.
3. *See* Guidelines, G-II-3.3.1, applied also in examination of Italian patents.

[B] Category 2: Invention of an AI Implementation

Creation of a system or process of broad application using known AI technology plus additional elements, such as a particular arrangement of filters or a particular interface, would be considered patentable as far as the additional elements are technical means. An interface for receiving user input or data would make the subject matter patentable.

[C] Category 3: A New Application of AI

A new application of AI can be patentable if it involves technical means. In general, any AI application would involve technical means: a computer running the AI algorithm taking input data and producing an output. Such technical means would make the AI application eligible for being patented.

[D] Category 4: Inventions Made Using AI

According to the Italian law,[4] as for subject matter patentability, it is not important how the invention is made or conceived, rather the focus is on the claimed invention. If the claimed invention has a technical character, for example, a better performing robot or a new chemical compound, then the invention will be eligible for being patented, regardless of the manner ('made using AI') in which that claimed invention was obtained.

[E] Category 5: Inventions Made by AI

In this case, there is not a problem of subject matter patentability (for which the above applies) but a problem related to the designation of the inventor, who can only be a natural person (an invention made only by an AI algorithm would be objected as the inventor should be a human being, see Section §10.06, *infra*).

§10.04 INVENTIVE STEP

There are no special rules in the IIPC for AI-related inventions regarding the assessment of the inventive step requirement. Therefore, as with all other types of inventions, the invention in question 'shall be considered as involving an inventive step if, having regard to the state of the art, it is not obvious to a person skilled in the art' (Article 48 which mirrors Article 56[5] EPC).

---

4. Art. 45 IIPC lists the subject matter that is not considered to be an 'invention', but does not make any reference to the way the invention is conceived.
5. Art. 56 EPC: 'An invention shall be considered as involving an inventive step if, having regard to the state of the art, it is not obvious to a person skilled in the art. If the state of the art also includes documents within the meaning of Article 54, paragraph 3, these documents shall not be considered in deciding whether there has been an inventive step.'

According to Italian practice, and mirroring the EPO approach, the requirement in question is assessed based on whether the solution would have been obvious to the average person skilled in the art in the relevant technical field. Indicia of non-obviousness (also called secondary considerations, such as the satisfaction of a long-felt need or an important technical surprising effect) may also be considered. The case law of the EPO also often resorts to the so-called 'problem-solution approach'.[6] With regard to AI related inventions, in determining the objective technical problem, only features which provide a technical contribution are considered. Therefore, features relating to business, games or mathematical methods are not considered. As an example, a new AI algorithm (Category 1) that is run on a computer would not be considered inventive as the only technical feature is the computer, i.e., a well-known device.

The person skilled in the art is a practitioner in the relevant field of technology. If the problem prompts the skilled person to search for a solution in another technical field, then the person skilled in the art is assumed to be a practitioner of that other field of technology as well.

Regardless of whether the invention is made by a human being in a traditional way (Categories 1–3), or is made using AI (Category 4), or is made by AI (Category 5), the approach does not change. Current case law does not provide for any different approach in the evaluation of inventive step.

The use of AI for making inventions, i.e., the use of computer programs that can calculate solutions in a much faster and complex way compared to a human person, does not change the fact that the person skilled in the art is always a practitioner (or a group of practitioners). The skilled person is assumed to have unlimited access to the prior art and to the common general knowledge (i.e., know everything that was made public, in any way and in any language, in the relevant field of technology) but to have no inventive skills (in the sense of a person with average intellectual skills, and average capacity for elaboration and experimentation). Therefore, the capabilities of AI impact the assessment of the skillset of the person skilled in the art as long as such AI capabilities are publicly available and thus part of the common knowledge in the art.

§10.05 ADEQUACY OF DISCLOSURE

There are no special rules in the IIPC for AI-related inventions relating to assessment of the adequacy of disclosure requirement. Therefore, as with all other types of patent applications, an AI-related patent application 'shall disclose the invention in a manner sufficiently clear and complete so as to be carried out by a person skilled in the art' (Article 51 IIPC mirrors Article 83 EPC). Hence, the use of AI does not change the standard of sufficiency of disclosure.

With reference to the five different AI categories, the following considerations apply:

6. Guidelines, G-VII-5, also applied in examination of Italian patents.

[A] Category 1: Invention of AI

If the invention is a new AI algorithm, the algorithm shall be disclosed in detail, providing all the formulas and details relating to the invention. Known steps or procedures do not need to be disclosed in detail. As an example, if the invention relates to a new combination of two known algorithms, such as a Support Vector Machine for classifying data and providing one class of data as a dataset for an XGBoost algorithm, the two algorithms do not need to be explained in detail because the person skilled in the art of AI would know these algorithms. On the other hand, if the invention relates to a new model of a model-based ML algorithm, the new model should be explained in detail.

[B] Category 2: Invention of an AI Implementation

If the invention consists in the creation of a system or process of broad application using known AI technology plus additional elements, such as a particular arrangement of filters or a particular interface, then the additional elements should be disclosed in detail, as well as the way they are used in combination with the AI technology. If well-known, the AI technology does not need to be disclosed in detail because the person skilled in the art would know it.

[C] Category 3: A New Application of AI

When the invention is not in the AI algorithm (as in Categories 1 and 2), but in the application of a known algorithm for a new application, the description does not need to focus on the known algorithm, but should focus on the way the dataset is made and on the way the algorithm is trained.

With reference to the dataset, the disclosure should be sufficient to allow a person skilled in the art to retrieve similar data and construct a dataset which will cause the algorithm to converge to an output that solves the technical problem faced by the invention.

Very often the invention focuses on the way the dataset is created by selecting some data from among a larger original set of data. In this case, the disclosure is considered enabling if it is discloses how the data are selected, for example, by applying a classification algorithm.

If the dataset is not publicly available, the disclosure should clearly indicate to the person skilled in the art how to obtain such data. As an example, if a known AI algorithm is applied to blood data to detect a certain disease, the application should disclose how to obtain this data, for example, which process is applied and, if relevant for the AI to work, which population sample is used.

Disclosure of the training method could be as relevant as the description of the creation of the dataset. A known algorithm, applied to public data, but trained in a certain way, can provide unexpected results and turn out to be optimal for a new application. In this case it is important to describe the training phase and give evidence that such particular training provides the unexpected results. In this case, the provision of experimental data could be useful.

[D] Categories 4–5: Inventions Made Using AI or Made by AI

The way the invention is made does not change the way the invention shall be disclosed. If the invention generated using AI (Category 4) or generated by AI (Category 5) is a machine, the disclosure should enable a person skilled in the art to carry out the invention. Since Article 51 IIPC does not require disclosure of how the invention was made, but only how the invention can be carried out, there is no need to disclose which data have been used by AI or which AI algorithm has been used to make the invention. Rather, there is only a need to carefully and completely disclose the inventive solution.

§10.06 INVENTORSHIP

[A] Inventorship in General

The IIPC does not establish any specific requirement to be considered an inventor. However, doctrine has always confirmed that inventors are physical persons who have contributed to the inventive step.

Further, case law of the Italian Supreme Court (e.g., decision 5281/2000) has confirmed that the author is a 'physical' person or group of 'physical' persons who have used inventive skills to make an invention.

The term 'author' is also used with the same meaning in connection with the following Articles of the IIPC:

- Article 62, which relates to the moral rights of the author of an invention;
- Article 63, which relates to the patrimonial and non-patrimonial rights of the author of an invention;
- Article 64, which relates to employees' inventions;
- Article 65, which relates to inventions made by university researchers; and
- Article 83, which relates to the industrial property rights deriving from utility models.

It may be derived from these provisions that a person who simply carries out work under instruction from another, but has no role in research and development work, or simply has a managing role without providing any technical contribution to an invention, should not be considered an author, and hence not an inventor.

Stated differently, all individuals who contribute to devising an invention should be mentioned as inventors in a patent application.

[B] Determination of Inventorship for AI-Related Inventions

Concerning inventions falling under Categories 1 and 2, it appears that the contribution of a natural person is necessary. Hence, inventorship would no doubt be determined based upon the provisions of the IIPC mentioned above, supported by case law and doctrine.

The same approach also applies to Categories 3 and 4. In fact, in all proposed instances a person, namely a human being, is the subject having the idea of using

AI for an intended purpose, as well as the subject who selects and configures an AI technology to suit an intended purpose. Selection of data and of an optimal solution also require the contribution of a human being, the nuances mentioned above being mostly a matter of inventiveness rather than of inventorship.

Finally, with regard to Category 5, it does not appear to be possible to name AI (perhaps as a juridical entity) as an inventor or co-inventor according to the IIPC. In fact, Article 62 of the IIPC (Moral rights) states that the right to be recognized as 'author of an invention' belongs to the inventor or 'upon his/her death' to his/her heirs. This implicitly states that the inventor is a human being. Moreover, Article 62 refers to a moral right to be identified as an inventor, which is typical of a human being.

§10.07 AREAS FOR FURTHER DEVELOPMENT

We do not think that special provisions should be introduced in the Italian patent law for AI-related patent applications. We believe the general rules for evaluating patentability of inventions should apply regardless of the subject matter.

One area of attention that would need additional clarification is the identification of technical and non-technical features. Although the distinction could appear trivial, when speaking of AI this distinction is less and less obvious. When dealing with AI-related inventions, there are always technical data that are retrieved and processed and different training methods and algorithms can perform better than others. Therefore, applicants could claim that an improved AI algorithm for calculating a financial product also solves a technical problem, i.e., reducing running time and computational resources compared to known methods. Although the EPO[7] has already taken a position explaining that the reduction of computational resources does not change the fact that the method is a financial one, the provision of further clarifications and examples from the EPO seems to be the only way to provide clear guidelines to the applicants.

§10.08 RECOMMENDATIONS FOR PATENT APPLICANTS

Applicants shall be aware that the use of a known AI algorithm for a new application is not *per se* sufficient to obtain a patent.

First of all, applicants should bear in mind that business methods cannot be patented and the simple fact of using AI to calculate a financial product or to estimate the performance of a financial product is not sufficient to obtain a patent.

Secondly, having it clearly in mind that the invention must have a technical character, applicants shall also remember to clearly disclose the invention in an enabling way, namely such that it can be carried out by a person skilled in the art. This means that it is not sufficient to list a number of possible AI algorithms with

7. Guidelines, G-II-3.6: '...The presence of a further technical effect is assessed without reference to the prior art. It follows that the mere fact that a computer program serving a non-technical purpose requires less computing time than a prior-art program serving the same non-technical purpose does not on its own establish the presence of a further technical effect (T 1227/05, T 1784/06, T 1370/11)'.

a list of possible training methods (supervised or unsupervised) to obtain a patent, because not all possible combinations of algorithms and training methods will converge to an invention that solves the technical problem at issue.

In order to give evidence that the AI algorithm is actually effective in solving the technical problem faced by the invention, it can be useful to provide experimental data, such as showing that a classification AI algorithm classifies data or situations in the correct way.

An AI algorithm is, in its most basic sense, a method implemented on a computer. Therefore, very often a method claim could be very effective in protecting the invention. Nevertheless, when AI is used in a machine, it is also possible to claim the machine implementing the AI method.

It is not necessary to put lines of source code in the description, but use of flowcharts and block diagrams can be useful to improve understanding the invention.

§10.09 CONCLUSION

The Italian practice is no different from the practice of the EPO and thus similarly requires paying attention to patent eligibility, novelty and inventive step of a claimed invention, independently of the use of AI. AI is a tool that can be used by a human being to solve technical problems, thereby possibly leading to patentable inventions. The role of the patent system in facilitating disclosure of AI technology to the public is of the upmost importance to allow continued progress in this area of technology.

Chapter 11

Japan

Dr Yusuke Ichikawa & Takashi Nakazaki

§11.01 PATENTABILITY OF SOFTWARE AND COMPUTER-IMPLEMENTED INVENTIONS

Computer software-related inventions ('CSI') have been patentable in Japan since an amendment to the Examination Guidelines for Patent and Utility Model in 2000, followed by the amendment to the Japanese Patent Act ('the Patent Act') in 2002. After the 2002 amendment, a product used in the 'invention of a product' may include a 'computer program, *etc.*,' even though a computer program is an intangible item.[1]

In Japan, a considerable number of applications relating to CSIs are filed and granted each year. In particular, a substantial number of artificial intelligence ('AI') related patents have been obtained during the fourth industrial revolution era.[2] In Japan, the Internet of Things ('IoT') and AI-related inventions are fully protected and are generally more likely to be granted for patents (especially business-related inventions) than in many other jurisdictions. In fact, the allowance rate for business-related inventions was only 8% in 2000 but has recently increased to about 60–75%, which is almost the same percentage as inventions in other technical fields. These trends are expected to continue, especially with the broader implementation of new technologies such as big data analysis, IoT, and 5G.

The Japan Patent Office's ('JPO') report on AI-related patent applications in 2022[3] indicates that there were approximately 5,700 applications for AI-related inventions in 2020, including approximately 2,400 applications for AI-related inventions with classification G06N (the patent classification applied for inventions relating to 'computer systems based on specific computational models').

1. Japanese Patent Act Art. 2(3)(i).
2. Japan Patent Office, *Recent Trends in AI-Related Inventions*, Oct. 2022, available at: https://www.jpo.go.jp/e/system/patent/gaiyo/ai/ai_shutsugan_chosa.html.
3. *Ibid.*

Like other jurisdictions, Japanese authorities, including the JPO and the Intellectual Property High Court, have formulated and revised rules regarding the standards for examining CSI patent applications and have conducted claim construction and infringement comparisons in patent infringement litigations.

The Examination Guidelines for Patent and Utility Model[4] (the 'Guidelines') and the Examination Handbook[5] (the 'Handbook') include chapters on computer software-related inventions. These chapters were revised in 2018 and 2019 to include updated case examples of technologies relating to IoT, AI, 3D printing, etc., to clearly show the JPO's current examination practices in these technical fields.

At the JPO, the approach to assessing whether a CSI relates to a statutory 'invention' or ineligible subject matter is described in the Handbook, Annex B, Chapter 1, 2.1. There are two steps for making this assessment: first, a determination based on the Guidelines, Part III, Chapter 1; and secondly, a determination according to the 'idea based on the standpoint of software'.

Accordingly, it is first determined whether the claimed CSI is a 'creation of a technical idea utilizing a law of nature', based on the Guidelines, Part III, Chapter 1. During this review, the examiner does not need to take into consideration whether the claimed CSI is, in fact, implemented in software.

Part III, Chapter 1 of the Guidelines specifies examples of technical ideas:

> (i) Those concretely performing control of an apparatus (e.g., rice cooker, washing machine, engine, hard disk drive, chemical reaction apparatus, nucleic acid amplifier), or processing with respect to the control; or
>
> (ii) Those concretely performing information processing based on the technical properties such as physical, chemical, biological or electric properties of an object (e.g., rotation rate of engine, rolling temperature, relation between gene sequence and expression of a trait in a living body, physical or chemical relation of bound substances).[6]

Thus, in the determination based on the Guidelines, Part III, Chapter 1, those CSIs considered a 'creation of a technical idea utilizing a law of nature', irrespective of whether computer software is used (e.g., examples (i) or (ii) above), would constitute a statutory 'invention' without being examined from the viewpoint of computer software.

In the second step, where a determination is made on the 'idea based on the standpoint of software', it is further considered whether the claimed software-related invention falls under the 'creation of a technical idea utilizing a law of nature', and whether the 'information processing by software is specifically implemented by using hardware resources in a software-related invention' (i.e., whether a specific

4. Japan Patent Office, *Examination Guidelines for Patent and Utility Model in Japan*, revised April 2023, available at: https://www.jpo.go.jp/e/system/laws/rule/guideline/patent/tukujitu_kijun/index.html.
5. Japan Patent Office, *Examination Handbook for Patent and Utility Model in Japan*, revised April 2023, available at: https://www.jpo.go.jp/e/system/laws/rule/guideline/patent/handbook_shinsa/index.html.
6. Guidelines, Part III, Chap. 1, Sec. 2.2(1).

information processor or an operation method thereof, depending on the intended use, is constructed through the cooperation of software and hardware resources).

§11.02 SPECIAL PROVISIONS RELATING TO PATENTABILITY OF INVENTIONS RELATING TO AI

In 2018 and 2019, the JPO amended the Guidelines and the Handbook to clarify the examination standards in relation to AI and other algorithm-related inventions. These amendments were in response to the increasing number of patents and patent applications involving algorithms (for example, those related to artificial intelligence and big data, or features of business rules and methods). The amendments to the Guidelines and the Handbook provide specific rules for the examination of such patents and patent applications, inform the public of how such patent applications should be examined, and offer guidance on how to draft patent applications for such types of inventions.

To enhance the practical application of the Guidelines to patent applications for AI-related technology, twenty example cases (including fifteen cases on eligibility for patent and five cases on inventive step) are provided in Annex A of the Handbook. Any determination on the enablement and support requirements of AI-related inventions is made in accordance with 'Enablement Requirement' (Section 1, Chapter 1 of Part II) and 'Support Requirement' (Section 2, Chapter 2 of Part II) of the Guidelines. The inventive step aspects are assessed in the same way that they would be in other technical fields.

Types of AI-related inventions considered in the Guidelines and the Handbook include any inventions that take advantage of AI-related technology in various technical fields. Also considered is the specific case of claims to a product that is predicted to have a certain function or characteristic due to an AI prediction. For these inventions, the JPO has provided new case examples.

The Guidelines and the Handbook also clarify that for inventions relating to structured data or data structures, patentability shall be determined by whether the structured data or data structure is equivalent to a program. More specifically, it will be considered whether the structured data or data structure has characteristics similar to a program where the structure of the data specifies the processing of the computer. Structured data or data structure is determined to be software only when it is equivalent to a program.

These guidelines and examples for examination of AI-related inventions will be described in more detail in the sections that follow.

§11.03 SUBJECT MATTER PATENTABILITY

[A] Overview

The issue of subject matter patentability (or eligibility) in Japan is sometimes triggered for CSIs, particularly when an applicant seeks to claim an abstract invention with a broad scope. However, in most situations, subject matter eligibility issues can be solved in Japan if the specification describes the details of the computer system used to execute the invention and the claims are amended to incorporate at least some of those specific details. We will first provide an overview of the general rules regarding subject matter eligibility and then provide specific examples related to AI-related inventions.

[B] Category of Patentable Invention

As described above, the Patent Act stipulates that an invention of a 'computer program, etc.' is regarded as a product invention.[7] Such 'computer program, etc.' is defined as 'a computer program (meaning a set of instructions given to a computer which work to produce a specific result...) and any other information that is to be processed by an computer equivalent to a computer program'.[8] The 'other information ... equivalent to a computer program' may also be a product invention, including data structures and learning models as described below.

Thus, a claim may be made directly for a computer program (or software) to cover an AI-related invention. This includes both core AI inventions as well as other types of products such as computer systems or information processing devices. It is noteworthy that Article 2 of the Patent Act treats any electronic communication of a computer program, such as by downloading, as an infringing action. This indicates that remedial relief in the form of an injunction based on a patent could effectively stop an actual patent infringer if the claimed invention is directed to a computer program.

[C] Relevant Rules and Guidelines to CSIs

Although computer programs are included in the statutory definition of patentable products, such computer programs must nonetheless comply with the relevant rules and guidelines to satisfy the subject matter eligibility requirement. Specifically, to be patent eligible, a claim to a CSI must satisfy the statutory definition of invention: a 'highly advanced creation of technical ideas utilizing the laws of nature'.[9] As described above, this test is performed by applying a two-step assessment. Application of this two-step assessment is illustrated in the Handbook as shown in Figure 1.[10]

First, satisfaction of the statutory requirement is determined based on Sections 2.1.1.1(1) and (2). Particularly, the criteria noted above from the Guidelines, Part III, Chapter 1, and repeated in Section 2.1.1.1(1) provide a helpful framework to assist applicants in passing the subject matter eligibility requirement:

> (i) Those concretely performing control of an apparatus (e.g., rice cooker, washing machine, engine, hard disk drive, chemical reaction apparatus, nucleic acid amplifier), or processing with respect to the control; or

7. Patent Act Art. 2(3)(i), English translation at: www.japaneselawtranslation.go.jp/en/laws/view/3118/en.
8. *Ibid.*, Art. 2(4).
9. *Ibid.*, Art. (2)(1).
10. Handbook, Annex B, 2.1.1.1.

Figure 1. Process of determining eligibility for patent for a software-related invention

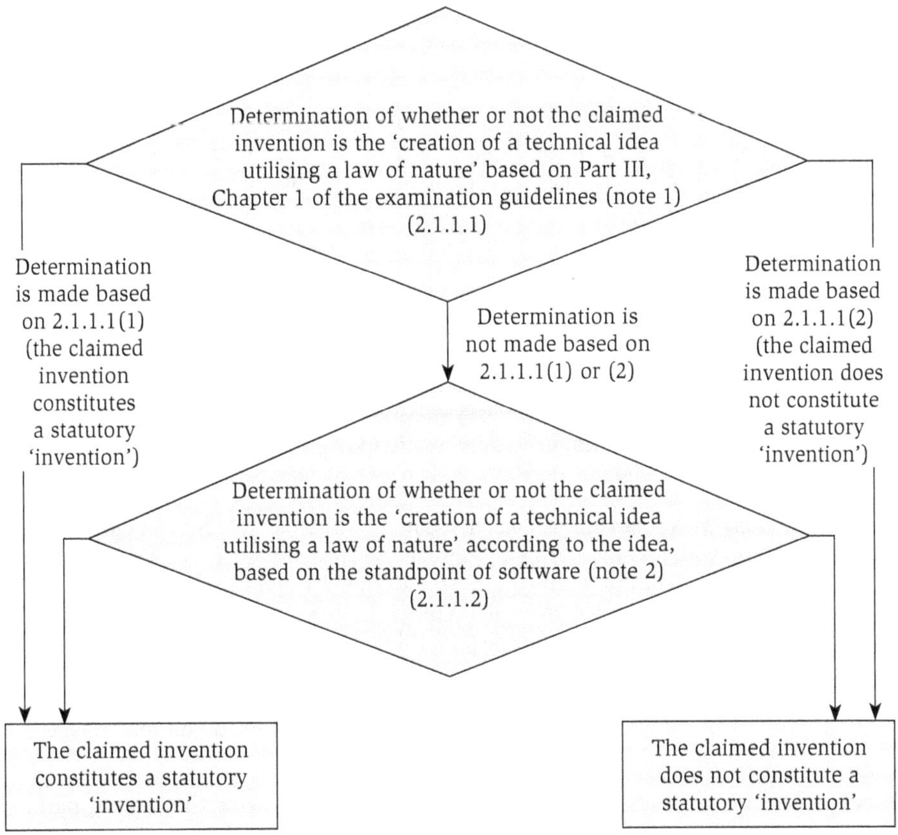

(ii) Those concretely performing information processing based on the technical properties such as physical, chemical, biological or electric properties of an object (e.g., rotation rate of engine, rolling temperature, relation between gene sequence and expression of a trait in a living body, physical or chemical relation of bound substances).

The Handbook, Annex B, provides examples of such inventions. Specifically, examples of inventions falling under (i) above are:

(i-1) Those performing control of a target apparatus … based on a structure, system component, composition, action, function, nature, property, operation, etc. of the control target apparatus or any other apparatus related to the control target apparatus.

(i-2) Those performing control in a way that realizes operations according to the purpose of an apparatus.

> (i-3) Those performing integrated control of a whole system comprising multiple related apparatuses.

Similarly, examples are provided of inventions that would normally fall under category (ii) above:

> (ii-1) Those obtaining intended numerical values, images, etc. by calculation or processing of numerical values, images, etc. showing the technical properties of an object, which is performed according to said technical properties.
>
> (ii-2) Those performing information processing by utilizing a technical correlation between a state of an object and a phenomenon corresponding thereto.

In short, if an AI-related invention controls something or handles information processing based on technical properties, such AI-related invention would satisfy the subject matter eligibility requirement. On the other hand, if an AI-related invention is found to neither control anything nor handle information processing based on technical properties, including situations where the AI-related invention involves business methods, financial activity, mental activity or games, the following 2.1.1.1.(2) issue may arise:

> When a claimed invention is considered as any of (i) to (v) shown below, the claimed invention is not deemed to utilize the laws of nature, and thus, is not considered as a statutory 'invention' (see Example 1 and Example 2).
>
> (i) Any laws other than the laws of nature (e.g., economic laws)
> (ii) Arbitrary arrangements (e.g., a rule for playing a game as such)
> (iii) Mathematical formulas
> (iv) Mental activities of humans
> (v) Those utilizing only (i) to (iv) (e.g., methods for doing business as such)[11]

Mere presentations of information are not technical ideas using the laws of nature. However, examples are provided where a technical idea resides in how information is presented, rendering the invention patent eligible:

> Mere presentation of information (where the feature resides solely in the content of the information, and the main object is to present information)
>
> Example 1: A written manual for instructing an operation of a machine or directing a use of a chemical substance
>
> Example 2: An audio CD the feature of which resides solely in music recorded thereon
>
> Example 3: Image data taken with a digital camera
>
> Example 4: A program of an athletic meeting made by a word processor
>
> Example 5: A computer program list (mere representation of computer programs by means of printing them on paper, displaying them on a screen, etc.)
>
> If a technical feature resides in presentation of information (presentation per se, means for presentation, a method for presentation, etc.), a claimed invention is not considered as mere presentation of information.

11. Handbook, Annex B, Sec. 2.1.1.1.(2)a.

Example 6: A test pattern for use in checking the performance of a television set

Explanation: The technical feature resides in the pattern per se.

Example 7: A plastic card on which information is recorded with characters, letters and figures embossed on it

Explanation: The information is printed on the plastic card by emboss processing and the printed information on the card is copied by affixing the card on paper. The technical feature resides in the means for presentation.[12]

Given that mere presentation of information is not patentable, mere presentation of a computer program also is not patentable and should not be claimed as such. However, a description of a computer program in the specification is sometimes helpful to argue disclosure and inventive step requirements. Further, as described above, information itself is not patentable, but information may have a substantial role from the viewpoint of inventive step when, for example, the invention is based on treating, using a conventional computer system, information or data differently from a conventional usage of that information or data.

For example, sometimes a CSI includes generation of information or data. If the generation of such information has some technical meaning, such generation of information, without providing the usage of such information in a claim, makes the claim broad and useful from a practical point of view. Therefore, in some cases, it is possible to satisfy the subject matter eligibility requirement not by the usage of the generated information (such as identifying the target to be controlled by such information) but by the process of generating the information.

As the above diagram shows, if the subject matter eligibility cannot be determined by the criteria of 2.1.1.1(1) and (2), then the 2.1.1.2 criteria are applied to determine the subject matter eligibility:

(i) When for software of a software-related invention, 'information processing by the software is concretely realized by using hardware resources,' said software is a 'creation of a technical idea utilizing the laws of nature.'

'Information processing by the software is concretely realized by using hardware resources' means that 'a specific information processor or an operation method thereof depending on intended use is constructed through cooperation of the software and the hardware resources.[13]

Two points are worthy of note with respect to the phrase, 'cooperation of software and hardware resources'. First, this criterion is not an issue of description of the specification but rather an issue of what is claimed. Therefore, even if the specification describes a detailed hardware system, this may not be enough to satisfy the subject matter eligibility requirement unless the claims can be amended to incorporate at least some of these details. Secondly, this criterion is not automatically satisfied merely by addition of a generic element such as a computer, CPU, or memory to the claim. However, from a practical point of view, addition of such elements would tend to increase the probability of passing this criterion.

12. *Ibid.*, 2.1.1.1(2)b.
13. *Ibid.*, 2.1.1.2.

[D] Application to the Five Categories of AI-Related Inventions

AI-related inventions under all five categories would be tested using the above criteria and all can potentially be patentable. For example, if an AI-related invention directly controls a machine as described under the 2.1.1.1 criteria, a claim directed to that invention would easily satisfy the subject matter eligibility requirement. On the other hand, if an AI-related invention does not control a machine and instead is, for example, incorporated into a field that involves a business method, a financial method, a human mental process or the like, such AI-related invention would need to pass the 2.1.1.2 criteria.

[1] Category 1 (Invention of AI)

Category 1 inventions relate to the invention of new algorithms or models for the AI itself, independent of the data to which it is applied and independent of any particular use case ('core AI'). Subject matter eligibility of core AI depends on the degree of abstractness of the algorithms or models. Even if the subject matter of the invention involves an algorithm or a model, a claim to the invention may be patent eligible to the extent 'a specific information processor or an operation method thereof depending on intended use is constructed through cooperation of software and hardware resources'.[14]

The Handbook provides the following relevant examples:

1. Example of an invention with a mathematical formula[15]

This first example does not directly relate to AI-related inventions. However, the example is helpful for understanding the meaning of the criterion of 'a specific information processor or an operation method thereof depending on intended use is constructed through cooperation of the software and the hardware resources'. In addition, this example shows that subject matter eligibility may be satisfied without limiting the claim to specific applications or industrial fields, so long as it provides some technological idea. Thus, when a given AI-related invention can be broad enough to apply to many kinds of applications or industrial fields, it is advisable to describe the technical concepts residing in the invention in the specification in order to provide support for subject matter eligibility is based on such technical ideas.

> Case 2-1 in Examination Handbook, Annex B
>
> [Claim 3]
>
> A computing device to compute the formula
>
> $$s = \frac{(m + n)^2 - (m - n)^2}{4}$$
>
> comprising means for inputting natural numbers 'n' and 'm' (where $1 \leq n \leq m < 256$), arithmetic means, and means for outputting a result 's' by the said arithmetic means.

14. *Ibid.*
15. *Ibid.*, Case 2-1.

[Claim 4]

A computing device to compute the formula

$$s = \frac{(m + n)^2 - (m - n)^2}{4}$$

comprising, means for inputting natural numbers 'n' and 'm' (where $1 \leq n \leq m < 256$), a square values table wherein square values k^2 (where $0 \leq k < 511$) is stored at the k-th position, arithmetic means comprising of an adder-subtracter and a bit shifter, and a means for outputting a result 's' by said arithmetic means, wherein the formula is computed, without using a multiplier-divider, but using square values read by the said arithmetic means from the said square values table.

In this example, Claim 3 does not fall within the definition of invention because 'it cannot be said that concrete means or procedure is used for implementing specific calculation or processing of information depending on the intended use, i.e., computing a formula.'[16]

On the other hand, Claim 4[17] falls within the definition of invention because 'specific calculation or processing of information depending on the intended use, i.e., computing a formula on a device which does not have any multiplier-divider unit, is implemented by concrete means or procedure through cooperation of software and the hardware'.[18]

A recent decision is helpful in recognizing the degree or extent of a technological idea necessary to satisfy the statutory definition of invention, even though it does not relate to an AI-related invention. The decision involved a system used to deliver steaks. The problem to be solved by the invention was found by a court to be the misidentification of meat for customers, and the invention specified the use of several tangible items, including a card with the customer's table number, a scale to measure the amount of meat for the customer, and a sticker to identify the amount of meat and the table number, all of which were found by the court to contribute to solving the problem.[19] Thus, this case illustrates the importance, for eligibility purposes, of including in the specification a logical explanation of the technical idea and how it is applied to solve a problem.

2. Example of an invention related to a learning model[20]

The next example shows a claim to a learning model that is considered to be patent eligible. This example demonstrates that a learning model itself can be eligible subject matter if the specification and the claim show that the learning model is equivalent to a computer program.[21]

---

16. *Ibid.*
17. The specification explains that 'The invention performs calculation of values $(m + n)^2$ and $(m - n)^2$ by referring to a square function table of 0 ~ 510, without using a multiplier device. It therefore requires shorter time for calculation than adding natural number m n-times, and guarantees to perform such calculation process within a certain time.'
18. Handbook, Annex B, Case 2-1.
19. 2017 (Gyo ke) 10232. Note that inventive step was not raised or determined.
20. Handbook, Annex A, Case 2-14.
21. The Examination Guidelines indicate that the specification describes 'the trained model is supposed to be utilized as a program module which constitutes a part of artificial

The practical value of claiming a 'learning model' as such is unclear because the specification should explain that the 'learning model' is a computer program or software, and it is very likely that the 'learning model' in the claim would be construed to be just a computer program in a claim construction at court for a patent infringement case.

However, there have been no court decisions on this point to date and future decisions may adapt a new construction of such claim. Thus, until that time, the 'learning model' is recommended to be included in the specification and the claims thereof in order to protect AI-related inventions from various aspects.

Case 2-14 in Examination Handbook, Annex A

[Claim 1]

A trained model for causing a computer to function to output quantified values of reputations of accommodations based on text data on reputations of accommodations, wherein;

the model is comprised of a first neural network and a second neural network connected in a way that the said second neural network receives output from the said first neural network;

the said first neural network is comprised of an input layer to intermediate layers of a feature extraction neural network in which the number of neurons of at least one intermediate layer is smaller than the number of neurons of the input layer, the number of neurons of the input layer and the number of the output layer are the same, and weights were trained in a way each value input to the input layer and each corresponding value output from output layer become equal;

weights of the said second neural network were trained without changing the weights of the said first neural network; and

the model causes the computer function to perform a calculation based on the said trained weights in the said first and second neural networks in response to appearance frequency of specific words obtained from the text data on reputations of accommodations input to the input layer of the said first neural network and to output the quantified values of reputations of accommodations from the output layer of the said second neural network.

3. Example of an invention related to a data structure[22]

AI-related inventions can be protected from the perspective of data structure (or structured data). An invention of data structure can be eligible subject matter if it satisfies the two requirements: (1) the data structure can be categorized as a statutory computer program, and (2) the data structure can be a creation of technical idea.

---

intelligence software' and 'the CPU of the computer operates, in accordance with instructions from the trained model stored in the memory, in a way that it performs a calculation based on trained weights and response functions in the first and second neural networks in response to data input to input layers of the first neural network (appearance frequency of specific words obtained from text data of reputations of accommodations, e.g., by performing morphological analyses) and outputs results from output layers of the second neural network (quantified values of reputations, e.g. "10 stars")'.

22. Handbook, Annex A, Case 2-13.

In the example below, the data structure of Claim 1 determines the processing from (1) to (5) based on the relation of the data elements in the data structure. The data structure includes plural branch information, each of which connects with the dialogue corresponding to a candidate answer based on the answer from a user, which has similar properties to computer programs in that it defines a processing flow. For this reason, it is assessed to be equivalent to the computer program. Furthermore, voice dialogues in accordance with branch information included in dialogue units are recognized by a series of processing steps performed by a voice interactive system composed of the server and clients' devices, which satisfies the creation of a technical idea.

Case 2-13 in Examination Handbook, Annex A

[Claim 1]

A data structure of dialogue scenarios utilized in a voice interactive system composed of a client's device and a server, comprising:

unit IDs that identify dialogue units constituting dialogue scenarios;

messages including contents of utterances and information presented to users;

a plurality of candidate answers in response to answers from users;

information on communication mode; and

a plurality of branch information mapped to each of the candidate answers and information on communication mode, wherein the branch information indicates the following dialogue unit which contains messages corresponding to the said candidate answers and whose data size is corresponding to the said information on communication mode;

wherein, the said data structure of dialogue scenarios is utilized for the following processing performed by the said client's device:

(1) outputting a message included in the current dialogue unit;
(2) acquiring an answer from the user in response to the said message;
(3) specifying the said candidate answer based on the answer from the said user;
(4) selecting one branch information based on the said candidate answer and information on communication mode; and
(5) receiving from the server a following dialogue unit indicated by the selected branch information.

Accordingly, inventions in Category 1 may generally be patent eligible provided they are claimed in a manner consistent with these examples and satisfy the other requirements for patentability.

[2] Categories 2 and 3 (Inventions of AI Implementations and New Applications of AI)

Category 2 AI-related inventions are directed to a particular implementation of Category 1 'core AI'. Category 3 AI-related inventions are directed to a particular implementation of AI, i.e., application to a particular use case. In both cases the same assessment of patent eligibility as described above with respect to Category 1 would be applied. It can be assumed that construction of a specific information processor or an operation method thereof depending on intended use through cooperation of the software and the hardware resources by a particular implementation (Category 2) or application to a particular use case (Category 3) will make the case for eligibility much stronger.

[3] Categories 4 and 5 (Inventions Made by or Using AI)

Category 4 and 5 AI-related inventions are situations where what is claimed was invented by a human using AI or, theoretically, by AI itself. Unless AI is being used to invent AI (which is possible), Category 4 and 5 claims would not relate to AI at all. The claims could be directed to a product or process in any field. Therefore, the normal patent eligibility standards would be applied, based on what is claimed, without regard for the manner in which the invention was made.

§11.04 INVENTIVE STEP

[A] General Rules and Guidelines on Inventive Step

The Patent Act provides inventive step as a statutory requirement as follows:

> A person may not obtain a patent if prior to the filing of the patent application, a person of ordinary skill in the art of the invention would have easily been able to make that invention based on an invention [in the prior art].[23]

The Guidelines characterize this requirement as follows:

> Article 29(2) provides that a patent shall not be granted for an invention (an invention lacking an inventive step) where a person ordinarily skilled in the art of the invention (hereinafter referred to as 'a person skilled in the art' in this Part) would have been easily able to make the invention based on the prior art.[24]

A 'person skilled in the art' is not defined in the Act but is explained in the Guidelines as follows:

> In this Part, 'a person skilled in the art' means a hypothetical person who meets all the following conditions (i) to (iv). In some cases, it is appropriate to consider a person skilled in the art to be a 'team of experts' in several technical fields rather than an individual person.
>
> (i) A person who has the common general knowledge ... in the technical field of the claimed invention at the time of filing.
>
> (ii) A person who is able to use ordinary technical means for research and development (including document analysis, experiment, technical analysis, manufacture, etc.).
>
> (iii) A person who is able to exercise ordinary creativity in selecting materials and modifying designs.

23. Patent Act, Art. 29(2).
24. Guidelines, Part III (1).

(iv) A person who is able to comprehend all the matter in the state of the art … in the technical field of the claimed invention at the time of filing, and comprehend all technical matters in the field relevant to problems to be solved by the invention.[25]

The general rule of inventive step based on the Guidelines is as follows:[26]

> The examiner selects the prior art most suitable for the reasoning (hereinafter referred to as 'the primary prior art' in this Chapter), and determines whether it is possible to reason that a person skilled in the art would easily arrive at the claimed invention from the primary prior art by following the steps (1) to (4) …:
>
> (1) The examiner determines whether or not the reasoning is possible based on the various factors in support of the non-existence of an inventive step … for the differences between the claimed invention and the primary prior art by adopting other pieces of prior art (hereinafter referred to as 'secondary prior art' in this Chapter) or considering the common general knowledge.
>
> (2) If the examiner determines that the reasoning is impossible based on the above step (1), the examiner determines that the claimed invention involves an inventive step.
>
> (3) If the examiner determines that the reasoning is possible based on the above step (1), the examiner determines whether the reasoning is possible by comprehensively assessing various factors which includes factors in support of the existence of an inventive step …
>
> (4) If the examiner determines that the reasoning is impossible based on the above step (3), the examiner determines that the claimed invention involves an inventive step. If the examiner determines that the reasoning is possible based on the above step (3), the examiner determines that the claimed invention does not involve an inventive step.

Figure 2. Main factors for reasoning

Factors in support of the non-existence of an inventive step	Factors in support of the existence of an inventive step
Motivation for applying secondary prior art to primary prior art. (1) Relation of technical fields. (2) Similarity of problems to be solved (3) Similarity of operations or functions. (4) Suggestions shown in the content of prior art Design, variation of primary prior art Mere aggregation of prior art	Advantageous effects Obstructive factors. Example: it is contrary to the purpose of the primary, prior art to apply the secondary prior art to the primary prior art

25. Guidelines, Part III, Chap. 2, Sec. 2(2).
26. *Ibid.*, Sec. 2(3).

The Handbook provides several guidelines pertinent to inventive step for AI-related inventions. For example, the inventive step determination should include consideration of general issues in the computer technology field, such as 'sophistication of a determination through AI':

> Issues involved in software or computerization are often general issues common to the computer technology field. For example, they include 'sophistication of a determination through AI or fuzzy logic,' 'facilitation of input through GUI' or the like. The examiner shall make a determination on inventive step based on these general issues that have been known in the field of computer technology.[27]

The Handbook also addresses application of CSIs to different technical fields:

> A procedure or means used in a software-related invention related to a specific field has often a common function or action irrespective of an applied field. As such, when the function or action is common, an attempt to apply a procedure or means of a software-related invention related to a specific field to another specific field falls under exhibition of normal creation capabilities of a person skilled in the art.
>
> Example 1:
>
> If a prior art of a 'file search system' is present, creating a 'medical information search system' by applying means (specific configuration for searching) whose function or action is common falls under exhibition of normal creation capabilities of a person skilled in the art.[28]

[B] Relation Between Subject Matter Eligibility and Inventive Step

In assessing inventive step, all the elements of a claimed invention are compared with the primary prior art, and every differentiating element derived by the comparison is evaluated in light of the secondary prior art or common general knowledge. Therefore, when AI-related inventions involve a business method, mathematical formula, or a mental step, and are eligible subject matter, all of the elements in the claimed AI-related invention are compared with the primary prior art, and the differentiating elements are evaluated even when such differences are intangible elements and not pure technical matters.

[C] Application to AI-Related Inventions

Based on the above criteria, each of the five categories of AI-related inventions will now be considered.

27. Handbook, Annex B, Chap. 1, Sec. 2.2.3.1(4).
28. *Ibid.*, Sec. 2.2.3.2(1).

[1] Category 1 (Inventions of AI)

This category relates to the invention of new algorithms or models for the AI itself, independent of the data to which it is applied and independent of any particular case. A skilled person for this type of invention would be a skilled person in the area of researching new algorithms or models.

Inventive step for claims to inventions falling in this category would be determined based on the prior art of algorithms or models for the AI at the time of the priority date of filing of the patent application. Therefore, if the claimed algorithms or models would not have been easily conceivable for the person skilled in the field from the prior art AI algorithms or models, the claims would satisfy the inventive step requirement.

[2] Category 2 (Inventions of AI Implementations)

As illustrated by Handbook, Annex B, Sections 2.2.3.1(4) (discussed above) and 2.2.3.2(2),[29] a mere AI implementation using known core AI is unlikely to satisfy inventive step because a skilled person in the art would be assumed to understand all the matters of the specific field and of the general field of AI. However, additional elements added to the AI implementation would increase the probability of passing inventive step, depending on the nature of the additional elements.

For example, if a particular arrangement of filters or a particular interface is new or, even if such filter or interface is known but some technical reasons exist to combine such known filter or interface with the AI to reach the claimed invention, the inventive step requirement may be satisfied. Here, descriptions in the prior art indicating difficulty or obstacles to, lack of motivation to, and/or teaching away from combining the prior art in the manner claimed would be crucial to overcome the inventive step issue.

Handbook Case 36 relates to a dementia stage estimation apparatus and the inventive step relating to AI technology is explained:[30]

> [Claim 1]
>
> A dementia stage estimation apparatus comprising:
>
> a speech information obtainment means for obtaining a speech information on a conversation between a questioner and a respondent;
>
> a speech information analysis means for analyzing the speech information, and then specifying a speech section by the questioner and a speech section by the respondent;
>
> a speech recognition means for converting, through speech recognition, the speech information on the speech section by the questioner and the speech section by the respondent into text and then outputting a character string;

29. 'Addition of what is usually used (well-known commonly used means) as a system component or replacement of a part of the system component by the publicly known equivalent means falls under exhibition of normal creation capabilities of a person skilled in the art.'
30. Handbook, Annex A, case 36.

> a question topic specification means for specifying a question topic by the questioner based on the result of the speech recognition; and
>
> a dementia stage determination means for inputting, to a trained neural network, the question topic by the questioner and the character string of the speech section by the respondent to the question topic in an associated manner with each other, and then determining a dementia stage of the respondent,
>
> wherein *the neural network is trained through machine learning using training data so as to output an estimated dementia stage, in response to an input of the character string of the speech section by the respondent in an associated manner with the question topic by the questioner.* (Emphasis added).

The AI aspect of the invention is set forth in the highlighted portion, namely, the neural network is trained, using training data, to output an estimated dementia stage in response to an input of the character string of the speech section by the respondent in an associated manner with the question topic by the questioner.

The example assumes that the cited prior art discloses a neural network which is configured to output a dementia stage, based on an input of a character string that has been converted into text through a speech recognition, without a classification between a speech section by a questioner and a speech section by a respondent.

Based on this assumption, Claim 1 is considered to have inventive step for the following reasons:

> A person skilled in the art would conceive a modification of a training data, which is an input to a neural network for machine learning, through a certain pre-processing in order to improve an accuracy of estimation by the neural network.
>
> However, there is no prior art found that discloses a specific technique related to dementia stage assessment, in which a speech information on a conversation between a questioner and a respondent is converted into text, a question topic by the questioner is specified in a character string in the text, the specified question topic and a response to the question by the respondent is associated with each other to assess a dementia stage. Further, it is not a common general technical knowledge at the time of filing. …
>
> Furthermore, the invention of Claim 1 brings about a significant effect, that is, a highly accurate dementia stage estimation by specifying a question topic by a questioner and a response by a respondent (corresponding character string) to the question topic in an associated manner with each other. It is because a neural network can effectively learn know-how of a well-trained doctor from a training data.[31]

Suppose a new service relating to AI is launched with the concept of applying a known AI system to an existing conventional system. If a patent is applied for in order to protect such system, it is likely to have no new or inventive points from an abstract perspective.

However, from a technical implementation and a patent view, an introduction of the known AI system to an existing conventional system is very likely to affect

31. *Ibid.*

other minor points in the existing conventional system, such as the treatment of data, processing of data, timing of processing, or storing data for future machine learning. Such minor, but important, changes in the existing conventional system may be used to argue inventive step to obtain a patent.

[3] Category 3 (New Application of AI)

Inventions relating to new applications of AI are evaluated under the general rules explained above, regardless of whether they are a 'decision maker' or 'decision aid'. As always, the question would be whether the new application would have been easily able to make the invention based on the prior art and common general knowledge.

The Handbook explains, for example, that a simple application of computer technology known in one field to another field would lack inventive step:

> [I]f the claimed invention simply applies a procedure, means, or the like of a computer technology applied in a specific field to another specific field, without demonstrating any other technical feature, and if the advantageous effect obtained through this application does not exceed what is predictable based on the state of the art at the time of filing, there is a factor in support of the non-existence of the inventive step.[32]

Case 34 from the Handbook, 'Estimation system of hydroelectric generating capacity',[33] provides an example of this:

> [Claim 1]
>
> An estimation system of a hydroelectric power generating capacity of a dam comprising:
>
> a neural network that is built by means of an information processor, the neural network having an input layer and an output layer, in which an input data to the input layer containing a precipitation amount of the upper stream of a river, a water flow rate of the upper stream of the river, and a water inflow rate into a dam during a predetermined period between a reference time and a predetermined time before the reference time, and an output data from the output layer containing a hydroelectric power generating capacity in the future after the reference time;
>
> a machine learning unit that trains the neural network using a training data corresponding to actual values of the input data and the output data; and
>
> an estimation unit that inputs the input data to the neural network that has been trained by the machine learning unit with setting a current time as the reference time, and then calculates an estimated value of a future hydroelectric power generating capacity based on the output data of which reference time is the current time.

32. *Ibid.*, Annex B, 2.2.3.3.
33. *Ibid.*, Annex A, Case 34.

> [Claim 2]
>
> The estimation system of a hydroelectric power generating capacity as in Claim 1, wherein the input data to the input layer further contains a temperature of the upper stream of the river during the predetermined period between the reference time and the predetermined time before the reference time.

In this case, the prior art discloses an estimation of a hydroelectric power generating capacity using a regression equation model. Also, it is found that '[i]n the technical field of machine learning, it is well-known that an estimation process of an output in the future is carried out based on an input of time series data in the past, by using a trained neural network which has been trained with training data containing an input of time series data in the past and a certain output in the future.'

Under such assumptions, Claim 1 is found to lack inventive step because a skilled person in the art could easily substitute a trained neural network instead of the regression equation model by applying the well-known art to the prior art.

Note the level of abstractness of the neural network in the well-known art. The neural network of the well-known art is not specific to the area of generating capacity, but just in the 'technical field of machine learning'. Currently, possible applications of AI are discussed in virtually every conceivable field. This would indicate that if the difference is only application of the known AI to some new application, it would fail the inventive step requirement.

On the other hand, the invention as recited in Claim 2 calculates an estimated value of a future hydroelectric power using a parameter of 'a temperature of the upper stream of the river', which Claim 1 does not have. Here, the prior art does not disclose 'a temperature of the upper stream of the river', the parameter has improved the accuracy of estimation, and it is evaluated to be not expected by a skilled person in the art based on the prior art. Thus, introduction of a new parameter not disclosed in the prior art would be one possible way to pass the inventive step.

[4] Categories 4 and 5 (Inventions Made by or Using AI)

For inventions of Categories 4 and 5, where the AI is involved in the process of inventing but not (necessarily) present in the claims, inventive step would be determined in accordance with general rule of inventive step based on a person of ordinary skill in the art to which the claims are directed.

At the outset, it is important to note that, according to the Guidelines, the person of ordinary skill in the art would be one or more humans, not an AI system. Also, if AI is known in the technical field such that the AI can try every possible option to determine an optimal solution, such known AI technology would affect the inventive step negatively since the person of ordinary skill in the art would easily been able to use such known AI to produce the claimed result. Accordingly, if the level of AI technology is sufficiently developed such that (1) the identification of the problem or need, (2) the selection of the AI technology to be used, and (3) the selection of proper training and input data can be easily performed, such level of technology would be used as prior art to assess the inventive step.

Therefore, as AI technology continues to develop and to be applied to more fields, it may become more difficult to pass the inventive step requirement since a skilled person would be able to use such AI technology.

§11.05 ADEQUACY OF DISCLOSURE

[A] General Rules for Disclosure Requirement

The Patent Act sets forth the following provisions[34] relating to adequacy of disclosure:

> Enablement Requirement:
>
> Article 36(4)
>
> The statement of the detailed explanation of the invention as provided in item (iii) of the preceding Paragraph shall comply with each of the following items:
>
> (i) in accordance with Ordinance of the Ministry of Economy, Trade and Industry, the statement shall be clear and sufficient as to enable any person ordinarily skilled in the art to which the invention pertains to work the invention
>
> Support Requirement:
>
> Article 36(6)
>
> The statement of the scope of claims as provided in paragraph (2) shall comply with each of the following items:
>
> (i) the invention for which a patent is sought is stated in the detailed explanation of the invention

The support requirement was clarified by a Grand Panel case[35] of Intellectual Property, which stated:

> Whether the statement of the scope of claims satisfies the Support Requirement of a Description should be determined by considering, through comparison of the statement of the scope of claims and the statement of the detailed explanation of the invention, whether the invention described in the scope of claims is the invention described in the detailed explanation of the invention that is within the scope for which a person ordinarily skilled in the art can recognize, based on the statement of the detailed explanation of the invention, that the invention can solve the problem to be solved by the invention, and also by considering whether the invention described in the scope of claims is an invention within the scope which a person ordinarily skilled in the art can recognize, in light of the common general technical knowledge as of the time of filing the application, that the invention can solve the problem to be solved by the invention, even without the statement and indication thereof.

Examples of AI-related inventions below provide some guidance for analysing the above criteria. When the invention involves a relationship of data, such as inventions including an input and output of AI, an explanation of such data relationship is

34. Patent Act, Art. 36.
35. 2005 (Gyo ke) 10042.

required to satisfy the enablement and support requirements to the extent that a skilled person in the art could understand the invention based on the specification and a common general technical knowledge.

Generally speaking, training data is used to take advantage of AI technology in a wide range of different fields. That training data may involve many different types of data and may vary widely from one field to the next. Describing the training data with adequate specificity may present a challenge for adequacy of disclosure. Generally, one of two conditions must be met: (1) it can be recognized that there is a certain relation (such as a correlation) between the multiple types of data based on the disclosure in the specification; or (2) it can be presumed that there is a certain relation (such as a correlation) between the multiple types of data based on common general technical knowledge.

Similarly, for inventions relating to products that include a function carried out by AI, in order to satisfy the description requirement either the patent specification must include an explanation of how the function carried out or a skilled person must be able to estimate a similar, substitute result.

[1] Categories 1, 2 and 3

The inventions in Categories 1, 2 and 3 include claims to the AI itself, to an implementation of AI, and/or to an application of AI. If the AI uses a certain correlation between data, such correlation must be specifically explained in the patent application. This may be information such as statistical data or experimental data, or may be common technical knowledge to the extent that a skilled person in the art would understand the correlation.

The Handbook provides a useful example, 'an estimation model that estimates a body weight of a person based on a feature value representing a face shape and a body height of the person',[36] including claims and a detailed explanation of the content and degree of the adequate disclosure in the specification.

> [Claim 1]
>
> A body weight estimation system comprising:
>
> a model generation means for generating an estimation model that estimates a body weight of a person based on a feature value representing a face shape and a body height of the person, through machine learning using training data containing feature values representing face images as well as actual measured values of body heights and body weights of people;
>
> a reception means for receiving an input of a face image and body height of a person;
>
> a feature value obtainment means for obtaining a feature value representing a face shape of the person through analysis of the face image of the person that has been received by the reception means; and
>
> a processing means for outputting an estimated value of a body weight of the person based on the feature value representing the face shape of the person

36. Handbook, Annex A, Case 49.

that has been received by the feature value obtainment means and the body height of the person that has been received by the reception means, using the generated estimation model by the model generation means.

[Claim 2]

The body weight estimation system as in Claim 1, wherein the feature value representing a face shape is a face-outline angle.

Figures

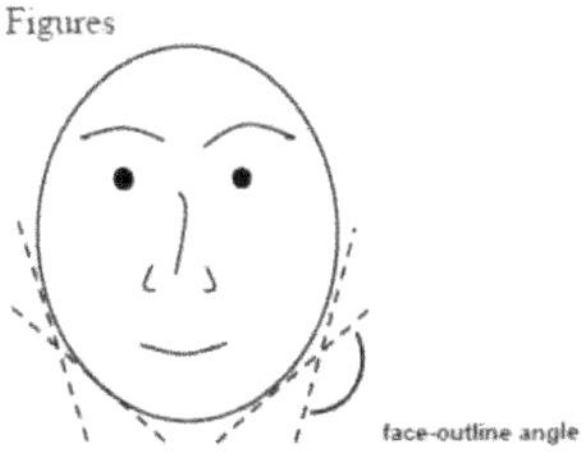

Fig. 1

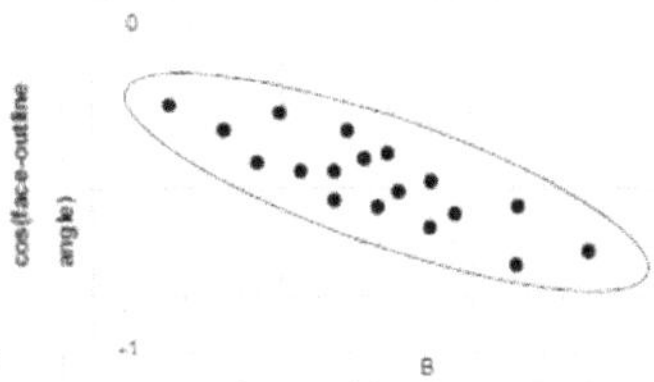

Fig. 2

Note:

In this case, it is assumed that, even in view of a common general technical knowledge at the time of filing, a person skilled in the art can presume a certain relation such as a correlation ... between (i) a body height, weight, and the like of a person and BMI based on these and (ii) a feature representing a face shape such as a face-outline angle was not a common general technical knowledge at the time of filing.

In the specification of this example, only a correlation between a feature value of a face-outline angle and BMI (defined as a body weight divided by the square of a body height) of a person is described as depicted in Fig. 2, in which the horizontal axis represents BMI and the vertical axis represents a cosine of a face-outline angle. Other than such a face-outline angle, the specification mentions that the correlation is not limited to the face-outline but '[a]ny feature value representing a face shape may be obtained from a face image and used'.

Considering this disclosure in the specification and the assumption of the common general knowledge, the Handbook concludes the disclosure requirement is satisfied for Claim 2, but not for Claim 1. Particularly, the Handbook reasons that a skilled person in the art, based on the specification and common general knowledge, would not have been able to understand a correlation between 1) a feature value *other* than a face-outline angle representing a face shape and 2) a body height, weight, and the like of a person and BMI based on these.

In this case, the actual data is explained in the style of graph. Therefore, if it is possible, the actual data should be explained in the patent application to support the claim. If the actual data is not possible to be described in the patent application, the next example will be helpful.

The next example, 'Method for estimating allergy incidence rate of test substance',[37] shows another way to satisfy the disclosure requirement where the result of the AI model performance is evaluated.

37. *Ibid.*, Case 50.

> [Claim 1]
>
> A method for estimating an allergy incidence rate of a test substance in a human being comprising:
>
> inputting a training data to an artificial intelligence model to train the model, the training data including a group of data representing a shape change of a human X cell in culture solution and a scoring data on incidence rates of human allergic reaction caused by each substance, in which each of the substances is separately added to the culture solution and the incidence rates of human allergic reaction caused by each of the substances are already known;
>
> obtaining a group of data representing a shape change of a human X cell that has been measured in culture solution to which a test substance is added;
>
> inputting, to the trained artificial intelligence model, the group of data representing a shape change of a human X cell that has been measured in the culture solution to which the test substance is added; and
>
> causing the trained artificial intelligence model to calculate a scoring data of an incidence rate of human allergic reaction.
>
> [Claim 2]
>
> The method for estimating an allergy incidence rate as in Claim 1, wherein the group of data representing a shape change of a human X cell is a combination of a shape change in an ellipticity, rugosity, and oblateness of the human X cell; and the allergic reaction is contact dermatitis.

In the Specification, experimental data is shown. An inventor performs an experiment to train an AI system by inputting data of a combination of a shape change in an ellipticity, rugosity, and oblateness of the human X cell and contact dermatitis as an allergic reaction, and the difference between the estimated score by the training model and the actual score is explained in the experiment result. On the other hand, the specification does not disclose other parameters to show a shape change except for such ellipticity, rugosity, and oblateness of the human X cell, or other allergic reaction other than the contact dermatitis, which leads Claim 1 to fail the disclosure requirement. Claim 2, which includes these limitations, is found to meet the disclosure requirement.

As described in the cases above, statistical data / experimental data or the substituted evaluation of the AI should be explained in the patent application. In the case where correlation between the data and evaluation of AI are absent, the Handbook describes one example of an AI invention where the description requirement is satisfied based on a common general technical knowledge.

In Case 47, 'Business plan design apparatus',[38] the invention estimates future sales quantity based on a web advertisement data and online 'mention data'. The claim recites, *inter alia*:

> an estimation model that has been trained through machine learning with a training data containing a web advertisement data and mention data of a similar product that has been sold in the past and a sales quantity of the similar product,

38. *Ibid.*, Case 47.

> simulating and outputting a future sales quantity of the specific product estimated based on the web advertisement data and mention data of the specific product.

In such a situation, even if the patent application does not disclose a specific correlation between the web advertisement data, the mention data and the sales data, the example explains that 'it can be presumed that there is a correlation ... between them in view of a common general technical knowledge at the time of filing' and the disclosure requirement of this claim is satisfied though the definition of data such as web advertisement data and mention data should preferably be explained.

Note that even though common technical knowledge can be useful to satisfy the disclosure requirement, such arguments may detrimentally affect the novelty or inventive step requirements. Accordingly, reliance on common technical knowledge for details of an AI application is generally not advisable.

[2] Categories 4 and 5

Inventions in Categories 4 and 5 are made by or using AI and thus the claims do not necessarily include the AI. To the extent the claims include AI, the disclosure requirements would be the same as described above.

On the other hand, when the AI is not claimed, the normal disclosure requirements attach to whatever is claimed and not to the AI that was used to assist with the inventive process. Indeed, there is no duty to disclose the manner by which an invention was made and thus, apart from the inventorship issue discussed below, there need be no mention of AI in the specification at all.

The Handbook provides an interesting example, 'Anaerobic adhesive composition',[39] of a product claim (with no mention of AI) where the specification indicates a neural network was used to estimate curing strength:

> [Claim 1]
>
> An anaerobic adhesive composition comprising:
>
> a 0.08 - 3.2 mass % compound A,
>
> a 0.001 - 1 mass % compound B, and
>
> a residue containing an anaerobically curable (meth)acrylate monomer,
>
> wherein the anaerobic adhesive composition shows the curing strength equal to or exceeding 30 % of the curing strength after 24 hours have passed, within 5 minutes from the start of curing.

It is explained that Claim 1 does not satisfy the enablement and support requirements because: 1) the patent application neither shows that the claimed composition in fact has the effect as provided in the claim nor shows that the accuracy of the estimation by the trained model was verified; and 2) there was no common technical knowledge that an estimation result by a trained model can be a substitution for an actual experimental result.

Thus, in cases of inventions in Categories 4 and 5, the above criteria should be satisfied. Please note that in the future, if such assessment could be also automatically

39. *Ibid.*, Case 51.

performed by AI, then the criteria of enablement and support requirements could be more easily passed.

§11.06 INVENTORSHIP

[A] Inventorship in General

Recent decisions in Japanese courts, based on the statutory definition of invention and on a Supreme Court decision,[40] have defined an inventor as 'a person who actually involves a creation of technical idea of an invention, namely, a person who involves a creative activity to constitute a feature portion of the invention concretely and objectively to the extent that a skilled person in the art exercises implement'.[41] Similarly, the courts have defined a co-inventor as a person who 'substantially contributes under an united and successive cooperative relationship with other co-inventors through a creative activity to constitute a feature portion of the invention concretely and objectively to the extent that a skilled person in the art exercises implement'.[42]

On the other hand, a manager who manages a subordinate researcher, a general adviser or an assistant who takes data or who performs experiments under the instruction of a researcher, or a person who supports the completion of an invention by providing funding or a research environment for an inventor, is not an inventor,[43] because they do not contribute to the creative activity.

In Japan, an inventive contribution is determined for each claim. For example, in one dispute over inventorship, the plaintiff was held to be the inventor of Claims 1 and 3, while the defendant was held to be the inventor of Claim 2.[44]

[B] Determination of Inventorship for AI-Related Inventions

[1] Categories 1 and 2

A person who develops the idea of a new algorithm or model for the AI itself, or who has an idea regarding the additional element for an implementation of known AI, is an inventor.

[2] Categories 3 and 4

The same criteria for inventorship shall also be applied to AI-related inventions in Categories 3 and 4, namely, those who made the actual contribution, as explained above.

---

40. 1976 10 13.
41. 2014 (Gyo ke) 10275, and a similar decision in 2013 (Ne) 10100.
42. 2013 (Ne) 10100.
43. 2007 (Ne) 10037.
44. 2015 (Gyo ke) 10230.

Thus, in the case of a new application of AI or use of AI to produce a new invention, the following people would be considered as inventors:

(1) a person who has the idea of using the AI for this intended purpose, because to identify some intended purpose is considered to be a part of a contribution to the invention;
(2) a person who selects an AI technology and configures it to suit the intended purpose, because the selection and configuration are considered to be a part of a contribution to the invention;
(3) a person who selects the data to be used to train the AI because the selection of the data to be used to train is also considered a contribution, assuming the selected data type is a part of an element of claim;
(4) a person who selects the input data fed to the trained AI system, because the input data fed to the trained AI system is equivalent to the above (3); and
(5) a person who recognizes the value of and selects one optimal solution from a large number of potential solutions produced by the AI, because it is likely to be viewed as actual involvement in the completion of invention. (Please note that Japanese patent law admits invention by selection.)

[3] Category 5

Category 5 AI-related inventions are inventions 'invented' by AI, without a human innovator.

The Patent Act does not clearly state whether inventors are limited to human inventors or include AI. In this regard, Japanese Patent Office has announced that it will consider the inventors of patentable inventions to be limited to human inventors and thus patent applications describing that AI is the inventor should be rejected based on the interpretation of Patent Act Article 36(1) and other relevant Articles.

Accordingly, under Japanese current practice, patent applications describing AI as the inventor would be rejected.

§11.07 AREAS FOR FURTHER DEVELOPMENT

The Guidelines and the Handbook as well as recently provided examples have provided sufficient guidance for each of the requirements, which is very helpful in preparing patent applications and responses to Office Actions for AI-related inventions.

As described mainly in the disclosure requirements section, the current examples focus on the correlation between data as a type of machine learning and other types of machine learning are not explained. Therefore, further development of examination examples for other types of machine learning would be useful.

§11.08 RECOMMENDATIONS FOR PATENT APPLICANTS

AI-related inventions involve many areas including business, finance, mental activity, or games and all of these kinds of areas would potentially be patentable in Japan. Further, such patents are likely to be practically enforceable in Japan.

For example, the Intellectual Property High Court ('IPHC') in Japan sustained[45] an injunctive remedial decision of patent infringement found by Tokyo District Court regarding a patent that involved equipment for managing the transaction of a financial product. The patent-in-suit involved a system to enhance the usability of the financial product transaction and included a certain level of concept of a business method.

The satisfaction of such subject matter eligibility is sufficiently possible by delicately realizing the cooperation of software and hardware resources to some degree as well as maintaining the scope of the patent to be practically enforceable, particularly when a technical idea is incorporated with that invention. Therefore, without limitation to the field of the invention, any and all kinds of inventions can be included in Japanese patent applications.

Further, the Patent Act recognizes computer programs and learning models as categories of inventions. Thus AI-related inventions may be claimed in many different styles including computer programs, learning models, computer systems, information processing devices, methods, and data structures. These styles should be adequately described in the specification to be prepared for the incorporation into claims by amendment or future divisional applications.

§11.09 CONCLUSION

From the perspective of protection of AI technologies, as explained above, the Patent Act, the Guidelines and the Handbook from the JPO have provided user-friendly guidance and provided a variety of examples to assist patent applicants with patent prosecution. This includes adaptations for any kind of AI-related inventions, such as computer program claims, learning model claims, and data structure claims, which are suitable categories to protect AI-related inventions.

From the perspective of enforcement of patents, injunctive relief can be obtained in Japanese courts if injunctive relief is sought and patent infringement is found, without needing to satisfy additional requirements such as irreparable injury. For example, the IPHC found patent infringement and admitted an injunctive relief based on a patent related to the invention of financial instruments and exchange apparatus.[46]

Further, the Japanese Patent Act has promoted and realized a pro-patent policy. For example, from May 2020, the amendment of Patent Act introduced an inspection system to support an evidence collection system, which aimed to support software patents including AI-related patents. In the inspection system, a fair and neutral expert appointed by a court is provided with the authority to collect evidence related to patent infringement. This authority includes requests of inquiries, production of documents, operations of equipment, measurements and experiments against alleged infringers to understand and analyse the operation of the software because the mere production of the source code related with the software patent would not be sufficient to analyse the function or operation of the source code without the help of the programmer or operator.

45. 2018 (Ne) 10085.
46. *Ibid.*

Under such pro-patent policy, AI-related patents in Japan are expected to increase in value in the Japanese market, with more and more developments of AI technologies.

Chapter 12

Mexico

Héctor E. Chagoya-Cortes

§12.01 PATENTABILITY OF SOFTWARE AND COMPUTER-IMPLEMENTED INVENTIONS

The Mexican Industrial Property Law ('IPL')[1] was enacted in 1991 and has been modified several times, including an extensive modification in 1994. However, it was not changed substantively until 1 July 2020, when a new Federal Law for the Protection of Industrial Property ('FLPIP')[2] was published. The FLPIP entered into force on 5 November 2020. At the time of writing this chapter, examination of applications under the new FLPIP is still scarce. Therefore, most of the changes in the new FLPIP have been considered in this chapter based on an interpretation of the new statutory provisions. However, the actual interpretation of the law and any changes in the Mexican practice for computer-implemented inventions will take place in the months and years to follow.

Most of the provisions in both laws are equivalent in the field of computer-implemented inventions ('CIIs'). However, because some sections were changed, all articles were renumbered. Therefore, throughout this chapter reference is made to both laws using as main reference the new FLPIP. The former law is referenced using parentheses. The exception will be when both laws are discussed because there are significant differences between them.

It is also important to consider that the two laws will coexist for a while because, to avoid retroactive application of the law, the FLPIP expressly states in its transitional articles that patent applications filed before the date of entry into

1. *Ley de la Propiedad Industrial*. Diario Oficial de la Federación. Mexico, 27 Jun. 1991 (latest reform of 18 May 2018).
2. *Ley Federal de Protección a la Propiedad Industrial*. Diario Oficial de la Federación. Mexico, 1 Jul. 2020.

force will be prosecuted under the IPL. This means that the new criteria are only developing and might not mature into more robust rules for some years to come.

[A] A Unique Definition of Invention

Mexican law is unique in that, unlike many national or regional laws, it includes a specific definition of 'invention' for the purposes of the law in Article 46 of the FLPIP (formerly Article 15, IPL), as follows:

> Article 46. – Any human creation that allows the transformation of matter or energy that exists in nature, for use by mankind and to meet its specific needs, is considered an invention.

This definition is the most important guideline for CIIs in Mexico. It comprises three requirements that must be very clear in a patent application in order for a claim to be considered patentable subject matter. These requirements are, therefore, also crucial to artificial intelligence ('AI') inventions:

- it has to be a human creation;
- it has to allow transforming matter or energy existing in nature; and
- a specific need of mankind has to be met or satisfied.

For CIIs the first requirement was not typically an issue until the emergence and growth of AI, which will be discussed *infra*.

Regarding the matter and energy transformation requirement, computer signals are considered a transformation of energy. Hardware configuration and selection have also been considered in practice to be compliant with this requirement. Further, it is important to note that while the creation must *allow* transformation of matter or energy, this does not mean that the invention itself must transform matter or energy. Unfortunately, this is just a practice as there are no court decisions supporting such interpretation. However, the practice is very stable in this regard and the transforming of matter or energy is in general not used as an eligibility argument by Mexican examiners.

As for the third requirement, it is extremely important to identify in a patent application a need of mankind that is actually solved, not only the technical implications of the solution to such need. For example, if there is an algorithm that is implemented in a computer system, it is extremely important to identify something happening beyond the system that will benefit some aspect of human needs, such as a health matter, the ability to access resources, save energy, an impact on food, or controlling something in the tangible world. If the invention is described only as a set of steps that are implemented in a computer with no consequence in the real world, very likely there will be eligibility objections, based mainly on non-eligible subject matter as explained in the next section.

[B] Ineligible Subject Matter

Article 47 of the FLPIP (formerly Article 19 of the IPL) describes a list of subject matter that is not considered an invention and, therefore, is not patent eligible:

Article 47. - The following shall not be considered inventions, in particular:

I. - Discoveries, scientific theories or their principles;

II. - Mathematical methods;

III. - Literary, artistic works or any other aesthetic creation;

IV. - Schemes, plans, rules and methods for the exercise of intellectual activities, for games or for economic-commercial activities or for conducting business;

V. - Computer programs;

VI. - Ways of presenting information;

VII. - Biological and genetic material, as found in nature, and

VIII. - The juxtaposition of known inventions or combination of known products, except in the case of their combination or fusion that cannot function separately or that their characteristic qualities or functions are modified to obtain an industrial result or a non-obvious use for a technician in the field.

The subject matter provided for in Sections I to VIII above shall not be considered as an invention whenever the application exclusively claims it as such or in itself.

The changes in the FLPIP with respect to the IPL include certain drafting changes that at first sight might seem to be clarifications to the current practice. However, any actual impact on the criteria for patentability for patents filed on or after November 5, 2020, will depend on how this language is interpreted by examiners, and possibly courts, in the months and years to follow.

In order to understand if a CII is eligible, it is important first to understand:

- the category of the claims, particularly if the invention can be considered a scheme, plan, rule, method or computer program; and
- the purpose for which it was created, namely, the field of the invention.

The specific exceptions from IPL Article 19 were generally maintained in FLPIP Article 47 and will be analysed below. However, before analysing the specific cases, it is important to link the statutory provisions of ineligible matter to the general definition of invention in Mexican law. Because of that, when analysing a description to determine whether it is an invention under the IPL, the field of the invention must first be determined and then the nature thereof considered. If it is found from the field analysis that the patent is directed to matters relating exclusively to the mind or understanding, to entertainment, to the conduct of commercial transactions that report a profit or loss, or to the relationship between abstract entities, the study of the nature of the invention would otherwise not apply the relevant exceptions of Article 47 of the FLPIP (Article 19 IPL).

As an example, it can be easily understood that a mathematical formula *per se*, with abstract variables (x,y,z), or the rules of a game, in principle do not *allow* transformation of matter or energy even though they might address a need (such as entertainment). A method for helping a person to develop fast reading, i.e., a method of performing a mental act, also does not allow transformation of matter or energy. However, a process, product or device that operates using a mathematical formula that allows such process, product or device to transform matter or energy for use by mankind should be considered an invention under the FLPIP (or the IPL). A device to perform a trick that transforms matter or energy to amuse an audience, or a method that allows commercial or financial operations to be carried out by using less energy or fewer human resources, are examples of this. In other words, although the category may be similar to that of ineligible matter that cannot be considered an invention, a specific application solving a need of mankind may be considered an invention.

[1] Intellectual Activities

Article 19 of the IPL specified as ineligible any scheme, plan, rule, method 'to perform mental acts', a term which was changed to 'to exercise intellectual activities' in Article 47 of the FLPIP. A mental act, in the Spanish definition, would be considered any action relative to the mind or understanding. An action relative to mind or understanding is inherently human. In other words, it is understood that only a human being can perform mental acts and, therefore, whenever the invention has effect only on a person, it can be considered a mental act. Therefore, if the effect of the invention is on a human (e.g., hypnosis or fast reading) it likely would be considered ineligible. Conversely, an invention that has effects on computer systems or tangible objects, and not on humans, cannot be considered an intellectual activity (or mental act), and therefore may not fall into this exception to patentability. The change to 'exercise intellectual activities' does not seem to change this fundamental analysis, because in Spanish 'intellectual' refers to the concept of 'understanding', which in turn relates to 'human reason'.

[2] Games

In the field of CIIs this may be perhaps the most difficult area because of the importance of games in the software industry. Under the Spanish definition of 'game', any scheme, plan, rule, method 'to perform games' is not eligible for patent protection. However, all hardware or tangible elements of games potentially may be protected, having in mind the general rule that when the method has effects only on a person it will not be eligible.

[3] Business Methods

For technologies related to the financial world (fintech) this exception to patentability is one of the most relevant. A 'business' under the Spanish definition is something related to performing a commercial transaction that reports a profit or a loss. Article 19 of the IPL made reference to ineligible schemes, plans, rules and methods 'to perform business', but the new Article 47 of the FLPIP broadens the exception to 'economic-commercial activities'. The interpretation of this term is one of the biggest uncertainties currently in Mexican IP law, particularly given the importance of fintech. The term 'economic' in Spanish refers to management of goods, while 'commercial' refers to the exchange of goods and services.

With the new changes, terms such as 'transaction', when used with reference to goods, services or money, will be very likely objected to, particularly when described as an essential feature of the invention and used in a claim. Nevertheless, it is important to consider that the exception is related only to schemes, plans, rules and methods to perform such businesses or economic-commercial activities. As a consequence, there is a need to have two parties and an exchange of money or goods/services, which is not necessarily the case of all fintech methods. Furthermore, a method of inventory control, package tracking, process optimization, or the like, involving only one entity, under these concepts, would not have the objective of conducting business, and would allow transformation of matter or energy more efficiently for use by humans.

Under the limited restriction to 'business methods' of Article 19 of the IPL, there are situations where it would not be clear whether this exclusion of patentability is met or not, such as when the objective is not to conduct business but to manage it. For example, a collection tracking method is not intended to get business done between two parties because, by the time the method is applied, the business has already been done. Rather, this method would aim to let only one of the parties know how many transactions were done, how much was received, and when it was paid. However, in such cases the line is very subtle, as it could also be said that the business does not end until the goods or money transfers are finished and that, therefore, the monitoring of collection is part of the process of the business. However, the language of new Article 47, which adds the concept of 'economic-commercial,' would seem to be broader than the prior 'business methods' and thus it is expected that the Mexican Institute of Industrial Property ('IMPI') will start rejecting this type of subject matter when applying the new law as cases are examined.

[4] Mathematical Methods

According to its Spanish definition, if the field is related to obtaining a result through deductive reasoning and the use of the properties of abstract entities, numbers, geometric figures, etc., and their relationships, then the subject matter might be considered to be mathematical. Evidently, the keyword here is 'abstract', as opposed to 'tangible' in the sense of the definition of invention of Mexican law (see above).

Additionally, it is necessary to consider that 'software' is a broader term than 'computer program', which is nothing more than a set of relationships between abstract entities that have a certain purpose. That purpose is achieved through comparisons (set theory), arithmetic operations, variable definitions, etc., all of which fall within the mathematical field. Therefore, if a claim only describes how to relate to such abstract entities, its nature may be defined as mathematical.

For CIIs this may be the hardest objection to overcome. Therefore, the human need that is solved through the computer-implemented method becomes very relevant because it has the possibility to transform the method into something with a concrete tangible effect as opposed to being purely abstract. Similarly, a claim directed only to a mathematical formula *as such* could be regarded as a way of relating abstract entities, since the relationship itself does not allow transformation of matter or energy. However, anything that can transform matter or energy in the tangible world (as opposed to being kept as an abstraction) and that, for such purpose, uses (is characterized by) a mathematical formula or a mathematical model, should be considered as an invention. This is because the formula or mathematical model is precisely what allows such transformation to occur.

[5] *Computer Programs*

Another area of ineligible subject matter under Article 47 of the FLPIP (Article 19, IPL) is computer programs. This is under the basic rationale that they are eligible for copyright protection. However, it is important to note that the more general notion of 'software' is not mentioned in the law; only the reference to the more limited concept of computer program, which implies computer code. In this respect, under the interpretation of Article 19 of the IPL that is typically applied by the IMPI, when a computer program is part of the claims, the claim is typically rejected as ineligible matter. However, many patents are granted to what could be considered 'software' when the computer program is not expressly mentioned. This narrow interpretation of the term computer program is expected to prevail under the new FLPIP.

[6] *Technical Problem and Technical Features as a Requirement*

One of the notable changes in the FLPIP with respect to the IPL is the concept of 'essential technical feature' in Section VI of Article 45 of the FLPIP:

> VI. – Essential technical features are those necessary for the invention to solve the technical problem.

In addition, new Article 94, Section V of the FLPIP states that the patent application must include:

> V. – One or more claims that must be clear and concise, define the subject matter for which protection is sought based on its essential technical features, and have support in the description, so that they may not exceed the content of the same;

The IPL did not include a definition of essential technical feature although, in practice, most examiners issued objections based on the lack of technical character or technical effect of the claimed invention, particularly for CIIs, without a clear legal basis, influenced by the European practice. The new FLPIP does provide a definition, discussed in more detail below, based on a 'technical problem'. In any event, under a strict interpretation of the matter and energy transformation concept, the requirement that claims should be based on essential technical features that solve a technical problem should not represent a major change in practice.

[7] *Matter Ineligible Only If Claimed 'as Such'*

Another interesting addition in the FLPIP is the final paragraph in Article 47 that reads:

> The subject matter provided for in sections I to VIII above shall not be considered as an invention whenever the application exclusively claims it as such or in itself.

A possible interpretation *a contrario sensu* (in the opposite sense) is that whenever the application claims the ineligible matter in combination with or as part of a different invention, such an invention would be eligible. The final interpretation of this new language will be known only once the law has been applied to a number of concrete cases in the future. But, in the meantime, it seems proper to interpret this provision the same way that its equivalent provision from the European Patent Convention is interpreted.

There is not an equivalent provision in Article 19 of the IPL and therefore this is another of the key new elements of the FLPIP that will need interpretation in practice in the years to come. In any case, if the ineligible matter is claimed as part of an invention that *does* transform matter and energy, such as a system, apparatus, machine or set of machines, *even if* the operation depends on a scheme, rule plan or method or has a purpose to implement a scheme, plan, rule or method, such an invention has been and should continue to be considered a patent-eligible invention, despite being characterized by something that according to the law is not invention. The protection afforded by such a patent would be on the system, apparatus, machine or set of machines rather than on the scheme, plan, rule or method itself.

When it comes to machinery, equipment or process control systems, the practice is the same. There are countless patents claiming electronic systems characterized by a CPU or simply processing means that include a computer program that performs certain functions. That is, the computer program is considered a technical characteristic, although by itself it cannot be considered as an invention. In this case, the difference between different control systems is precisely the functions performed by the program, and therefore it is this program that allows the system to perform a different transformation of matter or energy relative to the prior art, thus giving it the technical character.

§12.02 SPECIAL PROVISIONS RELATING TO PATENTABILITY OF INVENTIONS RELATING TO AI

Patent rights exist in Mexico under the assumption that intellectual creations can only happen as a result of the creative effort of a human being and are granted as a fundamental right in the Mexican Constitution. Artificial intelligence is putting pressure to this paradigm.

A completely new object can be designed through an AI system, based on prior design data, to comply with certain technical features or specifications. The new design may be automatically printed in a 3D printer and converted into a tangible thing without the intervention of a human being. Nevertheless, either at the data collection, the learning process or the programming of the algorithm there is still a lot of intervention by human beings and, therefore, the time when something is made totally without intervention by a human being whatsoever seems still far away.

This is perhaps why the new FLPIP did not include any new provisions dealing specifically with artificial intelligence. Under the FLPIP, AI-related inventions are examined and treated like any other invention in accordance with the definition of 'invention' under Mexican law.

As previously explained, the first element of the definition of an invention under Article 46 of the FLPIP (formerly Article 15, IPL) is that it must be a *human creation*. Accordingly, if in the context of a description of the invention it turns out that the invention was made merely through the use of artificial intelligence, without intervention of a person, this would definitely mean that the resulting output is not a human creation, and therefore it would not be patent eligible under the current law.

For all other AI-related inventions, the general rules for computer-implemented inventions are applied in Mexico.

§12.03 SUBJECT MATTER PATENTABILITY

[A] Category 1: Invention of AI

It is important to consider that, under Mexican law, an invention has to solve a human need and have the potential to transform matter or energy. A new AI system that is characterized solely by its algorithm will likely face objections related to its nature and be considered a mere mathematical method. However, systems must be analysed case-by-case in order to understand if the definition of invention under Mexican law is complied with or not. If the system makes it apparent that a contribution to any aspect of artificial intelligence systems (such as a new structure of a neural network, learning algorithm or data manager) can have a tangible effect in the systems to which it is applied, it might be eligible subject matter. The drafting of the claims for such purposes is very important. It is a fact that the ineligible categories by statute relate mainly to methods and not systems, which themselves are considered tangible. Therefore, if the claims and the description are made using different elements of a system in tangible terms, it is possible under Mexican law to obtain patents.

An example of a granted patent under Mexican law of this kind is Mexican Patent No. 233907 'Dynamic Synapses for Signal Processing in Neural Networks',[3] which is claimed as a system in terms of its processing elements, the communication between such elements, and particular signal processing, without limitation to a specific application or use of the system.

Another example is Mexican Patent No. 357374 'Neural Network and Neural Network Training Method'.[4] Interestingly, the claims in this patent refer specifically to a 'neural network' that is defined in terms of inputs and outputs and the relationships through synapses and information distribution through the network, not as a system. Considering that the independent claim is not directed to a method, this example shows that by correctly defining the category of the claim in the preamble it is possible to obtain protection if all the elements of the network are clearly defined and functionally related.

In practice, some examiners might object to system claims by focusing on the fact that computers or other standard elements are used in the claimed systems. However, the applicant must make it clear that the invention is made of a set of features that cannot be analysed in isolation. The new paragraph of Article 47 of the FLPIP, which did not exist under the IPL, can be useful in order to overcome such kinds of objections by pointing out that the invention must be analysed as a whole.

3. Liaw, Jim-Shih, et al. 'Sinapsis dinamica para procesamiento de señales en redes neuronales', *Gaceta Oficial Patentes, Registros de Modelos de Utilidad y de Diseños Industriales*, Instituto Mexicano de la Propiedad Industrial. Jan. 2006.
4. Marc' Aurelio Ranzato et al., 'Sistemas y métodos para la representación facial', *Gaceta Oficial Patentes, Registros de Modelos de Utilidad y de Diseños Industriales*, Instituto Mexicano de la Propiedad Industrial. Feb. 2019.

[B] Category 2: Invention of an AI Implementation

If we consider now the use of AI technology in conjunction with other elements that will make it function differently or with a specific function, the criteria are the same as for Category 1 discussed above. Namely, under Mexican law, the claims must be directed to the system or another eligible category and particularly to the elements that are used in conjunction with the AI.

For example, Mexican Patent No. 362983 'Systems and Methods for Facial Representation' claims how to build a deep neural network based on 2D images in order to obtain a 3D facial image. This is done through the use of a characteristic vector with the identity of the facial 2D images. The claims are directed to a system defined in terms of its elements, inputs, processing and outputs and not to the vector itself.

Another example is the configuration of a trained neural network that, given certain parameters in the production of certain resources (such as gold, petroleum or the like), the network is able to predict future production intervals, as claimed in Mexican Patent No. 359360. This is another example where claims are directed to the network itself.

[C] Category 3: A New Application of AI

The broad applicability of AI systems across industries makes such new applications easier to justify in terms of eligibility under Mexican law, as it is easier to demonstrate the tangible effects of the results. Method, apparatus or product claims are possible for these applications depending on their nature, from the automotive industry to health care.

For instance, Mexican Patent No. 366201[5] claims a method for processing signals in a flame detector in a boiler that includes a step of using an artificial intelligence system for processing one of the claimed features. The claimed method is directed to the acquisition of the flame data but is a good example of how AI systems can be incorporated into the claims as an actual technical feature of invention.

Another example that shows how AI systems can be claimed as an element embodied in an apparatus is Mexican Patent No. 240954.[6] In this patent, a device is claimed for monitoring the colour of fluids in real time. One of the 'modules' of the claim includes the use of an AI system, showing that an AI system can be a claimed feature of an application-specific device. Furthermore, the patent includes claims directed to an AI module that uses colour values as learning data and colour formulae as outputs.

5. Antonio Trejo-Morales et al., 'Método para el procesamiento combinado de señales de un detector de flama', *Gaceta Oficial Patentes, Registros de Modelos de Utilidad y de Diseños Industriales*, Instituto Mexicano de la Propiedad Industrial. Jul., 2019.
6. Craig McClanahan, 'Sistema y método para organizar valores de color, usando un modelo de grupo basado en una inteligencia artificial', *Gaceta Oficial Patentes, Registros de Modelos de Utilidad y de Diseños Industriales*, Instituto Mexicano de la Propiedad Industrial. Oct., 2006.

Additional examples include methods that are implemented in machinery, as it is the case of Mexican Patent No. 240561.[7] This patent claims a procedure for optimizing the width of a band that is passed through a lamination train, where the width is adjusted by an artificial intelligence system while the machine is in operation.

As for health care applications, a good example is Mexican Patent No. 370077 'Automated Processing and Interpretation of Mastographic Images for the Assignment of the Level on the Birads Scale'[8]. The claims of this patent are directed to a method that includes processing by an AI system with a multilayer perceptron trained through back-propagation based on the Birads scale. In this case, the claims are drafted as a method with steps that include the use of AI.

[D] Category 4: Inventions Made Using AI

In practice, it is very difficult to establish if there are patent applications or granted patents in Mexico that somehow result from the use of AI because the claimed output of the AI system is not necessarily traceable to the use of AI. The reason is that, typically, the invention would be a result that is not linked to the AI system used in its design. In fact, the claimed invention may be (and should be) completely described in terms of how it is constructed, its advantages and the problems solved by the claimed invention. In other words, the duty to describe the claimed invention attaches to what is claimed, not the manner by which the invention was made. AI might be used as a tool by a human inventor as an aid to invent new devices or processes in any imaginable field. The important point for AI-related inventions in this category is to understand that what is claimed is the result of that use, not the use of AI to make the invention (a claim to the use of AI for a particular purpose would fall into Category 3, discussed *supra*). A human inventor might use AI as a tool to invent a mechanical device, which would clearly be eligible subject matter. A human inventor might also use AI as a tool to invent an abstract concept or process, which would not be eligible subject matter. Thus, the determination of subject matter eligibility for inventions in Category 4 will be dependent entirely on what is claimed, applying the definition of 'invention' under Mexican law as explained *supra*.

[E] Category 5: Inventions Made by AI

Assuming for the sake of the argument that inventions made by AI exist, and setting aside for the moment the inventorship issues this would raise (discussed *infra*), the analysis of subject matter eligibility for inventions in Category 5 would be exactly

---

7. Einar Broese et al., 'Procedimiento para optimizar la distribución de ancho de banda en los extremos de una banda que pasa por un tren de laminación', *Gaceta Oficial Patentes, Registros de Modelos de Utilidad y de Diseños Industriales*, Instituto Mexicano de la Propiedad Industrial. Sep., 2006.
8. Eduardo Gasca-Alvarez et al., 'Procesamiento e interpretación automatizado de imágenes mastográficas para la asignación del nivel en la escala de Birads', *Gaceta Oficial Patentes, Registros de Modelos de Utilidad y de Diseños Industriales*, Instituto Mexicano de la Propiedad Industrial. Nov., 2019.

the same as that of Category 4. This is because, in Category 5, like in Category 4, what is being claimed is the output from the AI, not the AI (or use thereof) itself.

For instance, consider an AI system that is trained using clinical data of patients, including their genomes, and also with a variety of treatments and corresponding outcomes. Based on this learning, the system identifies a certain compound that is effective to treat a certain disease for people expressing a certain gene. In this hypothetical example, the identification was made by the system, but the determination of whether such treatment will work is not dependent on the AI system (even though it was programmed for that purpose). We could say that the fundamental hypothesis was proposed by the AI system, but certainly a patent covering the use of the compound to treat a disease in patients having that certain genetic information would not be credited to the AI system because, at a minimum, a human would have to recognize and verify the proposal with experimental evidence for a patent to be filed and granted.

One can imagine many examples of these types of scenarios, but the fundamental rationale is that an invention will not be reduced to practice or become tangible or real unless there is a human intervention that makes it real, based on an abstract proposition of an AI system. Therefore, it is very likely we would never know upon such reduction to practice whether the invention was made by a human or by the AI system that proposed it. Therefore, patentability of these types of inventions should not be determined on the basis of the use of the AI but on rather on the nature of the invention that is obtained using AI as a tool.

For these inventions there is also a rationale related to the sufficiency of the description that is addressed in the sections below.

§12.04 INVENTIVE STEP

The definition of inventive step under Mexican law is expressly stated in Article 45 Section III of the FLPIP (Article 12 Sec. III, IPL) as 'the creative process which results are not obviously or evidently deduced from the prior art for those skilled in the art'.

The new definition of inventive step under Mexican law incorporated the concept of obviousness, which was not included in the definition of the IPL, but it does not change the fundamental issue that something inventive must not be the result of a deductive process by those skilled in the art.

At a first impression, it might seem that anything obtained through an AI system can be considered a deduction. AI systems work based on learning algorithms that get inputs related to outputs, which are afterwards used to obtained proposed outputs based on new inputs. It could be said that AI systems deduce outputs based on certain inputs. However, in practice this issue is more nuanced.

Unfortunately, Mexican law does not define the concept of 'skilled in the art' and there are no court decisions that formally establish an interpretation of this term. However, there is an isolated decision by one court[9] – a decision that does not

9. 9th Era, Decision Reg. 163706, Circuit Courts, Isolated Thesis I. 4o. A. 727 A, *Inventive step. Its notion for the purposes of patent applications for inventions filed before the Mexican Institute of Industrial Property*; Idea AG, Proponent Judge: Jesus Antonio Nazar Sevilla, Oct. 2010.

have mandatory legal effect for other courts under Mexican law[10] – that relates the concept of inventive step expressly to prior art by emphasizing that the notion that inventive step must be evaluated in the context of the prior art:

> A patent application filed before the Mexican Institute of Industrial Property, is the result of inventiveness, understood as that arising from a creative process that results in a technique, that is, a set of successive practices that give rise to something new, called invention, the results of which are not deduced from a set of knowledge made public by oral or written description, by exploitation or any means of dissemination or information in Mexico or abroad and which is not of obvious knowledge to a technician in this field.

The only other relevant precedent ('*Coflex*'),[11] which also is not mandatory law under Mexican rules, is a ruling that proposes a standard of 'reasonable doubt' in favour of the patent applicant in the evaluation of obviousness:

> if the comparison between the elements of the patent at issue and the evidence provided at administrative authority cannot be clearly noted, as a requirement to declare their nullity, that it is only the juxtaposition of inventions or mixture of known products, their variation in form, size or materials in order to obtain an industrial result not obvious to a technician in this field, it follows that it is necessary to operate the aforementioned 'reasonable doubt', since it is not possible to distinguish with certainty whether the invention analysed does not imply an inventive activity, especially where it is for that authority, where appropriate, as a specialized authority, to issue its decision as an expert in the field would have.

The principles and definitions of Mexican law applied to AI systems, therefore, depend on whether the AI system is itself the claimed subject matter or is used as a tool. If the AI system is the claimed subject matter, as is the case for AI-related inventions in Categories 1–3, then the prior art to evaluate must be other close AI systems, and the skilled person in the art must be an AI systems designer, either in general, or for the field of application of the AI system.

However, for inventions that are the result of the use of AI systems (Categories 4–5), the prior art to be assessed in terms of the invention will not necessarily be an AI system, but rather the prior art related to the claimed outcome, regardless of whether that prior art was obtained through another AI system.

Under the reasonable doubt principle proposed by the Court in the *Coflex* case, the burden for an examiner to demonstrate that, by using an AI system, the invention

---

10. Mexico has a civil law system where precedents are only mandatory to all courts if they are so declared by the Supreme Court (jurisprudence), which happens only if five similar decisions were issued by different courts in the same law matter or opposing decisions in the same law matter by two courts.
11. 9th Era, Decision Reg., Circuit Courts, Isolated Thesis I. 4o. A. 698 A, *Intellectual property. In view of the impossibility of clearly noting the novelty of a patent for which its invalidity was administratively declared, the regional chamber specializing in the matter of the federal court of fiscal and administrative justice must apply the principle of 'reasonable doubt' in favour of its holder*. Coflex, S. A. de C. V. Proponent Judge: Jean Claude Tron Petit, Mar. 2010.

could be obtained by anyone skilled in the art would be extremely high. This is because even if the examiner could cite prior art proposing the use of AI for solving certain problem, it would be extremely unlikely that the examiner could demonstrate deductively that the use of the AI system will necessarily lead to the specific invention that is described and claimed in a given patent application. Furthermore, this would be impossible for the examiner if the description of the invention under examination is such that it does not mention at all the use of an AI system as the source of the invention, which is regularly the case in practice.

That said, an invention may be obvious if the prior art undoubtedly teaches that an AI system – trained a certain way to solve the same specific problem that the invention solves – can be used to establish a specific solution whose optimization will necessarily lead to the claimed invention. In such a case, there would be a way to demonstrate, deductively, that those skilled in the art could reach the invention. Such optimization has to be described in the prior art in order to be used against a patent claim.

This could be the case for AI systems that are designed to rapidly process large amounts of data and select data based on specific parameters that always lead to the same decision. In such a case, it could be demonstrated that there is a single solution for solving the same problem. The decision-making process could be demonstrated by a deductive argument that is optimized by the AI but that anyone skilled in the art could reach it, even if it would take a lot of time for that skilled person.

Otherwise, considering that, in practice, the AI systems that will potentially lead to inventions are those that propose unpredictable outputs, it is very likely that objections related to the inventive step of such outputs will be very weak, even if the description recites that the invention was obtained with the use of AI as a tool. The reason is that such an objection would not have enough force if the principle of 'reasonable doubt' does prevail.

§12.05 ADEQUACY OF DISCLOSURE

The standard for the description of the invention in Mexico is established in Article 94, Section IV of the FLPIP (Article 47 Sec. I, IPL). This article changed in the drafting relative to the IPL, but the essence is kept by establishing that a patent application must contain:

> IV. – The description, which must disclose the invention in a sufficiently clear and complete way so that it can be carried out by a person skilled in the art, and the best method known to the applicant to implement it, as well as the information supporting the industrial application of the invention.

On one hand, as evidenced by the examples provided in Section §12.03 above, the Mexican Patent Office does not object to AI-related inventions in terms of sufficiency of disclosure merely because AI is mentioned in the description and claims. Such objections must be based on the fact that the description is insufficient to put the invention into practice. It is important, therefore, to establish first what the invention is, in order to verify whether the disclosure is complete.

First, the basic rules of the category of the invention must be followed. If a method is claimed, a sequence of steps is expected to be specifically described, including any features that are necessary to reduce the invention to practice. For systems, networks, apparatuses or products, the specification of the parts thereof and their relationships and functions that are necessary for a person skilled in the art to carry out the invention must be included in the description.

Therefore, if the claimed invention is directed to an AI system itself (Categories 1 and 2), it is assumed that those skilled in the art know how to build an AI system, and because the invention is either the AI system itself, or a specific configuration, training or handling of data as input or output of the AI system, the description must specify the features that are necessary to operate the system and solve a technical problem related to the system. Therefore, there is no need for a steady or determined outcome that is repeatable, but rather it is necessary to specify clearly whatever is necessary to obtain the system with the functions as described.

Regarding patents that claim new applications of known AI systems (Category 3), such as those particularly configured to reach a desired outcome, as evidenced by the examples in Section §12.03[C], *supra*, it is enough to describe how the AI system is configured, trained or used, because the invention still lies in the system itself. Therefore, the description must enable those skilled in the art to build the system -- not necessarily to obtain a single outcome -- but to solve an evident problem of the prior art based on the performance of the system. The problem solved will determine case-by-case the necessary level of description of the features of the system, depending on the prior art available and the described contribution of the invention.

As another example, an AI system may be described as one of the features of an apparatus, product or procedure. In this case, the AI system is not the main or key feature, but for those skilled in the art, the incorporation of an AI system to perform a determined function within the other category is enough. A person skilled in the art for this case would not be an AI system designer but rather someone skilled in the field of the claimed apparatus, product or procedure. In this case, the features of the AI system must be established clearly in terms of a selection of the system to be incorporated into the broader invention.

For inventions obtained by AI systems or through its use (Categories 4 and 5), it is again important to determine first what the claimed invention is. In these cases, the invention is an outcome or result of the use of the AI system. Therefore, in order to assess the sufficiency of the disclosure of the invention it is important to assess whether the invention can be reduced to practice by those skilled in the art, and not necessarily the way that the invention was obtained. In fact, those skilled in the art likely would not be AI system experts. However, chemists can obtain a compound proposed by an AI system just like engineers that can build products with the features proposed by an AI system. In most inventions of this kind, the invention would not need the AI system at all to be reduced to practice and, therefore, the fact that the invention was obtained through the use of AI systems is not relevant to sufficiently disclose what is claimed.

There could be a case where the outcome of the invention is not certain and, rather, a number of variable outcomes are possible. Typically, this type of AI-related invention will not claim or describe the specific outcome and, therefore, will be claimed as an AI system and not as an invention obtained by an AI system.

One additional general rule to AI systems, which applies to all kinds of inventions, is related to the provision of information that is not necessarily relevant for reducing the invention to practise but for supporting improved performance, synergistic effects or the like. If the AI system is providing an advantage over other AI systems, or their outputs or results, comparative examples are required to prove such described effects.

There are no rules, practices or court precedents related to the need to disclose specific details of databases or the like because the standard for the description is to allow those skilled in the art to reproduce the invention. Therefore, sufficiency of disclosure may be complied with by describing the main features that will allow a skilled person to obtain the described results at a general level. Accordingly, disclosure of confidential or very specific information that those skilled in the art may obtain without undue experimentation such as training data, outputs or even algorithms, should not be necessary in principle.

Regarding undue experimentation, it is important to note that new technologies related to big data, Internet of Things and cloud computing often involve acquisition, curation and selection of massive amounts of data. This may make the concept of 'undue experimentation' different in the field of AI systems. Accordingly, the description may include means or ways to acquire large amounts of information and to treat such information, which will make evident to the examiners and those skilled in the art that the acquisition of the necessary information for the AI system is feasible without undue experimentation. For example, this may be done by registering in real time sensor information in equipment or analysing information from patients with certain specific conditions through thermometers, glucometers or other medical devices connected to databases. Accordingly, the actual data need not be disclosed, rather, the specification must sufficiently explain the kind of data to be used and how it is related at a level that would allow a skilled person to practise the invention. This, of course, is important given that including the data itself in the patent application would be impractical given the large amount of data that most AI systems need to function.

§12.06 INVENTORSHIP

[A] Inventorship in General

Under Article 39 of the FLPIP (Article 13, IPL), the inventor is presumed to be the natural person or persons indicated as such in the patent application. For inventions made by more than one person, Article 38 (Article 10 Bis, IPL) establishes that, if the invention has been made jointly by two or more persons, the right to obtain the patent or registration shall belong to them jointly. Finally, Article 36 of the FLPIP (Article 9, IPL) establishes that the right to obtain a patent belongs primarily to the natural person that obtains the invention, or to his assignee.

In addition, the same Article 39 referred to above establishes that inventors have the inalienable and irrevocable right to be named in the patent application. Accordingly, it can be concluded that, under Mexican law, in order to be recognized as an inventor, the inventor must be a natural person who has made an invention, which in turn as discussed in the eligibility section above, has to be a human creation.

There are, to date, no court precedents in Mexico that can illustrate an interpretation on how to determine inventorship based on the claimed matter. The only guide is the presumption of inventorship established in the law based on the patent application. In practice, however, as the invention is defined as a human creation, it follows that any person who participated in such a creation must be recognized as an inventor and, in practice, the conflicts on inventorship have been solved on the basis of logs or registers of the persons who participated during the development process.

[B] Determination of Inventorship for AI-Related Inventions

[1] Categories 1–4

In all of Categories 1–4 the inventor is presumed to be a human. Otherwise, it could not be considered an invention under the current definitions of Mexican law. Therefore, the Mexican law of inventorship applies directly in the conventional manner. It is worthy of note, however, that in the case of inventions in Category 3, where a new application of known AI is claimed, part of the invention may lie in selection of training or input data. Therefore, while no change of law is implied or needed, inventors of inventions in Category 3 may include those who select and curate data, which might be considered unusual for inventions in other fields. The legal implications of the use or ownership of such data is beyond the scope of this chapter, as there might be contractual or data protection law issues involved in the use of the data in the system. However, that might or might not affect the ability of filing for a patent depending on the specific contracts and laws involved, particularly related to the collection of the data.

[2] Category 5

The hypothetical case of inventions in Category 5, where the invention has been made *by* AI, raises clear problems for inventorship. Based on the general rules of Mexican law and the definition of invention, it is not possible to name an AI system as an inventor. This is because it is inherent in the definition of invention under Mexican law that the inventor must be human. Moreover, if an AI system is proposed as an inventor, the applicant would be recognizing that whatever is claimed is not patent eligible because it would not be a human creation. Finally, an AI system would not be eligible to hold a patent right because patent rights are reserved to natural persons who create an invention or to their assignee. It logically follows also that an AI system also cannot be considered a co-inventor.

Accordingly, a discussion of inventorship for AI-related inventions has to take into account these basic facts, and therefore, the definition of whatever it is the invention is of the essence to determine inventorship. In the absence of any rules or decisions in Mexico interpreting the inventorship concept, it may follow that whenever an invention would not have been obtained without the intervention of a human, the humans that did intervene must be considered inventors, and this is not only a rule but a right for all these persons who participated in obtaining the invention.

It follows, therefore, that it is impossible for an invention not to have at least one human inventor under Mexican law, because if that were the case, it would not be considered an invention. Therefore, if an AI system is designed, used to design or achieve certain goals, or otherwise obtained by a human or used as a tool by a human, the role that would be assigned to such AI system is either an invention itself or a tool used by a human to obtain an invention, in which case, the contribution to the invention by humans would in turn determine who will be considered inventors.

Furthermore, whoever is named as an inventor will be presumed to be the actual inventor. This means that whoever claims that someone is not an inventor in an issued patent application has the burden of proving it, and of course an AI system will not take such an action to claim any rights. Therefore, because there is no need or burden to prove inventorship in Mexico, the only way to question an AI-related invention in terms of inventorship would be to prove that no human intervened at all for reducing the invention to practice, which seems very unlikely.

Regarding the determination of inventors as the natural persons who did participate in the creation that constitutes an invention, the analysis must go back to defining what the invention is, and every person who contributed to it must be recognized as an inventor. If the invention is a training method, all the persons who intervened in the training must be named, from data selection to the training algorithm, and depending on whatever is novel or contributes to the solution of a technical problem, the inventors would need to be recognized in every activity thereof. This recognition includes all kinds of contributions, such as the idea of using AI for a determined purpose, a new configuration of AI technology for achieving a novel result, selection or curation of data for training AI systems, or the identification of the invention as an outcome of an AI system.

In conclusion, the nature of the contribution made to an invention by a natural person is not relevant to being recognized as an inventor; it matters only that a contribution was made to the claimed invention.

§12.07 AREAS FOR FURTHER DEVELOPMENT

The new provisions of the FLPIP, excluding from patentability mathematical methods or computer programs 'as such', but in practice allowing inclusion of such matters as part of the features of claimed inventions, provide enough flexibility to obtain protection of AI-related inventions in all modalities, which provides certainty under the Mexican patent system.

Therefore, the development of the Mexican patent system regarding AI technology is more dependent on the criteria of the IMPI and the implementation of the FLPIP than on further law changes at this point in time.

Other more radical changes, mainly related to the possibility of naming or providing certain recognition or rights to AI systems, do not seem to be relevant or useful at this point in time for the patent system. They will have to evolve, as the legal recognition of non-human entities in terms of rights and obligations is solved by the national and international legal systems at large.

§12.08 RECOMMENDATIONS FOR PATENT APPLICANTS

The main recommendation for AI technology patent applicants is to consider the basic rules for CIIs, which imply showing that there is a tangible effect of the invention in the solution of a problem for mankind.

Whenever a patent application is to be filed in Mexico, it is important to take into account the unique definition of invention that we have in our law, which includes what can be known as the 'matter or energy transformation potential test' in order to determine if the invention will be considered as such under Mexican law.

Having in mind such definition, the application can be drafted in a way that will not fall into any of the categories of ineligible subject matter, which include computer programs and mathematical methods claimed as such. When this is properly taken into account, patents to all aspects of AI systems, from its design, modification, configuration or use, may be obtained under Mexican law and practice.

Finally, it is important to consider also that minimum damages in Mexico for patent infringement, which used to be a minimum of 40% of the selling price to the public of the infringing goods under the IPL, is still very attractive as a venue for infringement actions. The new standards of the FLPIP provide damages of a minimum of 40% of what is now called a 'legitimate value indicator', with standards based on typical damages for lost profits, undue enrichment or retail or market price. Another enforcement improvement of the FLPIP includes the fact that the damages may now be claimed directly before a civil court without the need to first obtain an infringement declaration by the IMPI, as was required under the IPL. Therefore, the possibilities of more quickly obtaining both remedies and damages have increased in Mexico under the new FLPIP.

§12.09 CONCLUSION

In practice, the current Mexican patent system seems to have the fundamental definitions and provisions necessary to provide a solid ground for patentability of AI-related inventions. For the time being, the developments of the Mexican patent system in this technology area will be dependent on the AI-related inventions themselves rather than on changes in the fundamental patent law.

As AI technology continues developing and spreading rapidly, the temptation to discuss the possibility that an AI system could own a patent becomes more and more common. However, the possibility that AI systems can own patents is not straightforward, nor simple. Such possibility requires a broader legal framework to provide legal certainty regarding an artificial legal entity that can both be a rights holder and responsible for actions. In patent matters alone, it will imply determining how such an entity could be liable of infringing rights of third parties, how such an entity could be considered a person skilled in the art or how such an entity will exercise its rights in case of infringement. All these issues do not depend on patent law alone, but are part of a more complex determination on how such an artificial person can be given legal standing overall for all the rights and obligations that natural or even legal persons can acquire under the legal framework in Mexico and internationally.

The evolution of AI-related inventions does not seem to differ from the evolution of the patent system for all areas of technology at large: the prior art makes the innovation burden rise, but the variety of the developments make it possible to innovate more. What is new today is prior art the minute after, and also becomes knowledge available to those skilled in the art. This makes the criteria for evaluating both enablement and inventiveness evolve just as rapidly as the technology.

Chapter 13

Middle East

Ishraqa Abutaha, Tamara El-Shibib, Nevin Jacob Koshy, Sarmad Hasan Manto & Ahmad Saleh

The authors of this chapter are practitioners licensed in the United Arab Emirates ('UAE'). Due to general similarities of the relevant laws among the countries in the Middle East region, this chapter addresses laws and approaches of the region generally and, where appropriate, addresses the specific laws of a particular country. It should be understood that not every law of every country can be addressed herein and further that variations in local laws may exist that are not specifically mentioned.

§13.01 PATENTABILITY OF SOFTWARE AND COMPUTER-IMPLEMENTED INVENTIONS

The governing statutes in the United Arab Emirates that deal with the patent domain are Federal Law No. 11 of 2021 and its implementing regulation, Resolution No. 6 of 2022 (the 'UAE Patent Law').[1] Article 1 of the UAE Patent Law provides a definition of 'invention':

> Invention: An innovative idea conceived by an inventor in any technical field in relation to a product, a method of manufacturing, or both of them, in a way that practically leads to a new addition or a solution to a specific problem in such a field.

Article 5 provides a list of conditions for patentability:

> 1. A patent shall be granted for each novel invention resulting from an innovative idea or innovative improvement, which involves an inventive step and is susceptible to industrial application.

1. Federal Law No. 11 of 2021.

2. A patent shall be granted independently for any novel application, modification, improvement, or addition related to a previously patented invention if it meets the conditions provided for in this Law.

3. An invention shall be considered new if it is not preceded by any earlier technology previously disclosed to the public in writing or orally, through use, or by any other means which have made such invention known before the date of filing the patent application or of the legally claiming priority.

Article 7 indicates subject matter that is not patent-eligible under the UAE Patent Law:

a. Plant and animal research and species or biological methods of plant and animal breeding, except for microbiological methods and their products in accordance with the Executive Regulations of this Law.

b. Diagnostic methods, medications, and surgical operations related to the treatment of humans and animals.

c. Scientific principles, discoveries and theories, and mathematical methods.

d. Plans, rules, software, methods of carrying out commercial activity, performing a purely mental activity, or playing games.

Therefore, under Article 7(d), software in and of itself would not be patentable in the UAE. However, although not explicitly written in the law, regulations, or examining guidelines, if a software program is linked to hardware and is claimed as a technical solution to a technical problem, it is generally considered patentable provided the technical aspect of the solution meets the substantive patentability criteria. This is the general practice in countries such as the UAE and Saudi Arabia.

§13.02 SPECIAL PROVISIONS RELATING TO PATENTABILITY OF INVENTIONS RELATING TO AI

None of the current governing statutes, regulations, and examining guidelines in the Middle East region provide any special provisions for patents on artifical intelligence ('AI')-related inventions.

§13.03 SUBJECT MATTER PATENTABILITY

Common law jurisdictions rely on case law for guidance on how patent examiners and the courts will treat AI-related inventions and patents thereon. However, all Middle East countries are civil law jurisdictions and there is little formal guidance in the regional patent laws and regulations on the patentability of AI-related inventions. With few cases published and no system of binding precedent, it is a challenge to predict how patent offices in the region will treat the different categories of AI-related inventions.

At most, the patent laws in the region will include specific provisions relating to the exclusion of software or computer programs and mathematical formulae. These exclusions are generally harmonized with international patent laws.

Although 'computer programs' are explicitly listed as not patentable in the UAE Patent Law, the International Center for Patent Registration Ministry of Economy ('UAE Patent Office') has allowed applications for software-related inventions to be granted, including those relating to AI, provided the invention is a technical solution to a technical problem and meets the criteria of novelty and inventiveness.

Examiners trained by the Korean Intellectual Property Office ('KIPO') carry out substantive examination at the UAE Patent Office. Therefore, concerning the categories of AI-related inventions, the UAE Patent Office is likely to follow the approach adopted by the KIPO. In January 2022 the KIPO updated its examination guidelines by issuing *Examination Guidelines for Specific Technical Fields* ('STF Guidelines')[2] that include a chapter for Computer-Related Inventions.[3] In the STF Guidelines, the KIPO outlined specific guidelines on the description and novelty/inventiveness requirements for different categories of AI-related inventions in addition to eligibility requirements for computer-related inventions. We would expect UAE patent examiners to follow this approach. For more detail on the STF Guidelines and the KIPO's approach to examination and patentability of AI-related inventions, please refer to the Korea chapter of this book.

Further, applicants who have successfully prosecuted an AI-related application in a foreign patent office (in particular, one of the major offices, i.e., KIPO, United States Patent and Trademark Office, European Patent Office ('EPO'), Japan Patent Office or China National Intellectual Property Administration) can expect the UAE Patent Office to handle examination similarly. In fact, applicants are encouraged to submit copies of successfully prosecuted 'allowable' claims to the UAE Patent Office as, in most cases, this helps to expedite the examination and grant of the UAE application if the local requirements are met.

Similarly, Saudi laws do not have special provisions on patentability of AI-related inventions. When considering the patentability of AI inventions, the focus is placed on the technical contribution that the invention makes to the state of the art.

In Egypt, AI-related inventions involving a hardware system that provide a technical contribution or effect that goes beyond mere computer automation may be patentable. There is also a requirement for AI claims to be directed to the hardware system.

In summary, and based on extensive research of regional laws and practice, the general position in the region as to the five categories of AI-related inventions is as follows:

[A] Categories 1 and 2

Inventions of AI (e.g., new algorithms or models for the AI itself) and inventions of an AI implementation (e.g., creation of a system or process of broad application using AI technology) are both potentially patentable. Although algorithms and mathematical formulas are excluded from patentability when claimed as such, computer-implemented inventions ('CIIs') including AI-related inventions are not excluded if they are of a technical nature, i.e., are claimed as a technical solution to a technical problem. This may be more difficult to achieve in the case of Category 1 inventions, which are, by definition, not tied to a particular implementation. However, this would be evaluated on a case-by-case basis.

2. Examination Guidelines for Specific Technical Fields ('STF Guidelines'), KIPO, Jan. 2022.
3. *Ibid.*, pp. 53–84.

[B] Category 3

A new application of AI would be evaluated for subject matter eligibility on the same basis as described above for Categories 1 and 2. Here, however, eligibility is likely given that, in the case of Category 3 AI-related inventions, the AI has been applied in a particular field for a particular purpose. Provided that field is technical and the purpose is to solve a technical problem, claims directed to such inventions would be patent eligible.

[C] Categories 4 and 5

AI-related inventions in Categories 4 and 5 have claims directed to the result of application of AI, rather than to the AI itself. Thus, the claims could be directed to any type of product or process in any field. The determination of patent eligibility would accordingly be made based upon what is claimed, without regard for the manner in which the invention was made. Notably, this is merely theoretical for inventions in Category 5, because, as discussed *infra*, regional patent laws require the inventor to be a natural person.

§13.04 INVENTIVE STEP

Regional patent laws and regulations provide general definitions for the person of ordinary skill in the art but are all silent on the requirements for inventive step as it specifically relates to AI-related inventions or the categories of AI inventions that are likely to meet the requirement.

In the UAE, Article 5 of the UAE Patent Law[4] states that an invention will be deemed to involve an inventive step 'if it is not axiomatic in the opinion of the ordinary craftsman, due to the previous condition of the industrial technology related to the application of patent'.

Article 44 of the Saudi Patent Law[5] states that 'an invention is deemed to involve an inventive step if, with regard to prior art related to the patent application, it is not obvious to a person with ordinary skills in the art'.

In Egypt, Article 1 of the Egyptian Patent Law[6] requires an invention to be 'inventive' to the 'person having expertise in the art'.

In general, the person skilled in the art should be presumed to be a hypothetical person having ordinary skill in the art and being aware of what was common general knowledge in the art at the relevant date. He or she should also be presumed to have had access to everything in the 'prior art', and to have had at his or her disposal the normal means and capacity for routine experimentation.

4. Federal Law No. 11 of 2021. Art. 5(5).
5. Law of Patents, Layout Designs of Integrated Circuits, Plant Varieties, and Industrial Designs No. 27 of 2004. Art. 44.
6. Egyptian Intellectual Property Protection Law No. 82 of 2002. Art. 1.

[A] Categories 1–3

While no specific guidance exists at the time of this writing, it may be considered that for inventions of AI, inventions of AI implementations, and inventions of new applications of AI, the skilled person would be a person of ordinary skill in the art of AI system design and/or AI system use and implementation. In this respect, the inventive step analysis would be no different from an inventive step analysis for any other CII.

[B] Category 4

As noted in the previous section, AI-related inventions in Category 4 (invention made *using* AI) have claims directed to the result of an application of AI, rather than to the AI itself. Thus, the claims may be directed to any field imaginable and need not (and usually would not) claim AI at all. Indeed, the fact that AI was used to develop an invention may not be mentioned in the patent specification and hence it would not be apparent from the patent application or issued patent that AI had been used during the inventive process (just like it is not necessary to explain when other tools such as computer-aided design are used to assist the inventive process). Accordingly, the skilled person would be a person of ordinary skill in the art of what is claimed, and the inventive step inquiry would be conducted in the same manner as it would for any other invention. The determination of patent eligibility would accordingly be made based upon what is claimed, without regard for the manner in which the invention was made.

[C] Category 5

In the hypothetical case of claims to inventions made *by* AI, the question of inventive step would not be reached because it is likely the regional Patent Offices will uphold the position of most major jurisdictions (including the US and Europe) that AI itself cannot invent or be an inventor. This is considered further in Section §13.06 below.

§13.05 ADEQUACY OF DISCLOSURE

Article 11 of the UAE Patent Law[7] sets forth the conditions for applying for a patent or utility certificate in the UAE, including requirements for adequacy of disclosure:

> The patent specification should include the title of the invention, summary, detailed description, claims, abstract, and the drawings (if any).
>
> The description of the invention should be written as well as possible at the time of filing the patent specification to enable a person skilled in the art to understand the claimed invention.
>
> The patent specification should include claims and description and illustrations that can be used in the description to explain the claims in detail.

7. Federal Law No. 11 of 2021, Art. 11.

> The claims should be clear, concise and based on the description.
>
> The claims should be supported by the description.
>
> In case of any amendments, support for each amendment should be included in the originally filed patent specification.

In simple terms, the UAE Patent Law defines a broad criterion for defining the adequacy of disclosure, i.e., the claimed invention must be fully and particularly disclosed in the patent specification. The patent specification should be clear and should sufficiently disclose the working of the invention to enable a person of ordinary skill in the art to comprehend the invention by referring to the description of the invention.

In view of the above, the adequacy of disclosure of a claimed invention is determined based on whether the patent specification clearly and sufficiently discloses the working of the invention and on whether the claim is sufficiently described in the description. This is true for AI-related inventions as well as for all other types of inventions.

AI-related inventions may include or be related to machine learning systems, neural networks, algorithmic systems, etc. The scope of the patent specification for such inventions should be clear and should include detailed examples to support the claims. Currently, there is no clear provision in the UAE Patent Law that defines a specific requirement for adequate disclosure of such inventions. Due to this, we recommend that the applicant follow the best practices adopted in the US, Korea and at the EPO.

Some of the provisions that can be followed by local applicants in the UAE are:

United States of America, Section 112(a):[8]

> The specification shall contain a written description of the invention, and of the manner and process of making and using it, in such full, clear, concise, and exact terms as to enable any person skilled in the art to which it pertains, or with which it is most nearly connected, to make and use the same, and shall set forth the best mode contemplated by the inventor or joint inventor of carrying out the invention.

From the above provision, it is clear under the US law that a patent specification must disclose the manner or a process of making and using the invention in such full, clear, concise, and exact terms as to enable any person skilled in the art to make and use the same. Given that software *per se* cannot be registered as a patent under the UAE Patent Law, and thus must be tied to some sort of hardware, adequacy of disclosure could be determined by considering whether the algorithm performed by the hardware is sufficiently disclosed in the written description to enable a person ordinally skilled in the art to make or use the AI-related invention without undue experimentation.

European Patent Convention ('EPC'), Article 83:[9]

8. 35 U.S.C. 112(a).
9. Art. 83 EPC.

> The European patent application shall disclose the invention in a manner sufficiently clear and complete for it to be carried out by a person skilled in the art.

From the above provision it is apparent the EPC also provides essentially the same standard for determining the adequacy of disclosure. However, the handling of such inventions can be different because the EPO has issued Guidelines for examining AI and machine learning inventions (the 'EPO Guidelines').[10] The EPO Guidelines define AI and machine learning as 'based on computational models and algorithms for classification, clustering, regression and dimensionality reduction, such as neural networks, genetic algorithms, support vector machines, k-means, kernel regression and discriminant analysis'. For a complete discussion of the EPO approach and the EPO Guidelines, reference is made to the EPO chapter of this book. However, it is sufficient to say that an application that meets the EPO standards for sufficiency of disclosure is likely to also meet the standards in the Middle East region, including the UAE.

Republic of Korea:

The KIPO refers to the aforementioned STF Guidelines[11] to provide sufficiency requirements for AI-related inventions. The KIPO determines the sufficiency of disclosure requirement based on whether a description of the invention is clearly and concisely described so that a person skilled in the art can easily implement the invention. The actual improvement relating to the AI that is embodied in the claimed invention should be disclosed so that a person skilled in the art clearly understands, in particular, a certain means, a technical problem of the invention and the means to solve the same. A certain means for implementing an AI-related invention may encompass a description of training data, a data processing method, a training model, a loss function, etc. However, a submission by the Republic of Korea to a WIPO study noted:

> even without a substantial description or a drawing of certain means for implementing an AI-related invention, it is possible that the invention can fulfil the enablement requirement if a person skilled in the art according to their general technical knowledge can clearly understand and implement the invention.[12]

In light of these standards from other major jurisdictions, and in the absence of any specific guidelines to handle AI-related inventions and the requirements to examine the adequacy of disclosure requirement by the UAE Patent Office, generally, patent specifications should follow the best practices adapted in other foreign jurisdictions. In addition, the description of the patent specification should be as detailed as possible to meet the requirement of Article 11 of the UAE Patent Law.

The five categories of AI-related inventions will now be considered to the extent possible based on available guidance.

10. EPO Guidelines for Examination, Part G, Chapter II, Section 3.3.1, 'Artificial intelligence and machine learning'.
11. *STF Guidelines*, KIPO, Jan. 2022.
12. WIPO SCP/34/5 p. 27, available at: https://www.wipo.int/edocs/mdocs/scp/en/scp_34/scp_34_5.pdf.

[A] Categories 1 and 2

The standards for adequacy of disclosure for AI-related inventions in Categories 1 and 2 would be the same way as for any other CII. Namely, the invention of core AI or of an AI implementation would need to be disclosed sufficiently to enable a person skilled in the art to understand the claimed invention. Importantly, the technical problem and how it is addressed should be disclosed and the interaction between the various elements of the invention (algorithms, hardware, etc.) must be clearly explained. The level of required detail would, of course, depend on what a person skilled in the art would know and understand. Thus, for example, a new algorithm would need to be described in more detail than a known algorithm being implemented in a new way (where the new implementation would need to be described in detail). If, on the other hand, the hardware or software that implements the function of an AI-related invention is explained only at a high level with functional block diagrams or generalized flow charts, the disclosure may not enable the skilled person to understand the invention and hence the patent may not meet the enablement requirement.

[B] Category 3

With regard to Category 3 where the claimed subject matter of the patent is a new application of known AI, it is advisable to disclose what type or types of AI may be used for the particular application, how that AI interacts with hardware components (e.g., how it receives input data and generates output data) along with a detailed process description of the invention. Particular attention must be paid to the description of training data to ensure that a skilled person can use the claimed invention based on what is described.

[C] Category 4

Sufficiency of disclosure requirements for an invention made using AI (Category 4) would be based on what is claimed without regard to the AI tools used to arrive at the invention. In fact, as noted *supra*, a claim to an invention in Category 4 would not, in most cases, recite AI and similarly the specification may not mention AI at all. As the use of AI tools expands into more and more fields, a human may use AI tools to assist in making inventions in an ever-increasing variety of areas. Thus, the duty to 'to enable a person skilled in the art to understand the claimed invention' is just that: a duty relating to the *claimed* invention. For example, if a human uses an AI tool to design a mechanical device, and that mechanical device is claimed, then the disclosure must describe that mechanical device – how it is made and how it is used – sufficiently to enable the person skilled in the art to understand it. This does not include explaining how to *invent* the mechanical device using AI, which is irrelevant to this inquiry.

[D] Category 5

Turning to the hypothetical case of Category 5, where an invention is claimed that was made *by* AI, the requirements for sufficiency of disclosure would be the same as those described above with respect to Category 4 inventions, i.e., the *claimed invention* (not the manner by which the invention was made) would need to be sufficiently described. However, of course, in the case of a Category 5 invention the AI itself would be an inventor and this raises a different set of issues as discussed in Section §13.06 below.

As stated above, the UAE Patent Office has not established any practice or formulated guidelines for handling AI-related inventions. Until it does, applicants are advised to follow the best practices adopted by other jurisdictions to meet the disclosure requirements for AI-related inventions. As AI-related inventions become increasingly complex, examination of the adequacy of disclosure requirements will become challenging in the coming days.

§13.06 INVENTORSHIP

[A] Inventorship in General

The UAE Patent Law provides specific provisions to protect the 'rights of inventors'. Although the UAE Patent Law has not explicitly defined the terms 'inventor' and 'inventorship', the UAE Patent Office determines inventorship based on a basic principle of law. The general connotation of inventorship implies a person who contributes to the conception of the invention, meaning to at least one claim of a patent.

UAE Patent Law, Article 8, defines the provisions for determining the rights to an invention. The right to the invention shall belong to the inventor or to the legal successor of the inventor.[13] If the invention contains one or more essential elements and is obtained from another invention, all rights to the invention will belong to the person of the other invention as an original inventor.[14] Further, if a single invention is a combined effort of two or more inventors, the right to the invention shall belong to all the contributing inventors. However, in this case, the right to the invention will be limited to portion of the invention to which the conception applied. Also, a person whose efforts are limited to assisting in the implementation of the invention without participating in any inventive step shall not be considered an inventor.[15] Furthermore, if two or more persons perform the same invention individually, the person who files a patent application or a utility certificate before the other, or who first claims priority over the invention, shall be entitled to obtain a patent or a utility certificate.[16] That means, the UAE follows the first to file system.

Referring to Article 10 of the UAE Patent Law, if an organization made a contract with a person who contributes to the conception of the invention, the right to the invention shall belong to the employer of the organization. If the invention has some

13. UAE Patent Law, Art. 8(2).
14. UAE Patent Law, Art. 8(3).
15. UAE Patent Law, Art. 8(4).
16. UAE Patent Law, Art. 8(5).

economic value that exceeds the expectations of the buyer or third party at the time of signing the contract, the inventor shall be entitled to additional compensation. Further, if a worker whose work contract does not provide for an inventive activity makes an invention related to the employer's field of activity, using the employer's expertise, documents, tools, or raw materials placed at worker's disposal through work, the right to that invention belongs to the worker (inventor worker) after four months from the date of submitting the report to the employer about the invention, or as of any date during which the employer otherwise learned about the invention, and whereof the employer did not provide a written notice of a desire to acquire the invention. Additionally, if the employer indicates the desire to acquire the invention within the period, the employer shall be entitled to the right in the invention as of its inception, and the worker shall be entitled to a fair compensation and any other benefits arising from such acquisition. In case of any dispute between the parties, the compensation shall be determined by a court of law.

[B] Determination of Inventorship for AI-Related Inventions

The UAE Patent Law clearly defines the inventorship, transfer of inventorship in view of the employer-employee relationship and any compensation arising out of such acquisition. However, the UAE Patent Law does not include any provisions specific to inventorship of AI-related inventions. In the absence of such provisions, it is expected that the inventorship defined under Articles 8 and 10 shall be applicable to AI-related inventions.

While no explicit guidance exists at this time, certain conclusions may be drawn from logical application of Articles 8 and 10:

- For AI-related inventions in Categories 1 and 2, inventorship would be determined as it is for any other hardware or hardware/software combination invention.
- For AI-related inventions in Category 3, like Categories 1 and 2, inventorship would be determined as in other CII cases. However, in Category 3 cases there may be factual issues around whether certain roles in the development process – such as curating training data for example – are inventive or are mere implementation under UAE Patent Law, Article 8(4). Further guidance on this point will be needed in the future.
- For AI-related inventions in Category 4, even though what is claimed is the product or process that results from use of the AI, the human or humans who had the concept to employ the AI in that manner would be presumed to be the inventor(s).
- Lastly, with regard to the hypothetical case of Category 5 inventions – where what is claimed was made *by* AI without human input or direction – the current state of the UAE law would not permit a patent and thus inventorship would be irrelevant. An interesting and as yet unanswered issue would be the case where a human inventor used AI as part of an inventive process and the AI performed an activity that, if that activity had been done by a human, would have qualified that human as a co-inventor. It is not clear at this time

whether a patent could be issued naming only the sole human inventor, or if patent coverage would be unavailable due to the AI's 'co-inventive' activity.

§13.07 AREAS FOR FURTHER DEVELOPMENT

As noted *supra*, Article 7 of the UAE Patent Law explicitly excludes software from patentability. The UAE Law currently provides no further guidance on exceptions to the software exclusion.

Since the law is silent with respect to the patentability of CIIs and there is nothing in the law that excludes the patentability of these, the current situation is that CIIs are in general eligible for patent protection under the law as long as they meet the criteria of novelty, inventiveness and industrial applicability. The UAE patent examiners are influenced by the examination of equivalent applications filed in other countries, especially those filed in the US, Europe and South Korea.

Though the new industrial property law has come into force recently (in 2022), the new law fails to address some key aspects including the patentability of CIIs. We do recommend legislative amendments to the law whenever possible to align with public policy considerations in terms of the aspirations of the UAE to grow the digital economy and attract high-tech companies and innovators to the country.

Until legislative changes are adopted, it is recommended that the UAE Patent Office adopt examination guidelines pertaining to the patentability of CIIs, including specific guidance for AI-related inventions, in order to provide clarity and predictability to patent applicants in this field.

As digitalization and digital technology in general are among the core industries within the focus of the UAE leadership, including AI and blockchain, and to strengthen this industry inside the country, it is recommended that the UAE adopt a tolerant and flexible approach to the patentability of CIIs and AI-related inventions – such as is the case in South Korea and Japan. This also aligns well with the current dynamics because, as noted *supra*, the UAE has a collaboration agreement with the KIPO and most UAE patent applications are currently being examined by South Korean examiners.

§13.08 RECOMMENDATIONS FOR PATENT APPLICANTS

[A] Preparation of the Patent Application

The foundation of any patent protection is the preparation of the patent application. For CIIs, including AI-related inventions, and until more detailed legal positions are defined, it is recommended that patent applications pertaining to such inventions are drafted thoroughly with as much support in the specification as possible with respect to the technical implementation of the invention and related technical features supported by block diagrams and flow charts. The specification should clearly show the technical features of the claimed invention, the technical problem solved, and explain the claimed invention so as to be understandable by the skilled person.

[B] Global Patent Protection Strategy

A global patent protection strategy needs to take into consideration the position and dynamics in the UAE. In this light, it is highly recommended to align the patent specification and claims as much as possible with any equivalent applications filed in the US, Europe and/or South Korea. An allowance or grant in one or more of these countries is likely to positively influence the examination of the UAE application (though will not be legally binding).

§13.09 CONCLUSION

It is critical that the UAE's regulatory and legislative framework be strengthened to keep up with the acceleration of digital technology. It is time to adopt amendments to the industrial property law and, in the meantime, to implement new examination guidelines on CIIs and AI-related inventions in order to attract high-tech companies and innovators to the UAE. There is a need for more legal clarity from the UAE Patent Office in this regard and a positive approach to patentability of these types of inventions will benefit applicants as well as the economy at large.

Chapter 14

South Africa

Stephen Middleton

§14.01 PATENTABILITY OF SOFTWARE AND COMPUTER-IMPLEMENTED INVENTIONS

The Patents Act No. 57 of 1978 (the 'Patents Act') governs patentability of inventions in South Africa. Section 25 of the Patents Act sets out the requirements for patentability, which include that '[a] patent may, subject to the provisions of this section, be granted for any new invention which involves an inventive step and which is capable of being used or applied in trade or industry or agriculture.'[1]

The Patents Act does not say what an invention is, but rather states:

> [a]nything which consists of:
> (a) a discovery;
> (b) a scientific theory;
> (c) a mathematical method;
> (d) a literary, dramatic, musical or artistic work or any other aesthetic creation;
> (e) a scheme, rule or method for performing a mental act, playing a game or doing business;
> (f) a program for a computer; or
> (g) the presentation of information,
>
> shall not be an invention for the purposes of this Act.[2]

The above provisions, however, prevent an invention from being treated as an invention for the purposes of the Patents Act only to the extent to which it relates to that thing *as such*.[3]

1. Patents Act No. 57 of 1978, s. 25(1).
2. *Ibid.*, s. 25(2).
3. *Ibid.*, s. 25(3).

Software and computer-implemented inventions therefore, in addition to meeting the requirements of novelty and inventiveness, will have to be shown to be drawn to more than scientific theories, mathematical methods, schemes, rules or methods of performing mental acts or to programs for a computer, as such.

The above provisions are very similar, but not identical, to the corresponding provisions of Section 1(2) of the UK Patents Act 1977,[4] which themselves are very similar to the corresponding provisions of Article 52 of the European Patent Convention.[5]

However, unlike in the UK and Europe, there is no case law to guide as to how these provisions of the Patents Act are to be interpreted.[6] British and European judicial precedent can be helpful when dealing with situations for which there is no case law in South Africa, but it should be approached with caution.[7]

In addition to the dearth of case law on these particular provisions, South Africa implements a so-called patent registration system in terms of which the registrar of patents examines each patent application including the accompanying specification to ensure that it complies with the prescribed formalities, and if it complies with the requirements of the Patents Act, it shall be accepted.[8] There is no substantive examination as to the patent application's compliance with Section 25 of the Patents Act. Consequently, there is currently uncertainty as to how Sections 25(2) and (3) of the Patents Act would be applied to software and computer-implemented inventions.

[A] Transition to Substantive Search and Examination

South Africa is, however, taking steps towards implementing substantive search and examination, with a number of patent examiners being hired and trained in 2016. Phase one of an IP policy dated 2018[9] notes that the Companies and Intellectual Property Commission ('CIPC'), in which the Patent Office is housed, has onboarded a capable cohort of patent examiners, with a significant number holding PhDs. The policy further notes that the CIPC has been working closely with the European Patent Office ('EPO') pursuant to a memorandum of understanding between the two offices.[10] Referred to as a 'reinforced co-operation programme', the memorandum of understanding was signed by the president of the EPO, Benoît Battistelli, and the Commissioner of the CIPC of South Africa, Rory Voller, on 27 June 2018. Mr Voller at the time commented that the CIPC 'now look[s] forward to forging an even stronger

4. T.D. Burrell, *Burrell's South African Patent and Design Law*, 4th edition (2016) ss 1.14 and 1.22.3.
5. *Ibid.*, s. 1.22.3.
6. Most of the patent litigation in South Africa relates to the technical fields of pharmaceuticals and mining; the patentability of a computer-implemented invention has not yet been considered by the South African courts.
7. Burrell, s. 1.14, referring to *Gentiruco AG v. Firestone SA (Pty) Ltd* 1971 BP 58(A) at 85G-86A and *Mossgas (Pty) Ltd v. Sasol Technology (Pty) Ltd* 1999 BIP 96 (W) at 106C-D.
8. Patents Act, s. 34 read with Regulations 40 and 41 of Patent Regulations, No. R6247 of 15 Dec. 1978 (the 'Patent Regulations').
9. Intellectual Property Policy of The Republic of South Africa, Phase 1, 2018, Department of Trade and Industry.
10. *Ibid.*, p. 18.

partnership through this reinforced co-operation, to build national capacity in the area of substantive search and examination, and to raise the levels of education and awareness in the protection of patent rights, in line with our National IP Policy.'[11]

However, the required legislative changes in the form of a new patents act, regulations and guidelines for the examination are still outstanding. To date, no draft bill has been circulated for comment.

Pending these changes, the examiners retained by the CIPC are currently being put to work in an 'Experiential Learning Programme' introduced to South African patent practitioners in a memorandum from the CIPC in January 2022.[12] In terms of the Programme, substantive search and examination of patent applications is carried out during a trial period for applicants who have elected to opt in to the programme. Work products are sent to the applicants' representatives who review and respond to the findings. The outputs of this Programme are legally non-binding and it is up to the applicants whether or not to respond to any report.[13]

In the January 2022 memorandum, the CIPC notes the training of the examiners by the EPO using a training curriculum and framework designed specifically for CIPC patent examiners based on EPO and international best practices. In addition, experienced examiners were appointed from the EPO as mentors for the South African patent searchers to train them on specific areas of patent examination and to ensure quality work output.[14]

This close relationship with the EPO is clear from the outputs of examiners in examination reports on applications for computer-implemented inventions. In such reports, examiners tend to identify the closest prior art, identify the differences between the claimed invention and the closest prior art, and then proceed to analyse the distinguishing features to identify any excluded subject matter and to identify whether a technical solution to a technical problem is present.[15] Yet, despite these exciting signs of progress towards substantive examination, best estimates are that South Africa is at least one year but more likely many years away from binding substantive search and examination.

In the meantime, patent applicants in the field of software and computer-implemented inventions can view this as an opportunity to play a part in defining how South Africa one day views such applications by partaking in the Experiential Learning Programme and litigating when commercially relevant.

11. *EPO launches first-ever reinforced co-operation programme with South Africa*, European Patent Office (29 June 2018), https://www.epo.org/news-events/press/releases/archive/2018/20180629.html.
12. *Companies and Intellectual Property Commission (CIPC) Substantive Search and Examination (SSE) Experiential Learning*, CIPC Memorandum (4 January 2022).
13. *Ibid.*, pp. 2–3.
14. *Ibid.*, p. 2.
15. These are anecdotal observations from practice and not the findings of rigorous analysis.

§14.02 SPECIAL PROVISIONS RELATING TO PATENTABILITY OF INVENTIONS RELATING TO AI

There are no special provisions relating to patentability of inventions relating to artificial intelligence ('AI') in South Africa.

§14.03 SUBJECT MATTER PATENTABILITY

Categories 1 to 3 of AI-related inventions (as defined in the Introduction to this book) would have claims directed to inventions of AI itself, implementations of AI, and new applications of AI, respectively. In each of these cases, to be subject matter eligible the claims would need to overcome the excluded subject matter provisions of Section 25(2) of the Patents Act as detailed above. Given the lack of case law and the fact that patent applications are not examined substantively in South Africa, it is not possible to say with any clarity as to how such inventions might be shown to overcome these exclusions. Ultimately, for reasons that should be apparent from Section §14.01 above, an approach similar to that of Europe might be followed. But that remains to be seen.

Category 4 AI-related inventions – inventions made by a human inventor using AI as a tool – may contain claims directed to literally anything. The claims could be, but need not be, directed to a computer-implemented invention. For example, a human may use AI as a tool to assist with inventing a mechanical device, an industrial process, or anything else under the sun. Thus, while Category 4 AI-related inventions would need to overcome the same subject matter exclusions as mentioned *supra*, the degree to which this would be a problem would depend entirely on what is being claimed.

Category 5 AI-related inventions – inventions made, hypothetically, by AI without human control or direction -- would, from a subject matter eligibility standpoint, be treated the same as Category 4 above. Like Category 4 inventions, in a hypothetical situation where an AI entity invents something without human control or direction, that 'something' could be anything under the sun and need not relate to AI or computer-implemented inventions at all. For example, one of the claimed inventions in the famous DABUS case, discussed *infra*, alleged to have been invented by an AI entity, is directed to a beverage container – completely unrelated to the AI by which it was supposedly invented. Category 5 inventions would, of course, also have to overcome the inventorship obstacles as detailed below.

§14.04 INVENTIVE STEP

There are two enquiries for determining inventive step between which South African courts seem to switch.[16] The first, and earliest enquiry formulated for the Patents Act, considers three factors: (1) what the art is to which the invention relates; (2) what the state of this art was at the relevant time; and (3) who is to be regarded as a 'person

16. Burrell, s. 4.12.

skilled in the art'.[17] The second and later enquiry constitutes four considerations: (1) What is the inventive step said to be involved in the patent in suit? (2) What, at the priority date, was the state of the art (as statutorily defined) relevant to the step? (3) In what respect does the step go beyond, or differ from, that state of the art? (4) Having regard to such development or difference, would the taking of the step be obvious to the skilled person?[18]

Regardless of the inquiry applied, the analysis of AI-related inventions in Categories 1–3 should be the same as in any other technology. Namely, in all three of these categories, one or more human inventors have claimed an invention that will need to be deemed as having, or not having, inventive step based on the state of the prior art at the relevant time and considered through the eyes of the skilled person in that art.

AI-related inventions in Category 4, where a human inventor has employed AI as a tool to make an invention, would be subject to the same standard. However, here we have the question of whether the level of skill in the art includes the level of skill of a person employing an AI tool. Because AI can generate a universe of possible solutions to any problem, a net effect of this may be a heightening of the effective level of skill in the art. However, to be clear, this is conjecture as no such cases have yet arisen in South Africa.

Finally, considering the hypothetical case where the AI itself is an inventor, and setting aside for the moment the inventorship obstacles that hypothetical brings, a question arises under either enquiry as to how to define the person skilled in the art. Ultimately, if an AI entity were allowed to be an inventor, then perhaps the level of skill in the art would be another AI entity having training and capabilities as of the filing date. Again, this is pure conjecture.

In summary, for the time being and at least until sentient machines take the stage, inventive step in South Africa will be judged according to one of the two enquiries noted above, considering the state of the art as of the priority date and the knowledge of the person (human) skilled in that art.

§14.05 ADEQUACY OF DISCLOSURE

A South African patent can be revoked for failing sufficiently to describe, ascertain and, where necessary, illustrate or exemplify the invention and the way it is to be performed in order to enable the invention to be carried out by a person skilled in the art of such invention.[19] The patentee need only describe the way the invention is to be performed; no explanation or theory as to how the invention works is required.[20] Further, the addressee of the patent is presumed to know the art and they are expected to read the directions in the specification in the light of all technical and

17. *Roman Roller CC and another v. Speedmark Holdings (Pty) Ltd* 1995 BP 199 (A) and Burrell, s. 4.12.
18. *EnsignBickford (South Africa) (Pty) Ltd and others v. AECI Explosives and Chemicals Ltd* 1998 BIP 271 (SCA).
19. Patents Act, s. 61(1)(e).
20. Burrell, s. 4.28 referring to *Lego M Lemelstreich Ltd v. HydroPlan Engineering Ltd* 1981 BP 1 (CP) at 9BC.

factual knowledge in the art.[21] A specification should not be held to be insufficient if the person to whom it is addressed would be able to carry out the process claimed, without any difficulty and with the aid of simple or routine experiments not requiring any prolonged researched or inquiry.[22]

Without any law specifically relating to the categories of AI-related inventions under consideration here, it is difficult to theorize how these principles would be applied. Although there is no case law that specifically concerns inventions in Categories 1 and 2, these are software, hardware, algorithms, and combinations thereof and it is safe to assume that the principles discussed above can be complied with. While there may be eligibility issues depending on how technical they are, it is unlikely that inventions in these categories will present new issues from a sufficiency of disclosure standpoint.

Category 3 inventions, which are applications of known AI to a new use case (recognizing a face, causing a car to navigate, and many, many others), may not be as straightforward. The vast majority of AI-related patent applications fall in this category. However, in many, particularly when the AI is 'off the shelf', the defining feature of what makes the AI suited to purpose is the data with which it is trained. Questions that may arise in this context, and which will have to be settled through case law, may include: how much detail must be given to describe the training data? Is it enough to generally say what type of data should be used? What if the training data is data that only a small number of people would have access to (like internet search data)? Is the duty of disclosing the data heightened in that case? At this point, these are open questions in South Africa.

For inventions in Categories 4 and 5, what is being claimed is whatever invention the human used AI to make (or, theoretically, the AI made itself). It could be a hammer. A shoe. A beverage container. As mentioned above, in South Africa, the patentee need only describe the way the invention is to be performed. No explanation or theory as to how the invention works is required. It follows that there is no duty to disclose the manner by which an invention was made. So, apart from the inventorship issue with Category 5 inventions, there might be no indication in the patent application that AI was used at all. It can be expected that the sufficiency of disclosure issues will be no different from a comparable case that did not involve an AI in the making of the invention.

§14.06 INVENTORSHIP

[A] Inventorship in General

The Patents Act does not define an inventor. Nor does it stipulate requirements for being named as an inventor. However, certain rights are conferred by the Patents Act on to the inventor. Section 27 of the Patents Act specifies that an inventor may apply for a patent in respect of an invention or, alternatively, any other person acquiring from the inventor the right to do so may apply for the patent. It is also

21. Burrell, s. 4.32 referring to *Weiss v. Viljoen NO* 1956 BP 205 (CP) at 214F-215A.
22. *Unilever Ltd v. Colgate-Palmolive Co.*, 1977 BP 200 (CP) at 204G-205A.

possible that both the inventor and such other person can apply.[23] In the absence of an agreement to the contrary, joint inventors may apply for a patent in equal and undivided shares.[24] Generally, then, the invention is the inventor's to pursue either him- or herself, or to allow another party to pursue.

In the case of a person other than the inventor making or joining an application for a patent, that person must furnish such proof of his title or authority to apply for a patent in the prescribed manner.[25] The manner in which to furnish such proof as prescribed in the Patent Regulations is 'an assignment or other proof, to the satisfaction of the registrar, of the right of the applicant to apply'.[26]

In practice, for applications made by an employer for an invention made by his employee acting within the course and scope of his duties, no assignment of invention is necessary. The Registrar typically requires proof of the relationship between the employer and employee either by providing a copy of the contract of employment or by affidavit.[27]

A register is kept at the Patent Office in which, amongst other details, the names and addresses of applicants for and grantees of patents and of the inventors of the relevant inventions are entered.[28]

Where a dispute arises between persons as to their rights to obtain a patent for an invention, or as to the right to or title in a patent, any such party may apply to the commissioner who will decide the matter in dispute.[29]

Further, available grounds of revocation of a patent relating to the question of inventorship include that 'the patentee is not a person entitled under section 27 to apply for the patent';[30] that 'the grant of the patent is in fraud of the rights of the applicant or of any person under or through whom he claims';[31] and that 'the prescribed declaration lodged in respect of the application for the patent contains a false statement or representation which is material and which the patentee knew to be false at the time when the declaration was made'.[32]

The courts however tend to be pragmatic in this regard. For example, omitting an inventor's name through clerical error can be rectified by way of a correction to stave off an application for revocation based on the ground that the prescribed declaration lodged in support of the application for the patent contains a false statement or representation which is material and which the patentee knew to be false at the time when the declaration was made.[33]

Where a patent is revoked on the ground of fraud, or a patent fraudulently obtained has been surrendered and revoked, the inventor of the relevant invention or

23. Patents Act, s. 27(1).
24. *Ibid.*, s. 27(2).
25. *Ibid.*, s. 30(4).
26. The Patent Regulations, Regulation 22(1)(d).
27. Burrell s. 2.18 referring to *Firm Construction Co Ltd v. Kusel* 1997 BIP 25 (CP) at 30E.
28. Patents Act, s. 10(10).
29. *Ibid.*, s. 28(1). This section also covers the right to make, use, exercise or dispose of an invention.
30. *Ibid.*, s. 61(1)(a).
31. *Ibid.*, s. 61(1)(b).
32. *Ibid.*, s. 61(1)(g).
33. *Hokuriku Pharmaceutical Co Ltd v. Cipla-Medpro (Pty) Ltd* 1999 BIP 384 (CP).

his assignee or legal representative may apply to have the grant of a patent directed to him for the whole or any part of the invention.[34]

Inventorship therefore plays an important part in South African patent law. However, as mentioned above, the Act does not define 'inventor'. Historically, and much like the UK, in South African patent law an inventor included an 'importer' who had imported the invention into the country.[35] This changed in 1896[36] in the decision of *Hay v. African Gold Recovery*[37] in terms of which the words 'first and true inventor' were taken in their natural sense, not limited to persons in the country, but rather to signify the person who made the discovery before anyone else in any part of the world.[38]

Since then, the actual question of what is required to be listed as an inventor in South Africa has not been considered by South Africa's courts.

[B] Determination of Inventorship for AI-Related Inventions

As mentioned above, the South African Patents Act does not define an 'inventor' and the lack of case law makes it difficult to theorize on how the different categories of AI-related inventions might be dealt with by South African courts. With respect to AI-related inventions in Categories 1–4 – all of which involve a human inventor – it is reasonable to assume that inventorship would be treated no differently than with respect to non AI-related inventions.

Regarding Category 5, however, it may be possible to name AI as an inventor or co-inventor. There is no explicit requirement in the Patents Act, the Patent Regulations, or case law that the inventor be a natural person, although the Patents Act does use the pronouns 'him' and 'he' when dealing with inventors and applicants. This could simply be because nothing other than a human inventor was contemplated as being possible in 1978.

The Patents Act allows a person acquiring from an inventor the right to apply for a patent to lodge an application for an invention made by that inventor, provided such person can furnish such proof of his title or authority to apply for the patent in the prescribed manner. Employers can file patent applications for inventions made by employees without an assignment agreement, and in practice just need to evidence the employer-employee relationship.[39]

Until there is case law that confirms otherwise, it could therefore be submitted that a person having made and controlling the AI could 'acquire from the AI' the right to lodge a patent application for an invention made by the AI. Of course, similar such arguments have been debunked by courts in the UK and Australia in the case of applications listing DABUS as an inventor in patent applications.

---

34. Patents Act, s. 63.
35. Burrell, s. 2.2.
36. In what was then the Cape Colony, which would be united with three other colonies in 1910 to become the Union of South Africa.
37. (1896) 3 OR 338 (Dutch text), (1896) 3 OR 244 (English translation at 277), discussed in Burrell at s. 2.2.
38. Burrell, s. 2.2.
39. *See* preceding section.

Yet, the South African patent application lodged by the Artificial Inventor Project listing DABUS as the inventor was granted by the South African Patent Office.[40] This may have been because of a technicality found in a 2009 'Practice Note' issued by the South African Patent Office, in terms of which 'Proof of Assignment of Invention with regard to PCT Applications ... will not be required ...[w]here the applicant recorded on the PCT Pamphlet is the same as the applicant recorded on the priority application thereof'.[41] This requirement was met in the case of the DABUS application, so all formal requirements of the application were met and the patent was accepted and granted. It is not clear how the Patent Office would have reacted had it not been for the Practice Note and had the applicant lodged an affidavit setting out the proof of entitlement to apply for an invention made by DABUS.

In discussing this grant, Thaldar et al.[42] argue that the point of departure when interpreting the Patents Act in South Africa is that South African law prescribes a purposive approach to statutory interpretation. They submit that the patenting of inventions by AI systems should be allowed. They arrive at this conclusion by considering that the Patents Act recites its objective as being to 'provide for the registration and granting of letters patent for inventions and for matters connected therewith' together with the IP Policy[43] stating that IP is an important policy instrument in promoting innovation and the like.[44] Policy reasons that might be against such an interpretation are not dealt with.

The validity of this decision by the Patent Office could be challenged in court. Until then, the South African patent stands.

§14.07 AREAS FOR FURTHER DEVELOPMENT

South Africa is in need of case law and guidelines from the Patent Office once substantive search and examination has commenced.

§14.08 RECOMMENDATIONS FOR PATENT APPLICANTS

Indications are that an approach similar to what is applied in Europe will be followed in South Africa once substantive search and examination has commenced. However, this is not a foregone conclusion. Applicants should therefore be careful not to dismiss filing in South Africa for fear that a particular invention that might not be treated

40. Acceptance of patent application no. 2021/03242 listing DABUS as the inventor was published in the *South African Patent Journal*, Vol. 54, No. 07, Part 2, p. 255.
41. This Practice Note was replaced by a new one in January 2023 in which the provision discussed here is no longer present. The new Practice Note does however allow for, 'where the rights to the invention have been transferred from the inventor to the applicant by virtue of operation of law, a statement by the applicant on form P3 that the rights to the invention made by the inventor have been transferred to the applicant by virtue of the provisions of the relevant Act,' to satisfy the requirements as to proof of entitlement to apply for the patent.
42. D. Thaldar and M. Naidoo, 'AI inventorship: The right decision?', *S. Afr. J. Sci.* vol. 117 no. 11/12 (2021).
43. Phase 1 of the South African IP Policy.
44. Thaldar et al., p. 2.

favourably in Europe would receive the same treatment in South Africa. There is scope for different interpretation in South Africa and until we have case law and guidelines from the Patent Office, applicants have the opportunity to play a part in determining where the boundaries of subject matter eligibility, inventorship and sufficiency of disclosure lie.

§14.09 CONCLUSION

South Africa's Patents Act contains subject matter exclusions which are similar to those of the UK and Europe. However, South African case law has not yet interpreted these provisions for the South African context. The issues of inventorship and adequacy of disclosure are similarly undeveloped in so far as they relate to the categories of AI-related inventions under discussion here. Until such time as these issues have been settled, applicants can adopt a more generous interpretation of these provisions while keeping in mind that a UK or European-centric approach may ultimately be adopted by South Africa's courts.

Chapter 15

South Korea

Seong Tahk Ahn, Peter Sungjin Chun & Dr Mincheol Kim

§15.01 PATENTABILITY OF SOFTWARE AND COMPUTER-IMPLEMENTED INVENTIONS

The Korean Patent Act (the 'Patent Act') provides that inventions having industrial applicability may be patentable, subject to prior art considerations:

> (1) inventions having industrial applicability may be patentable unless they fall under any of the following subparagraphs:
>
> 1. Inventions publicly known or worked ... prior to the filing of the patent application;
> 2. Inventions described in a publication distributed ... prior to the filing of the patent application...
>
> (2) Notwithstanding paragraph (1), where an invention could easily be made prior to the filing of the patent application by a person having ordinary skill in the art to which the invention pertains ... no patent shall be granted. [1]

The Patent Act does not provide specific guidance as to patentability of software and computer-implemented inventions. However, the Korean Intellectual Property Office ('KIPO') has issued Examination Guidelines for Specific Technical Fields ('STF Guidelines')[2] that include a chapter for Computer-Related Inventions.[3] The STF Guidelines introduce the general state of law in Korea regarding the patentability of software and computer-implemented inventions.

1. Patent Act, Republic of Korea, Art. 29.
2. *STF Guidelines*, KIPO, Jan. 2022.
3. *Ibid.*, pp. 53–84.

[A] Eligibility of an Invention

The assessment of eligibility is summarized in the STF Guidelines as follows.[4]

For computer-related inventions where information processing by software is concretely implemented by using hardware resources, the following are considered patent-eligible subject matter as a creation of technical ideas utilizing a law of nature:

- an information processing apparatus (machine) that cooperatively operates with the software; a method for operating the same;
- a computer-readable medium having the software recorded thereon; and
- a computer program recorded on the medium.

However, a computer program *per se* is considered to be a mere list of instructions to operate a computer and, therefore, is not patent eligible. The phrase 'information processing by software is concretely implemented by using hardware resources' means that, 'the information processing apparatus (machine) or a method for operating the same particularly suitable for a use purpose is constructed by implementing arithmetic operation or manipulation of information depending on the said use purpose through concrete means or methods in which software and hardware are cooperatively working, i.e., the combination of software and hardware is used.'

Meanwhile, when an invention is merely created by: (i) laws other than a law of nature (such as economic laws); (ii) arbitrary arrangements (such as design of cryptographs); (iii) mental activity or offline behaviour (such as an invention mainly constituting of human behaviour using the general functions of a computer or internet system); or (iv) mere presentation of information (such as computer program listings); the invention is not a creation of technical ideas utilizing a law of nature. Therefore, in these cases, patent eligibility of the invention is denied.

In general, the patent eligibility of computer-related inventions is not strictly assessed under Korean patent practice. The patent eligibility of the invention is satisfied even if technical ideas are embodied in a general-purpose computer. Also, whether technical ideas are specifically claimed tends to be assessed in terms of novelty/inventive step rather than in terms of eligibility.

[B] Novelty/Inventive Step of an Invention

When assessing novelty/inventive step of computer-related inventions, the STF Guidelines provide for consideration of the following issues.[5]

Technical problems in connection with 'software implementation' or 'computerization' are common to computer/software technologies. The problems include, for example, 'to improve the level of decision-making by using Artificial Intelligence (AI) or Fuzzy Logic' or 'to make input-operation easier by using a Graphical User Interface (GUI).' Novelty and inventive step of a given invention are assessed taking into consideration the fact that such problems are generally known problems in the related art.

4. *Ibid.*, pp. 61–76.
5. *Ibid.*, pp. 76–83.

Also, general technical effects such as, 'can be processed quickly', 'can process a large amount of data', 'can reduce errors', and 'can obtain uniform results' are often naturally obtained as a result of computerization. Thus, novelty and inventive step of a given invention are assessed taking into consideration the fact that such effects are generally known effects in the related art.

When the invention corresponds to exercise of ordinary creativity by a Person of Ordinary Skill in The Art ('POSITA'), novelty/inventive step can be denied. The STF Guidelines provide some examples of what would be considered ordinary creativity by a POSITA:

(i) a 'file retrieval system' described in the prior art is applied to an information system in a specific industrial field;
(ii) functions that are otherwise performed by hardware are implemented by software;
(iii) human transactions or business methods are implemented by a system;
(iv) a known event is reproduced in a computerized virtual space such as virtual reality and augmented reality;
(v) a differentiating feature between the claimed invention and the prior art merely exists in data contents, or only a limitation of 'recording a program or data on a computer-readable storage medium' is added to the claim;
(vi) a claimed invention is only specified by features unique to the information transmission medium, for example, 'a medium which can transmit certain information such as a program and a data'; and
(vii) the prior art or a well-known technique in the art is merely implemented by Artificial Intelligence (AI) technology.[6]

§15.02 SPECIAL PROVISIONS RELATING TO PATENTABILITY OF INVENTIONS RELATING TO AI

As noted above, the Patent Act does not provide special provisions regarding the patentability of AI-related inventions. The STF Guidelines were published in December 2020 and updated in January 2022. The STF Guidelines include a chapter on AI-related inventions,[7] which explains: i) description requirements including enablement requirements; ii) patentability requirements such as eligibility requirements, novelty and inventive step; and iii) examples of examination cases of AI-related inventions. Specifically, the examples of examination cases include five examination cases of AI-related inventions, discussed in more detail below, directed to machine learning and provide examples of determining description requirements and inventive step. In the STF Guidelines, under a chapter titled, 'Cases of assessing inventive step of the 4th Industrial Revolution-related applications,' examples of assessing inventive step of AI-related inventions are further cited.[8]

The STF Guidelines regarding AI-related inventions are applicable to inventions that require AI technology based on machine learning. The STF Guidelines divide

6. *Ibid.*, pp. 78–80.
7. *Ibid.*, pp. 1101–1432.
8. *Ibid.*, pp. 127–134.

machine learning-based AI-related inventions into AI learning modelling inventions and AI applied inventions. The basic overview diagram of AI-related inventions used in these STF Guidelines is as follows:[9]

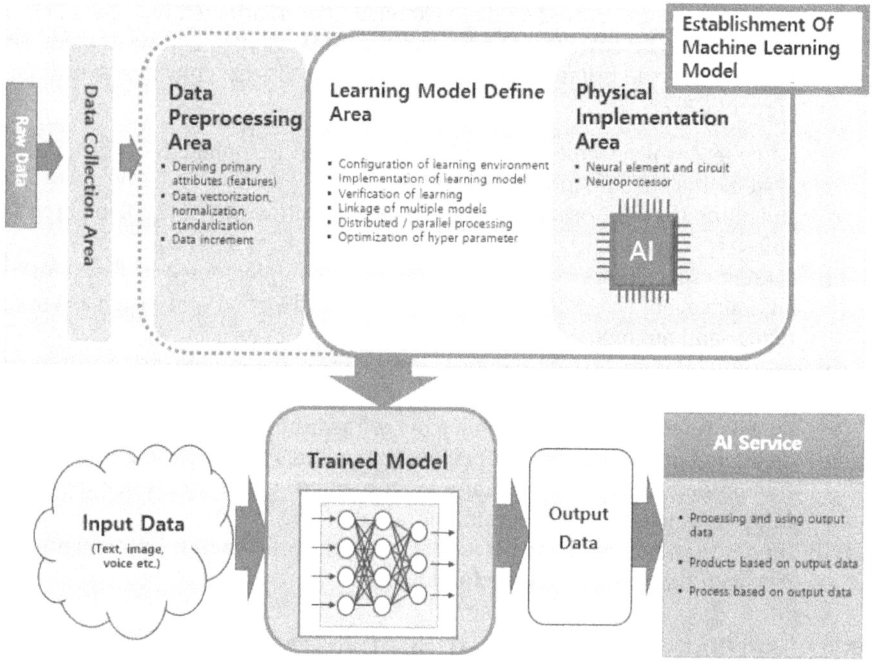

AI learning modelling inventions are inventions whose feature resides in creating a model that is trained based on learning data (i.e., raw data collected for use in learning) and learning models (which includes learning methods such as learning algorithms and/or data preprocessing). Examples of such inventions include a method for accelerating learning model computation, a data normalization method, and an automatic generation method of learning models. Accordingly, AI learning modelling inventions as defined by KIPO would fall under Category 1 or 2 as defined in this book.

AI application inventions are inventions whose feature resides in performing specific functions by applying learning data and/or trained models to solve problems in various fields. These fields are determined by apparatus (hardware) that implements operations according to the purpose of use. Examples of such inventions include AI autonomous mobile robots, AI medical appliances, or business method inventions utilizing AI. Accordingly, AI application inventions as defined by KIPO would fall under Category 3 as defined in this book.

For any issues not addressed in the specific guidelines for AI-related inventions, KIPO will examine an invention according to the guidelines for Computer-Related

9. *Ibid.*, p. 1101.

Inventions in the STF Guidelines, which also contain some points relating to AI-related inventions.

For example, the assessment of inventive step of 'an invention where prior art or well-known or commonly used art is implemented with AI technology' is described. When claims of an invention specify the unique processing of information obtained from a model that is trained so that the AI technology can perform specific tasks, and the invention has an effect better than the prior art or well-known or commonly used art in view of the detailed description and common sense, inventive step of the invention will be recognized. However, when the invention is merely an implementation of the prior art or well-known or commonly used art using AI technology while not specifying any unique processing of information obtained from a learning model, and when such invention is not recognized to have an effect better than the prior art or well-known or commonly used art, it is unlikely that the invention would be considered to have inventive step.[10]

The technical problems in connection with 'software implementation' or 'computerization' are often common to computer/software technologies. An invention for improving the level of decision-making by using AI is an example of addressing such problems. The assessment of inventive step should be made taking into consideration whether improving the level of decision-making by using AI is a generally known problem.[11]

The eligibility of AI-related inventions ultimately depends on whether such inventions correspond to a 'creation of a technical idea utilizing the laws of nature', which involves considering whether the claims recite 'a specific means or a specific method in which software and hardware cooperate to realize the computation or processing of specific information according to the purpose of use' to obtain the same repetitive effects without intervention of the mental activity of a natural person.[12]

§15.03 SUBJECT MATTER PATENTABILITY

[A] Eligibility Criteria in Korea

As noted *supra*, Article 29, Paragraph 1 of the Patent Act[13] stipulates that an invention having industrial applicability is patentable. In this regard, the General Examination Guidelines for Patent and Utility Model[14] interpret 'invention having industrial applicability' as specifying two separate requirements: the statutory invention requirement and the industrial applicability requirement. The statutory invention requirement means that a patentable invention must fall under 'invention' as defined under the patent law. The industrial applicability requirement means that an invention is patentable only if the invention is considered industrially applicable. There is no doubt that all inventions should be industrially applicable since the purpose of the Patent

10. *STF Guidelines*, p. 83.
11. *Ibid.*, p. 77.
12. *Ibid.*, p. 75.
13. Patent Act, Art. 29, para. 1.
14. *The General Examination Guidelines for Patent and Utility Model*, KIPO, Dec. 2021.

Act is to contribute to the development of industry.[15] Therefore, the above-specified statutory invention requirement would be considered essential in determining patent eligibility under Korean patent law.

Regarding the definition of statutory invention, Article 2 of the Patent Act[16] stipulates that 'invention means the highly advanced creation of a technical idea using the laws of nature'. In other words, Korean patent law has a direct definition as to what an invention is and, therefore, analysis of this definition is a starting point of discussion regarding patent eligibility in Korea. The General Examination Guidelines for Patent and Utility Model provide detailed explanations as to the meaning of statutory invention under the patent law as explained in Section §15.01, *supra*.

[B] Types of Statutory Inventions

Under the STF Guidelines, a computer-related invention can be claimed as either a method or a process. Accordingly, AI-related inventions can also be claimed in the same manner. However, in Korea, software or a computer program itself cannot be a statutory type of invention.

[1] Method Invention

A computer-related invention can be claimed as a method by specifying a series of processes or operations connected in a time sequence, namely steps.

[2] Product Invention

A computer-related invention can be claimed as a product, such as a computer device, or computer system by specifying multiple functions performed thereby. A computer-related invention can also be claimed as a computer readable medium having program code recorded thereon to install, execute or distribute the program, or a computer program recorded in a medium to accomplish a specific task or a specific need when combined with hardware.

[C] Actual Operation in Eligibility Examination in the KIPO

The eligibility test according to the statutory invention requirement does not appear to operate well in Korean patent practice. In order to find the reason for this, it is necessary to go back to the history of how the Patent Act came to have such a definition. The Patent Act introduced the definition, 'invention means the highly advanced creation of a technical idea using the laws of nature' by revision of the law in 1963.[17] That definition apparently was based on an academic definition by

15. The industrial applicability requirement has been used, for example, to deny the patentability of medical method inventions for treating a human disease under Korean patent practice.
16. Patent Act, Art. 2.
17. Amendment to Patent Act of Mar. 5, 1963.

nineteenth century German jurist Aller Kohler.[18] In other words, the definition in the Patent Act was drafted very long ago and has been maintained so far without any revision. On the other hand, human technology has undergone so much change and innovation compared to the 19th century. Therefore, at first glance, doubts arise over whether the 19th century's invention definition correctly and effectively defines inventions being created by modern science and technology.

In addition, the definition of 'technical idea using natural laws' is so compressed that it is difficult to understand what it means in detail, and courts in South Korea have avoided drawing a clear line between the area in which statutory inventions belong and those in which they do not belong. Therefore, ordinary patent practitioners are not confident to clearly understand the boundaries derived from such definition and it is hard to avoid the perception that the definition is rather vague.

For these reasons, the provisions on statutory invention in the Patent Act are often criticized, treated as outdated, excluded from deeper research, and are poorly utilized in practice. On the other hand, as explained in detail below, some argue that this statutory definition of invention summarizes the current requirements in a very sophisticated way, and therefore it is effective to judge the eligibility of inventions using this definition.[19]

In Korean practice, even if eligibility of the invention is suspect, most examiners do not directly deny the eligibility of the invention under the statutory invention requirement of Article 29 paragraph 1. Rather, they prefer to give reasons for rejection on the grounds that the descriptions are unclear or that inventions lack novelty or inventive step by finding prior art. Such practices have been going on for a long time and there seems to be no movement within KIPO to change them. However, eligibility is the root of the matter inherent in the invention, and not a matter that can be overcome by clarifying descriptions of inventions or by clarifying the difference between the invention and the conventional technology. Sometimes, this practical opportunism happens to give exclusive rights to mathematical algorithms close to natural laws, economic laws, and artificial human decisions, mental process or human activity that should not be given exclusive rights.

Korean examiners typically do not proactively judge the statutory invention requirement due to one or more of the following factors:

1. They have not been doing that for a long time;
2. It is convenient for them to bypass the statutory invention requirement and apply another type of rejection, such as description requirements;
3. It is difficult to determine whether the invention conforms to the definition of invention; and
4. The definition of invention is often criticized as being out of date for failing to adapt to new technologies, so it is unlikely that the examiners will be criticized due to incomplete examination even if they do not seriously consider whether the invention conforms to the definition of invention.

18. *Understanding the Patent Act of the Republic of Korea*, KIPO, Chap. 3, s. 1, part II, available at: https://www.kipo.go.kr/upload/en/download/Understanding_the_Patent_Act_of_the_Republic_of_Korea.pdf.
19. Park, Jun-seok, 'A Study on the Definition for Invention in the Korean Patent Act', *Seoul Law Journal* Vol. 54, No. 3, pp. 763–841 (Sept. 2013).

On the other hand, the General Examination Guidelines for Patent and Utility Model have developed and set the specific criteria for this statutory invention requirements since 2006. These Guidelines clarify the statutory eligibility criteria by saying that if a claimed invention does not involve logic or mathematical principles themselves, or methods directly using them, but instead involves technical devices or methods that give useful, concrete and tangible results by increasing or controlling the performance of a certain technical tools with the data which has been transformed by such mathematical algorithm, and if the technical devices or technical methods are considered as universal, repeatable and objective as a reasonable means for resolving a specific problem, they are deemed to be a statutory invention, i.e., a 'highly advanced creation of a technical idea using the laws of nature'.

In order for a software-related device or method to meet the requirements for statutory invention, the STF Guidelines require that 'information processing by software is concretely implemented by using hardware in the claimed invention'. In other words, if software and hardware resources are working cooperatively to provide a concrete means by which an arithmetic operation or manipulation of information depending on a purpose is actually realized, and information processing equipment or its operational method is constructed with a specific purpose, the claimed invention constitutes 'a creation of a technical idea using the laws of nature'.

The United States Patent and Trademark Office ('USPTO') published revised guidelines regarding eligibility requirements under US law in January 2019 based on experience gained after the famous *Alice* case from the U.S. Supreme Court in 2014.[20] According to the revised USPTO guidelines, the eligibility criteria can be summarized in three steps: a first step is to determine if the invention belongs to a judicial exception (mathematical algorithm, human activity, mental process), a second step is to determine whether the invention has a practical application, and the last step is to determine if there is there is 'something significantly more' in the invention. In comparison, the Korean Patent Act, as interpreted by the General Examination Guidelines for Patent and Utility Model, defines a 'technical idea using natural laws' to mean:

(i) an invention should not be a technical idea using a human's decisions or mental process which is not a natural law;
(ii) natural laws should be 'used' for the invention but cannot be the invention itself and, therefore, the invention should have a specific technical problem to be solved and achieve technical effect objectively and repeatedly, but it should not be an academic achievement, such as a mathematical algorithm without such a specific application; and
(iii) an invention should be a technical idea, not an artful or artificial creation.

It is important to note that the revised U.S. examination guidelines do not substantially differ from the current Korean examination guidelines, and therefore the eligibility definition in Korea largely mirrors the current USPTO standard. Accordingly, the Korean Patent Act's definition of invention and the practical support by the General Examination Guidelines for Patent and Utility Model not only express the traditional ideas of eligibility standards established and developed in the U.S. through the *Deener*

20. *Alice Corp. v. CLS Bank International*, 573 U. S. 208 (2014).

case,[21] the *Benson* case,[22] the *Flook* case,[23] and the *Diehr* case,[24] but also share the same thoughts with the recently revised USPTO eligibility guidelines.

Notwithstanding the above, Korean patent examiners tend to apply the statutory invention requirement less strictly when reviewing the eligibility of AI inventions even though the requirement itself does not differ substantially from that of other countries such as the United States. Against this backdrop, we look at the eligibility of the five Categories of AI inventions presented in this book.

[D] Categories 1 and 2

Algorithms, in general, are often made up of a combination of basic natural laws, which may be regarded as something that use natural laws themselves. However, algorithms themselves are mathematical and/or logical tools that are not yet applied to industry, regardless of whether they are specific or general, or simple or complex. Further, regardless of whether the algorithms are using other natural laws or other algorithms, they are classified as natural laws themselves, and do not belong to the statutory invention under patent law.

Regardless of whether an AI is a core algorithm or a system equipped with a filter or interface, such AI may remain as a 'natural law', not as a 'technical idea using natural law' unless it is used to solve any particular problem. However, if it can be shown that an AI's core algorithm, or a system with a filter or interface, is being used to solve certain problems, and if its technological effects have universality, repeatability, and objectivity, such AI invention would meet the statutory invention requirement.

With respect to an invention of AI training which does not recite any specific target or purpose of the training in claims, it would be a difficult question to determine whether such invention is equivalent to a pure algorithm that does not have eligibility, or whether the method of training itself is considered to be an application with eligibility. Korean examiners are currently granting patents for inventions regarding how to train AI unless there is obviousness in view of a prior art, thus the current tendency is to recognize its eligibility in Korea.

[E] Category 3

If AI inventions are specifying applications to address specific problems, chances are high that they will satisfy eligibility. Eligibility issues may arise in a case where AI is simply applied to conventional solutions. However, if technical effects obtained by applying AI are predictable by ordinary technicians, it should be an issue of inventive step, not an issue of eligibility.

21. *Cochrane v. Deener*, 94 U.S. 780 (1876).
22. *Gottschalk v. Benson*, 409 U.S. 63 (1971).
23. *Parker v. Flook*, 437 U.S. 584 (1978).
24. *Diamond v. Diehr*, 450 U.S. 175 (1981).

[F] Categories 4 and 5

Unlike in Categories 1–3, where AI or an application of AI is being claimed, in Categories 4 and 5 what is being claimed is what was created by or using AI not AI itself. Even if AI contributes to the creation of an invention, patent eligibility is a question on the created invention itself, i.e., what is claimed, not a question on inventorship. So, there is no room for discussion of inventorship to affect the determination on eligibility. Even if a general AI is developed and inventions in Category 5 are devised in the future, the determination of eligibility will remain focused on the claimed invention, i.e., what was created by AI and not on the AI itself.

§15.04 INVENTIVE STEP

According to the STF Guidelines,[25] when comparing an invention set forth in the claims to a cited invention, novelty and inventiveness should be determined by extracting the corresponding points and differences between technical constituents of both inventions with regard to the concrete means (learning data, data preprocessing method, learning model, loss function, *etc.*) of implementing the AI-related invention.

An AI-related invention, including a specific trained model, may have different outcomes or effects depending on the applied industrial field. Novelty and inventiveness are not necessarily denied for there being no difference in technical constituents between the claimed invention and cited prior art in cases where an AI-related invention overcomes a problem which had been unsolved for a long time in a specific industrial field, or overcomes a technical difficulty in a specific industrial field, or achieves superior effect by changing the industrial field.

An AI-related invention may have different learning model outcomes and performance depending on the learning data. It is difficult to recognize inventiveness only by the difference in learning data between the claimed invention and cited prior art, and it is appropriate to determine novelty and inventiveness in consideration of whether specific information processing on the learning data adopted in the claimed invention is recited, and whether better effects have occurred due to the difference in learning data.

When an AI-related invention specifically sets forth in its claims the configuration using the results output through the trained model, the products based on the output result, and the processing method based on the output result, and has remarkable effects therefrom, its inventiveness may be recognized.

[A] Categories 1–3

In 2010, the Korean Patent Court issued a decision[26] defining a POSITA as, 'a virtual natural person who can obtain all the published material, regardless of whether it is domestic or foreign, in the technical level of the relevant technical field at the time of the patent application and make them his or her own knowledge, and can use such

25. *The STF Guidelines*, pp. 1311–1324.
26. Patent Court decision 2008HER8150, Mar. 19 2010.

knowledge freely for research and development.' If that definition of POSITA is applied to the field of AI, a POSITA of an AI-related invention is a person who is expected to have common general knowledge both in the applied field of AI software-related inventions and computer technology (e.g., AI systematization technology); use ordinary technical means for research and development; exercise ordinary creative activity in design modification; and be able to comprehend all the state of the art in the field of AI technology as of the filing date. In addition, a POSITA is presumed to be able to comprehend as his/her own knowledge all technical matters in the field of AI technology relevant to a problem to be solved by an invention.

There are many cases in which steps or means for implementing the function used in computer-related inventions are common in function or operation, regardless of the applied field to which the invention belongs. In such cases, it is within the ordinary creative activity expected of a POSITA to apply such steps or means of AI-related inventions used in certain applied fields to other fields to implement the same function or operation.

Since alleged general effects such as 'can be processed quickly', 'can process a large amount of data', 'can reduce errors', 'can obtain uniform results' are often obtained as a result of computerization, these types of results usually cannot be said to be unforeseeable from the knowledge of the state of the art. Inventive step of a claimed invention is therefore assessed taking the aforementioned general effects into consideration.

The novelty and/or inventive step of a claimed invention cannot be affirmatively inferred when it is ascertained that a different feature between the AI invention and the closest prior art exists merely in data contents. For example, if there exists the closest prior art of 'apparatus for detecting an image feature', inventions of 'apparatus for detecting an apple image feature' or 'apparatus for detecting a banana image feature' would be denied novelty and/or inventive step because the difference lies only in the contents of the data.

According to examination examples in the STF Guidelines, Korean examiners compare claimed inventions and prior technologies in terms of (i) technical field, (ii) learning data, and (iii) learning models. There are several examples that recognize a difference in effect and thus recognize inventive step when the claimed invention has different learning models compared to the prior art, even when the claimed invention has conventional learning data. In those cases, the learning model was recognized to have inventive step because it changed the way the conventional artificial neural network is arranged and/or had a difference in the method of pre-processing learning data even though it was not a new core AI such as a Category 1 invention.

In one example from the STF Guidelines, inventive step of an invention relating to an urban traffic prediction system is recognized because the system predicts the average speed of vehicles more accurately in a particular section by clustering learning data in similar patterns and individually performing local Artificial Neural Network ('ANN') learning on input pattern vectors within each cluster. Similarly, in another example, inventive step is recognized for an invention relating to bone age estimation because the invention applied additional sub-neural networks to improve reliability and accuracy in bone age readings while using a conventional ANN or Convolutional Neural Network ('CNN').

As another example, an invention of a real-time welding quality inspection device using AI had the same technology field and learning model compared to those of Reference 1, with differences existing in the learning data only. Reference 2 disclosed the same learning data as the claimed invention (e.g., characteristic data such as the width between a valley and a hill of the welding bud and the determination value of defect). The examiner denied inventive step on the grounds that it was easy to combine References 1 and 2 and that the invention had no noticeable effect when compared to the prior art. This example illustrates that, in determining inventive step of AI, if the technology field, learning data, and learning model are disclosed in several prior art references separately, the general inventive step judging method should be applied to examine the difficulty of combining the prior art and the remarkability of the technical effect, if any, of the claimed invention compared to that of the prior art.

[B] Categories 4 and 5

As noted *supra*, for AI-related inventions in Categories 4 and 5, what is claimed is the output of the use of AI, not the AI itself. Therefore, what is claimed could be in any field and, unless AI is being used to invent new AI, the AI would not be recited in the claim. Accordingly, inventive step for these types of inventions would be judged under the general rule, considering a POSITA having common general knowledge in the field that is claimed. Thus, inventive step of Category 4 inventions should be determined by whether the claimed solution would have been obtained from the state of art at the time of the filing from the view of the POSITA and by whether the technical effects derived from the claimed solution are noticeable or unexpected.

With respect to Category 5 inventions, i.e., inventions that do not involve a human inventor, as described *infra*, no one can be considered an inventor according to current law – neither AI nor an owner or manufacturer of the AI. Because it is not possible to grant exclusive rights to anyone, there currently is no guidance regarding determination of inventive step of a Category 5 invention.

§15.05 ADEQUACY OF DISCLOSURE

According to Korean law, the description of an invention shall be stated in such a manner that a POSITA in the field of AI-related inventions can carry out the claimed invention on the basis of the description in the specification and drawings and the common general knowledge as of the filing.[27]

If the description of an invention states technical steps or functions corresponding to those recited in a claim in an abstract manner, but does not disclose how the steps or functions can be implemented or performed by hardware or software, thus making it impossible or very difficult to perform the claimed invention, such disclosure does not meet the enablement requirement under the Korean patent law. For example, when an information processing system to execute an application of AI is recited in a claim, if there is no disclosure in the description of the invention

27. Patent Act., Art. 42, para. 3.

on how to implement such application on a computer, then the invention is unable to be carried out and such disclosure does not meet the enablement requirement.

According to the STF Guidelines,[28] the detailed description of the invention should specifically describe a correlation between input data and output data from a trained model to implement AI-related inventions. Cases in which the correlation is specifically described include those where: 1) learning data is specified; 2) there is a correlation among the characteristics of learning data to solve the technical problems of the invention; 3) the learning model or learning method to be trained using the learning data is specifically described; and 4) a trained model for solving the technical problems of the invention is generated by the learning data and the learning method.

When data preprocessing, which converts collected raw data into learning data, is a characteristic technology of the invention, and (i) the invention does not describe how to perform and embody the steps and functions of data preprocessing, or (ii) the invention does not specifically describe the correlation between the raw data and the learning data, or a POSITA has difficulty estimating or figuring out the correlation, then the enablement requirement is not satisfied.

If an AI-related invention based on reinforcement learning does not specifically describe a method of reinforcement learning, including the correlations among agent, environment, state, action, and reward, or if a POSITA has difficulty estimating or figuring out the learning method, then the enablement requirement is not satisfied.

[A] Categories 1 and 2

Adequacy of disclosure for AI-related inventions in Categories 1 and 2 would be judged the same way as any other computer-implemented invention. Namely, the invention of core AI or of an AI implementation would need to be disclosed sufficiently such that a POSITA would be able to carry out the claimed invention. Therefore, if, for example, the hardware or software that implements the function of an AI-related invention is explained only with functional block diagrams or general flow charts in the description of the invention, and the explanation is not sufficient to understand how the hardware or software is structured so that the invention can be carried out, then such disclosure does not meet the enablement requirement.

[B] Category 3

Inventions in Category 3, applications of AI, are often defined largely by the data with which they are trained and, thus, the correlation between input data and output data during use. According to examination examples of the STF Guidelines, it may be judged that a specification does not meet the description requirement if the explanation of the invention does not specify the correlation between the input data and the output data of the trained model but instead lists only training data and if it is therefore difficult for a POSITA to estimate such correlation in light of the state of the art at the time of the filing or from examples in the specification. In addition,

28. *STF Guidelines*, pp. 1201–1211.

it may be judged that the claim is not supported by the specification if the specific composition corresponding to the claims is not described in the description of the invention, or if the contents of the description of the invention cannot be extended or generalized to the full extent of the claimed invention in light of technical common sense at the time of filing an application.

For example, in an example case from the STF Guidelines of an invention regarding an AI-based automatic home temperature control system, the description of the invention and the preferred embodiments of the invention only described the correlation between some input data (temperature, humidity information) and output data of the learned model (information that automatically controls the temperature of the house). The description did not disclose the correlation between the other input data (wind, cloud, fine dust concentration information) included in claims and the output data of the learned model. In the example, the examiner judged that a POSITA could understand the correlation between wind and cloud information and temperature control of house, despite not having a specific disclosure, based on common technical knowledge or examples in the specification. However, the examiner denied that a POSITA could estimate the correlation between fine dust concentration information and temperature control of house since it was not described in the specification nor obvious to a POSITA. The examiner also found that the contents of the description of the invention could not be extended to the full extent of the claimed invention, i.e., information including fine dust concentration in light of technical common sense at the time of filing the application. Therefore, the enablement requirement was not met for the claimed invention.

Generally, considering that the current STF Guidelines do not specify precise requirements and that KIPO has already granted many patents for AI-related applications without disclosure of specific input data, it should be sufficient for the purposes of the disclosure requirement to describe input data in terms of types or general categories provided that the disclosure is directed to a technical idea that is feasible and understandable. Of course, if the specification discloses examples of real data, a claimed invention would have a higher chance of being granted a patent.

[C] Categories 4 and 5

As noted *supra*, for AI-related inventions in Categories 4 and 5, what is claimed is the output resulting from the use of AI, not the AI or the use of AI. That output could be anything: a mechanical device, a new drug, a new manufacturing method, etc. The adequacy of disclosure requirements would thus attach to what is claimed, not the manner in which the invention was made. Said another way, the patent application must enable the POSITA to use the claimed invention, but need not enable the POSITA to replicate the manner in which the invention was made.

§15.06 INVENTORSHIP

[A] Inventorship in General

[1] Limited to Natural Persons

In Korea, only a natural human being can be an inventor. Article 33 of the Patent Act specifies that a natural person who makes an invention, or his/her successor, shall be entitled to a patent. Article 42 of the Patent Act requires that an inventor's name and address be furnished at the time the patent application is filed. A patent application without the name and address of at least one inventor will not be accepted in Korea.

According to the Patent Act, an animal or a legal entity, such as a company, cannot be an inventor of a patented invention since it is not a natural person.[29] A tool or a facility that is used to create an invention cannot be an inventor either.

It is true that many inventions are made through the help of a company that employs a human inventor. A company may provide funds, experimental facilities and tools necessary to successfully realize the invention. Sometimes, the contribution to the invention made by the company is much greater than that made by the human inventor. However, no matter how much the company contributes, it is not considered to be a co-inventor. And no matter how little a human inventor contributes, so long as there is contribution to at least one claim, the human inventor is considered to be the inventor or co-inventor.

When determining the compensation an employee should receive for creating an invention, Korean courts consider how much the human inventor (employee) contributed and how much the company (employer) contributed to the invention. For example, in the case of a 2003 Seoul Northern District Court decision,[30] the contribution of a human inventor to an invention was found to be only 5% while the company contribution was found to be 95%. While this impacts the amount of compensation to the employee, it has no impact on inventorship. Thus, even in a case where a non-human entity contributes 95%, and a human inventor contributes only 5%, the non-human entity cannot be an inventor and only the natural person can be an inventor.

[2] A Person Substantially Contributing to an Invention

Whether a particular person is considered to be an inventor of an invention depends on the significance of the contribution and is determined on a case-by-case basis. According to Korean court decisions,[31] a deciding factor is whether the contribution by the person is substantial or not.

29. Korean Supreme Court decision 91Hu1113, rendered 27 Dec. 1991.
30. Seoul Northern District Court decision 2002KaHab3727, rendered 3 Jul. 2003.
31. Korean Supreme Court decision 2009Hu2463, rendered 29 Sep. 2011; Korean Supreme Court decision 2012Da67705, rendered 27 Dec. 2012.

According to the Korean Patent Court,[32] a human person is at least a co-inventor of an invention when the person substantially contributes to an invention. Adding or complementing a technical idea to solve a technical problem, completing a technical idea through an experiment, or providing specific means or methods to realize an invention are substantial contributions. A person who contributes in any of these ways is at least a co-inventor. Merely suggesting a problem to solve, generally managing a researcher, merely organizing data, only conducting an experiment, providing money, or providing an experiment facility are not substantial contributions. A person who contributes in any of these or similar ways is not an inventor.[33]

[3] A Person Contributing to at Least One Claimed Invention

A person who contributes to at least one claimed invention is qualified to be an inventor or co-inventor. Inventorship is always determined based on what is claimed, because the disclosure of a patent may include descriptions of unpatentable technical features in addition to the description of the claimed invention.

When a person argues that he/she should be added as a co-inventor of a patented invention, the Korean court examines whether the person substantially contributed to at least one claimed invention of the patent.[34]

[B] Determination of Inventorship for AI-Related Inventions

[1] Weak AI and Strong AI

Weak artificial intelligence (weak AI)[35] is artificial intelligence that implements a limited part of a mind or is focused on one narrow task, while strong artificial intelligence (strong AI) is defined as a machine with the ability to apply intelligence to any problem, rather than just one specific problem, sometimes considered to require consciousness, sentience and mind.

The discussions throughout this book consider AI-related inventions through the lens of five Categories. Of these, Categories 1–4 involve weak AI. In all Category 1–4 cases, there is at least one human inventor. Therefore, as illustrated above with regard to the employee/employer cases, inventorship will be determined based upon the human or humans who made a contribution to at least one claimed invention, regardless of the percentage of that contribution. Category 5 inventions, which most people consider to not yet exist, would involve strong AI where AI invents on its own without human participation.

---

32. Korean Supreme Court decision 2012Da67705, rendered 27 Dec. 2012, Korean Patent Court decision 2013Heo5551, rendered 19 Dec. 2013.
33. Korean Patent Court decision 2013Heo5551, rendered 19 Dec. 2013.
34. Korean Supreme Court decision 2011Da77313, rendered 13 Nov. 2014.
35. https://en.wikipedia.org/wiki/Weak_AI.

[2] *Inventorship of Category 1–4 AI*

A person can use Category 1–4 AI to create an invention. Category 1–4 AI cannot invent without a person directing it. Category 1–4 AI can be thought of as a tool that can be used by a person to make an invention, regardless of how powerful the AI is.

According to the current Korean Patent Act, only a human can be an inventor. Therefore, Category 1–4 AI cannot be an inventor under Korean law, no matter how much the Category 1–4 AI contributes to the invention.

A human inventor may use equipment, programs, or other tools to make an invention. With an average tool, the inventor may fail. With a better tool, the inventor may succeed. With a better tool, the inventor may save time or create a better invention.

In fact, many inventions have been made with the help of many tools. Sometimes, the tools play a very important role in the creation of the invention. In some cases, the invention could not have been made without the tools. However, a tool is never considered to be a co-inventor, no matter how much the tool contributes to the completion of the invention.

In the lawsuit[36] regarding compensation to be given to the employee for creating an invention mentioned *supra*, the Korean Court determined human contribution was 5% and company contribution was 95%. As that case shows, even if the human inventor contributed much less to the invention than the company, the human inventor is named as an inventor and the company is not. Likewise, no matter how much a tool contributes it can never be an inventor; only a human inventor can be named as an inventor.

[3] *Inventorship of a Person Using Category 1–4 AI*

A human person can be involved in various ways in the making of an invention using Category 1–4 AI. For example, a person can 1) bring the idea of using AI for the intended purpose; 2) select an AI technology and configure it to suit the intended purpose; 3) select the data to be used to train the AI; 4) select the input data fed to the trained AI system; and 5) recognize the value of an optimal solution and select the optimal solution from a large number of potential solutions produced by the AI.

According to the Korean courts, a person is at least a co-inventor of an invention when the person substantially contributed to the invention. Substantial contribution can be adding or complementing a technical idea to solve a technical problem of an invention, completing a technical idea through an experiment, or providing specific means or methods to realize an invention. Non-substantial contribution is, for example, merely suggesting a problem to solve, generally managing a researcher, merely organizing data, or conducting an experiment, providing money, or providing an experiment facility.[37]

The inventorship of a person involved in an invention created by or with assistance of Category 1–4 AI should be determined based on whether the person made any contributions and whether the contribution was substantial considering

36. North Seoul District Court decision 2002KaHab3727 rendered on 3 Jul. 2003.
37. Korean Patent Court decision 2013Heo5551, 19 Dec. 2013.

various aspects of that specific case. Sometimes, the person who brings the idea of using AI for the specific intended purpose can be an inventor if the idea is a substantial part of the invention. The person could not be an inventor if the idea is not a substantial part of the invention. Likewise, a person who selected the input data fed to the trained AI system may be an inventor if the selection is a substantial part of the invention. The person cannot be an inventor if the selection is not a substantial part of the invention.

An invention created by a person assisted by Category 4 AI sometimes solves a problem the human inventor did not intend to solve. That is, the invention may solve a problem unrelated to the inventor's original goals. In this case, it might be argued that the invention was made 'accidentally' using AI. Under Korean law, whether a person can be named as an inventor or not for this kind of accidental invention is also determined based on whether the person substantially contributed to the invention considering the various aspects of that specific case. This actually does happen. The product Viagra™ is an example of an accidental invention for which a person is named as an inventor. Likewise, even if the human inventor is using the AI for another purpose, and the AI produces an invention the inventor did not intend to create, the person can be named as inventor if it is determined that what the person contributed is substantial considering the various aspects.

[4] *Inventorship of a Person Who Makes the Category 1–4 AI Used to Make the Invention*

When an invention is made with the assistance of Category 1–4 AI, can a person who made the AI be named as a co-inventor?

Many inventors use experimental equipment, a computer, software, and other such tools. No matter how much the tools contribute to the invention, the inventors or developers of the tools are not considered to be co-inventors of the invention made by means of the tools.

As discussed before, Category 1–4 AI is regarded as a tool regardless of how much it contributes to the invention. Therefore, a person who creates an AI system is not an inventor or a co-inventor under the current Korean law.

[5] *Inventorship of a Company Related to Category 1–4 AI*

There may be a company that employs a person who invents an AI system or a company that employs a person who makes an invention using AI.

Under Korean law, only a natural person can be an inventor and a company cannot be an inventor. Therefore, a company that employs a person who invents an AI system and a company that employs a person who makes an invention using an AI system cannot be an inventor.

[6] *Inventorship of a Category 5 AI*

Category 5 inventions, which most people consider to not yet exist, would involve strong AI. In this hypothetical scenario, AI can invent on its own without direction by a human person. That is, Category 5 AI does not need assistance from a person to create something. It can identify problems to be solved and create an invention for the purpose of solving the problems. Unlike Category 1–4 AI, the fact that Category 5 AI can invent without human intervention means that Category 5 AI is self-motivated to create. A person does not control or bring out motivation in Category 5 AI.

According to the current Patent Act, only a natural person can be an inventor. Therefore, Category 5 AI cannot be an inventor under Korean law, even if it is able to invent on its own without human intervention.

Currently, there is no Category 5 AI in existence. It is an imaginary thing. Even if we imagine that a Category 5 AI is created, it would be difficult to answer the question of inventorship of a Category 5 AI with respect to policy. Under the current law, Category 5 AI cannot be an inventor; however, a law or policy can be revised. Whether or how to revise Category 5 AI policies relates to whether humans will let Category 5 AI be created and operated, supposing it becomes technically possible to create Category 5 AI, and whether we will give full autonomy to Category 5 AI or only partial autonomy when limitation is possible. Revision is also related to whether Category 5 AI is capable of being responsible for its actions. If Category 5 AI is given rights, it must also take on responsibility since rights and responsibilities go together. Will this be possible?

It is therefore too early to give a concrete answer to the question of Category 5 AI inventorship. We will have to watch and wait. The answer will be given at some point. The answer might even come from Category 5 AI and not us. Who knows?

§15.07 AREAS FOR IMPROVEMENT

There are AI methods available to be used to generate new prior art. An example of such would be 'All Prior Art'.[38] This AI service crawls publicly published documents on the internet and makes new prior art based on the crawled data. The new prior art is then published on the internet.

It is uncertain whether such documents are eligible as prior art that can be cited against a patent application to show that the application lacks novelty and inventive step.

Under Article 29 of the Patent Act, the following are regarded as prior art that can be a basis to deny a patent application:

1. An invention publicly known or practised in the Republic of Korea or in a foreign country prior to the filing of a patent application;
2. An invention published in a publication distributed in the Republic of Korea or in a foreign country or an invention disclosed to the public via telecommunications lines prior to the filing of a patent application.

Under Korean law, prior art that is generated using AI is eligible as prior art, since it is disclosed to the public via the internet, which is determined by Korean courts to be a type of telecommunications line.

38. https://allpriorart.com/.

However, we must think carefully about allowing the eligibility of AI-generated prior art. What problems might there be in allowing AI-generated prior art without limitation? AI can crawl a huge number of documents on the internet with extraordinary speed and produce a huge number of new prior art documents. If this becomes popularized and widely adopted, there might be no invention to be patented in the future.

Weak AI does not understand what it generates. AI-generated prior art may be just a combination of phrases and clauses. Should we then, even in such case, still maintain the position that AI-generated prior art is eligible as prior art which can be cited against a patent application?

§15.08 RECOMMENDATIONS FOR PATENT APPLICANTS

As discussed in the previous sections, the STF Guidelines require that information processing by software should be concretely implemented by using hardware in AI-related inventions. However, the patent eligibility of AI-related inventions is not strictly assessed under Korean patent practice. The patent eligibility of the invention is satisfied even if technical ideas are embodied in a general-purpose computer. This relaxed examination trend seems to have partially resulted from the KIPO's policy to facilitate the granting of patents in 4th industrial revolution fields. Whether technical ideas are specifically claimed or novel tends to be assessed in terms of novelty/inventive step rather than in terms of eligibility.

Korean examiners compare claimed AI-related inventions and prior art in terms of (i) technical field, (ii) learning data, and (iii) learning models to determine an inventive step of the claimed invention. An applicant is recommended to describe in detail a technical feature(s) distinguishable from the prior art in at least one of those three items. In addition, adding an element into an AI-related invention to provide a unique effect distinguishable from that of the prior art, even if the element is not directly related to the AI, can enhance the possibility that the inventive step of the AI-related invention can be recognized. For example, in the case of an independent claim pertaining to a method for controlling a robot cleaner comprising setting a path for the cleaner, despite the difference of the learning model CNN used therein from an ANN of the prior art, the inventive step thereof was not acknowledged since the difference could be derived from a simple design modification by a POSITA. However, for the dependent claim thereof comprising a specific element (that the robot cleaner can recognize its current location through the learned CNN and reestablish its travel path based on its current battery residual quantity), in addition to the learning data and learning model, inventive step thereof was acknowledged because the effect of preventing the situation that a robot cleaner cannot return to the charging area was recognized.

Regarding preparation of the detailed description of the invention, the hardware or software that implements the function of the AI-related invention can be explained using block diagrams or general flow charts to the extent that a POSITA may understand how the hardware or software works in order to achieve a purpose of the invention in light of the state of the art or other examples or description in the specification. Meanwhile, it is recommended that, for learning data enumerated in the detailed description, the correlation between the input data and the output data from the learned model be specifically disclosed, or related working examples be added. If an examiner issues a rejection on the basis that no explanation of the correlation has been provided, it would be advisable to argue that a POSITA would be able to determine the correlation from the common technical knowledge at the time of filing the relevant application. If such an argument is not available, it would be necessary to delete the limitation to the relevant learning data (input data) that lacks the correlation. In this regard, adding an explanation about the correlation or related working examples in response to the rejection would not be allowed due to the issue of addition of new matter.

§15.09 CONCLUSION

As mentioned above, while Korea has patent examination guidelines dedicated to determining the patentability of AI-related inventions, there are no court precedents regarding infringement issues related to them yet. The KIPO has reviewed AI-related inventions according to the STF Guidelines. The KIPO seems to have recently examined 4th industrial revolution technologies in the pro-patent direction. As such, it will be quite interesting to see how the guidelines address real patent issues specific to AI technologies. Meanwhile, some topics introduced in this book, such as inventorship regarding Category 4 and 5 inventions, have never been at issue in an actual case. However, AI technology is one of the core technologies leading the 4th industrial revolution, and the number of AI-relevant patent applications has been increasing substantially. Therefore, court precedents are expected to be established soon to effectively support the development of core future technologies by addressing new features of cutting-edge technologies while following the existing patent law system.

Chapter 16

Switzerland and Liechtenstein

Thomas Kretschmer & Dr Sébastien Ragot

Switzerland and the Principality of Liechtenstein form a unified territory of protection for the purposes of patent law. Once granted, a patent is valid in both Switzerland and Liechtenstein. Similarly, a European patent may only be obtained for Switzerland and Liechtenstein by joint designation as provided in Article 142 of the European Patent Convention ('EPC'). Accordingly, the following remarks apply to both Switzerland and Liechtenstein, also referred to as the 'Unified Territory' herein.

Switzerland and the Principality of Liechtenstein are contracting states of the EPC. In Switzerland, the Federal Patent Court ('FPC') has exclusive jurisdiction over validity and infringement disputes. In Liechtenstein, the Princely High Court is the designated court (single instance) in civil cases regarding patents. In each case, decisions can be appealed to the Federal Supreme Court ('FSC'). The validity of European patents validated in the Unified Territory is independently assessed by national courts under Swiss law, which refers to the EPC (Article 109, Federal Act on Patents for Inventions, hereafter 'PatA').[1] Accordingly, the law applicable to the validity of such patents is the EPC and the case law of the Boards of Appeal ('BoAs') of the EPO has persuasive authority. The national courts are generally inclined to follow the case law of the BoAs of the EPO, even if they are not bound by such case law.

§16.01 PATENTABILITY OF SOFTWARE AND COMPUTER-IMPLEMENTED INVENTIONS

National patents in the Unified Territory are subject to Swiss patent law, which does not contain statutory provisions that specifically concern the patentability of software and computer-implemented inventions ('CIIs').

1. The Swiss Patent Act of 25 June 1954 (status as of 1 January 2022) addresses the rights on inventions, the prosecution of patent applications, and the effect of patents and patent applications, including patents granted by the European Patent Office.

The statutory provision relevant to patentability is Article 1 PatA, which merely states that patents are granted for 'inventions':

1. Patents for inventions are granted for new inventions applicable in industry.
2. Anything that is obvious having regard to the state of the art (Article 7 para. 2) is not patentable as an invention.
3. Patents are granted without the guarantee of the State.[2]

Article 1 PatA is consistent with Article 52 EPC, although more general. Like Article 52 EPC, Article 1 PatA does not define what is meant by 'invention'.[3] But unlike Article 52(2) EPC, Article 1 PatA does not provide examples of subject matter or activities that are not regarded as inventions.

While Article 1 PatA does not explicitly exclude any subject matter, *a priori*, the Swiss doctrine considers that the notion of 'inventions applicable in industry' implies the existence of an 'invention' as such and, in particular, an invention belonging to the field of technology.[4] This interpretation is confirmed in Section 2 of the Guidelines of the Swiss Federal Institute of Intellectual Property ('IPI'),[5] hereafter the 'IPI Guidelines'.

Echoing the Swiss case law, the IPI Guidelines further define the term 'invention' as implying technical character, similar to EPO practice. In particular, an invention must make a technical contribution to the state of the art, just like at the EPO. Namely, the IPI Guidelines provide:

> From the frequently used definition of an invention as a '(new and non-obvious) rule for a technical activity', it follows that only objects which make a technical contribution to the state of the art can be validly patented. They must therefore have technical character by their nature.[6]

The IPI Guidelines further provide a non-exhaustive list of examples of abstract subject matter, which are not regarded as inventions, similar to that of Article 52(2) EPC. For instance, mathematical methods and computer programs as such are deemed to lack technical character and thus are not considered patentable inventions. Besides, other abstract inventions, such as methods for performing mental acts and methods for doing business, are not patentable either. Swiss courts consistently follow this line.

Importantly, however, the IPI Guidelines clarify that abstract subject matter is excluded from patentability only to the extent to which a patent application relates to such subject matter or activities *as such*, consistent with Article 52(3) EPC. In particular, the IPI Guidelines provide that 'calculation programs, computer programs

2. English is not an official language of the Swiss Confederation. A translation into English is nevertheless provided by the publication platform for federal law ('Fedlex'), for information purposes.
3. The legislator has purposely not provided any definition of the notion of invention, a task that is devoted to case law and doctrine. *See* N. Gillard, F. Marchetto, S. Bettschart, N. Iynedjian, O. Niggli, A. Thevenaz, *Brevets d'invention – quarante ans de jurisprudence fédérale*, CEDIDAC, Lausanne, 1996, pp. 27-3.
4. PatA, Art. 1, para. 1.
5. Revised Patent Examination Guidelines from 1 Jan. 2021.
6. IPI Guidelines, Sec. 2.1.

or software as such are not patentable on their own'.[7] For example, a 'method claim that does not contain any other feature besides the characters of the computer program is not acceptable because such a claim relates only to the computer program as such. Similarly, purely economic activities are considered non-technical: they are therefore not patentable as such.'[8]

A natural corollary is that a mix of technical and non-technical features is accepted, as long as the claimed subject matter as a whole has technical character. Namely, 'technical character [...] is in no way destroyed [...] by the introduction of non-technical characteristics alongside technical characteristics'.[9] And for what specifically concerns CIIs, the IPI Guidelines emphasize that 'the characteristics of the objects considered must in no case all be of a purely technical nature in order to satisfy the condition of technicality'.[10,11]

In general, a patent application claiming a technical solution to a technical problem and involving technical features is considered having technical character. However, such a condition is implicitly described as a sufficient condition and not a necessary condition. Indeed, according to the IPI Guidelines, the IPI applies a global (or 'holistic') approach to determining the technical character, whereby, in principle, 'each of the task/problem, means, solution/effect can already justify on its own the technical character of the invention, even though, ultimately, this is the global assessment of the subject of the invention which is decisive in judging its technical character'.[12] Note, the global (or 'holistic') approach applied by the IPI to assess the technical character of the invention is independent of the categories of the claims.

For what specifically concerns CIIs, technical character may notably result from:

- the problem at the basis of the claimed CII, which problem is solved thanks to the invention;
- the means, in other words the technical features, constituting the solution to the problem posed;
- the effects produced by the solution of the problem;
- the need to carry out technical reflections in order to grasp the CII claimed.[13]

However, the IPI Guidelines make it clear that the technicality criterion can also be satisfied when the four points are not fulfilled simultaneously.[14] That is, the above conditions are not cumulative conditions.

Thus, according to the IPI Guidelines, the technical character of CIIs can, in principle, be derived on the basis of the problem solved by the invention, the means (i.e., the technical features) involved to solve the problem, the effects achieved by the claimed solution, and/or the technical considerations involved.

7. *Ibid.*, Sec. 2.1.1.
8. *Ibid.*, Sec. 2.1.2.
9. *Ibid.*, Sec. 2.1.1.
10. *Ibid.*
11. According to the IPI Guidelines (Section 2.1.2, generally), 'technicality' and 'technical character' are synonymous.
12. IPI Guidelines, Sec. 2.1.
13. *Ibid.*, Sec. 2.1.1.
14. *Ibid.*

Importantly, 'the mere implementation of a non-technical activity on a computer system does usually not suffice to justify a technical character'.[15] Thus, the IPI rejects patent applications where the sole technical features claimed consist of general computer means, e.g., a personal computer or a computer network. Originally, this is justified by the fact that the term 'invention' in 'computer-implemented invention' must imply technical character, even before its implementation by a computer.[16]

Note, such an approach is stricter than the first hurdle in the EPO approach, which compensates for the fact that the IPI does not examine patent applications for novelty and inventive step.[17] Rather, the IPI examination focuses on formal matters, with emphasis put on clarity, something that certainly facilitates the granting of patents, including for CIIs.

Closely related, a computer program that merely produces standard physical effects does not have sufficient technical character to be patentable. Namely, 'such physical effects are considered normal and cannot in themselves suffice to confer technical character on the computer program'.[18] Thus, a method claim that merely recites the execution of the computer program by a computer will likely be considered to lack sufficient technical character. For example, a computerized system that merely executes an algorithm (i.e., a mathematical method) to optimize financial transactions would be rejected.

The IPI Guidelines provide a number of examples of CII-related activities or subject matter that are, as such, not considered patentable. These examples include:

- a method for sorting data;
- a functional analysis method;
- conversion programs;
- the modelling of non-technical processes and/or systems;
- pure translation programs, optimized mathematical algorithms used only for data analysis,
- a data-driven system for market arbitration and trend evaluation;
- an expert system defined only by functional relationships; and
- a terminal for the management of digital use rights (management of electronic tickets).[19]

To the contrary, the following examples would be considered patentable:

- a method for detecting and protecting against attacks on server systems of network service providers and operators;
- a method of operating a defined computer by means of a 'system program';
- a method of operating a multi-level hierarchical memory system of a data processing installation which simultaneously manages several processes, as well as a circuit for implementing said method;

15. *Ibid.*, Sec. 2.1.2.
16. Takata Herb, Arisa, *The protection of business methods by patent law Under European, French, Swiss, American and Japanese law*, University of Zurich, Faculty of Law (2015).
17. PatA, Art. 59.
18. IPI Guidelines, Sec. 2.1.1.
19. *Ibid.*

- a method allowing the management of track elements such as switches or signals in an electronic switch station;
- a method for controlling devices placed in a communication network;
- a semiconductor circuit and its application in an arithmetic logic unit, a measurement transducer and a signal processing system;
- a process allowing the capture of data by means of measuring instruments and their analysis;
- a process for controlling the quality of digital recordings of colour images;
- a method for controlling a flow of water in a purge system of an installation for galvanotechnics and for surface treatment; and
- a computer allowing the processing of tomography signals by nuclear magnetic resonance, as well as a nuclear magnetic resonance tomograph equipped with said computer.[20]

Such examples notably delineate two patentability criteria, which relate to: (i) the technical application; and (ii) the technical implementation, as further discussed in the next section.

As noted above, the IPI does not examine patent applications for novelty and inventive step. Thus, the Swiss jurisdiction has to cope with the duality arising from the lack of examination for novelty and inventive step by the IPI and adjudications by the Swiss courts. Accordingly, depending on requests and allegations of the parties and the case at hand, the courts have to potentially assess all patentability requirements, including those related to technical character, novelty, and inventive step.

Swiss case law with regard to CIIs is very scarce. Swiss scholars often used to rely upon an FSC decision of 1970[21] or an even older administrative decision of 1968. Both denied patentability of CIIs due to lack of technical character. In addition, a decision from the Federal Appeals Commission for Intellectual Property referring to an application entitled 'Technically real dimensorics'[22] relied on a global assessment of the technical character of the claimed invention, similar to the IPI approach, to conclude to a lack of technical character.

In this rather quiet context, the FPC decision *Hamilton Medical AG v. imtmedical AG*[23] and a subsequent FSC decision on appeal[24] were more than welcome. Basically, the FPC endorsed the 'any-hardware approach' and the 'COMVIK' approach (also known as COMVIK criterion) of the EPO, and notably referred to the decisions T 641/00 and T 258/03.[25] So did the FPC in its judgment on appeal.[26] As a result, a single technical feature is sufficient to ensure technical character, regardless of whether the invention involves a mix of technical and non-technical features or not. The rest is a question of inventive step, which must be assessed based on the sole features considered to contribute to the technical character, as discussed in detail in the EPO

20. *Ibid.*
21. *Canguilhem v. Federal Bureau of Intellectual Property*, BGE 98 Ib 396.
22. PA 01/04, in sic!, 589 (2005).
23. O2017_007, FPC decision of 1 Nov. 2019.
24. 4A_609/2019, FSC decision of 16 Jul. 2020.
25. EPO Decisions T 641/00 (Two identities/COMVIK) of 26 Sep. 2002 and T 258/03 ('Hitachi') of 21 Apr. 2004.
26. *Hamilton Medical*, para. 9.1.1.

chapter. Interestingly, the FSC formulated the COMVIK criterion as meaning that 'features (of a mixed invention) which neither have a technical effect nor interact with the other features in such a way as to result in a functional technical contribution cannot constitute an inventive step'.[27]

More generally, Swiss courts are inclined to follow the case law of the Boards of Appeal (BoAs) of the EPO, even though they are not bound by such case law. Thus, national courts generally apply the standard of the BoAs of the EPO. For example, in *A/S v. Y. AG* the court acknowledged that the 'case law of the Boards of Appeal of the European Patent Office may be relevant for the application of the Swiss patent law.'[28]

The standard for inventive step defined by Article 1(2) PatA, 'anything that is obvious having regard to the state of the art is not patentable as an invention', essentially corresponds to Article 56 EPC. Thus, following the above FPC and FSC decisions Swiss courts may well assess the technical character of CIIs as part of an EPO-like, two-hurdle assessment in the future (including for Swiss patents), even if this approach deviates from the global approach applied by the IPI.

Accordingly, the recommendations for applicants provided in the EPO chapter should remain generally valid for the Unified Territory.

§16.02 SPECIAL PROVISIONS RELATING TO PATENTABILITY OF INVENTIONS RELATING TO AI

As of this writing, the Swiss law and IPI Guidelines do not contain provisions specific to inventions relating to artificial intelligence ('AI') beyond those relating more generally to computer-implemented inventions, as discussed *supra*.

However, the provisions of the IPI Guidelines concerning CIIs can be applied to AI-related inventions involving machine learning models or algorithms executed on conventional computer platforms, inasmuch as such inventions remain fundamentally computer-implemented inventions.

In practice, for what specifically concerns AI and machine learning, IPI examiners strive to make a distinction between the abstract mathematical nature of the underlying computational models and/or algorithms and the technical aspects of a patent claim. This pivotal distinction is recalled in Section 2.1.1 of the IPI Guidelines, providing that it 'is fundamental to distinguish, on the one hand, the "abstract algorithm" and, on the other hand, its use in practice'.

This distinction is consistent with the two criteria identified in the previous section, which respectively concern the technical application and the technical implementation of the underlying algorithm, method, or computational model, similar to the EPO.

Concerning the technical application, the IPI Guidelines note that a functional analysis method implemented by means of a computer is not patentable.[29] However, in the example given, the corresponding description is assumed to include examples from technical as well as non-technical fields, which demonstrates that the problem solved by this mathematical method is independent of the field of application and

27. *Ibid.*, para. 9.1.2.
28. BGE 133 III 229.
29. IPI Guidelines, Sec. 2.1.1.

therefore belongs to mathematics and not to the technical field; there is therefore a lack of technicality. Similarly, the IPI Guidelines provide that 'optimized mathematical algorithms used only for data analysis' are not patentable when 'devoid of any input/measurement character, or without involving a processing of physical signals', and, more generally, when 'the field of application is devoid of any technical character, and therefore detached from practice'.[30]

One understands therefore, conversely, that an algorithm having a technical application (or otherwise anchored to a technical concept) would be considered to contribute to the technical character, similar to the EPO approach. For example, the IPI Guidelines acknowledge the technical character of a method for detecting and protecting against attacks on server systems of network service providers and operators, as noted in the previous section. That said, the examples provided in the IPI Guidelines suggest that the technical application must be specific, as is also the case at the EPO.

Concerning the technical implementation, the IPI Guidelines suggest that program-related features may contribute to the technical character, provided that such features sufficiently interact with other constitutive technical features. Namely, Section 2.1.1 of the IPI Guidelines provides that:

> A device can be defined by functional features.... When such characteristics appear in the form of a program integrated into the device, they are also admissible, provided that the claim contains other construction characteristics of the device with which the program is related in order to solve the technical problem posed by the invention, thus making it possible both to confer a technical character on the invention and to fulfil the condition of technicality.

More generally, where a claim combines technical and non-technical features, the non-technical features must be sufficiently linked to the technical features, for the non-technical features to contribute to the technical character. For instance, IPI Guidelines provide that a 'method whose definition includes, in addition to the features of the computer program, other features (of a technical nature) intrinsically associated with the claimed computer program and directly linked to the solution of the technical problem to be solved, may fulfil the condition of technicality applicable to CIIs'.[31] In particular, a 'method of operating a device comprising program features is admissible, because the presence of a device implies the existence of characteristics of a technical nature in the definition of the method'.[32]

To summarize, the teaching of the IPI Guidelines is generally consistent with EPO practice, where two essential criteria to assess the technical character of an AI-related invention (in particular a machine learning computational model) are whether the underlying method targets a specific technical application and/or whether it is adapted to a specific technical implementation, provided there is a sufficient link between the technical purpose and the method steps. Accordingly, the conclusions drawn in respect of the patentability of inventions relating to AI in the EPO chapter should remain generally valid for the Unified Territory.

30. *Ibid.*
31. *Ibid.*
32. *Ibid.*

§16.03 SUBJECT MATTER PATENTABILITY

The subject matter patentability of AI inventions directed to specialized hardware (e.g., neuromorphic hardware) is usually not an issue; such inventions are in principle patentable, just like any other physical machine. In practice, subject matter patentability issues mostly relate to AI-related inventions implemented in software running on conventional computer hardware. Under Swiss law, such inventions are treated as CIIs and their subject matter patentability is determined in accordance with the existence of a technical character, as explained *supra*.

[A] Category 1

AI-related inventions in Category 1 are directed to the 'core AI', i.e., new algorithms or models for the AI itself, independent of the data to which it is applied and independent of any particular use case. In view of the discussions *supra*, a claim directed in the abstract to a new algorithm or model having no particular technical purpose will be considered devoid of technical character by the IPI.

Moreover, even if such a claim recites that the model/algorithm is run by conventional computing means, it will be rejected by the IPI, due to the technicality criteria used by the IPI, whereby a computer-implemented invention must have technical character, even before its implementation by a computer, as discussed in Section §16.01, *supra*.

Following the two-hurdle approach of the EPO, however, Swiss courts would likely acknowledge the technical character of such a claim, although they would likely deny any technical contribution to the prior art as part of the subsequent inventive step assessment, in accordance with the recent FPC and FSC decisions discussed in Section §16.01, *supra*.

[B] Category 2

AI-related inventions in Category 2 relate to AI implementations, i.e., claim a system or process of broad application using known AI technology plus additional elements, e.g., a particular arrangement of filters or a particular interface.

Such an AI implementation would likely be considered by the IPI to have technical character, provided that it involves technical features that are specific enough, as opposed to generic computing means. Moreover, the underlying computational model or algorithm may be acknowledged to contribute to the technical character if there is a sufficient link between the model or algorithm and the specific, constitutive technical features, see Section §16.02, *supra*.

More generally, the technical character of CIIs may possibly be derived on the basis of the problem solved by the invention, the means (i.e., the technical features) involved to solve the problem, the effects achieved by the claimed solution, and the technical considerations involved, according to the IPI Guidelines, see the discussion in Section §16.01, *supra*.

[C] Category 3

AI-related inventions in Category 3 are applications of AI to a particular use case, e.g., causing a car to stop at a stop sign, performing facial recognition, or identifying candidates for new pharmaceutical products. AI-related inventions in this category may be a 'decision-maker' application that causes a result to occur, or a 'decision aid' application that provides advice or a plurality of choices to a human user.

Again, the technical character of CIIs may be derived from the problem solved by the invention, the means involved to solve the problem, the effects achieved by the claimed solution, and the technical considerations involved.

So, AI-related inventions in Category 3 may be acknowledged as having technical character if the application (or use case) itself is technical, provided that the use case is reflected in the claim so as to limit the claim accordingly, otherwise the claim may be construed to potentially have non-technical applications as discussed in Section §16.01 *supra*.

Moreover, the underlying computational model or algorithm may be acknowledged to contribute to the technical character if it sufficiently links to this application; see Sections §16.01 and §16.02, *supra*.

[D] Category 4

The result of an application of AI may be, in and of itself, a patentable invention (Category 4), just like a new aircraft designed by computer-aided design ('CAD') is.

For AI-related inventions in Category 4, what is claimed is the *result* of the use of AI, not the use of AI itself. That result could possibly be an invention in Category 1, 2, or 3, as discussed above, or anything else from, e.g., a mechanical device to a new industrial process to a new drug.

Accordingly, the technical character and thus the patentability of the resulting invention will be assessed regardless of the tool used to arrive at the invention, just like parts or products designed by CAD. It will, in fact, be irrelevant that this invention was obtained using AI.

[E] Category 5

According to the current doctrine and case law, an inventor is a human being. Naming an AI entity as inventor will likely not permit issuance of a patent to an invention in Category 5; the invention will not even be prosecuted in that case, as discussed *infra*, such that the question of subject matter patentability would not even be assessed by the IPI in that case.

Still, an invention 'made'[33] by an AI entity (Category 5) may be prosecuted, assuming the corresponding application names human inventors only (without

33. That an AI entity can invent is highly controversial, *see*, e.g., the Report of the Swiss AIPPI group on the '*Inventorship of Inventions made using Artificial Intelligence (Q 272)*; Sic! 10|2020.

naming the AI entity as inventor at all). In that case, the same conclusion as reached for Category 4 holds for inventions in Category 5.

The above conclusions are generally consistent with the conclusions drawn in the EPO chapter. As the technical contribution of the invention will be properly examined as part of the inventive step assessment by the Swiss courts, the question of which subject matter is susceptible of patent protection is intimately linked to the inventive step, as discussed in the next section.

§16.04 INVENTIVE STEP

Under current Swiss law, the IPI does not examine if an invention is new or whether it is obvious with regard to the state of the art.[34] However, novelty[35] and inventive step[36] are examined by the courts, e.g., in a civil action such as a request for nullity[37] of a patent.[38]

Swiss courts are generally inclined to follow the EPO case law and, in particular, use the 'problem-solution' approach. Thus, the inventive step discussion in the EPO chapter remains generally valid for the Unified Territory, especially since the recent endorsement of the 'any-hardware approach' and the COMVIK criterion[39] by the FPC and FSC as discussed *supra*.

According to the COMVIK criterion, only the claimed features considered technical participate in the assessment of the inventive step, while non-technical features are disregarded, as discussed *supra* in Section §16.01. This approach requires identifying all the novel technical features of a claim, including features that indirectly contribute to the technical character of the invention, and then assess the inventive step of the sole features considered to contribute to the technical character. Therefore, the question to answer is whether the residual differences identified with respect to the prior art make a technical contribution that is non-obvious.[40]

[A] Category 1

The IPI will likely deny sufficient technical character for core AI inventions (Category 1) that boil down to reciting a new ML algorithm or a new computational model, e.g., a model based on a new neural network architecture, such as a transformer architecture.

Swiss courts may perhaps consider that such an invention clears the first hurdle of the two-step approach of the EPO, because the underlying method is implemented by a computer, which is technical *per se*. However, they will likely not acknowledge any non-obvious contribution to the prior art in that case, for reasons discussed in

34. PatA, Art. 59, para. 4.
35. *Ibid.*, Art. 1, para. 1.
36. *Ibid.*, para. 2.
37. PatA, Art. 26.
38. Information on the criteria of inventive step and sufficiency of disclosure (circular C. 8403), IPI.
39. EPO decision T 641/00 ('COMVIK' decision).
40. EPO Guidelines, G-VII, 5.4.

Sections §16.01 and §16.02, *supra.*, i.e., the sole inventive contribution (in a colloquial sense) will typically be non-technical in that case.

[B] Category 2

The key criterion for a new AI implementations (Category 2) to be considered inventive is the non-obviousness of those claimed features that are considered to contribute to the technical character.

Because new AI implementations (Category 2) typically involve non-conventional technical elements, compared with inventions in Category 1 inventions in Category 2 may potentially involve more technical features that will favourably participate in the inventive step assessment. In addition, the interactions between the underlying computational model or algorithm and such elements may be regarded as contributing to the technical character too, which will also favour the inventive step.

In particular, new AI implementations (Category 2) may benefit from a specific technical implementation whereby the adaptation of the underlying method to that specific implementation may be acknowledged as having an inventive step if it is non-obvious in view of the prior art.

[C] Category 3

In principle, a claim directed to a new application of known AI technology (Category 3) may possibly be novel because: (i) a known AI technology (e.g., a known computational model) is used for the first time in an application that is not novel *per se* (the combination, however, is novel); and/or (ii) the application itself is novel. As in the EPO, the latter case disposes the claim favourably toward inventive step, assuming that the application has technical character and is recited so as to have a limiting effect on the claim.

The former case, however, is less likely to succeed. Indeed, applying known AI technology (Category 3) to a known application may likely be perceived by the Swiss courts as being a common design option for the skilled person, even more so where the sole residual novel feature is the use of an ML model in place of another mathematical function. That is, applying known AI technology to a known use case will likely be perceived to be in line with the general trend in technology and thus not considered inventive, much like automation.

[D] Categories 4 and 5

Where the result of application of AI is, in and of itself, a patentable invention having technical character, the inventive step of the resulting invention will likely be assessed regardless of the AI tool used to arrive at the invention, normally by using the problem-solution approach.

The same conclusion holds for inventions claimed to be made by an AI entity (Category 5). This, however, assumes that the corresponding patent application reaches the stage of inventive step examination by a Swiss courts, which is unlikely (see the discussion *infra* in Section §16.06), unless the patent application names human inventors only.

Of course, all such scenarios must be assessed on a case-by-case basis.

§16.05 ADEQUACY OF DISCLOSURE

Article 50 PatA provides that the 'invention must be disclosed in the patent application in such a manner that it can be carried out by a person skilled in the art'. This definition is in line with that of Article 83 EPC.

As set out in Article 26, paragraph 5, of the Swiss Patents Ordinance ('PatO'),[41] the description 'must contain at least one embodiment of the invention unless the former is disclosed sufficiently in another manner.' That is, it is possible to disclose the invention not only in the description or in the drawings but also in the claims should the latter be submitted on the date when the application was filed.

While Swiss law does not expressly require the description to include an example of an embodiment, a concrete example may be required by the IPI examiner, especially where the claims involve abstract or functional features.[42]

The IPI examines the disclosure of the invention.[43] The disclosure 'may be considered sufficient where it appears plausible to the examiner that a person possessing average professional knowledge of the field at issue could reproduce the invention by logical thought and without unreasonable effort'.[44] Depending on requests and allegations of the parties and the case at hand, the Swiss court may have to assess the sufficiency of disclosure, according to Article 26 paragraph 1 b PatA, whereby a court may declare the nullity of the patent if 'the invention is not described in the patent specification in a manner sufficiently clear and precise for it to be carried out by a person skilled in the art'.

For completeness, examination of industrial applicability also requires that the invention can be repeated as often as desired.[45] The technical documents must make plausible the non-random nature of the defined invention and the certainty of being able to repeat it. This requirement applies to all fields of technology.

Concerning CIIs, a criterion set forth in the IPI Guidelines is that the 'person skilled in the art must always be able to directly deduce the technical rule or the rules targeted for a technical activity; they must therefore be sufficiently explained'.[46]

Interpreting such provisions in the context of AI-related inventions in Categories 1–3, one may expect Swiss courts to require minimal indications as to the type and architecture (or topology) of the computational model involved, the training algorithm, and the training dataset, as discussed in detail in the EPO chapter. The explanations provided in the EPO chapter are believed to remain generally valid for the Unified Territory.

41. Ordinance relating to patents of invention (Ordinance on patents) of 19 Oct. 1977 (status on 1 January 2022).
42. *See* IPI Guidelines, Sec. 4.2.
43. PatO, Art. 67, para. 2.
44. IPI Guidelines, Sec. 4.2.
45. ATF 120 II 312.
46. IPI Guidelines, Sec. 2.1.1.

With respect to inventions in Categories 4 and 5, sufficiency of disclosure would be based on what is claimed, regardless of the means by which the invention was made.

§16.06 INVENTORSHIP

Swiss patent law is formulated in a technology-neutral manner and has proven to be sufficiently flexible to reasonably address inventorship issues in various technological areas. Now, as far as intellectual property protection is concerned, AI-related inventions do not fundamentally differ from other types of invention. Thus, there is no specific inventorship requirement applying to AI-related inventions. Accordingly, AI-related inventions in Categories 1–4, which have a human inventor, would be treated under the patent law like any other area of technology. While there may be some new types of human inventorship roles for inventions in these categories, such as a person who selects or curates training data, this implies no problems with the current standards. As in other fields of technology, several types of human interventions or acts may potentially be acknowledged as inventorship, provided that such contributions include inventive inputs that are sufficiently reflected in at least one of the patent claims. Decisive for legal inventorship, and hence patent protection overall, are the occurrence and extent of such contributions. Whether or not these contributions are sufficient to be acknowledged as inventorship has to be assessed on a case-by-case basis.

Inventions in Category 5 – those hypothetically made by an AI system without a human inventor -- raise a different question. According to Article 3 PatA, an inventor is a person originating the technical creation constituting an invention. The statute and commentaries thereon presuppose that an inventor is a human being. In addition, various provisions of Swiss law implicitly assume that inventors are human beings. For example, the 'patent applicant must provide the IPI with written confirmation of the name of the inventor',[47] it being noted that 'the mention of the inventor is made [...] indicating his surname and first name as well as his domicile'.[48]

As in the EPC, inventors are usually perceived as human beings who have sufficiently contributed to an invention, with inventive inputs, such that their respective contributions reflect in at least one claim of the corresponding patent application.

The PatA does not expressly state any particular threshold of human inputs to the inventive process. Rather, the wording of the statute frames inventorship in terms of human creation, justness and importance of rewarding human efforts, and stimulating human creativity.[49]

Such provisions manifestly exclude the possibility for an AI entity to be named as inventor in a patent application. So, in practice, a patent application directed to an invention made using AI has to name a human inventor in accordance with PatA Article 5 paragraph 1.

---

47. PatA, Art. 5 para. 1.
48. PatO, Art. 34.
49. *See*, e.g., the reports of the Swiss AIPPI group on the '*Inventorship of Inventions made using Artificial Intelligence (Q 272)*', Sic! 10|2020, and the '*Inventiveness and sufficiency of disclosure in AI inventions*', Sic! 11|2021.

However, inventorship is assessed independently of how the invention was done or which tools were used.[50] Thus, nothing in the Swiss law prevents an applicant from filing a patent application directed to an invention made by human beings using AI technology so long as the application contains the designation of a human inventor.

So far, the Swiss courts never have had the opportunity of deciding whether an IA entity can be designated as inventor or co-inventor in Switzerland. However, as noted above, several provisions of the Swiss patent law suggest that the inventor must be a natural person. Therefore, inventorship would likely be denied to an AI entity in Switzerland, just like in the EPO.

§16.07 AREAS FOR FURTHER DEVELOPMENT

The Federal Council intends to adapt the Swiss PatA to international standards and make the patent system more attractive to SMEs and individual inventors. The current proposal[51] is to increase legal certainty through a compulsory patent search for all patent applications and make the patent examination more flexible by providing an optional examination of all patentability requirements including novelty and inventive step. In the long run, this possibility should reinforce the convergence between the approaches of the IPI, the national courts of the Unified Territory, and the Examining Divisions and BoAs of the EPO.

§16.08 RECOMMENDATIONS FOR PATENT APPLICANTS

Given the current lack of provisions and guidance concerning the patentability of AI-related inventions in the Swiss patent law, it is recommended to handle such inventions in the same way as mathematical methods, computer programs, and CIIs. The recommendations provided in the EPO chapter are believed to remain generally valid for the Unified Territory.

§16.09 CONCLUSION

AI-related inventions are ever more relevant. Therefore, inventors and applicants should be encouraged to protect innovation in the area of AI and machine learning in the Unified Territory, provided that such innovation has technical character.

50. *See* FPC decision S2018_003, 24 Aug. 2018.
51. The Federal Council wants to strengthen the Swiss patent. Bern, 16 Nov. 2022.

Chapter 17

United Kingdom

Dr Julian Potter & Ranveer Rivat

§17.01 PATENTABILITY OF SOFTWARE AND COMPUTER-IMPLEMENTED INVENTIONS

The law relating to the patentability of computer implemented inventions ('CIIs'), such as artificial intelligence ('AI') and machine learning ('ML') inventions, derives from the statutory provisions found in Section 1(2) of The Patents Act 1977 ('PA77'):

> (2) It is hereby declared that the following (among other things) are not inventions for the purposes of this Act, that is to say, anything which consists of ...
>
> (c) a scheme, rule or method for performing a mental act, playing a game or doing business, or a program for a computer;
>
> ... only to the extent that a patent or application for a patent relates to that thing as such.[1]

It will come as no surprise to the reader that the words 'as such' have great importance as it is how those words influence the implementation of the exclusion that determines the patentability of CIIs.

Aerotel Ltd v. Telco Holdings Ltd[2] is currently treated as the definitive statement of the law in the United Kingdom concerning patentable subject matter having comprehensively considered the previous cases in this area. In *Aerotel*, the UK Court of Appeal set out the following four step test that subject matter is required to pass in order to be considered patentable subject matter:

1. Patents Act 1977, S. 1(2).
2. *Aerotel Ltd v. Telco Holding Ltd and others, and Neal William Macrossan's application* [2006] EWCA Civ 1371.

Step 1: Properly construe the claim

The approach to construction under English law set out in PA77 Section 125(1)[3] and Section 125(3)[4] should be adopted. This is to take a construction, based on the teaching of the specification and any drawings, that is neither a strict, literal meaning of the words used in the claims, where the description and drawings are used only to resolve ambiguity, nor a loose interpretation where the claims serve only as a guideline and the actual protection extends to what, in light of the description and drawings, the patent proprietor has contemplated. On the contrary, a proper claim construction is one that defines 'a position between these extremes which combines a fair protection for the patent proprietor with a reasonable degree of legal certainty for third parties'.[5] Note should be taken of the Protocol on the Interpretation of Article 69 EPC, referred to in Section 125, requiring due account to be taken of equivalents.[6] This might be a challenging requirement for applying the *Aerotel* test so far as looking to authoritative guidance on equivalents is concerned because the case law on equivalents in UK law has its genesis in infringement cases in which an alleged infringement falling outside a normal construction of a claim, a '*variant*', is determined to be or not be equivalent subject matter to that set out in the claim alleged to be infringed.[7] That is to say, the leading cases on construction of claims determine their scope relative to an alleged infringement. An alleged infringement is not something that will necessarily be in the case in many circumstances where the *Aerotel* test is to be applied.

Step 2: Identify the actual contribution

In *Actavis UK Limited v. ICOS*[8] the Court held that the 'improvement approach' is the correct approach for determining the scope of a patent claim. This is useful in that no test against an alleged infringement or other thing is brought into the test. This approach seeks to identify the technical problem that the invention solves and determine whether the solution provides a technical contribution that is not obvious to a person skilled in the relevant field. That is to say, the inventive feature has to be technical, and the check for whether it is technical and not excluded subject matter is the subject of the next two tests. It is notable too that *Actavis v. ICOS* uses language very similar to that used in the European Patent Office's formulation of the problem-solution approach to the assessment of inventive step.

Step 3: Ask whether it falls solely within the excluded subject matter

It was noted by Jacob LJ in *Aerotel* that the list of excluded subject matter set out in Section 1(2) of PA77 is non-exhaustive and so the general principle of taking a restrictive and limited view of the exclusions does not apply. The items in the list

3. PA77, S.125(1) 'an invention … shall … be taken to be that specified in a claim of the specification … as interpreted by the description and any drawings contained in that specification, and the extent of the protection … determined accordingly.'
4. *Ibid.*, S.125(3) 'The Protocol on the Interpretation of Article 69 of the European Patent Convention … shall … apply for the purposes of subsection (1) above as it applies for the purposes of that Article.'
5. Protocol on Interpretation of Article 69 EPC, Art. 1 (revised 29 Nov. 2000).
6. *Ibid.*, Art. 2.
7. *Actavis UK Limited & Ors v. Eli Lilly and Company* [2017] UKSC 48 (12 Jul. 2017).
8. *Actavis UK Limited v. ICOS Corporation* [2019] UKSC 15.

are non-limiting examples of excluded subject matter. If the construction of a claim includes both an embodiment which makes a technical contribution and one which does not, the claim is bad for encompassing excluded subject matter. However, the test is whether the subject matter *as such* falls under the exclusions and something which appears to fall under the exclusions may not do so when considered *as such*.

Step 4: Check whether the actual or alleged contribution is technical in nature

This test invokes the notion of technical *effect* developed by the Court of Appeal in *Merrill Lynch*[9] when assessing the patentability of a computer-implemented trading system. It is of course particularly applicable to CIIs in which the involvement of a computer may misdirect the enquiry under step 3 to find non-excluded subject matter merely due to the involvement of a computer.

It is helpful to consider steps 3 and 4 together when considering the patentability of CIIs in particular since it is whether or not the CII makes a technical contribution other than merely involving a computer that determines whether or not it is a patentable invention.

Determining when a CII constitutes a *technical* contribution has been a long-standing and complex issue, as evidenced by a series of Court of Appeal rulings, including *Merrill Lynch* and *Aerotel/Macrossan* as discussed above, but also cases such as *AT&T Knowledge Ventures*,[10] *Symbian*[11] and *HTC v. Apple*.[12] The Court of Appeal has acknowledged the difficulty in defining what qualifies as a technical contribution and what does not. While there is no comprehensive or precise test to answer this question, *AT&T Knowledge Ventures* introduced the following set of 'signposts' to assist courts in deciding whether there is the required contribution:

(1) whether the claimed technical effect has a technical effect on a process which is carried on outside the computer;
(2) whether the claimed technical effect operates at the level of the architecture of the computer; that is to say whether the effect is produced irrespective of the data being processed or the applications being run;
(3) whether the claimed technical effect results in the computer being made to operate in a new way;
(4) whether there is an increase in the speed or reliability of the computer;
(5) whether the perceived problem is overcome by the claimed invention as opposed to merely being circumvented.

The fourth signpost was modified later by the Court of Appeal in *HTC v. Apple* to encompass more broadly a technical effect which makes the computer 'better', which in the case of AI and ML inventions could encompass improving or enhancing existing AI/ML systems. Such an application of the modified fourth test is confirmed in the recent guidance given by the UK Intellectual Property Office ('UKIPO') on examining AI-related inventions, discussed in the following section.

9. *Merrill Lynch's Application* [1989] RPC 561.
10. *AT&T Knowledge Ventures/Cvon Innovations v. Comptroller General of Patents* [2009] EWHC 343 (Pat).
11. *Symbian Ltd v. Comptroller-General of Patents* [2009] RPC 1.
12. *HTC Europe Co Ltd v. Apple Inc* [2013] RPC 30.

Having set out the main principles relating to the patentability of CIIs (and it should be noted the foregoing is not an exhaustive discussion of the law relating to CIIs, let alone excluded subject matter in general), the discussion can now turn to how those principles are applied in the realm of AI and ML.

§17.02 SPECIAL PROVISIONS RELATING TO PATENTABILITY OF INVENTIONS RELATING TO AI

In general, the patentability requirements for AI and ML-related inventions are the same as for any other software or computer-implemented invention. The invention must be new, inventive, and have industrial applicability. The technical contribution of the invention is also an important factor in determining its patentability. However, the UKIPO recognizes that there may be some unique considerations for AI and ML-related inventions.

To address these considerations, the UKIPO has issued two-part guidance on the patentability of AI and ML-related inventions, comprising an explanation of the statutory and jurisprudence basis ('the Guidance')[13], and then a series of scenarios ('the Scenarios)[14] to illustrate the application of the law which includes the following:

[A] Technical Character

Unsurprisingly, the UKIPO will consider whether an AI or ML-related invention has a technical character. In other words, does the invention solve a technical problem using AI or ML techniques? If the invention is purely mathematical or abstract, it may not be patentable. Such considerations are likely to follow the law as applied to assessing the patentability of inventions and of CIIs in particular.

[B] Contribution[15]

The UKIPO will also consider whether an AI or ML-related invention makes a technical contribution to the field. This means that the invention should go beyond just implementing a mathematical algorithm or ML model and should provide some practical application or benefit. A technical contribution is likely to exist if the AI invention runs on a computer and its instructions:

- embody a technical process which exists outside the computer; or
- contribute to the solution of a technical problem lying outside the computer; or
- solve a technical problem lying within the computer itself; or
- define a new way of operating the computer in a technical sense;

---

13. *Examining patent applications relating to artificial intelligence (AI) inventions: The Guidance* (22 Sept. 2022).
14. *Examining patent applications relating to artificial intelligence (AI) inventions: The Scenarios* (22 Sept. 2022).
15. *The Guidance*, executive summary.

which are signposts familiar from the foregoing discussion.

[C] Data Training[16]

If an AI or ML-related invention involves training data, the UKIPO will consider whether the data is itself novel and inventive. In other words, does the data represent a new and inventive contribution to the field? This includes the development of new datasets for training AI models, as well as innovations in the data preparation and processing methods used to train these models.

[D] Disclosure[17]

Applicants seeking to patent AI or ML-related inventions should ensure that their application discloses the technical features and components of the invention in a clear and complete manner. While this may seem an obvious statement of the law, it is particularly important that applications and patents for subject matter at risk of being considered, or even just related to, excluded subject matter include a disclosure rich with technical and technically described features that are necessary to provide the benefits, advantages, and improvements ascribed to the invention. Describing how a technical feature works and how it is applied; addressing problems, particularly technical ones; and a formulation of the invention focusing on its technological aspects are all very important. It may help to substitute the term 'technological' for 'technical' when thinking about these things, as 'technological' tends to convey a sense of real things whereas the term 'technical' can include abstract things, for example a 'technical' financial instrument.

One of the main concepts introduced by the UKIPO Guidance is the categorization of AI to be used when assessing AI inventions, namely into the two categories of 'Applied AI' and 'Core AI'.

Applied AI[18] inventions are defined as those that utilize AI as a tool to solve technical problems outside of a computer process, control such processes, or improve computer performance.

Core AI[19] inventions pertain solely to the advancement of AI technology itself, such as an improved AI model, algorithm, or mathematical method, without specifying any particular application or use-case. The UKIPO considers a computer-implemented core AI invention to be an application program that performs the stated functions of the core AI.

§17.03 SUBJECT MATTER PATENTABILITY

The process of patenting an invention that utilizes AI technology can be a complex and challenging endeavour, particularly when it comes to meeting the stringent

16. *Ibid.*, Points 71–73.
17. *Ibid.*, Points 83–86.
18. *Ibid.*, Point 13.
19. *Ibid.*, Point 14.

requirements of patent law. For example, an invention that is described in broad mathematical terms and implemented in a generic manner may not qualify for patent protection, as it could be viewed as simply claiming a mathematical algorithm or abstract idea.

However, there are steps that can be taken to ensure that an AI invention is both innovative and patent eligible. Specifically, by describing the invention in precise technical terms and highlighting the unique hardware and software features that set it apart, it can improve the chances of drafting successful patent claims.

In order to provide an overview of the patentability of the five different categories of AI as defined in the Introduction to this book, the following sections will examine each category briefly. While example scenarios will be referenced, readers are encouraged to refer to the UKIPO Scenarios for a more detailed analysis of each scenario. Each scenario includes a simplified assessment of how each AI invention would likely be assessed in respect of Section 1(2) PA77. The focus of these scenarios is on the question of excluded matter only. It is assumed that the claimed inventions are novel and non-obvious, and that each scenario is sufficiently disclosed. The assessments of excluded matter provided in these scenarios follow a simplified application of the four-step *Aerotel* approach mentioned in Section §17.01.

[A] Category 1 (Invention of AI)

This category pertains to the creation of a new algorithm or model for the AI system itself, without regard to the data it is applied to or any specific use case, but instead represents an advance in the field of AI itself. This constitutes the core AI inventions mentioned in Section §17.02, *supra*.

The patentability of such inventions will depend upon how they are described and claimed in the patent specification. The UKIPO Guidance emphasizes that inventions of this nature must meet the third *AT&T* signpost. However, the Guidance also acknowledges the difficulty of relying on this signpost due to the lack of explicit examples in case law. Despite this uncertainty, the Scenarios provide three examples each of patentable and non-patentable subject matter to provide a better understanding of what may or may not be allowable. It is important to note that meeting the third signpost also leads to meeting the fifth signpost.

The three examples of where a patent could be granted interestingly all include some aspect of hardware interaction:[20]

- 'Processing a neural network on a heterogeneous computing platform' discusses adjusting clock speeds to allow heterogeneous elements to complete calculations at the same time;
- 'Special purpose processing unit for machine learning computations' discusses a system that collates memory address locations for non-zero memory values; and
- 'A multiprocessor topology adapted for machine learning' discusses the adaptation of an ML technique to a non-standard multiprocessor topology.

20. *The Scenarios*, examples 16–18.

In contrast, the examples where the likelihood of obtaining a patent is lower tend to pertain more to the software aspect:[21]

- 'Avoiding unnecessary processing using a neural network' can be considered as reducing the computing resource required to run a neural network; and
- 'Active training of a neural network' relates to the selection of training data.

Therefore, in the realm of UK patent law, inventions that involve unique and precise hardware, particularly those that interact with software architecture in a novel and technically advantageous manner, may qualify for patent eligibility through the drafting of corresponding apparatus and process claims, even if their application is not explicitly defined. This is particularly true when these novel features provide significant technical advantages, such as surmounting previous AI systems' limitations and presenting a 'technical solution' to a 'technical problem'. However, it is *critical* to establish in the specification that the invention represents a substantial improvement in computer technology.

[B] Categories 2 and 3 (Invention of AI Implementation and New Application of AI)

The UK guidance specifies that *Applied AI* can be divided into two subcategories: inventions that focus on improving the performance of the computer system itself, and those that address external problems, thus falling into the 'invention of AI implementation' and 'new application of AI' categories of this section.

According to the Guidance, the first and fifth *AT&T* signposts are relevant for determining patentability of *Applied AI* inventions performing processes or solving problems lying outside the computer. The scenarios provided in the guidance list six examples of patentable subject matter and three examples of non-patentable subject matter.

Regarding patentable subject matter, the guidance clarifies that the first signpost is not limited to inventions that control physical entities outside the computer but also extends to 'input'-side connections with the real world, as demonstrated in scenario 3: 'Analysing and classifying movement from motion sensor data'.[22] This is helpful for examiners who may have had a narrow view of the first signpost.

However, regarding the non-patentable subject matter, the guidance confirms that controlling purely business/administrative processes, as shown in scenario 7: 'Automated financial instrument trading', and mere classification of computerized data, as shown in scenario 9: 'Identifying junk e-mail using a trained AI classifier', are non-allowable subject matter.[23]

For 'new AI implementations' or, equivalently, 'Applied AI: improving computer functionality,' the path to grant primarily lies in the second and fourth *AT&T* signposts. The scenarios presented in the UK guidance offer valuable insight into how the second and fourth *AT&T* signposts can be applied. Specifically, the guidance provides three scenarios that demonstrate different ways in which computers can be made to work

21. *Ibid.*, examples 14–15.
22. *Ibid.*, example 3.
23. *Ibid.*, examples 7, 9.

better, with each scenario meeting the fifth signpost. These scenarios include cache management using a neural network (scenario 10), continuous user authentication (scenario 11), and a virtual keyboard with predictive text entry (scenario 12).[24] Notably, scenario 10 meets both the second and fourth signposts, while scenarios 11 and 12 only meet one of the two signposts.

[C] Category 4 (Inventions Made Using AI)

Unless the claim to the invention is directed to a method of designing or producing the invention using AI (in which case it would be a Category 3 claim) there is no reason or duty to claim the AI at all and subject matter eligibility rests entirely on what is claimed. To be eligible for patent protection, the claims must meet the same patentability criteria as any other invention.

It is worth noting that, as with any patent application, it can be challenging to demonstrate that an invention made using AI meets these patentability requirements. For example, demonstrating an inventive step may require showing how the AI system produced a result that was unexpected or not obvious to a person skilled in the relevant field. Moreover, the 'black box' issue, where the reasoning behind an AI's distinct solution may be opaque, can make it difficult to establish an inventive step in the first place. This will be discussed further in Section §17.04, *infra.*

[D] Category 5 (Inventions Made by AI)

In the UK, an invention that is made by AI would not currently be considered patentable, as the law requires that an inventor must be a human. However, if in the future AI is able to make inventions on its own, there may be changes to the law to accommodate such inventions. In an event, as to the subject matter patentability of a claim to an invention made, hypothetically, by AI, as is the case with Category 4 this would depend entirely on what is claimed without regard to the manner by which the invention was made.

§17.04 INVENTIVE STEP

There is no special rule of law on inventive step in relation to AI inventions in the categories set out above. The relevant prior art would be considered, and the question of whether the invention would have been obvious to a person skilled in the art at the time of filing would be assessed.

The person of ordinary skill in the art for inventions related to AI would depend on the specific technical field or application area of the invention. For example, the person of ordinary skill in the art for an AI invention in the field of computer vision would likely be someone with expertise in computer vision and ML.

For inventions in Categories 4 and 5, the fact that AI could try every possible option to determine an optimal solution potentially affects the assessment of inventive step if it means that the invention is merely the result of the application of routine

24. *Ibid.*, examples 10-12.

computer algorithms and techniques trying various combinations and options to find the best one. In this case it would be difficult to argue in favour of inventive step because merely selecting the best option, whether selected by the machine or a human looking at the output from the machine, would be an obvious thing to do. In such cases, it may be argued that the invention would have been obvious to a person skilled in the art as all they had to do was select the best option. Of course, not choosing the best option if based on cogent reasoning may in itself be an invention or at least inventive selection. However, if the AI is designed to use non-obvious or unexpected techniques, or if the invention is the result of a creative insight by the inventor, then it may still meet the inventive step requirement by virtue of the non-obvious programming of the AI.

§17.05 ADEQUACY OF DISCLOSURE

Section 14(3) of the Patents Act 1977[25] requires:

> The specification of an application shall disclose the invention in a manner which is clear enough and complete enough for the invention to be performed by a person skilled in the art.

Eli Lilly v. Human Genome Sciences[26] provides a summary of the key principles that should be considered when determining whether a patent application satisfies the disclosure requirement outlined in Section 14(3):

> The specification must disclose the invention clearly and completely enough for it to be performed by a person skilled in the art. The key elements of this requirement which bear on the present case are these:
>
> (i) the first step is to identify the invention and that is to be done by reading and construing the claims;
> (ii) in the case of a product claim that means making or otherwise obtaining the product;
> (iii) in the case of a process claim, it means working the process;
> (iv) sufficiency of the disclosure must be assessed on the basis of the specification as a whole including the description and the claims;
> (v) the disclosure is aimed at the skilled person who may use his common general knowledge to supplement the information contained in the specification;
> (vi) the specification must be sufficient to allow the invention to be performed over the whole scope of the claim;
> (vii) the specification must be sufficient to allow the invention to be so performed without undue burden.

When it comes to considering the sufficiency of disclosure for all inventions, including those related to AI, the principles outlined above are the ones that should be applied. The law in the UK does not require any additional disclosures specifically for AI-related inventions beyond these principles. Whether an AI-related invention

25. PA77 S.14(3).
26. *Eli Lilly v. Human Genome Sciences* [2008] RPC 2, para. 239.

meets the disclosure requirements is determined on a case-by-case basis, taking into account the individual circumstances of each case.

Therefore, for Categories 1 and 2, the disclosure requirements would be similar to any other patent application and follow the principles set out above. The application should describe the invention in sufficient detail to enable a person of ordinary skill in the art to make and use the invention without undue experimentation. The disclosure should include a clear description of the AI algorithm or implementation, including any unique features or elements that distinguish it from prior art.

For Category 3, the disclosure requirements may be more challenging, particularly if the distinguishing features of the invention relate to the specific training or input data used. In these cases, it may be difficult or impossible to directly describe the parameters within the AI in a clear manner such that the subject matter of the invention is directly and unambiguously derivable from the description. It may be tempting to include an annex to the application comprising a data file for the learning set, but this may still not provide a teaching that supports a claim across its whole breadth.

The patent application must contain a comprehensive explanation of the process and methodology used to train the AI, including the types of input data employed, how the data is utilized, why it is used, and how to apply the disclosed methods to other AI systems. This level of detail enables a skilled addressee not only to learn the specific teachings but also to apply them effectively in other scenarios.

The level of description required will depend on the specific circumstances of the invention and the technology involved. In general, the more complex the AI system and training methodology, the more detailed the description will need to be. If the input data is proprietary and not publicly available, the application should still provide as much detail as possible about the type of data used and how it was obtained, to enable a person of ordinary skill in the art to replicate the invention using similar data. If the input data has value to the proprietor, it is unlikely they will publish it through the patent system. This fear of having to disclose learning sets may dissuade AI innovators from patenting their innovations and seek to rely on confidentiality and secrecy instead, which will of course have the effect of reducing knowledge about innovations in this area and may be more challenging, particularly if the distinguishing features relate to the specific training or input data used.

The UKIPO Guidance reinforces the importance of describing an AI invention, including the training dataset, in sufficient technical detail so that the invention can be performed by someone skilled in the art without undue burden.

As noted previously, this has been set out in UK case law, *Eli Lilly v. Human Genome Sciences*, and the UKIPO considers these principles to be consistent with a recent decision of the European Patent Office's ('EPO') Board of Appeal, *T 0161/18*.

In reason 2.2 of decision *T 0161/18*[27] the Board stated that:

> The application does not disclose which input data are suitable for training the artificial neural network according to the invention, or at least one dataset suitable for solving the present technical problem. The training of the artificial

27. EPO Board of Appeal *T 0161/18*, at [2.2].

neural network can therefore not be reworked by the person skilled in the art and the person skilled in the art therefore cannot carry out the invention.

It should be noted that, in *T 0161/18*, the training of the neural network was a feature of the claim and was required to differentiate the invention from the prior art. The requirement for a sufficient disclosure of the claimed invention is a fundamental requirement of patent law that applies equally to AI-related inventions.

This case seems to concern an application that could have been written in a different way, such as by describing the type of data to be used in detail not merely general references to gender, age or cardiac history, and how and why it is used, to avoid the rejection of the application. It does not therefore make a convincing case for the inclusion of input data, such as a learning set, in a patent specification.

Regarding Categories 4 and 5, the primary distinction for the purposes of this section is that the claims would be directed *to whatever was made using* AI (or, hypothetically, by AI) *rather than to the AI itself*. The claim could thus be directed to literally anything: a mechanical device, a new industrial process, a beverage container,[28] software, or even AI (if AI is used to invent AI). Accordingly, the same rules of sufficiency would apply to these claims as well and the practicalities of complying with those rules would depend upon the particular subject matter being claimed, without regard to the manner in which the invention was made. Notably, unless the AI is claimed, *there is no duty to mention that AI was used in the inventive process at all*. It may, however, at least in theory, raise questions of inventorship as discussed in the next section.

§17.06 INVENTORSHIP

[A] Inventorship in General

In the UK, the law of inventorship is governed by Section 7 of PA77.[29] Under this law, an inventor is defined as the 'actual deviser' of an invention. This definition is generally straightforward for 'traditional patents', but becomes more contentious when AI is involved, as demonstrated by the notable DABUS applications that will be discussed in more detail below.

Once an invention is defined, it is necessary to determine who 'actually devised' it. In general, individuals who contribute to the conception of the invention, whether through initial ideas, experimentation, problem-solving, or data interpretation, may be considered inventors. However, those who simply carry out work under instruction, have no part in the research, or serve as project managers or supervisors without contributing technically to the invention would not be considered inventors. All individuals who contribute to the conception of the invention should be listed as inventors on the patent application.

In *Rhone-Poulenc Rorer International Holdings Inc v. Yeda Research & Development Co Ltd*,[30] the House of Lords clarified that Section 7 of PA77 determines who is

28. One of the two alleged DABUS inventions discussed *infra*.

29. PA77 S. 7(3)

30. *Rorer International Holdings Inc and others* [2007] UKHL 43.

entitled to a patent, with the actual deviser being *the natural person* who conceived the inventive concept.

Furthermore, Section 13(2) of PA77[31] requires patent applicants to file a statement:

> (a) identifying the person or persons whom he believes to be the inventor or inventors; and
> (b) ... indicating the derivation of his or their right to be granted the patent ...

Failure to do so means that the application will be withdrawn.

Section 13(2) aims to ensure that unintentional errors concerning inventorship and ownership of patents do not hinder or invalidate the granting of patents.

[B] Determination of Inventorship for AI-Related Inventions

For Categories 1 and 2, inventorship would be determined based on the contributions made to the invention in the traditional manner. The person or persons who conceived the idea of the invention or who contributed to the practical implementation of the invention would be considered inventors.

For Categories 3 and 4, inventorship may be more complex. The person or persons who had the idea of using AI for the intended purpose or who selected the AI technology and configured it to suit the intended purpose may be considered inventors. However, the person or persons who selected the data to be used to train the AI or the input data fed to the trained AI system may not necessarily be considered inventors unless they made a significant contribution to the inventive concept of the invention. Similarly, the person who recognized the value of and selected one optimal solution from a large number of potential solutions produced by the AI may not necessarily be considered an inventor unless they made a significant contribution to the inventive concept of the invention.

Regarding Category 5, an interesting case involving the AI machine DABUS, listed as the inventor,[32] has recently gained notoriety. The UKIPO was the first to reject these applications, as they found that the wording of Sections 7 and 13 of PA77[33] indicated a 'clear expectation' that the terms 'inventor' and 'person' referred to a natural person, i.e., a human, and not an AI machine.[34]

The English High Court of Justice (hereinafter 'High Court') affirmed the UKIPO's rejection.[35] The High Court did not distinguish between ownership and inventorship. Instead, the Court's analysis relied on the fact that DABUS had no legal personality and therefore lacked the legal capacity to transfer its rights to Dr Stephen Thaler, the individual seeking the patent:

31. PA77 S. 13(2).
32. UK Intellectual Property Office decision not to grant: BL O/741/19.
33. PA77 S. 7,13.
34. UKIPO decision at para. 18.
35. *Thaler v. The Comptroller-General of Patents, Designs And Trade Marks*, [2020] EWHC 2412 (Pat) (21 September 2020).

> There must either be an application by the inventor within section 7(2)(a) (which cannot be made because DABUS is not an inventor nor a person) or the inventor must have transferred the right to apply enabling Dr. Thaler to apply under one of section 7(2)(b) or (c) (which again cannot be in this case).[36]

The Court of Appeal has since rejected Thaler's appeal and upheld the UKIPO's and the High Court's decisions.[37]

At the time of writing, the UK Supreme Court is hearing Thaler's appeal as he challenges whether PA77 necessitates a natural person to be credited as the inventor in all circumstances. Furthermore, the Court will examine whether a patent can be issued without a designated human inventor, and whether an AI machine's owner, creator, and user is eligible for a patent if the machine produces an invention. A hearing in Thaler's case was held on 2 March 2023, with a decision expected in the coming months. The outcome of this case could have significant implications for the future of patent law in the UK as AI continues to advance and play an increasingly important role in innovation.

§17.07 AREAS FOR FURTHER DEVELOPMENT

[A] Inventorship

With the DABUS case having reached the Supreme Court as of the time of writing this chapter (March 2023), it is hoped that there will soon be clarity on whether or not an AI system may be named as the inventor of an invention that is the subject of a UK patent.

Whatever the decision of the Supreme Court may be, the law will have to consider the implications of such a decision. For example, if an AI system may be named as an inventor, then the notion of the first inventor having ownership of an invention is likely to require modification, unless the law is comfortable with a non-person – neither human nor legal entity – having property rights. On the other hand, if an AI system may not be named as an inventor for a valid patent, then the question of who is entitled to the property right in an invention involving the use of an AI system would seem to arise. For inventions in which the AI system may be properly described as a tool, it seems reasonable that a natural person would continue to be the logical choice for the inventor. However, as AI systems become more and more generative to the point where human intervention is minimal or unnecessary – as alleged in the case of DABUS – there may be no natural person having the necessary interaction with the machine to qualify as an inventor. In such a case, the concept of inventor and the naming of the inventor under English law would require modification. Alternatively, a simple solution may be to deem the person having a supervision or management right over the machine as the inventor. Amendment to or clarification of UK law to permit a legal person to be designated an inventor would allow a business entity to be first owner of an invention produced by a machine thereby coupling the economic benefit of the machine output to the

36. *Thaler v. Comptroller* at para. 49.
37. *Thaler v. Comptroller* Appeal at paras 54–55, 102, 116.

business, consistent with public policy behind the patent system to incentivise investment in technology.

[B] Sufficiency

While it may seem appealing to require a learning or teaching set to be included with a patent application or patent for AI systems, challenges may arise in circumstances where the AI system is not configured by supervised learning. For instance, the situation of an AI system utilizing unsupervised learning, capture of the learning data would need to be recorded for inclusion in any patent application or patent. However, if the AI system continues to learn from the data that it is collecting, then including a learning set input to the AI system representing the dataset up to a specific instance in time does not define the AI system and may fail a sufficiency test. This is because the configuration of the AI system due to subsequently collected data would not be disclosed by the inclusion of that learning data in the patent application or patent.

It appears that specifying the nature and type of the data to comprise the learning set in a sufficiently rigorous manner should provide instruction to the skilled person to configure an AI system using a learning set suitable for agreeing AI system in accordance with the invention. One may consider such an approach to have a number of advantages. Notably, there would be no need to have appendices comprising many gigabytes of learning set data. Additionally, the generation of learning sets can require substantial financial resources and have significant financial value. Therefore, innovators may be dissuaded from filing patent applications if they have to disclose a learning set, thereby reducing the dissemination of knowledge with respect to AI systems. Great care needs to be given to the matter of sufficiency for inventions in the AI and ML field.

§17.08 RECOMMENDATIONS FOR PATENT APPLICANTS

When describing an ML/AI invention, it is necessary to describe the actions and processes from the perspective of what the computer does and its interaction with the outside world (to the extent that it is relevant). The description of such actions and processes should be detailed and focused on technological aspects. Merely describing the outcomes that are achieved is very unlikely to result in the grant of a patent.

Additionally, the applicant must be sure not to give the computer human qualities. For instance, a machine cannot 'think', 'process' or 'identify'. They should always be thought of as machines that undertake technological activity to produce output signals in response to receiving input signals.

Finally, it is helpful to ask the applicant what aspects of their innovation they think will cause customers to purchase or use their invention. Even if those things are non-technical, it is nevertheless useful to know what they are because they may be implemented by technological elements. Drafting a patent application to the technological elements that are technically necessary to produce those things that attract customers may protect non-technical aspects of the invention indirectly by protecting their essential technical features and implementation.

§17.09 CONCLUSION

The legal landscape surrounding the use of AI in technology creation and the assignment of rights to the resulting outputs is an area that must continue to evolve and develop over time. A sober and reflective approach needs to be taken and emotive issues such as who or what may be an inventor need to be carefully considered from a public policy perspective, including the purpose of patents and their value in society. Would that purpose be met by or include AI inventorship?

Chapter 18

United States

James Carlson, Dr Kate Gaudry, Jonathan P. Osha, Dr Ian Schick & Dr Leron Vandsburger

§18.01 PATENTABILITY OF SOFTWARE AND COMPUTER-IMPLEMENTED INVENTIONS

In the United States, the statute that governs what types of inventions are eligible for patent protection, 35 U.S.C. §101, provides in its entirety:

> Whoever invents or discovers any new and useful process, machine, manufacture, or composition of matter, or any new and useful improvement thereof, may obtain a patent therefor, subject to the conditions and requirements of this title.[1]

Notably, the statute identifies *inclusion criteria* for patent eligibility, setting forth four patent-eligible statutory categories: process; machine; manufacture; and composition of matter. Under a literal reading of the statute, *any* new and useful invention falling in any of these four categories, and *any* new and useful improvement thereof, should be patent eligible. However, the US Supreme Court has interpreted §101 as being subject to three *exclusion criteria*: laws of nature, physical phenomena, and abstract ideas, as explained in more detail below.

In 1980, the US Supreme Court in *Chakrabarty*[2] considered the breadth of the inclusion criteria in the context of determining whether a human-made, genetically engineered bacterium falls within the 'manufacture' or 'composition of matter' categories of §101. Although considering a very different technology, the *Chakrabarty* decision provides an intriguing foreshadowing of the current issues surrounding patentability of inventions relating to artificial intelligence ('AI').

1. 35 U.S.C. §101.
2. *Diamond v. Chakrabarty*, 447 U.S. 303 (1980).

First, the Supreme Court considered the plain language of the statute, concluding:

> In choosing such expansive terms as 'manufacture' and 'composition of matter,' modified by the comprehensive 'any,' Congress plainly contemplated that the patent laws would be given wide scope.[3]

Next, the Court considered the legislative history of §101, noting the statute was originally written by the famous American Thomas Jefferson[4] in 1793 and has survived to the present time with a change of only one word: a change from 'art' to 'process':

> The relevant legislative history also supports a broad construction. The Patent Act of 1793, authored by Thomas Jefferson, defined statutory subject matter as 'any new and useful art, machine, manufacture, or composition of matter, or any new or useful improvement [thereof].' Act of Feb. 21, 1793, §1, 1 Stat. 319. The Act embodied Jefferson's philosophy that 'ingenuity should receive a liberal encouragement.' 5 Writings of Thomas Jefferson 75–76 (Washington ed. 1871). See Graham v. John Deere Co., 383 U.S. 1, 383 U.S. 7–10 (1966). Subsequent patent statutes in 1836, 1870, and 1874 employed this same broad language. In 1[9]52, when the patent laws were recodified, Congress replaced the word 'art' with 'process,' but otherwise left Jefferson's language intact. The Committee Reports accompanying the 1952 Act inform us that Congress intended statutory subject matter to 'include anything under the sun that is made by man.' S Rep. No. 1979, 82d Cong., 2d Sess., 5 (1952); H.R.Rep. No. 1979, 82d Cong., 2d Sess., 6 (1952).

The Court also noted that the principal draftsman of the 1952 recodification of the patent law, P.J. Federico, used similar language when testifying to Congress about the new statute:

> [U]nder section 101, a person may have invented a machine or a manufacture, which may include anything under the sun that is made by man....[5]

To balance this, the Court noted that the breadth of §101 is not limitless and, specifically, that laws of nature, physical phenomena, and abstract ideas are excluded from patentability ('exclusion criteria'):

> This is not to suggest that §101 has no limits, or that it embraces every discovery. The laws of nature, physical phenomena, and abstract ideas have been held not patentable. Thus, a new mineral discovered in the earth or a new plant found in the wild is not patentable subject matter. Likewise, Einstein could not patent his celebrated law that $E = mc^2$; nor could Newton have patented the law of gravity. Such discoveries are 'manifestations of ... nature, free to all men and reserved exclusively to none.'[6]

---

3. *Ibid.* at 308.
4. Thomas Jefferson was the principal author of the US Declaration of Independence and the third president of the United States (1801–1809).
5. Hearings on H.R. 3760 before Subcommittee No. 3 of the House Committee on the Judiciary, 82d Cong., 1st Sess., 37 (1951).
6. *Chakrabarty*, 447 U.S. 303, 309. (Internal citations omitted.)

Based on this construction of §101, the Court found Chakrabarty's bacterium to be patent-eligible subject matter:

> Judged in this light, respondent's micro-organism plainly qualifies as patentable subject matter. His claim is not to a hitherto unknown natural phenomenon, but to a nonnaturally occurring manufacture or composition of matter – a product of human ingenuity 'having a distinctive name, character [and] use.'[7]

Perhaps most interestingly for the subject matter of this book, the Court responded to two arguments made by the petitioner and *amici* opposing patent eligibility of the micro-organism: 1) Congress was not considering genetic engineering when it passed §101 in 1952 and, therefore, it cannot cover genetically engineered materials; and 2) genetic engineering is a new, unknown and unpredictable technology that may wreak havoc on human society so should not be patentable for policy reasons. Responding to the first argument:

> The petitioner's ... argument is that micro-organisms cannot qualify as patentable subject matter until Congress expressly authorizes such protection. His position rests on the fact that genetic technology was unforeseen when Congress enacted §101.
>
> ... The subject matter provisions of the patent law have been cast in broad terms to fulfill the constitutional and statutory goal of promoting 'the Progress of Science and the useful Arts' with all that means for the social and economic benefits envisioned by Jefferson.
>
> ...This Court frequently has observed that a statute is not to be confined to the 'particular application[s] ... contemplated by the legislators.' This is especially true in the field of patent law. A rule that unanticipated inventions are without protection would conflict with the core concept of the patent law that anticipation undermines patentability. Mr. Justice Douglas reminded that the inventions most benefiting mankind are those that 'push back the frontiers of chemistry, physics, and the like.' Congress employed broad general language in drafting §101 precisely because such inventions are often unforeseeable.[8]

Responding to the second argument, the Court explained:

> ... [P]etitioner, with the support of amicus, points to grave risks that may be generated by research endeavors such as respondent's. The briefs present a gruesome parade of horribles. Scientists, among them Nobel laureates, are quoted suggesting that genetic research may pose a serious threat to the human race, or, at the very least, that the dangers are far too substantial to permit such research to proceed apace at this time. We are told that genetic research and related technological developments may spread pollution and disease, that it may result in a loss of genetic diversity, and that its practice may tend to depreciate the value of human life. These arguments are forcefully, even passionately, presented; they remind us that, at times, human ingenuity seems unable to control fully the forces it creates – that, with Hamlet, it is sometimes better 'to bear those ills we have than fly to others that we know not of.'

7. *Ibid.*
8. *Ibid.* at 314–315. (Internal citations omitted.)

> ... [W]e are without competence to entertain these arguments – either to brush them aside as fantasies generated by fear of the unknown or to act on them. The choice we are urged to make is a matter of high policy for resolution within the legislative process after the kind of investigation, examination, and study that legislative bodies can provide and courts cannot. That process involves the balancing of competing values and interests, which, in our democratic system, is the business of elected representatives. Whatever their validity, the contentions now pressed on us should be addressed to the political branches of the Government, the Congress and the Executive, and not to the courts.[9]

The parallels to current discussions regarding AI-related inventions are quite clear.

Unfortunately, the *Chakrabarty* 'anything under the sun' view of patent eligibility has not persevered through a sequence of subsequent decisions on §101. While a complete review of this progression is beyond the scope of this chapter, it is sufficient to say the judicial pendulum has swung toward a narrower and more convoluted reading of §101.

Unlike the Supreme Court, which has the benefit of time and extensive briefings from the parties (and the public, through *amicus* filings) when considering whether a particular claim is patent eligible, federal district courts (the courts of first instance in US patent cases) have varying levels of patent experience and crowded dockets (these courts also hear, e.g., federal criminal cases and other federal civil matters; some district courts see a patent matter only very rarely) yet must endeavour to apply the nuances of §101 to the facts of their case. Similarly, patent examiners at the United States Patent and Trademark Office ('USPTO') must, in the relatively short period of time allotted for examination of a single case, not only review and apply the prior art but also make an assessment as to eligibility. In light of this, the United States Court of Appeals for the Federal Circuit (hereinafter 'Federal Circuit')[10] has attempted repeatedly to interpret the Supreme Court's eligibility case law in a manner that provides a predictable framework. Thus far, the Supreme Court has rejected such attempts.

One such attempt was in the Federal Circuit's 1998 *State Street Bank*[11] decision, which found a claim to a 'Data Processing System for Hub and Spoke Financial Services Configuration' to be patent eligible. *State Street* did two important things: first, it did away with a line of prior cases that had applied a 'business method exception' to patent eligibility ('[w]e take this opportunity to lay this ill-conceived exception to rest ... business methods have been, and should have been, subject to the same legal requirements for patentability as applied to any other process or method')[12]. Secondly, it held that mathematical algorithms would be eligible if claimed as a practical application and if the invention produces 'a useful, concrete and tangible result':

---

9. *Ibid.* at 316–317. (Internal citations omitted.)
10. The Federal Circuit hears all appeals from US district courts relating to patent matters. *See Gunn v. Minton*, 568 U.S. 251 (2013).
11. *State Street Bank & Trust Co. v. Signature Financial Group, Inc.*, 149 F.3d 1368 (Fed. Cir. 1998).
12. *Ibid.* at 1375.

> Today, we hold that the transformation of data, representing discrete dollar amounts, by a machine through a series of mathematical calculations into a final share price, constitutes a practical application of a mathematical algorithm, formula, or calculation, because it produces 'a useful, concrete and tangible result' - a final share price momentarily fixed for recording and reporting purposes and even accepted and relied upon by regulatory authorities and in subsequent trades.[13]

Removal of the business method exception was widely misunderstood by the public at the time to mean business methods were now patentable *per se* (as opposed to the actual holding, that such processes would be held to the same standards as all other processes). As a result, the *State Street Bank* decision was followed by a flood of business method and other questionable process patents. Perhaps partially in response to public backlash to these types of patents, and to several particularly egregious examples[14], the Federal Circuit, sitting *en banc* 10 years later, proposed a new framework: rejecting the 'useful, concrete and tangible result' test in favour of the 'machine or transformation' test:

> [W]e agree that future developments in technology and the sciences may present difficult challenges to the machine-or-transformation test, just as the widespread use of computers and the advent of the Internet has begun to challenge it in the past decade. Thus, we recognize that the Supreme Court may ultimately decide to alter or perhaps even set aside this test to accommodate emerging technologies. And we certainly do not rule out the possibility that this court may in the future refine or augment the test or how it is applied. At present, however, and certainly for the present case, we see no need for such a departure and reaffirm that the machine-or-transformation test, properly applied, is the governing test for determining patent eligibility of a process under §101.[15]

In less than two years, however, the ground shifted again when the Supreme Court in *Bilski*[16] overruled the Federal Circuit, rejecting the machine-or-transformation test as a bright-line standard:

> This Court's precedents establish that the machine-or-transformation test is a useful and important clue, an investigative tool, for determining whether some claimed inventions are processes under §101. The machine-or-transformation test is not the sole test for deciding whether an invention is a patent-eligible 'process'.[17]

The Supreme Court did not propose an alternative test. Rather the Court indicated that limitations should not be imposed on §101 and reference should be had to the statute and the 'guideposts' of its prior decisions. This left the lower courts and the USPTO, once again, without clear guidance.

---

13. *Ibid.* at 1373.
14. *See*, e.g., US Patent No. 6,368,227 'Method of swinging a swing' and US Patent No. 7,261,652 'Method of holding a putter and putting a golf ball'.
15. *In re Bilski*, 545 F.3d 943, 956 (Fed. Cir. 2008).
16. *Bilski v. Kappos*, 561 U.S. 593 (2010).
17. *Ibid.* at 604.

A pair of additional §101 decisions followed thereafter at two-year intervals: *Mayo Collaborative Services v. Prometheus Laboratories, Inc.*[18] in 2012 ('*Mayo*') and *Alice Corp. v. CLS Bank Int'l*[19] in 2014 ('*Alice*'). *Mayo* was an appeal from a Federal Circuit decision finding a claim to a 'method for optimizing therapeutic efficacy for treatment of an immune-mediated gastrointestinal disorder' patent-eligible under §101. The Supreme Court reversed, finding the claims recited natural laws without 'significantly more':

> The question before us is whether the claims do significantly more than simply describe these natural relations. To put the matter more precisely, do the patent claims add enough to their statements of the correlations to allow the processes they describe to qualify as patent-eligible processes that apply natural laws? We believe that the answer to this question is no.[20]

An unfortunate result of the *Mayo* decision, and specifically the 'significantly more' inquiry, was the introduction of a prior art analysis into the §101 inquiry. Determining whether the claims recite 'significantly more', according to *Mayo*, involved first dissecting the claim into the excluded portion (here, the natural law portion) and the non-excluded portion, and then comparing the non-excluded portion with the prior art because '[p]urely conventional or obvious [pre]-solution activity is normally not sufficient to transform an unpatentable law of nature into a patent-eligible application of such a law'.[21] The Court recognized that this inquiry would potentially cause overlap with the novelty and obviousness inquiries:

> We recognize that, in evaluating the significance of additional steps, the §101 patent-eligibility inquiry and, say, the §102 novelty inquiry might sometimes overlap. But that need not always be so. And to shift the patent-eligibility inquiry entirely to these later sections risks creating significantly greater legal uncertainty, while assuming that those sections can do work that they are not equipped to do.[22]

What the Court could not have envisioned in making this statement is the capriciousness with which the 'significantly more' inquiry would be applied in future cases and the lack of consistency that would result. This conflation of §101 (the eligibility threshold) with §102 (the novelty standard) and §103 (the obviousness standard) set US patent eligibility law off on an uncertain course that it navigates still today.

Two years later, the Supreme Court in *Alice* applied the *Mayo* test, which previously had been applied to claims reciting a natural law, to claims reciting an abstract idea. The outcome was the same. The *Alice* Court characterized the *Mayo* test as establishing a two-step framework for determining patent eligibility:

> In *Mayo Collaborative Services v. Prometheus Laboratories, Inc.*, we set forth a framework for distinguishing patents that claim laws of nature, natural phenomena, and abstract ideas from those that claim patent-eligible applications of

18. *Mayo Collaborative Services v. Prometheus Laboratories, Inc.*, 566 U.S. 66 (2012).
19. *Alice Corp. v. CLS Bank Int'l*, 573 U.S. 208 (2014).
20. *Mayo*, 566 U.S. at 77.
21. *Ibid.* at 79.
22. *Ibid.* at 90.

> those concepts. First, we determine whether the claims at issue are directed to one of those patent-ineligible concepts. If so, we then ask, '[w]hat else is there in the claims before us?' To answer that question, we consider the elements of each claim both individually and 'as an ordered combination' to determine whether the additional elements 'transform the nature of the claim' into a patent-eligible application. We have described step two of this analysis as a search for an 'inventive concept' – *i.e.*, an element or combination of elements that is 'sufficient to ensure that the patent in practice amounts to significantly more than a patent upon the [ineligible concept] itself.'[23]

Applying this test to claims directed to a computer-implemented method for mitigating settlement risk, the *Alice* Court applied the first step of the *Mayo* framework and found, yes, the claims recite 'the abstract idea of intermediated settlement'.

Moving to the second step, the Court again made reference to the need to find an 'inventive concept' as part of the §101 inquiry: 'we must examine the elements of the claim to determine whether it contains an "inventive concept" sufficient to "transform" the claimed abstract idea into a patent-eligible application.'[24] Applying this to the case at hand, the Court found, 'the method claims, which merely require generic computer implementation, fail to transform that abstract idea into a patent-eligible invention.'[25] In light of this, the Court unanimously held that the claims were merely claiming an abstract idea and were thus ineligible for patent protection.

The *Mayo/Alice* two-step framework remains the controlling law today. However, it has proven difficult to apply consistently in practice, resulting in a lack of clarity and predictability as to what is or is not patent eligible. Accordingly, many different courts and government agencies have openly admitted that the judicial precedents are confusing and contradictory in the aftermath of the *Alice* decision, especially for software and computer-implemented inventions.[26]

A first difficulty with application of the *Mayo/Alice* test is that, at some level of generalization, any method can be considered an 'abstract idea'. Thus, practically any method can be distilled down to something abstract, satisfying the first step of the test. A second difficulty is that the second step, looking for an 'inventive concept' sufficient to 'transform' the abstract idea into something eligible, involves a prior art inquiry based on a standard that is neither novelty nor obviousness and thus not time-tested by case law. As explained by the Federal Circuit in *Berkheimer v. HP Inc.*:[27]

---

23. *Alice*, 573 U.S. at 217–18.
24. *Ibid.* at 221.
25. *Ibid.*
26. *See*, e.g., *Athena Diagnostics v. Mayo Collaborative Services*, 927 F. 3d 1333 (Fed. Cir. 2019) ('This is not a case in which the judges of this court disagree over whether diagnostic claims, like those at issue in *Athena*, should be eligible for patent protection. They should. None of my colleagues defend the conclusion that claims to diagnostic kits and diagnostic techniques, like those at issue, should be ineligible. The only difference among us is whether the Supreme Court's *Mayo* decision requires this outcome. The majority of my colleagues believe that our hands are tied and that *Mayo* requires this outcome. I believe *Mayo* does not.').
27. *Berkheimer v. HP Inc.*, 881 F.3d 1360, 1367–1369 (Fed. Cir. 2018).

> At step two, we 'consider the elements of each claim both individually and "as an ordered combination" to determine whether the additional elements "transform the nature of the claim" into a patent eligible application.' The second step of the Alice test is satisfied when the claim limitations 'involve more than performance of "well-understood, routine, [and] conventional activities previously known to the industry."'...

Whether something is well-understood, routine, and conventional to a skilled artisan at the time of the patent is a factual determination. Whether a particular technology is well-understood, routine, and conventional goes beyond what was simply known in the prior art. The mere fact that something is disclosed in a piece of prior art, for example, does not mean it was well-understood, routine, and conventional.

A stark illustration of how the generalization of a claim under step 1 can go awry is provided by the Federal Circuit's decision in *American Axle*,[28] where a claim to a manufacturing method for a very physical item – a propellor shaft for an automobile – was generalized down to a mathematical relation that wasn't even recited in the claim. While this example is, indeed, far afield from the subject of artificial intelligence, it is a stark illustration of capriciousness of the current US eligibility standard.

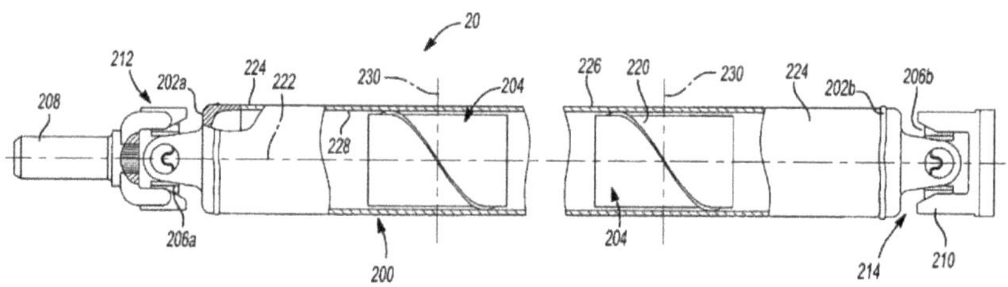

The claim read:

> 22. A method for manufacturing a shaft assembly of a driveline system, the driveline system further including a first driveline component and a second driveline component, the shaft assembly being adapted to transmit torque between the first driveline component and the second driveline component, the method comprising:
> - providing a hollow shaft member;
> - tuning a mass and a stiffness of at least one liner, and
> - inserting the at least one liner into the shaft member;
> - wherein the at least one liner is a tuned resistive absorber for attenuating shell mode vibrations and wherein the at least one liner is a tuned reactive absorber for attenuating bending mode vibrations.[29]

28. *American Axle & Manufacturing, Inc. v. Neapco Holdings LLC*, 967 F.3d 1285 (Fed. Cir. 2020).
29. US Patent No. 7,774,911.

In considering step 1 of the *Mayo/Alice* test, the Federal Circuit generalized claim 22 to use of a natural law, namely 'Hooke's law':

> [C]laim 22 of the *'911 patent* is directed to the use of a natural law: Hooke's law. As in *Flook*, where the claimed method did not specify how variables were measured or how the alarm system functioned, claim 22 here does not specify how target frequencies are determined or how, using that information, liners are tuned to attenuate two different vibration modes simultaneously, or how such liners are tuned to dampen bending mode vibrations. Claim 22 here simply instructs the reader to tune the liner to achieve a claimed result, without limitation to particular ways to do so. This holding as to step 1 of *Alice* extends only where, as here, a claim on its face clearly invokes a natural law, and nothing more, to achieve a claimed result.[30]

Once distilled down to a natural law in step 1, the actual limitations of the claim were found to be simply those necessary to carry out that law and thus insufficient to transform the 'natural law' (which isn't even in the claim) into patent-eligible subject matter. The Court reiterated the 'ineligible concept' found in step 1 cannot be used to show the 'inventive concept' required for step 2:

> [N]othing in claim 22 qualifies as an 'inventive concept' to transform it into patent eligible matter. [Patentee] contends that claim 22 includes numerous inventive concepts that were neither previously known, nor conventional or routine. ... This amounts to no more than a restatement of the assertion that the desired results are an advance. As we held in BSG Tech LLC v. Buyseasons, Inc., 899 F.3d 1281 (Fed. Cir. 2018), 'a claimed invention's use of the ineligible concept to which it is directed cannot supply the inventive concept' required to cross the line into eligibility. Id. at 1290; see also Trading Techs., 921 F.3d at 1385 ('The abstract idea itself cannot supply the inventive concept, "no matter how groundbreaking the advance."' (quoting SAP, 898 F.3d at 1170)); ChargePoint, 920 F.3d at 775 ('[T]he abstract idea itself ... cannot supply the inventive concept at step two.').[31]

Thus, during application of the two-step test intended to establish the eligibility threshold, the court separates what it considers to be abstract from non-abstract elements, and then considers only the non-abstract elements for 'inventive concept'.

A similar outcome was encountered in *Yu v. Apple Inc.*,[32] where a claim to a digital camera was found to be ineligible.

30. *American Axle*, 967 F.3d at 1298.
31. *Ibid.* at 1298–99.
32. *Yu v. Apple Inc.*, 1 F. 4th 1040 (Fed. Cir. 2021).

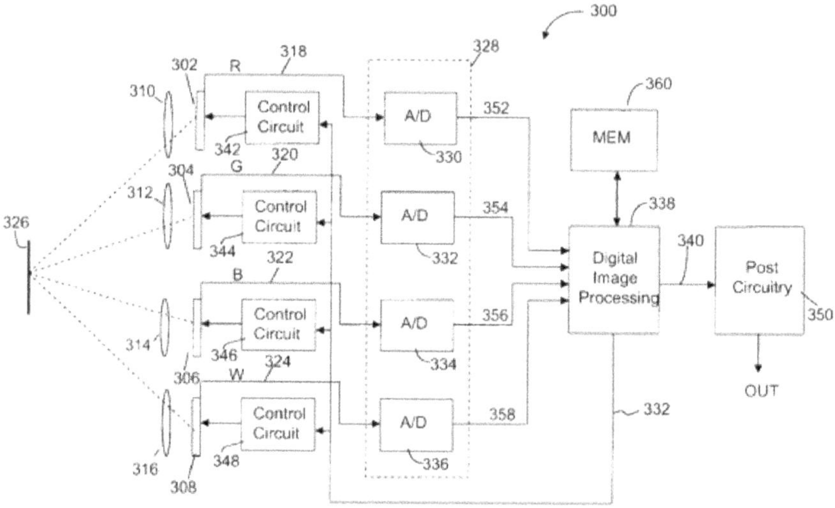

The representative claim reads:

1. An improved digital camera comprising:
   - a first and a second image sensor closely positioned with respect to a common plane, said second image sensor sensitive to a full region of visible color spectrum;
   - two lenses, each being mounted in front of one of said two image sensors;
   - said first image sensor producing a first image and said second image sensor producing a second image;
   - an analog-to-digital converting circuitry coupled to said first and said second image sensor and digitizing said first and said second intensity images to produce correspondingly a first digital image and a second digital image;
   - an image memory, coupled to said analog-to-digital converting circuitry, for storing said first digital image and said second digital image; and
   - a digital image processor, coupled to said image memory and receiving said first digital image and said second digital image, producing a resultant digital image from said first digital image enhanced with said second digital image.

The *Yu* Court, in step 1, affirmed the district court's finding that the asserted claims were directed to 'the abstract idea of taking two pictures and using those pictures to enhance each other in some way'.[33] In step 2, the Court found all the recited elements to be (individually) well-known and conventional and thus found the claim ineligible:

> Only conventional camera components are recited to effectuate the resulting 'enhanced' image – two image sensors, two lenses, an analog-to-digital

33. *Ibid.* at 1043.

> converting circuitry, an image memory, and a digital image processor. Indeed, it is undisputed that these components were well-known and conventional.[34]

The best reading from this case comes from the dissenting opinion of Judge Newman, who takes the opportunity to state the obvious:

> The invention described and claimed in U.S. Patent No. 6,611,289 ('the '289 patent') is a digital camera having two lenses mounted in front of separate image sensors, with analog to digital conversion circuitry, a memory that stores the images, and a digital processor that enhances the images. This camera is a mechanical and electronic device of defined structure and mechanism; it is not an 'abstract idea.' ...
>
> In the current state of *Section 101* jurisprudence, inconsistency and unpredictability of adjudication have destabilized technologic development in important fields of commerce. Although today's *Section 101* uncertainties have arisen primarily in the biological and computer-implemented technologies, all fields are affected. The case before us enlarges this instability in all fields, for the court holds that the question of whether the components of a new device are well-known and conventional affects *Section 101* eligibility, without reaching the patentability criteria of novelty and nonobviousness.
>
> The digital camera described and claimed in the *'289 patent* is a mechanical/electronic device that easily fits the standard subject matter eligibility criteria. Neither the panel majority nor the district court decided patentability under *Section 102* or *Section 103*, having eliminated the claims under *Section 101*. The *'289* claims warrant review under the substantive criteria of patentability – a review that they have never received.[35]

As one might imagine, if a propellor shaft and a digital camera can be ineligible under §101, what hope have claims to computer-implemented inventions ('CIIs')? Applying the *Mayo/Alice* test to CII claims can, indeed, lead to similarly unpredictable results. For example, in *McRO*,[36] the Federal Circuit found that a claim to a method for automating lip synchronization *did not recite an abstract idea at all*, and thus was eligible at step 1, without even reaching step 2. The representative claim read:

> A method for automatically animating lip synchronization and facial expression of three-dimensional characters comprising:
>
> - obtaining a first set of rules that define output morph weight set stream as a function of phoneme sequence and time of said phoneme sequence;
> - obtaining a timed data file of phonemes having a plurality of sub-sequences;
> - generating an intermediate stream of output morph weight sets and a plurality of transition parameters between two adjacent morph weight sets by evaluating said plurality of sub-sequences against said first set of rules;

34. *Ibid.* at 1044.
35. *Ibid.*, Newman J., dissent.
36. *McRO, Inc. v. Bandai Namco Games Am. Inc.*, 837 F.3d 1299 (Fed. Cir. 2016).

- generating a final stream of output morph weight sets at a desired frame rate from said intermediate stream of output morph weight sets and said plurality of transition parameters; and
- applying said final stream of output morph weight sets to a sequence of animated characters to produce lip synchronization and facial expression control of said animated characters.[37]

In reaching its conclusion that this claim does not recite an abstract idea, the *McRO* Court cautioned that courts 'must be careful to avoid oversimplifying the claims by ... failing to account for the[ir] specific requirements'.[38] However, this warning seems to be observed only sporadically. For example, in April 2023 the Federal Circuit in *Sanderling*[39] found claims to 'Dynamic Promotional Layout Management and Distribution Rules' to be ineligible. The representative claim read:

> A computerized method of distributing a digital image processing function, said computerized method comprising:
> - using at least one server having at least one hardware processor and over a network to access a database storing at least one digital image processing function associated with at least one distribution rule defining a geographic location;
> - receiving, over said network, a Global Positioning System (GPS) location indication from each of a plurality of mobile devices, each said location indication is determined according to a GPS module executed by one of said plurality of mobile devices;
> - matching, using said at least one hardware processor, each said GPS location indication with said geographic location; and
> - automatically forwarding, over said network and in response to receiving said Global Position System (GPS) location indication, said at least one digital image processing function to at least one mobile device of said plurality of mobile devices, said at least one mobile device having a respective said GPS location indication which matches said geographic location;
> - wherein said at least one image processing function is set to be used by an application executed on said at least one mobile device to process a digital image designated at said at least one mobile device to create an output digital image.

In step 1, the various recited hardware elements notwithstanding, the Court found the claim to be directed to the abstract idea 'of providing information ... based on meeting a condition'. In explaining its rationale, the Court explained that the key is whether the claims are directed to an improvement in computer functionality:

> Typically, as is true here, the step one analysis for computer-related inventions requires us to 'ask whether the claims are directed to an improvement to computer functionality versus being directed to an abstract idea.' The claims of the asserted patents are not directed to a specific improvement in computer

37. US Patent No. 6,307,576.
38. *McRO*, 837 F.3d at 1313.
39. *Sanderling Mgmt. Ltd. v. Snap Inc.*, 65 F.4th 698 (Fed. Cir. 2023).

> functionality but, instead, to the use of computers as a tool; here, a tool to identify when a condition is met and then to distribute information based on satisfaction of that condition. As the district court articulated, in a formulation we agree with, the claims are directed to the abstract idea '"of providing information – in this case, a processing function – based on meeting a condition," e.g., matching a GPS location indication with a geographic location.' Even though the information being distributed is of a particular variety – here, digital imaging processing based on a distribution rule that determines when a condition is met – distribution of information is an abstract idea.[40]

As noted *supra*, at this level of generalization any claim can be abstract because, once all the limitations are read out of the claim, what is left is typically an abstract idea. Predictably, after having reduced the claim to an abstract concept divorced from the language of the claim, in step 2 no 'inventive concept' was found to transform that concept into a patent-eligible invention:

> At the second step of the Alice inquiry, we must 'look to see whether there are any "additional features" in the claims that constitute an "inventive concept."' Such inventive features must be more than 'well-understood, routine, conventional activity.' Having undertaken this effort, we again agree with the district court: the elements of the representative claim, individually and as an ordered combination, do not constitute an inventive concept. 'If a claim's only "inventive concept" is the application of an abstract idea using conventional and well-understood techniques, the claim has not been transformed into a patent-eligible application of an abstract idea.'[41]

Both *McRO* and *Sanderling* involved rules and recited hardware elements to carry out those rules. In *McRO*, the rules were not considered to recite an abstract idea. In *Sanderling*, they were considered to be abstract, resulting in 'reading out' all the remaining limitations as conventional computing elements. *Sanderling* explained the difference as follows:

> In McRO, we found that patents for automatic animation of lip synchronization and facial expressions of 3D animated characters were not directed to an abstract idea. Those claims were, instead, directed to eligible subject-matter because they provided 'a combined order of specific rules that render[ed] information into a specific format.' The claims of the asserted patents here, by contrast, have a 'distribution rule' that merely receives, matches, and then distributes the corresponding function based on the user's location, a much more generic set of steps than McRO's specific claim language.[42]

Based on this explanation, it appears that breadth plays a part: a more 'generic' claim is more likely to be considered abstract while one limited with more detail may not be abstract at all. Of course, why any of this is a consideration under the eligibility threshold test, as opposed to under the novelty and obviousness standards, is difficult

40. *Ibid.*
41. *Ibid.*
42. *Ibid.*

to understand. As noted *supra*, the US law of patent eligibility continues to navigate the uncertain course on which it was launched by *Mayo* more than a decade ago.

As explained in detail in the following sections, while the US courts continue to be unpredictable on §101, the USPTO has put policies and procedures in place which, to the greatest extent possible within the confines of case law precedent, provides applicants and examiners alike some guidelines for eligibility.

[A] Comparison of Different US Venues that Determine Patentability

To understand the full picture of patent eligibility in the US it is important to understand the different venues in the United States where an eligibility challenge may be raised against a patent claim. To do so, a brief comparison is provided between the USPTO examination process for reviewing patent applications and the roles of various adversarial systems in patent enforcement.

Starting in 1836, the USPTO began examining patent applications to determine whether a patent claim satisfies various patent requirements of the United States Code.[43] Prior to this time, patents were granted as an administrative formality, and patent validity was determined by district courts. With the introduction of patent examination, the USPTO assumed a gatekeeper role using patent examiners to review patent applications for substantive requirements prior to issuance.[44] An examiner is assigned the role of analysing patent claims for both formalities and substance.[45] Given their technical background, an examiner can adequately review an invention's prior art for different patent requirements, such as novelty, non-obviousness, and enablement. Examiners are tasked in this examination process with following the USPTO's *Manual of Patent Examining Procedure* ('MPEP') rather than being independent arbiters between adversarial parties.[46]

At the USPTO, a patent examiner will undertake an initial review of the pending claims in a patent application. If a patent claim could be directed to an ineligible

43. *See* Patent Act of 1836, Ch. 357, 5 Stat. 117 (4 Jul. 1836).
44. *See Manual of Patent Examining Procedure* ('MPEP') §2103 (I) ('Under the principles of compact prosecution, each claim should be reviewed for compliance with every statutory requirement for patentability in the initial review of the application, even if one or more claims are found to be deficient with respect to some statutory requirement. Thus, examiners should state all reasons and bases for rejecting claims in the first Office action.').
45. *See* MPEP §706.01 ('The refusal to grant claims because the subject matter as claimed is considered unpatentable is called a 'rejection.' The term 'rejected' must be applied to such claims in the examiner's action. If the form of the claim (as distinguished from its substance) is improper, an 'objection' is made.').
46. *See* MPEP, Forward, Feb. 2023. ('[T]he [MPEP] contains instructions to examiners, as well as other material in the nature of information and interpretation, and outlines the current procedures which the examiners are required or authorized to follow in appropriate cases in the normal examination of a patent application.'). *See also* Purvis, S. A. 'The Role of the Patent Examiner.' Apr. 2013. ('Patent prosecution before the Office should not be adversarial, instead it should be cooperative investigation between the Examiner and the Applicant, which ensures an Applicant receives a patent only for that which they are entitled to in accordance with Patent laws.') *available at* https://www.uspto.gov/sites/default/files/about/offices/ous/04082013_StonyBrookU.pdf.

concept, the examiner issues a *prima facie* case of patent ineligibility against the patent claim.[47] Based on a patent applicant's response to the examiner's rejection, the examiner decides based on a preponderance of the evidence whether the patent claim is eligible for patenting.[48] Because patent eligibility is a question of law with possibly underlying factual issues, a higher burden is typically placed on the patent applicant for convincing patent examiners than in situations with purely factual issues.[49] If a patent examiner believes a claimed invention is not patent eligible as a matter of law, a patent applicant may be unable to overcome the examiner's rejection without an appeal.

In practice, patent applicants often use various strategies when faced with a patent eligibility rejection. One strategy is to cite to a patent claim from a similar technology previously indicated by a legal authority as being patent eligible. Such example claims may be found among the USPTO's guidance (the 'USPTO Guidance')[50] or claims from a precedential court case.[51] On the other hand, the patent applicant may also articulate various legal rationales for why the claimed invention is not directed to an ineligible concept or recites significantly more than the ineligible concept.[52] For example, a patent applicant may include support from their specification that indicates the claimed invention provides a technological solution to a technological problem.[53]

In contrast to the USPTO's cooperative examination process, US district courts apply an adversarial system between parties where a judge or other independent

47. MPEP §2106.07 ('The rejection should set forth a *prima facie* case of ineligibility under the substantive law. The concept of the *prima facie* case is a procedural tool of patent examination, which allocates the burdens going forward between the examiner and applicant. In particular, the initial burden is on the examiner to explain why a claim or claims are ineligible for patenting clearly and specifically, so that applicant has sufficient notice and is able to effectively respond.')
48. *In re Oetiker*, 977 F. 2d 1443, 1445 (Fed. Cir. 1992) ('After evidence or argument is submitted by the applicant in response, patentability is determined on the totality of the record, by a preponderance of evidence with due consideration to persuasiveness of argument.')
49. *See Berkheimer v. HP inc.*, 881 F. 3d 1360, 1368 (Fed. Cir. 2018) ('[W]hether a claim recites patent eligible subject matter is a question of law which may contain underlying facts').
50. *See* USPTO '2019 Revised Patent Subject Matter Eligibility Guidance,' 84 Federal Register 4 (7 Jan. 2019), pp. 50–57; USPTO 'October 2019 Update: Subject Matter Eligibility,' 84 Federal Register 202 (18 Oct. 2019), pp. 55942–55943.
51. *See Amdocs (Israel) Ltd. v. Openet Telecom, Inc.*, 841 F. 3d 1288, 1294 (Fed. Cir. 2016) ('[T]he decisional mechanism courts now apply [for determining patent eligibility] is to examine earlier cases in which a similar or parallel descriptive nature can be seen – what prior cases were about, and which way they were decided.').
52. *See*, e.g., MPEP §2106.05(a) ('In determining patent eligibility, examiners should consider whether the claim purport(s) to improve the functioning of the computer itself or any other technology or technical field.') (internal quotation marks removed).
53. *See Data Engine Technologies LLC v. Google LLC*, 906 F. 3d 999, 1008 (Fed. Cir. 2018) ('The Tab Patents solved this known technological problem in computers in a particular way – by providing a highly intuitive, user-friendly interface with familiar notebook tabs for navigating the three-dimensional worksheet environment ... Representative claim 12 recites precisely this technical solution and improvement in computer spreadsheet functionality.').

arbiter weighs evidence and arguments to determine which side is more persuasive.[54] For cases involving disputes on patent eligibility, courts apply a decisional mechanism that is best articulated in *Amdocs (Israel) Ltd. v. Openet Telecom, Inc.*,[55] (hereinafter '*Amdocs* analysis'). Under the *Amdocs* analysis, a plaintiff will submit several relevant appellate decisions that the plaintiff believes support its position on patent eligibility.[56] On the other hand, a defendant may also submit several alternative cases that reached an alternative holding on patent eligibility. Typically, both parties will agree on a representative claim for the patent-eligibility analysis and submit decisions that they believe are comparable to the claimed subject matter at issue.[57] Based on the underlying technology, the actual claim limitations, the type of invention, and other bases for comparison, the judge will find that the representative claim is patent eligible or ineligible.[58] The remaining claims will stand or fall based on the determination of this representative claim.

For an illustrative example, a patent owner seeking to enforce a software patent in a patent lawsuit may propose to a district court that a representative patent claim resembles the patent claims at issue in *DDR Holdings, LLC v. Hotels.com, L.P.*[59] and *Bascom Global Internet Services v. AT&T Mobility*[60]. In contrast, the alleged infringer may argue that the representative patent claim from the software patent most closely resembles the claims at issue in *Digitech Image Techs., LLC v. Elecs. for Imaging, Inc.*,[61] *Content Extraction & Transmission LLC v. Wells Fargo Bank, Nat'l Ass'n*,[62] and *In re TLI Commc'ns LLC Patent Litig.*[63] that courts found directed to ineligible subject matter. Based on a comparison among these different precedential decisions in view of the claim language, the original specification, and the prosecution history, the court then determines that the representative claim from the software patent is eligible or ineligible for patenting.[64]

---

54. *Hickman v. Taylor*, 329 U.S. 495, 516 (1947) (J. Douglas, concurring) ('[A] common law trial is and always should be an adversary proceeding.').
55. 841 F. 3d 1288 (Fed. Cir. 2016).
56. *See Chamberlain Group, Inc. v. Techtronic Industries*, 935 F. 3d 1341, 1346–1347 (Fed. Cir. 2019) (citing to *Amdocs* for explaining that courts typically examine earlier cases in which a similar or parallel descriptive nature can be seen to perform their abstract idea analysis).
57. *See Berkheimer*, 881 F. 3d at 1365 ('Courts may treat a claim as representative in certain situations, such as if the patentee does not present any meaningful argument for the distinctive significance of any claim limitations not found in the representative claim or if the parties agree to treat a claim as representative.')
58. *See*, e.g., *Data Engine Technologies*, 906 F. 3d at 1008–1009 (considering in the patent eligibility analysis the originally filed specification and contemporaneous articles from the prosecution history).
59. 773 F.3d 1245 (Fed. Cir. 2014).
60. 827 F. 3d 1341 (Fed. Cir. 2016).
61. 758 F.3d 1344 (Fed. Cir. 2014).
62. 776 F.3d 1343 (Fed. Cir. 2014).
63. 823 F.3d 607 (Fed. Cir. 2016).
64. *See*, e.g., *Amdocs*, 841 F. 3d at 1301–1302 ('Claim 1 is similar to the claims in *DDR Holdings* and *BASCOM*. As in *DDR Holdings*, when the claim limitations were considered individually and as an ordered combination, they recited an invention that is not merely the "routine or conventional use" of technology. Here, claim 1 solves a technological problem (massive data flows requiring huge databases) akin to the problem in DDR Holdings (conventional

Furthermore, patent eligibility can be challenged at different stages in litigation using different legal standards. A defendant may move to dismiss a patent lawsuit without any claim construction if the patent claims and the specification fail to describe any possible inventive concept that would be patent eligible under US case law.[65] A party may also move for summary judgment on this issue after claim construction.[66] Likewise, patent eligibility may also relate to underlying facts, such as whether the claimed invention can be performed using only well-understood, routine, and conventional technology.[67] Relevant factual inquiries have also been submitted to a jury trial in the United States to determine certain facts that might decide patent eligibility.[68]

Several administrative proceedings can also be used to render a patent invalid in view of claiming patent-ineligible subject matter. These different administrative tribunals also use different approaches to analysing patent eligibility. For example, the United States International Trade Commission ('ITC') may determine whether a patent is ineligible using an analysis similar to the *Amdocs* analysis for a §337 investigation.[69] On the other hand, a patent analysed in an America Invents Action ('AIA') trial proceeding may be analysed in view of USPTO guidance despite also being an adversarial proceeding.[70]

Internet hyperlink protocol preventing websites from retaining visitors).') (Internal citations removed).

65. *See*, e.g., *Simio, LLC v. Flexsim Software Products, Inc.*, 983 F. 3d 1353, 1364–1365 (Fed. Cir. 2020) ('The district court denied leave to amend as futile because it concluded that the new factual allegations in the PAC did not save the asserted claims from ineligibility at the pleadings stage.... We therefore see no error in the district court's determining ineligibility without first conducting claim construction.'); *Yu v. Apple Inc.*, 1 F.4th 1040, 1045–1046 (Fed. Cir. 2021).
66. *See California Inst. of Technology v. Broadcom Ltd.*, 25 F. 4th 976, 995 (Fed. Cir. 2022) (affirming a summary judgment finding of patent ineligibility after claim construction).
67. *See Berkheimer*, 881 F. 3d at 1368.
68. Dennis Crouch, 'Jury Verdict on Patent Eligibility (or its Underlying Factual Foundations),' Patently-O, Sept. 2019 (describing a jury instruction regarding whether the defendant proved by clear and convincing evidence that a patent claim only involved activities that were well-understood, routine, or conventional to a person of ordinary skill in the art).
69. *See*, e.g., *In the Matter of Certain Polycrystalline Diamond Compacts and Articles Containing Same*, Inv. No. 337-TA-1236 (Final), 26 Oct. 2022 ('The Federal Circuit has described the first-stage inquiry as looking at the focus of the claims, whether the claim, as a whole is directed-to patent-ineligible matter such as an abstract idea. This inquiry involves determining whether the claims focus on a specific means or method that improves the relevant technology or are directed to a result or effect that itself is the abstract idea and merely invoke generic processes and machinery. If a claim is directed to a patent-ineligible concept, the second step evaluates whether the claim's elements both individually and as an ordered combination of elements transform the nature of the claim into a patent-eligible application. The Federal Circuit has described the second-stage inquiry as looking more precisely at what the claim elements add, whether they identify an inventive concept in the application of the ineligible matter to which the claim is directed.') (citations and internal quotations removed) (unpublished).
70. *See*, e.g., *Supercell Oy v. Gree Inc.*, PGR2019-00018 (P.T.A.B. 20 Jun. 2020) (nonprecedential) ('[T]he U.S. Patent and Trademark Office published revised guidance on the application of §101.... Under the Guidance, we first look to whether the claim recites: (1) any judicial

§18.02 SPECIAL PROVISIONS RELATING TO PATENTABILITY OF INVENTIONS RELATING TO AI

The United States patent law statutes do not specifically address or target inventions relating to AI. To the extent that AI is involved in the subject matter of the invention, such subject matter would be analysed for novelty, non-obviousness, and other patentability requirements in the same manner as any other invention. However, the USPTO Guidance has provided one example of an AI invention indicated as being patent eligible.[71] This example, 'Example 39', is directed to a method for training a neural network for facial detection. An example claim described in Example 39 is provided below:

> A computer-implemented method of training a neural network for facial detection comprising:
> - collecting a set of digital facial images from a database;
> - applying one or more transformations to each digital facial image including mirroring, rotating, smoothing, or contrast reduction to create a modified set of digital facial images;
> - creating a first training set comprising the collected set of digital facial images, the modified set of digital facial images, and a set of digital non-facial images;
> - training the neural network in a first stage using the first training set;
> - creating a second training set for a second stage of training comprising the first training set and digital non-facial images that are incorrectly detected as facial images after the first stage of training; and
> - training the neural network in a second stage using the second training set.

To explain why Example 39 is considered patent-eligible, the USPTO states, '[t]he [example] claim does not recite any of the judicial exceptions' based on the USPTO's subject matter guidance. The USPTO further states that the example claim 'does not recite any mathematical relationships, formulas, or calculations' because '[w]hile some of the limitations may be based on mathematical concepts, the mathematical concepts are not recited in the claims'. Finally, the USPTO concludes that 'the claim does not recite a mental process because the steps are not practically performed in the human mind' and finds that the example claim does not recite any abstract ideas.

Example 39 provides an informative example of the USPTO's position on AI-related inventions. However, while this example is useful during prosecution before the USPTO, the courts consider the USPTO's guidance to be only instructive and not binding on patent eligibility determinations.[72]

---

exceptions, including certain groupings of abstract ideas (i.e., mathematical concepts, certain methods of organizing human activity such as a fundamental economic practice, or mental processes); and (2) additional elements that integrate the judicial exception into a practical application.').

71. 'Subject Matter Eligibility Examples: Abstract Ideas', USPTO (7 Jan. 2019).
72. *See Natural Alternatives Int'l v. Creative Compounds*, 918 F. 3d 1338 (Fed. Cir. 2017) ('The U.S. Patent and Trademark Office has adopted guidance on how examiners should determine whether a claim is eligible under §101 and provided examples of eligible and ineligible

§18.03 SUBJECT MATTER PATENTABILITY

Six days after the *Alice* decision was issued, the USPTO published Preliminary Guidance based on the Supreme Court case. The USPTO's guidance has been revised several times since, based on new case law. Currently, Examiners are to evaluate eligibility based on the USPTO Guidance[73] and the MPEP.[74] The following sections discuss: [A] the current USPTO test from USPTO guidance for evaluating subject matter eligibility; [B] the impact of the USPTO guidance on patent examination and patent issuance; [C] important judicial decisions impacting AI-related inventions; and [D] eligibility analyses for various AI-invention categories.

[A] Current USPTO Test from USPTO Guidance for Evaluating Subject Matter Eligibility

Under the USPTO Guidance, it is first to be determined *whether a claim recites (i.e., describes) a judicial exception*. With regard to the abstract idea exception, the guidance indicates that an abstract idea includes: (1) mathematical concepts (e.g., mathematical relationships, formulas or calculations); (2) certain methods of organizing human activity (e.g., fundamental economic principles or practices; commercial or legal interactions; or managing personal behaviour, relations or interactions between people); and (3) mental processes (e.g., concepts performed in the human mind, such as observations, evaluations, judgments and opinions).[75] Rarely, another claim concept may be determined to be an abstract idea, though an examiner is then to obtain approval from senior management at the USPTO.[76] Unlike at the courts, therefore, an examiner at the USPTO must choose only from a limited list of 'abstract ideas'.

If the claim does not recite a judicial exception, the claim is patent eligible. If the claim recites a judicial exception, next it must be determined *whether the exception is*

claims. Under these guidelines, a claim to a practical application of a natural product to treat a particular disease is patent eligible. The parties dispute the persuasiveness of this document and the weight we should afford.... The issue before us is a matter of law and the result is clear, thus this is not a case in which Skidmore deference would affect the outcome.').

73. *See* USPTO '2019 Revised Patent Subject Matter Eligibility Guidance,' 84 Federal Register 4 (7 Jan. 2019), pp. 50–57; USPTO 'October 2019 Update: Subject Matter Eligibility,' 84 Federal Register 202 (18 Oct. 2019), pp. 55942–55943.
74. The USPTO states that because the MPEP now incorporates the 2019 Revised Patent Subject Matter Eligibility Guidance (2019 PEG), October 2019 Patent Eligibility Guidance Update (October 2019 Update), and the Berkheimer Memo, the USPTO suggests all references to those materials should now be directed to citations within the MPEP. *See* USPTO, Subject Matter Eligibility, *available at* https://www.uspto.gov/patents/laws/examination-policy/subject-matter-eligibility (last visited March 5, 2023). However, the USPTO further notes that this incorporation of the guidance into the MPEP does not change current examination practice with respect to eligibility. *Id.*
75. *See* MPEP §2106.04(a)(2).
76. *See* MPEP §2106.04(a)(3).

integrated into a practical application.[77] For example, using the alleged abstract idea to improve the functioning of a computer or other technology or another technical field[78] would make the claim patent eligible. Importantly, the MPEP indicates that examiners must consider the specification to determine whether it 'provides sufficient details such that one of ordinary skill in the art would recognize the claimed invention as providing an improvement'.[79] If the specification clearly explains an improvement but the claims fail to include the features that produce such improvement, the specification sections are to be disregarded in the eligibility analysis.

If the claim does not recite a judicial exception or is integrated into a practical application in the claim, the USPTO Guidance indicates the claim should be determined to be patent eligible. If the claim does recite a judicial exception and is not integrated into a practical application, the examiner must then consider whether the claim as a whole amounts to 'significantly more' than the judicial exception. If the answer to this inquiry is 'yes', the claim is considered patent eligible. If the answer is 'no', the examiner will reject the claim as not patent eligible. In so doing, the examiner is required to provide a reasoned rationale that justifies this position.[80] The reasoned rationale may be based on available knowledge to those of skill in the art, case law precedent, the applicant's disclosure, or evidence.

[B] The Impact of USPTO Guidance on Patent Examination and Issuance

The 2019 USPTO Guidance and subsequent examiner training at the USPTO have drastically impacted the Patent Office's examination of software patent applications. In general, the *Alice* decision triggered an increase in patent-eligibility rejections and a decrease in allowance rates. However, the time at which these impacts occurred varied across examination art units (each of which include a group of examiners designated to examine particular types of technologies).

More specifically, data was received from LexisNexis® PatentAdvisor℠ to indicate, for each action issued by the USPTO since 1 January 2013, whether the action was an Office Action or an allowance; the corresponding art unit; the corresponding USPTO technology classification ('USPC') and action date. Four technology subgroups that related to AI technology were analysed: bioinformatics (corresponding to art unit 1631); image processing (corresponding to art unit 2665); business methods (corresponding to USPC class 705) and artificial intelligence (corresponding to USPC class 706).

Data was further segregated into calendar-year quarters (with respect to a date on which an action was sent). For each quarter and technology class, the percentage of the Office Actions that included patent-eligibility rejections was determined and the percentage of the actions that were allowances was determined. Notably, the allowance statistic (shown in Figure 1B) is distinct from the typically reported allowance rate statistic. The latter is defined to be the number of allowances divided by the sum of allowances and abandonments, whereas the statistic shown in Figure

77. *See* MPEP §2106.04(d).
78. *See* MPEP §2106.04(d)(1).
79. *See id.*
80. *See* MPEP §2106.07(a).

1B is equal to the number of allowances divided by the sum of allowances and Office Actions. The allowance-rate statistic depends on applicant decisions (as to whether to abandon an application), whereas the allowance statistic of Figure 1B is largely independent of applicant decisions. Further, if fewer allowances and more rejections are being issued by the USPTO, the allowance statistic of Figure 1B will immediately capture this happening, while the typical allowance rate will not (as it will take applicants some time to recognize the shift and to decide to abandon cases).

Figure 1

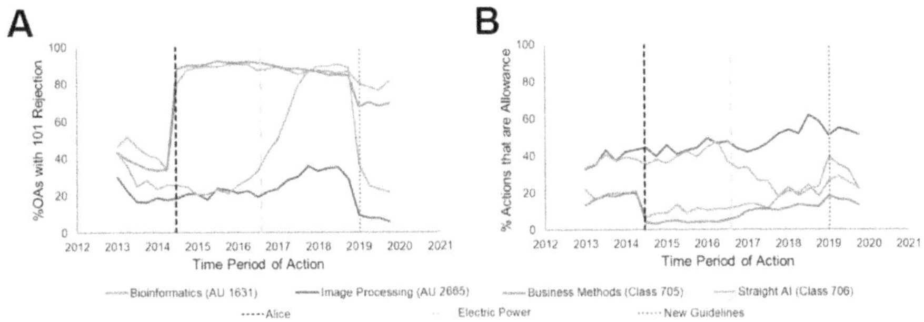

As illustrated in Figure 1, the *Alice* decision was quickly followed by a sharp rise in eligibility rejections and an equally dramatic drop in allowances. Interestingly, while these changes were dramatic with respect to business-method and bioinformatics technologies, examination of other types of software-focused patent applications (e.g., pertaining to AI and image-processing innovations) was unaffected.

However, approximately two years later, similar examination changes were observed in the AI class. Why the delay? Notably, the increase in eligibility rejections and the allowance-rate decrease in the AI class followed a decision from the Federal Circuit, *Electric Power Group, LLC v. Alstom S.A.*,[81] that held claims focused on monitoring and reporting on the performance of an electric power grid were ineligible.[82] The patents at issue had been examined in art units 2121 and 2125 at the USPTO, and those art units are in the same art unit group (the 2120s) as the art units examining patent applications in the AI class. Meanwhile, the patents at issue in *Alice* had been examined by business-method art units. Thus, one theory is that the USPTO uses art units of patents at issue in court cases to determine which art units and which examiners to train with guidance based on each case.[83]

As noted *supra*, the USPTO issued updated guidelines in 2019. It was in this USPTO Guidance update that the agency set forth the practical-application exception (by which a claim is to be considered eligible even if it is directed to an abstract idea so long as the abstract idea is integrated into a practical application). This was also

81. 830 F. 3d 1350 (Fed. Cir. 2016).
82. *Id.* at 1353–1356.
83. K. Gaudry and S. Hayim, 'Artificial Intelligence Technologies Facing Heavy Scrutiny at the USPTO' *IPWatchDog*. 2018.

the update that further restricted examiners' characterization of an abstract idea by specifying that any contention that a claim was directed to an abstract idea must tie the claim to one of three categories (mathematical concept, certain method of organizing human activity, or mental process) or be approved by a senior supervisor. As shown in Figure 1, the prevalence of eligibility rejections dropped after the updated guidelines.

What is particularly important to take away from this data is that eligibility and allowance statistics at the USPTO vary dramatically across art units and across time periods. In practice, it is possible that an 'AI patent application' will be assigned to the AI class, but these applications represent a small portion of the total number of AI-related patent applications examined at the USPTO. For example, each of the other art units and classes depicted in Figure 1 (and many other art units and classes) include many other AI applications (e.g., that may happen to pertain to a given type of technology, industry or technique that triggered an assignment to another art unit or class). In practice, it will also be impossible to predict with any certainty examination trends or shifts that may be influenced by court decisions and agency leadership. Even further uncertainty is present due to different tendencies across examiners within a single art unit. Thus, while this section and the book may offer some high-level predictions and updates, the realities of the practical eligibility assessments at the USPTO and even in the courts will depend on the particular decision-makers making the decision and the time and context of the decision.

[C] Important Judicial Decisions Impacting AI-Related Inventions

In 2021, two very important precedential court cases were decided for analysing AI-related inventions. These decisions were based on USPTO appeals of similar AI patent applications by Leland Stanford Junior University, i.e., *Stanford I*[84] and *Stanford II*.[85] *Stanford I* involves US patent application serial no. 13/445,925 ('the '925 application') filed on 13 April 2012, which describes methods and computing systems for determining haplotype phase.[86] More specifically, the '925 application claims the use of a hidden Markov model ('HMM') to predict inheritance states.[87] On the other hand, *Stanford II* involves US patent application serial no. 13/486,982 ('the '982 application') filed on 1 June 2012, which claims a similar invention as the '925 application.[88] However, while the '925 application describes an inference operation

84. *In re Bd. of Trustees of Leland Stanford Jr. Univ.*, 989 F.3d 1367 (Fed. Cir. 2021) (hereinafter '*Stanford I*').
85. *In re Bd. of Trustees of Leland Stanford Jr. Univ.*, 991 F.3d 1245 (Fed. Cir. 2021) (hereinafter '*Stanford II*').
86. *Stanford I*, 989 F.3d at 1369. Haplotype phasing is a process for determining the parent from whom alleles – i.e., versions of a gene – are inherited. *Id.*
87. *Id.* A hidden Markov model is a statistical tool that is used in various applications to make probabilistic determinations of latent variables. The claimed method in the '925 Application allegedly increases the number of possible haplotype phase predictions by factoring additional data into the analysis.
88. *Stanford II*, 991 F.3d at 1247.

that predicts haplotype data, the '982 application claims a training operation of the hidden Markov model prior to predicting haplotype data.[89]

In *Stanford I*, the Patent Trial and Appeal Board ('PTAB') applied the USPTO test referenced above for evaluating subject matter eligibility. First, the PTAB determined that the eight steps in claim 1 of the '925 application are directed to the abstract ideas of 'mental steps of receiving, storing, or providing information' and 'mathematical concepts'.[90] The PTAB further concluded that the abstract ideas recited in the claims were not integrated into a practical application and thus the claims were directed to abstract ideas. More specifically, the PTAB further found that the claimed invention did not improve computer technology but rather used off-the-shelf computing equipment to perform an improved mathematical analysis. While the PTAB agreed that the claims may provide a valuable contribution to science, the PTAB concluded that this contribution does not go beyond patent ineligible mental processes and mathematical operations.

On appeal, the Federal Circuit agreed with the PTAB's judgment in *Stanford I*. The appellate court held that the rejected claims were drawn to abstract mathematical calculations and statistical modelling, which are ineligible abstract concepts.[91] The Court determined that the claimed process may constitute a new or different use of a mathematical process by yielding a greater number of haplotype phase predictions.[92] However, the Federal Circuit did not believe the claimed process was an improved technological process warranting patentability.[93]

Turning to *Stanford II*, the '982 application had several material differences from the '925 application found ineligible by *Stanford I*. The '982 application described a parameterization algorithm in predicting haplotype phase data, where this embodiment could perform optimization on haplotypes rather than Markov chain Monte Carlo sampling used in the prior art. As such, the '982 application claimed various mathematical techniques that included 'building a data structure describing a hidden Markov model' and 'repeatedly randomly modifying at least one of the imputed initial haplotype phases to automatically recompute the parameters of the HMM until the parameters indicate that the most likely haplotype phase is found'.[94] Similar to *Stanford I*, the PTAB again reasoned that the claims recite steps

89. *See id.* at 1247–1248. In particular, independent claim 1 of the '982 application recites, in part, 'building a data structure describing a Hidden Markov Model, where the data structure contains [] a set of imputed haplotype phases … [and] a set of parameters comprising local recombination rates and mutation rates' and 'repeatedly randomly modifying at least one of the imputed initial haplotype phases in the set of imputed haplotype phases to automatically re-compute a new set of parameters comprising local recombination rates and mutation rates that are stored within the data structure.'
90. 989 F.3d at 1371.
91. *Id.* at 1369.
92. *Id.* at 1373.
93. *Id.* at 1374. The Court argued that simply storing information and providing that information upon request does not alone transform the abstract idea into patent eligible subject matter. In order words, a specific or different combination of mathematical steps may yield a greater number of haplotype predictions than previously achievable under the prior art, but this advantage is not enough to transform the claims into a patent eligible application.
94. *Id.* at 1250.

that humans could perform in their minds, or by mathematical algorithms. Thus, the PTAB concluded that the abstract ideas recited in the claims were not integrated into a practical application.[95]

On appeal in *Stanford II*, the Federal Circuit again found the claims of the '982 application to be drawn to the same concept of abstract mathematical calculations and statistical modelling as determined by the *Stanford I* Court.[96] While the patent applicant argued that the alleged increase in haplotype prediction accuracy renders the claimed invention integrated into a practical application, the *Stanford II* court found the claims did not involve any practical or technological improvements extending beyond improving the accuracy of a mathematically calculated statistical prediction.[97]

In view of *Stanford I and Stanford II*, a Texas district court case applied the *Amdocs* analysis referenced above to a particular AI invention.[98] In *Health Discovery Corp. v. Intel Corp.*[99] (hereinafter '*Health Discovery*'), a patent owner filed a complaint against Intel alleging that Intel had infringed US Patent No. 7,117,188 ('the '188 Patent') among other patents.[100] The '188 Patent relates to an innovative technology for using support vector machines ('SVMs') to identify relevant patterns in datasets.[101] In particular, the '188 Patent was directed to an improvement among support vector machines that used Recursive Feature Elimination ('RFE') to determine a selection of features within the datasets that best enable classification of the data. Because isolating valuable data presents a challenge for various machine learning architectures, several machine learning algorithms had attempted to solve the problem of sequencing genomic data. For example, artificial neural networks had been used to attempt to identify relevant patterns, but the artificial neural network solutions had produced 'crude models of the underlying processes,' and were limited by the 'curse of dimensionality,' i.e., as the dimensions of the data set increased, the processing time and power increased disproportionately for training the model.[102]

The '188 Patent proposed an SVM as a possible solution to these machine-learning problems. For example, the SVM could map input vectors into high dimensional feature space through non-linear mapping function. In this high dimensional feature space, an optimal separating hyperplane was produced that could be used to determine things such as class separations, regression fits, or accuracy in density estimation.

In the technical area of SVMs, the '188 Patent addressed a specific problem. When a machine learning algorithm like an SVM is trained with only a few training profiles that include a high number of features, the machine-learning algorithm risks

95. *Id.* at 1249.
96. *See id.*at 1250.
97. *Id.* at 1251.
98. This case is discussed to provide an illustration of how trial courts apply the law in this area and the challenges they face. A decision by a district court does not set national precedent.
99. 577 F. Supp. 3d 570 (W.D. Tex. 2021).
100. The other patents included US Patent Nos. 7,542,959, 8,095,483, and 10,402,685, which have a substantially common specification.
101. *Health Discovery*, 577 F. Supp. 3d at 573.
102. *Id.* at 574.

'overfitting' during training.[103] In other words, the SVM will accurately predict patterns for its training profiles but fails to do so when presented with new profiles. To address this problem, the '188 Patent proposed a reduction in feature size by ranking features and eliminating the lowest ranked features. This solution is referred to as RFE.

In *Health Discovery*, the Court applied the *Amdocs* analysis framework for evaluating whether the '188 Patent is patent eligible.[104] The patent owner and the defendant found claim 1 of the '188 Patent representative for purposes of an invalidity challenge, because claim 1 encapsulates the SVM-RFE.[105] After reviewing relevant case law, the court confined its *Amdocs* analysis to four Federal Circuit opinions, with *Stanford II* being identified as the most relevant precedential decision.[106] Importantly, the Court noted that when guided only by the two cases that found claims patent eligible, the Court would likely uphold the claims of the '188 Patent.[107] However, in view of *Stanford II* and the other case finding claims ineligible, the Court determined that closer judicial precedents precluded that outcome. Consequently, the Court found claims of the '188 Patent merely produced data with improved quality relative to that predicted data from conventional mathematical methods.[108] In other words, the Court held that the representative claim merely improved or enhanced an abstract idea. As in *Stanford II*, the Court also found nothing else in the claim salvaged patent eligibility under the second step of the *Alice* test.

In contrast to *Stanford I*, *Stanford II*, and *Health Discovery*, the PTAB designated *Ex parte Hannun* as an informative opinion that found a method of transcribing speech

---

103. *Id.*
104. The district court noted the difficulties in applying the Supreme Court's patent eligibility framework to abstract concepts. *See* 577 F. Supp. 3d at 575–576 ('This framework is almost impossible to apply consistently and coherently in the context of abstract ideas.... Members from every branch of the federal government have decried the uncertain state of §101 law and begged guidance from the Supreme Court, Congress, or both.') (Internal quotations and citations removed). For example, the Court characterized the first step of the *Alice* test as requiring answers to multiple overlapping and often conflicting questions. *See* 577 F. Supp. 3d at 577–578 ('At step one, the claims need to satisfy myriad overlapping questions to qualify as a non-abstract concept. For example, do the claims describe an improvement to relevant technology or an abstract idea that uses computers as a tool? Is the 'relevant technology' being improved itself an abstract concept? Is the relevant technology the functionality of computers and networks? ... Are the claims tied to the physical realm? Are the physical tethers too generic? Do the claims recite the practical application of an abstract idea? And is the practical application or improvement to relevant technology claimed with sufficient specificity?').
105. Claim 1 of the '188 Patent recites 'inputting into at least one support vector machine of a plurality of support vector machines a training set,' where the court interpreted the claimed support vector machine to mean 'a supervised mathematical learning algorithm that constructs an optimal separating hyperplane based on a subset of a training set and classifies data according to the optimal separating hyperplane.'
106. The other Federal Circuit opinions were (1) *SAP Am., Inc. v. InvestPic, LLC*, 898 F.3d 1161 (Fed. Cir. 2018), (2) *CardioNet, LLC v. InfoBionic, Inc.*, 955 F.3d 1358 (Fed. Cir. 2020), and (3) *Koninklijke KPN N.V. v. Gemalto M2M GmbH*, 942 F.3d 1143 (Fed. Cir. 2019). While the *SAP* court found patent claims ineligible, both *CardioNet* and *Koninkliike* found claimed inventions not directed to any abstract ideas and thus patent eligible.
107. *Health Discovery*, 577 F. Supp. 3d at 584.
108. *Id.*

using a trained neural network to be patent eligible.[109] The claims at issue related to 'a transcription of [an] input audio using ... predicted character probabilities outputs from the trained neural network constrained by a language model that interprets a string of characters' to transcribe speech.[110] The PTAB found that the claims did not recite any abstract-idea category under the USPTO's guidance. Specifically, it was held that the claims were not directed to a mental process because the claim elements could not 'practically be performed mentally', that the claims were not directed to organizing human activity as the claims did not relate to 'fundamental economic principles or practices, commercial or legal interactions, managing personal behaviour or relationships or interactions between people', and that the claims were not directed to a mathematical concept due to the claims not reciting a mathematical algorithm or formula.[111] The PTAB further found that the claims had a practical application due to the claims including specific transcription features 'specifically designed to achieve an improved technological result'.

While we note that the result in *Hannun* is a favourable decision for inventors of AI-related inventions, the PTAB's analysis may conflict with the reasoning in *Stanford I*, *Stanford II*, and *Health Discovery*. For example, the trained neural network would likely be an ineligible mathematical concept in a similar way that the claimed support vector machine was in *Health Discovery*.[112] However, integrating the trained neural network into a practical application could also save the patent claim under US case law.[113]

[D] Eligibility Analyses for AI-Invention Categories

The current eligibility framework at the USPTO provides the opportunity for applicants to assert that their claims are eligible by presenting one or more of the three arguments: (1) the claims do not recite any judicial exception (e.g., an abstract idea); (2) the claims integrate any judicial exception into a practical exception; and/or (3) the claims recite significantly more than the judicial exception.

Frequently, eligibility-focused content concentrates on potential eligibility arguments that may be made. However, it is important not to forget *that any and all eligibility arguments will be based on claim language.* Thus, care should be taken to prepare claims having a scope that supports a strong eligibility case. Overly broad claims risk limiting the opportunity to demonstrate that any judicial exception of the claims is integrated into a practical application, such as by demonstrating improved function and/or performance. Notably, if an improved function is only attributable to one or multiple embodiments covered by a claim, such an improvement would likely be insufficient to demonstrate eligibility. Overly broad claims further risk limiting the

109. Appeal No. 2018-003323, (P.T.A.B. April 1, 2019) (informative).
110. *Id.* at 2–3.
111. *Id.* at 9–10.
112. The *Hannun* panel addressed this possibility and states 'even if the claims were considered to recite a mathematical concept, under prong two of step 2A the claims are not directed to an abstract idea because the alleged judicial exception is integrated into a practical application'. *Id.* at 9.
113. *See, e.g., McRO, supra.*

opportunity to demonstrate that the claims are 'significantly more' than the judicial exception. Indeed, an empirical analysis of AI-focused US patent applications found, not surprisingly, that more specific and detailed claim language was associated with higher allowance prospects.[114]

Further, as noted above, courts frequently turn to the specification to determine whether a claimed invention provides an inventive concept, such as technological performance benefits indicating a technological improvement. Patent applicants should include a thorough description that explains technical benefits and how specific mechanisms (whether software or hardware) can achieve these benefits. Supporting such assertions using reasoned rationales, descriptions of the prior art, and comparative data based on improved technical performance may provide strong support for any down-the-line eligibility argument.[115] Thus, it would seem that an ounce of thoughtful application preparation is worth a pound of subsequent eligibility argument.

[1] Categories 1 and 2: Invention of AI and Invention of an AI Implementation

As noted *supra*, the 'Invention of AI' category corresponds to inventions that identify new algorithms or models for AI itself. For example, such an invention may include a new type of neural network. The 'Invention of AI Implementation' category corresponds to inventions that identify a system or process of broad application using known AI technology plus additional elements (e.g., that include a new type of pre-processing or post-processing technique).

Using the current eligibility test at the USPTO, an examiner would first need to determine whether a claim recites a judicial exception. The exception most likely to be invoked for inventions in these categories is the abstract-idea exception. The types of abstract idea most likely to relate to these AI categories are mental processes (e.g., concepts performed in the human mind, such as observations, evaluations or judgments) and mathematical concepts (e.g., formulas or calculations).

If a claim is sufficiently specific as to the approach used to process data, and if such processing is sufficiently complex, an applicant would likely be successful in arguing that the claim does not recite a mental process (or that such specifics amount to 'significantly more' than the abstract idea). If the claim lacks details about the approach and instead relies on high-level and/or rather vague language (e.g., 'determining X based on Y'), it may be harder to argue that such actions could not be performed in the human mind.

Meanwhile, this same specificity may (but need not) increase the chances that an examiner asserts that the claim recites a mathematical concept. This type of abstract idea is rather specific in that the claim must recite a mathematical relationship,

114. E. Sutton, 'Not Another AI Patent Article: Data-Driven Prosecution in the Field of Artificial Intelligence' *Patnotechnic*, Oct. 2019, *available at* http://www.patnotechnic.com/2019/10/not-another-ai-patent-article-data.html.

115. Under typical USPTO procedure, a patent examiner should issue a *prima facie* case of patent ineligibility if there is any doubt that the claimed invention may resemble a patent ineligible case. The primary mechanism for avoiding ineligibility challenges is to tailor the claims to fit strongly in a technology area that has few subject matter eligibility issues.

formula, or calculation. Thus, there is a fair bit of middle ground between a mental process that can be performed in the human mind and particular mathematical relationships, formulas, and calculations.

The practical-application caveat of the USPTO eligibility test may be particularly useful for asserting that Category 1 and 2 inventions are patent eligible. As noted above, a claimed invention that improves the functioning of a computer or of another technology is to be considered patent eligible. Many AI technologies are devised precisely for this purpose.

Once again, ideally, an application will include data that demonstrates its superior performance. Such data can include comparative data that shows both the performance of the claimed invention and the performance of state-of-the-art solutions and/or alternative approaches. Importantly, the scope of the claims should be considered while preparing such examples. Providing data that illustrates superior performance of a single configuration of a single type of model using a single data set may be insufficient to demonstrate superior performance of a claim of larger breadth. Thus, it may be advantageous to provide several examples that vary with respect to different potential uses and configurations within the scope of the independent claims.

Further, care should be taken to identify what particular aspects of the invention are novel. Demonstrating that these aspects are tied to improved performance, a particular machine, or a particular manufacture supports the argument that the invention has a practical application and is patent eligible.

Finally, particularly for Category 2 inventions, an applicant may be well-advised to emphasize how the invention is substantially more than just the judicial exception. Importantly, here, the claim is to be considered in its entirety. Thus, if a claim includes eight claim features and the examiner asserts that four claim features are directed to an abstract idea, the applicant can argue why the combination of all eight claim features amounts to substantially more than the abstract idea by itself if there is adequate specificity and adequate integration into the other features. Once again, it advisable to tie this argument to the novelty of the claim. However, the applicant should them be prepared to explain why these additional elements and/or the combination are not part of the judicial exception.

[2] Categories 3–5: New Application of AI, Invention Made Using AI and Invention Made by AI

The types of inventions in any of Categories 3 to 5 ('New Applications of AI', 'Inventions Made Using AI' and 'Inventions Made by AI') are not constrained to any field. For example, a new application of AI (Category 3) may include a technique for water-safety monitoring, an automated-driving system or auto-adjusting lighting system. As other examples, an invention made using AI and/or an invention made (hypothetically) by AI may include a pharmaceutical drug, a plant or battery. These types of AI-related inventions are especially suited for being connected to a particular machine or particular manufacture. Thus, for Category 3 inventions the same comments above with respect to Category 1 and 2 inventions will apply. However, Category 3 inventions, when properly claimed, are even more likely to benefit from the 'integration of any judicial exception into a practical exception' caveat of the eligibility test at the USPTO.

While inventions in Categories 4 and 5 relate to AI in terms of how they were generated, these types of inventions typically would not claim AI and thus would highly overlap with inventions made without using AI. Accordingly, subject matter eligibility would depend entirely on what is claimed without regard to the manner in which the invention was made. For these cases, therefore, an applicant can follow general advice as to how to demonstrate patent eligibility in the United States. Of course, for Category 5 cases where the invention was hypothetically made by an AI system, unless and until AI inventorship is permitted in the US, any such patent applications would not reach the examination stage.

§18.04 INVENTIVE STEP

Similar to determining whether a patent claim has an inventive step, US law applies an analogous doctrine that determines whether a person of ordinary skill in the art using common sense would find the claimed invention 'obvious'. The heart of the US statutory test of obviousness is found in the first sentence of AIA 35 U.S.C. §103, which states:

> A patent for a claimed invention may not be obtained, notwithstanding that the claimed invention is not identically disclosed as set forth in section 102, if the differences between the claimed invention and the prior art are such that the claimed invention as a whole would have been obvious before the effective filing date of the claimed invention to a person having ordinary skill in the art to which the claimed invention pertains. Patentability shall not be negated by the manner in which the invention was made.[116]

The first and leading Supreme Court interpretation of this 1952 statutory provision is found in the 1966 decision in *Graham v. John Deere*.[117] The *Graham* decision mandates three separate factual inquiries in a determination of the obviousness of an invention: 'Under §103, the scope and content of the prior art are to be determined; differences between the prior art and the claims at issue are to be ascertained; and the level of ordinary skill in the pertinent art resolved.'[118]

The obviousness or non-obviousness of the subject matter claimed is determined against the background of the results of these three factual inquiries. Objective evidence of non-obviousness, such as commercial success, long-felt but unsolved needs, failure of others, and other criteria also may be relevant for shedding light on the circumstances surrounding the origin of the subject matter sought to be patented.[119]

In *KSR International v. Teleflex, Inc.*, the US Supreme Court held that 'if a person can implement a predictable variation [of something found in the prior art], §103 likely bars its patentability'.[120] Additionally, if a technique has been used to improve a device in one area, it would be obvious to use the same technique to improve a

116. Pre-AIA 35 U.S.C. §103(a), which was identically re-codified simply as §103.
117. *Graham v. John Deere*, 383 U.S. 1 (1966).
118. *ACS Hosp. Sys., Inc. v. Montefiore Hosp.*, 732 F.2d 1572, 1575 (Fed. Cir. 1984) (citing *Graham*, 383 U.S. at 17–18).
119. *Graham*, 383 U.S. at 17.
120. *KSR Int'l v. Teleflex, Inc.*, 550 U.S. 398, 417 (2007).

device in a second area unless the application of the technique in the second area would be beyond the ability of one of ordinary skill in the art.[121] However, challenges 'on obviousness grounds cannot be sustained by mere conclusory statements; instead there must be some articulated reasoning with some rational underpinning to support the legal conclusion of obviousness'.[122]

In making an obviousness determination, the teachings of the references, their relatedness to the field of the applicant's endeavour, and the knowledge of persons of ordinary skill in the relevant art at the time of the alleged invention are all relevant considerations.[123] When the prior art references are in the same field as that of the claimed invention, knowledge of that art is presumed.[124]

AI-related inventions in Categories 1–3 follow the same requirements as other software inventions for non-obviousness under US law. The difficulty specific to these AI-related inventions is that the basis for non-obviousness may be the recitation of a new and improved abstract idea, such as a mathematical model or an improved data processing implementation. However, this new and improved abstract idea can also render the claimed invention ineligible for patenting. Accordingly, AI-related inventions typically need to walk a tightrope in claiming essentially abstract features, such as specific types of data processing and mathematical algorithms. On one end, a sufficient amount of AI technology needs to be claimed to render an invention non-obvious, while claiming the AI technology is such a manner that will not conflict with patent eligibility requirements.

Moreover, the *KSR* Court's consideration of 'predictability' for determining non-obviousness has particular significance for AI-related inventions. Software and other computer-implemented technologies are typically considered predictable arts under US patent law, but AI-related inventions are often multi-disciplinary inventions that include features from unpredictable arts. Therefore, an AI invention must not be a 'predictable variation' in view of the *KSR* Court's requirements for patentability, but 'predictable variation' will likely be determined to be one or more secondary technologies related to the main AI implementation.

As noted previously, AI-related inventions in Categories 4–5 claim the *result* of an AI application. Thus, the claim could be directed to any product or process in any field and, unless AI is being used to invent AI (which is possible), the claim would not include any language relating to AI at all. Thus, the US law for determining obviousness (or non-obviousness) would be applied to these claims in the same manner as it is to any other non-AI invention, looking through the eyes of the person skilled in the art to which the claims pertain.[125] Notably, however, as knowledge and use of AI tools continue to expand into increasingly diverse fields, it is likely that the person skilled in the art will be presumed to understand how to apply AI tools

121. *Id.*
122. *Id.* at 418 (quoting *In re Kahn*, 441 F.3d 977, 988 (Fed. Cir. 2006)).
123. *See In re Oetiker*, 977 F.2d 1443, 1447 (Fed. Cir. 1992); *In re Gorman*, 933 F.2d 982, 986–87 (Fed. Cir. 1991); *In re Young*, 927 F.2d 588, 591 (Fed. Cir. 1991).
124. *In re Dance*, 160 F.3d 1339, 1343 (Fed. Cir. 1998).
125. At the present time, as explained in §18.07, inventions made by AI (i.e, without a human inventor) are not patentable in the US and thus the obviousness analysis would not be reached. If, in the future, such inventions (Category 5) are patentable, then the obviousness analysis would be the same as that for Category 4.

in their field. Accordingly, while not changing the test for obviousness, AI may have the effect (like other new technologies in the past) of effectively raising the level of skill in the art.

§18.05 ADEQUACY OF DISCLOSURE

In the United States, a patent is required to include 'a *written description* of the invention, and of the manner and process of making and using it, in such full, clear, concise, and exact terms as to *enable* any person skilled in the art to which it pertains, ..., to make and use the same, and shall set forth the *best mode* contemplated by the inventor ... of carrying out the invention'.[126] This section has been interpreted as including a written description requirement, an enablement requirement, and a best mode requirement. Moreover, additional disclosure requirements may be imposed for claim limitations that are interpreted under the means-plus-function provisions of the United States Code.[127]

[A] Written Description Requirement

The written description requirement serves to demonstrate that the patentee possessed, at the time of filing, the invention claimed[128] and to promote the progress of the useful arts by requiring a clear and adequate description of the invention.[129] To satisfy this requirement, a patent specification must provide 'sufficient detail' to demonstrate possession of the invention to one of skill in the art, which may include identifying an actual reduction to practice or a clear and complete description of the claimed invention.[130] For generic claims, courts often consider the following factors in determining whether the written description is satisfied: (1) the existing knowledge in the particular field, (2) the extent and content of the prior art, (3) the maturity of the science or technology, and (4) the predictability of the aspect at issue.[131] For example, the level of detail for satisfying the written description requirement is strongly connected to whether the claimed invention is located in a technology field that is predictable or unpredictable.[132] For a predictable art, a lower level of detail

126. 35 U.S.C. §112 (emphasis added).
127. 35 U.S.C. §112(f).
128. *In re Barker*, 559 F.2d 588, 592 n.4 (CCPA 1977).
129. MPEP §2163.
130. *Pfaff v. Wells Elec., Inc.*, 55 U.S. at 66, 119 S.Ct. at 311, 48 USPQ2d at 1646.
131. *See AbbVie Deutschland GmbH v. Janssen Biotech, Inc.*, 759 F. 3d 1285, 1299 (Fed. Cir. 2014).
132. *See Hologic, Inc. v. Smith & Nephew, Inc.*, 884 F. 3d 1357, 1361 (Fed. Cir. 2018) ('We agree with the Board's finding that the field of this invention is a predictable art, such that a lower level of detail is required to satisfy the written description requirement than for unpredictable arts.'). See also *AK Steel Corp. v. Sollac and Ugine*, 344 F. 3d 1234, 1244 (Fed. Cir. 2003) ('An artisan's knowledge of the prior art and routine experimentation can often fill gaps, interpolate between embodiments, and perhaps even extrapolate beyond the disclosed embodiments, depending upon the predictability of the art.') (Internal quotation marks removed.)

may be required than an invention in a less predictable area.[133] Likewise, a patent applicant may typically rely on what is 'well-known in the art' to assist in satisfying the written description requirement.[134]

Written description issues typically arise as a result of amending a claim, adding a new claim and/or relying on a filing date of a priority application.[135] However, while there is a presumption of adequate written description of original claims, a contrary conclusion can be reached if the specification fails to adequately describe an essential feature that is not conventional or known in the art, or fails to show possession of a broad claim in an unpredictable art.[136]

[B] Enablement Requirement

The enablement requirement has similar factual issues as the separate written description requirement because they relate to similar underlying factual inquiries regarding the patent's disclosure.[137] The enablement requirement requires that the original specification include sufficient information to enable one of skill in the art to make and use the claimed invention. Whether a disclosure is deemed to provide sufficient information turns on whether one of skill of the art would be able to practise the invention without 'undue experimentation'.[138] Factors pertinent to assessing whether any necessary experimentation is 'undue' include: (A) the breadth of the claims; (B) the nature of the invention; (C) the state of the prior art; (D) the level of one of ordinary skill; (E) the level of predictability in the art; (F) the amount of direction provided by the inventor; (G) the existence of working examples; and (H) the quantity of experimentation needed to make or use the invention based on the content of the disclosure.[139]

[C] Best Mode Requirement

The Leahy-Smith American Invents Act ('AIA') of 2011 indicated that failure to disclose a best mode may no longer serve as a basis to cancel, invalidate or otherwise render unenforceable any claim of a patent. Thus, the AIA 'took the teeth' out of the best mode requirement. Nonetheless, the best mode requirement continues to be enforced at the USPTO during examination.

---

133. *See ibid.*
134. *See Ajinomoto Co., Inc. v. Intern. Trade Com'n*, 932 F. 3d 1342 (Fed. Cir. 2019) ('In some circumstances, we have added, a patentee may rely on information that is well-known in the art for purposes of meeting the written description requirement, because the specification is viewed from the perspective of one of skill in the relevant art.') (Internal quotations and citations removed.)
135. MPEP §2163.03.
136. MPEP §2163.
137. *See Centrak, Inc. v. Sonitor Technologies, Inc.*, 915 F. 3d 1360, 1366, 1369 (Fed. Cir. 2019) (finding genuine issues of material fact as to whether disclosure of the implementation details was necessary to satisfy the written description requirement, but declining to address similar issues of enablement on appeal for the first time).
138. *In re Wands*, 858 F.2d 731, 737, 8 USPQ2d 1400, 1404 (Fed. Cir. 1988).
139. *Id.*

At the USPTO, an examiner is to assume the best mode is disclosed unless there is evidence to the contrary.[140] If the examiner determines that, at the time of filing, the inventor knew that a particular mode of practising the invention was superior to another mode, then the examiner must determine whether the application's specification is sufficient to enable one of skill in the art to make and use the best mode.

Given that the best mode requirement cannot be used to invalidate a patent and Examiners at the USPTO are to assume disclosure of best mode unless there is contrary evidence, the bestmode requirement is rarely an issue in the US.

[D] Special Considerations for Means-Plus-Function Claim Limitations

Special disclosure requirements also exist for any claim term that is interpreted as a means-plus-function claim limitation. More specifically, AIA 35 U.S.C. §112(f)[141] expressly permits an element of a patent claim to be expressed as a 'means' or 'step' for performing a specified function:

> An element in a claim for a combination may be expressed as a means or step for performing a specified function without the recital of structure, material, or acts in support thereof, and such claim shall be construed to cover the corresponding structure, material, or acts described in the specification and equivalents thereof.

In other words, although a claim limitation written in 'means for' or 'step for' plus function language would appear to encompass every conceivable means for performing the recited function, a proper interpretation requires that one look to the patent specification and interpret the 'means' limitation to encompass only the structures or acts disclosed and equivalents thereof.[142]

When a §112(f) analysis is appropriate, a patentee must set forth in the specification an adequate disclosure showing what is meant by that language.[143] If the specification contains no such adequate disclosure of corresponding structure, material, or acts, the patent claim is invalid.[144] Furthermore, a structure disclosed in the specification qualifies as 'corresponding' structure only if the specification or prosecution history clearly links or associates that structure to the function recited in the claim.[145] While corresponding structure need not include all things necessary to enable the claimed invention to work, it must include all structure that actually performs the recited function.[146]

140. MPEP §2165.
141. The proper citation of this statute, when applied to pre-AIA patents, is 35 U.S.C. §112 ¶ 6. No changes were made to the statute after enactment of the AIA other than the change in designation from '§112 ¶ 6' to '§112(f)'.
142. *In re Donaldson Co.*, 16 F.3d 1189, 1196 (Fed. Cir. 1994) (*en banc*) (where the specification only describes a flexible wall structure, a claim covering a 'means responsive to pressure increases in said chamber' may not be interpreted to cover a rigid wall).
143. *In re Donaldson Co.*, 16 F.3d at 1195.
144. *See id.*
145. *Default Proof Credit Card Sys. v. Home Depot U.S.A., Inc.*, 412 F.3d 1291, 1298 (Fed. Cir. 2005).
146. *Id.*

Special consideration is given to software patents that use means-plus-function language.[147] It is well established that the corresponding structure for a function performed by a software algorithm is the algorithm itself.[148] When a patentee invokes means-plus-function claiming to recite a software function, it accedes to the reciprocal obligation of disclosing a sufficient algorithm as corresponding structure.[149] An incomplete algorithm is insufficient structure. For a 'means' claim limitation to be valid, the specification must disclose one or more complete algorithms to perform all functions associated with the claimed means.[150] What a person of ordinary skill in the computer software art would understand is insufficient to meet this duty unless algorithms to cover all functions are disclosed.[151]

[E] Special Disclosure Considerations for AI-Related Inventions

For AI-related inventions in Categories 1–3, the claims are likely to include or pertain to an entire new AI model, an improvement to an existing AI technology such as a new AI implementation, or a new application of an existing or new AI model. AI models in these types of inventions are closest to what the Supreme Court refers to as 'building blocks of human ingenuity', which require special care in drafting a disclosure that renders the claimed invention patent eligible. For example, identifying multiple practical applications for inventions under these three categories may be necessary to guarantee validity from patent issuance throughout the enforcement of the patent. Given the changing and confusing nature of US case law, one type of practical application may prove ineligible, while a different practical application may later prove patentable.[152]

Accordingly, several factors are particularly relevant for inventions under Categories 1–3: (1) to what practical and specific practical applications can the AI invention be tailored; (2) to what extent is an AI invention located in a predictable art; and (3) what structure is required for any means-plus-function limitations.

---

147. *See*, e.g. *EON Corp. v. AT&T Mobility LLC*, 785 F.3d 616, 620–23 (Fed. Cir. 2015); *Noah Systems, Inc. v. Intuit, Inc.*, 675 F.3d 1302, 1310–14 (Fed Cir. 2012) ('access means' invoked §112 ¶ 6); *Ergo Licensing, LLC v. CareFusion 303, Inc.*, 673 F.3d 1361, 1362–65 (Fed. Cir. 2012).
148. *EON Corp.*, 785 F.3d at 621.
149. *EON Corp.*, 785 F.3d at 623.
150. *Noah Systems*, 675 F.3d at 1310.
151. However, a standard microprocessor can serve as sufficient structure for functions that can be achieved by any general purpose computer without special programming. *See In re Katz Interactive Call Processing Patent Litig.*, 639 F.3d 1303, 1316–17 (Fed. Cir. 2011) (holding that a standard microprocessor can serve as sufficient structure for functions of a general but not special purpose computer).
152. *See*, e.g., *Athena Diagnostics v. Mayo Collaborative Services*, 927 F. 3d 1333, 1371 (Fed. Cir. 2019) (J. O'Malley, dissenting from *en banc* rehearing) ('I believe that confusion and disagreements over patent eligibility have been engendered by the fact that the Supreme Court has ignored Congress's direction to the courts to apply 35 U.S.C. sections 101, et seq ('Patent Act') as written. Specifically, the Supreme Court has instructed federal courts to read into Section 101 an 'inventive concept' requirement – a baffling standard that Congress removed when it amended the Patent Act in 1952.').

[1] Categories 1–3: Practical Applications

Given the mathematical nature of AI-related inventions in Categories 1–3, the disclosure needs to be prepared with multiple strategies for overcoming different types of eligibility challenges. For example, one strategy may include describing one or more technical problems in the specification within related technology areas. Thus, clear support for the claims reading on a technical solution to a technological problem is one possible basis for patent eligibility. For each problem, the specification may describe how the claimed invention provides specific features that overcome difficulties among prior art solutions for solving the identified problems. Examples of technical solutions may include an improved medical device, an improved data transmission within a computer network, or an improved graphical interface that uses the underlying AI invention.

Even where the AI invention operates within a single technology area, such as medical diagnostics or audio transcription software, the patent disclosure must provide sufficient support for the practical application beyond simply proposing that the AI invention could be 'applied' to this technology area. For an improved medical device, the disclosure may require significant domain knowledge of the relevant medical area, such as types of medical sensors, various medical control devices, and an adequate description of any necessary biophysics or biochemistry for implementing an improved medical device.

For some AI-related inventions, particularly those in Category 3 where a known AI system is applied to a new use case, the operation of the claimed invention may depend largely on the data with which the AI system was trained and/or the data input to the system. Here again, the manner in which the data is disclosed and described must be considered from the perspective of what would be known by a person skilled in the art. For example, there are many commercially available training data sets for a wide variety of applications. If such a training set is used, reference thereto together with an explanation of how it was used should be sufficient for adequate description purposes (together with disclosure of the rest of the claimed invention of course). On the other hand, where the data is not known or publicly available, it is likely that adequate description would require a more detailed explanation of the data so as to enable a skilled person to make and use the invention without undue experimentation.[153] This is similar to the sliding scale of disclosure required for predictable versus non-predictable technologies, discussed next.

[2] Categories 1–3: Predictability of the Relevant Technology

Software technologies used in many AI-related inventions are typically considered predictable arts under US patent law.[154] However, AI-related inventions are often

153. This is the authors' opinion; to the authors' knowledge no court decision has yet been rendered on this point.
154. *See*, e.g., *McRO, supra*, (finding computer animation software to be 'well-developed' and thus predictable for satisfying enablement); *Vasudevan Software, Inc. v. MicroStrategy, Inc.*, 782 F. 3d 671, 682–683 (Fed. Cir. 2015) (reversing a district court's invalidity finding on written description). *But see LizardTech, Inc. v. Earth Resource Mapping, Inc.*, 424 F. 3d

multi-disciplinary inventions that may combine inventor knowledge from both predictable and unpredictable arts.[155] Depending on the type of AI invention, a patent applicant may need to draft the patent disclosure without the certainty of which predictable or unpredictable technology area the claimed invention will fall inside. For a claimed AI invention with a nexus to different technologies, the disclosure should satisfy a level of detail for the written description and enablement requirements for the least predictable technology.

Moreover, the degree to which a particular AI invention builds on preexisting models and algorithms may determine the level of predictability for the AI invention. Because recurrent neural networks have been around for decades, a lower level of disclosure may be necessary under US case law than a newer type of artificial neural network, such as a transformer neural network.[156] For example, a unique algorithmic model may require a heightened detailed description than a novel application of a popular and well-known model type.

For illustration, a machine-learning use case can be relatively straightforward in some instances. For example, an input data set may have a modest number of input variables or familiar structure (e.g., an image). Also, an invention may also use a machine-learning model in a conventional way (e.g., a regression model to process a set of input variables or a convolutional neural net to process an image). As such, it may be well-understood in the technology area for one of ordinary skill in the art to explore different options and arrive at a well performing model. Some software toolkits even facilitate quickly exploring performance of many different types of models by easily facilitating changing hyperparameters, activation functions, learning techniques, and the like. In these cases, the enablement requirement may be satisfied merely by describing the input and output data types and identifying one or more types of models that may be used. On the other hand, in the absence of, for example, a familiar input data structure or a conventional use of a machine-learning model, more detail will certainly be required.

[3] Categories 1–3: Sufficient Structure for Means-Plus-Function Claiming

The black box nature of many AI models invites functional claim language and hence raises the possibility of claim limitations being interpreted under 35 U.S.C. §112(f).[157] Even where the underlying AI technology is in a predictable art such that routine

---

1336 (Fed. Cir. 2005) (finding a software invention failed to satisfy the written description requirement for a non-seamless discrete wavelet transformation ('DWT') algorithm by only describing seamless DWT algorithms in its written description).

155. *See*, e.g., *In re Bd. of Trustees of Leland Stanford Jr. Univ.*, 989 F.3d 1367, 1369 (Fed. Cir. 2021) (describing a machine learning invention based on computing systems and genetics).

156. *See* A. Vaswani et al., 'Attention Is All You Need,' *Advances in Neural Information Processing Systems*, Vol. 30, 2017, *available at* https://arxiv.org/abs/1706.03762.

157. While the use of the word 'means' creates a presumption of §112(f) interpretation and absence of the use of the word 'means' creates the opposite presumption, these are only presumptions. It is, in fact, quite common for USPTO examiners (and US courts) to interpret what they consider to be purely functional limitations using §112(f) even in the absence of the word 'means'.

and well-understood components normally would not need to be described, such components must be described to support interpretations under §112(f).

To illustrate the means-plus-function dilemma, a trained neural network model may include a large number of nodes that are trained on very large input data sets. Thus, it may be incredibly difficult to explain structurally how the trained model processes select inputs to arrive at particular decisions. Further, the model may be trained locally using different data types. Thus, the learned parameters and performance of one trained model may differ from that of another trained model. Therefore, it is no easy task to describe what weights, biases, hyperparameters, and activation functions form the trained model in one particular application. But, without some structural description, claim limitations to the trained model could run afoul of means-plus-function claiming if the model is claimed in terms of its function and if insufficient specificity exists in the specification as to a particular structure/algorithm.

Given that a trained model's input-output relationship may not be directly explainable, one way to show possession of the AI invention is to describe the training. A solid training description may identify input and output data types, a type of model, important hyperparameters (and/or other performance-influencing model characteristics), and specific training algorithms, such as backpropagation algorithms. Furthermore, describing how to collect and use training data can almost always suffice for an adequate description of the training process. For example, a specification may identify the specific hardware and/or software mechanisms that obtain the training data, such as particular sensors, software probes, and how the data is aggregated into a useable form through training and testing a model.

[4] Disclosure Considerations for Categories 4 and 5: Invention Made Using AI and Invention Made by AI

The types of inventions in Categories 4 and 5 ('Inventions Made Using AI' and 'Inventions Made by AI') correspond to inventions identified based on results of an AI model. Here, it is assumed that the claimed invention is the resulting product or process not the system or process by which it was made (otherwise, it would fall under Category 3 as an application of AI). Thus, the operation of the AI model would be irrelevant as to how to make or use the claimed invention. Rather, the factors noted in the above US disclosure requirements sections will be relevant as applied in the field of the resultant invention.

It is important to emphasize that the US requirements for adequacy of disclosure are tied to what is claimed, not the manner in which an invention as made. US law states explicitly: 'patentability shall not be negated by the manner in which the invention was made'.[158] Other than for purposes of determining inventorship (discussed *infra*), the manner in which an invention was made is *irrelevant* for adequacy of disclosure purposes. Consider, for example, a human inventor who uses an AI as a tool (Category 4) to facilitate invention of a novel mechanism for an auto-winding watch. Assuming the claim is to the watch mechanism and not to the method of designing a watch (which would be a Category 3 invention), the specification would need to describe the new auto-winding watch mechanism sufficiently

158. 35 U.S.C. 103.

that a person skilled in the art could make and use that mechanism without undue experimentation. There would be no obligation to even mention in the specification that the inventor had used an AI tool as part of the inventive process (just like there is no obligation to disclose the use of computer-aided design tools or other software tools in various fields).

As explained in the following section, Category 5 AI-related inventions, if they exist, are currently not patentable in the US. Should such inventions become patentable in the future, and unless new disclosure requirements are enacted for such inventions,[159] the analysis of the preceding paragraph would apply equally to claims to Category 5 AI-related inventions.

§18.06 INVENTORSHIP

[A] Inventorship in General

To be considered an inventor on a US patent, one must have contributed to at least one claim of the patent and must have made a significant contribution to the invention's conception. Inventorship is rooted in Article I, Section 8 of the US Constitution and codified in the Patent Act, which provides that '[t]he term "inventor" means the individual or, if a joint invention, the individuals collectively who invented or discovered the subject matter of the invention'.[160] 'Inventors may apply for a patent jointly even though (1) they did not physically work together or at the same time, (2) each did not make the same type or amount of contribution, or (3) each did not make a contribution to the subject matter of every claim of the patent.'[161]

Case law provides additional guidance on inventorship. In determining inventorship, '[t]he threshold question ... is who conceived the invention. Unless a person contributes to the conception of the invention, he is not an inventor.'[162] Joint inventorship is determined by assessing whether each claimed inventor contributed to the inventive concept.[163] To qualify as an inventor, an individual's contribution must be more than just a routine or ordinary task and must involve a significant contribution to the invention's conception. The contribution must also be original and not derived from others.[164] An inventor does not necessarily have to have

159. At the time of writing this chapter there are policy discussions ongoing as to whether there should be some obligation, above and beyond the current requirements of §112, to identify contributions made by AI. See, e.g., 'Request for Comments Regarding Artificial Intelligence and Inventorship,' 88 FR 9492 (14 Feb. 2023), question 6: ('Should the USPTO require applicants to provide an explanation of contributions AI systems made to inventions claimed in patent applications? If so, how should that be implemented, and what level of contributions should be disclosed? Should contributions to inventions made by AI systems be treated differently from contributions made by other (i.e., non-AI) computer systems?').
160. 35 U.S.C. §100(f).
161. 35 U.S.C §116(a).
162. *In re Hardee*, 223 USPQ 1122, 1123 (Comm'r Pat. 1984).
163. *Ethicon, Inc. v. United States Surgical Corp.*, 135 F.3d 1456 (Fed. Cir. 1998).
164. *Bd. of Educ. v. Am. BioScience, Inc.*, 333 F.3d 1330 (Fed. Cir. 2003).

reduced the invention to practice but must have made a significant contribution to the invention's conception.[165]

[B] Determination of Inventorship for AI-Related Inventions

For AI-related inventions in Categories 1, 2 and 4, i.e., inventions of AI itself (e.g., new algorithms or models), inventions of a new AI implementation (e.g., known AI technology plus additional elements), and inventions made using AI, inventorship is assessed like it would be for any other invention, using the law as set forth above.

The same is true for AI-related inventions in Category 3 (applications of AI), however it may be less clear which of multiple humans involved in an AI application development project qualify as inventors under the existing standards. Some 'inventor-like' roles in an AI application development project can be analogized to traditional inventor roles in other fields. For example, a human may have the idea to apply AI to a problem in a particular way, which could be analogized to any other 'tool' that could have been used to address the same problem. Similarly, selecting, arranging, or modifying AI models to use for an intended purpose may be analogized to combining elements into a new circuit. On the other hand, for certain roles of human involvement in AI application development projects, inventorship in the traditional sense is less clear. For example, humans may be involved in obtaining training data or input data (e.g., data collection, selection, labelling, curating), training the model (e.g., parameter optimization), model deployment (e.g., designing for real-world applications), selecting 'inventive' outputs from a larger set of outputs (e.g., some outputs better than others), or humans may recognize 'inventive' unintended outcomes. For these roles, while the legal standard is clear (contribution to at least one claim of the patent and must have made a contribution to the invention's conception), how that standard applies to these 'less traditional' roles is not yet clear as the case law has not yet developed in this area. It can be anticipated that case decisions will be forthcoming in this area and, possibly, additional guidance from the USPTO.

As for AI's place in inventorship, 'the Patent Act requires that inventors must be natural persons; that is, human beings' as held by the Federal Circuit in *Thaler v. Vidal*.[166] When there is no human in a traditional inventor role, and the AI would be considered an inventor if its inventive activity was performed by a human, the invention is not patentable.[167] Therefore, AI-related inventions in Category 5, assuming they exist, would not be patentable in the US. The court in *Thaler*, however, noted it did not address the question of 'whether inventions made by human beings with the *assistance* of AI are eligible for patent protection'.[168] Presumably, 'assistance' here means an action by an AI system (working with a first human) that, if done by a second human, would have qualified that second human as a co-inventor.[169] In

165. *See Ethicon*, 135 F.3d at 1463–1465.
166. *Thaler v. Vidal*, 43 F.4th 1207 (Fed. Cir. 2022) (cert. denied).
167. *See Thaler*, 43 F.4th at 1210.
168. *Thaler*, 43 F.4th at 1213 (emphasis in original).
169. This is presumed because human inventors use tools – both software and not – to assist with making inventions all the time; there is no suggestion that, for example, use of a CAD program should preclude a human inventor from obtaining a patent.

other words, a human-AI co-inventorship situation. It is indeed an open question as to whether, in that instance, a valid patent could be obtained by naming only the human inventor. Policy discussions on this point are ongoing[170] and development of future case law is expected.

§18.07 AREAS FOR FURTHER DEVELOPMENT

The most important area for further development remains a need for clarity and consistency on issues affecting subject matter eligibility. The differences between the eligibility analysis provided in the USPTO Guidance and the analysis performed by the courts presents a scenario where an applicant may be able to show eligibility at the USPTO and obtain a patent, only to have that patent later invalidated by a court applying a different standard. Further, there is little consistency in how the eligibility standard is applied from one district court to the next or even from one panel to the next within the Federal Circuit.[171] This lack of predictability is extremely detrimental to inventors, patent owners, software and AI-related businesses and, ultimately, to the US economy at large.

Moreover, the significant number of judicial decisions affecting each technology underlying AI-related invention makes it essential for any patent applicant to have access to US patent law expert. However, requiring each stakeholder to have a US patent law expert for each technology is an unrealistic requirement. Accordingly, predictable and, to the extent possible, 'bright line' rules for patentability are needed to assist both experts and non-experts in making decisions on developing AI technologies and allotting resources for future research.

In the areas of adequacy of disclosure requirements and determination of inventors for applications of AI (Category 3), while the legal standards appear to be apt, further guidance on both points would be highly beneficial for applicants to avoid later invalidity challenges. Updated guidance from the USPTO, together with development of case law in these areas, will be valuable for future patent applicants.

---

170. See, e.g., 'Request for Comments Regarding Artificial Intelligence and Inventorship,' 88 FR 9492 (14 Feb. 2023), question 3:

 3. If an AI system contributes to an invention at the same level as a human who would be considered a joint inventor, is the invention patentable under current patent laws? For example:
 a. Could 35 U.S.C. 101 and 115 be interpreted such that the Patent Act only requires the listing of the natural person(s) who invent(s), such that inventions with additional inventive contributions from an AI system can be patented as long as the AI system is not listed as an inventor?
 b. Does the current jurisprudence on inventorship and joint inventorship, including the requirement of conception, support the position that only the listing of the natural person(s) who invent(s) is required, such that inventions with additional inventive contributions from an AI system can be patented as long as the AI system is not listed as an inventor?
 c. Does the number of human inventors impact the answer to the questions above?

171. Except when hearing an appeal 'en banc' (with all judges participating), the Federal Circuit normally hears cases using a three-judge 'panel'.

§18.08 RECOMMENDATIONS FOR PATENT APPLICANTS

US patent-eligibility law in the CII space continues to evolve and the case law is only beginning to solidify a framework for addressing artificial intelligence. In particular, several pitfalls already exist for AI-related inventions as shown in the *Stanford I*, *Stanford II*, and *Health Discovery* line of cases. Nevertheless, some practice tips seem clear given the current eligibility framework and general leanings of US courts.

First, patent applications should draft claims and a specification with real world practical applications, such as ones that integrate the AI invention into embodiments that use well-understood, routine, or conventional components. However, having a practical application implemented only with a generic computer processor may not be sufficient. Furthermore, patent applicants should also draft a specification that indicates that the claimed innovation includes superior performance over particular state-of-the-art solutions. If possible, explain why and how such performance benefits can be achieved.

§18.09 CONCLUSION

The current practice at the USPTO with respect to AI-related inventions is a recent evolution from previous struggles in patenting software inventions. However, AI-related inventions also provide unique difficulties that have not yet been answered by US courts. For example, the advanced level of mathematics inherent to many AI-related inventions poses special concerns regarding subject matter eligibility. On the other hand, the multiple, distinct technologies used by many AI-related inventions provides special patent law questions relating to other patentability requirements, such as non-obviousness and written description. Additional uncertainty is added by the several distinct legal entities in the United States that examine patentability using their own special rules for these distinct patent law questions. Certainly, the US law in these areas will continue to evolve.

AIPPI LAW SERIES

1. Sanna Wolk, Kacper Szkalej (eds), *Employees' Intellectual Property Rights*, Second Edition, 2018 (ISBN 978-90-411-9230-1).
2. Jochen Bühling (ed.), *Patent Protection for Second Medical Uses*, Second Edition, 2020 (ISBN 978-94-035-0935-8).
3. Christopher V. Carani (ed.), *Design Rights: Functionality and Scope of Protection*, Second Edition, 2022 (ISBN 978-94-035-3210-3).
4. Eléonore Gaspar (ed.), *Genuine Use of Trademarks*, Second Edition, 2021 (ISBN 978-94-035-2833-5).
5. Jürgen Meier, Oswin Ridderbusch (eds), *Antibody Patenting: A Practitioner's Guide to Drafting, Prosecution and Enforcement*, Second Edition, 2023 (ISBN 978-94-035-3626-2).
6. Christian Czychowski, Jan Bernd Nordemann (eds), *Law of Raw Data*, 2021 (ISBN 978-94-035-3280-6).
7. John C. Todaro, Martin Bensadon, Brigitte Carion-Taravella (eds), *Pharmaceutical Test Data Exclusivity: A Multi-Jurisdictional Survey*, 2022 (ISBN 978-94-035-0106-2).
8. Jonathan P. Osha (ed.), *Artificial Intelligence and Patents: An International Perspective on Patenting AI-Related Inventions*, 2023 (ISBN 978-94-035-2215-9).

www.ingramcontent.com/pod-product-compliance
Lightning Source LLC
LaVergne TN
LVHW020644300926
849161LV00004B/811

Line 14—Other

Itemize on line 14, or on a separate sheet if more space is needed, the beneficiary's tax information not entered elsewhere on Schedule K-1. This includes the allocable share, if any, of:

- Payment of estimated tax to be credited to the beneficiary (section 643(g));
- Tax-exempt interest income received or accrued by the trust (including exempt-interest dividends from a mutual fund or other regulated investment company);
- Investment income (section 163(d));
- Gross farming and fishing income;
- Credit for backup withholding (section 3406);
- The information a beneficiary will need to figure any investment credit;
- The work opportunity credit;
- The welfare-to-work credit;
- The alcohol fuel credit;
- The credit for increasing research activities;
- The low-income housing credit;
- The renewable electricity production credit;
- The empowerment zone employment credit;
- The Indian employment credit;
- The orphan drug credit; and
- The information a beneficiary will need to figure any recapture taxes.

Note: *Upon termination of an estate or trust, any suspended passive activity losses (PALs) relating to an interest in a passive activity cannot be allocated to the beneficiary. Instead, the basis in such activity is increased by the amount of any PALs allocable to the interest, and no losses are allowed as a deduction on the estate's or trust's final Form 1041.*

Form **4970**

Department of the Treasury
Internal Revenue Service

Tax on Accumulation Distribution of Trusts

▶ Attach to beneficiary's tax return.

▶ See instructions on back.

OMB No. 1545-0192

1998

Attachment Sequence No. 73

A Name(s) as shown on return	B Social security number
C Name and address of trust	D Employer identification number

E Type of trust (see instructions) ☐ Domestic ☐ Foreign	F Beneficiary's date of birth	G Enter number of trusts from which you received accumulation distributions in this tax year . . . . ▶	

Part I Average Income and Determination of Computation Years

1	Amount of current distribution that is considered distributed in earlier tax years (from Schedule J (Form 1041), line 37, column (a)).	1	
2	Distributions of income accumulated before you were born or reached age 21	2	
3	Subtract line 2 from line 1	3	
4	Taxes imposed on the trust on amounts from line 3 (from Schedule J (Form 1041), line 37, column (b))	4	
5	Total (add lines 3 and 4)	5	
6	Tax-exempt interest included on line 5 (from Schedule J (Form 1041), line 37, column (c)) . . .	6	
7	Taxable part of line 5 (subtract line 6 from line 5)	7	
8	Number of trust's earlier tax years in which amounts on line 7 are considered distributed . . .	8	
9	Average annual amount considered distributed (divide line 3 by line 8) . . 9		
10	Multiply line 9 by .25 10		
11	Number of earlier tax years to be taken into account (see instructions)	11	
12	Average amount for recomputing tax (divide line 7 by line 11). Enter here and in each column on line 15	12	

		(a) 1997	(b) 1996	(c) 1995	(d) 1994	(e) 1993
13	Enter your taxable income before this distribution for the 5 immediately preceding tax years					

Part II Tax Attributable to the Accumulation Distribution

			(a) 19......	(b) 19......	(c) 19......
14	Enter the amounts from line 13, eliminating the highest and lowest taxable income years	14			
15	Enter amount from line 12 in each column	15			
16	Recomputed taxable income (add lines 14 and 15)	16			
17	Income tax on amounts on line 16	17			
18	Income tax before credits on line 14 income	18			
19	Additional tax before credits (subtract line 18 from line 17) . .	19			
20	Tax credit adjustment	20			
21	Subtract line 20 from line 19	21			
22	Alternative minimum tax adjustments	22			
23	Combine lines 21 and 22	23			

24	Add columns (a), (b), and (c), line 23	24	
25	Divide the line 24 amount by 3	25	
26	Multiply the amount on line 25 by the number of years on line 11	26	
27	Enter the amount from line 4	27	
28	Partial tax attributable to the accumulation distribution (subtract line 27 from 26) (If zero or less, enter-0-)	28	

General Instructions

Section references are to the Internal Revenue Code unless otherwise noted.

Changes To Note

For tax years beginning after August 5, 1997, the tax on accumulation distributions from trusts does not apply to most domestic trusts. The tax continues to apply to foreign trusts, certain domestic trusts that were once foreign trusts, and certain domestic trusts created before March 1, 1984. For more information, see section 665(c).

Important: If you received an accumulation distribution from a foreign trust, you must report the distribution and the partial tax on a 1998 Form 3520, Annual Return To Report Transactions With Foreign Trusts and Receipt of Certain Foreign Gifts. DO NOT file Form 4970 for distributions from any foreign trust, except to attach it as a worksheet to Form 3520 if those instructions direct you to. If the distributions are from a domestic trust that used to be a foreign trust, see Rev. Rul. 91-6, 1991-1 C.B. 89.

Purpose of Form

If you are the beneficiary of a trust that accumulated its income, instead of distributing it currently, use Form 4970 to figure the partial tax under section 667. The fiduciary notifies the beneficiary of an "accumulation distribution" by completing Part IV of Schedule J (Form 1041).

Thus, if you received a distribution for this tax year from a trust that accumulated its income, instead of distributing it each year (and the trust paid taxes on that income), you must complete Form 4970 to compute any additional tax liability. The trustee must give you a completed Part IV of Schedule J (Form 1041) so you can complete this form.

If you received accumulation distributions from more than one trust during the current tax year, prepare a separate Form 4970 for each trust from which you received an accumulation distribution. You can arrange the distributions in any order you want them considered to have been made.

Definitions

Undistributed Net Income (UNI). Undistributed net income is the distributable net income (DNI) of the trust for any tax year less: (1) the amount of income required to be distributed currently and any other amounts properly paid or credited or required to be distributed to beneficiaries in the tax year; and (2) the taxes imposed on the trust attributable to such DNI.

Accumulation Distribution. An accumulation distribution is the excess of amounts properly paid, credited, or required to be distributed (other than income required to be distributed currently) over the DNI of the trust reduced by income required to be distributed currently.

Generally, except for tax-exempt interest, the distribution loses its character upon distribution to the beneficiary. See section 667(d) for special rules for foreign trusts.

Specific Instructions

Item E-Type of Trust. If you received an accumulation distribution from a foreign trust, see Changes To Note above. Do Not file this form other than as an attachment to Form 3520.

Line 1. For a nonresident alien or foreign corporation, include only the part of the accumulation distribution that is attributable to U.S. sources or is effectively connected with a trade or business carried on in the United States.

Line 2. Enter any amount from line 1 that represents UNI of a domestic trust accumulated before you were born or reached age 21. However, if the multiple trust rule applies, see the instructions for line 4.

Line 4—Multiple Trust Rule. If you received accumulation distributions from two or more other trusts that were considered to have been made in any of the earlier tax years in which the current accumulation distribution is considered to have been made, do not include on line 4 the taxes attributable to the current accumulation distribution considered to have been distributed in the same earlier tax year(s).

For this special rule, only count as trusts those trusts for which the sum of this accumulation distribution and any earlier accumulation distributions from the trust, which are considered under section 666(a) to have been distributed in the same earlier tax year, is $1,000 or more.

Foreign Trust. If the trust is a foreign trust, see section 665(d)(2).

Line 8. You can determine the number of years in which the UNI is deemed to have been distributed by counting the "throwback years" for which there are entries on lines 32 through 36 of Part IV of Schedule J (Form 1041). These throwback rules apply even if you would not have been entitled to receive a distribution in the earlier tax year if the distribution had actually been made then. There can be more than 5 "throwback years."

Line 11. From the number of years entered on line 8, subtract any year in which the distribution from column (a), Part IV of Schedule J (Form 1041) is less than the amount on line 10 of Form 4970. If the distribution for each throwback year is more than line 10, then enter the same number on line 11 as you entered on line 8.

Line 13. Enter your taxable incomes for years 1993–1997, even if less than 5 years of the trust had accumulated income after you became 21. Use the taxable income as reported by you or as changed by the IRS. Include in the taxable income amounts considered distributed in that year as a result of prior accumulation distributions, whether from the same or another trust, and whether made in an earlier year or the current year.

If your taxable income as adjusted is less than zero, enter zero.

Line 17. Figure the income tax (not including any alternative minimum tax (AMT)) on the income on line 16 using the tax rates in effect for your particular earlier tax year shown in each of the three columns. Use the Tax Rate Schedules, etc., as applicable. You can get the Tax Rate Schedules and earlier year forms from many IRS offices or by calling 1-800-TAX-FORM (1-800-829-3676).

Line 18. Enter your income tax (not including any AMT) as originally reported, corrected, or amended, before reduction for any credits for your particular earlier year shown in each of the three columns.

Line 20. Nonrefundable credits that are limited to tax liability, such as the general business credit, may be changed because of an accumulation distribution. If the total allowable credits for any of the 3 computation years increases, enter the increase on line 20. However, do not treat as an increase the part of the credit that was allowable as a carryback or carryforward credit in the current or any preceding year other than the computation year.

To refigure these credits, you must consider changes to the tax before credits for each of the 3 computation years due to previous accumulation distributions.

If the accumulation distribution is from a domestic trust that paid foreign income taxes, the limitation on the foreign tax credit under section 904 is applied separately to the accumulation distribution. If the distribution is from a foreign trust, see sections 667(d) and 904(f)(4) for special rules.

Attach the proper form for any credit you refigure. The amount determined for items on this line is limited to tax law provisions in effect for those years involved.

Line 22. Use and attach a separate Form 4626, Form 6251, or the AMT schedule for Form 1041 to recompute the AMT for each earlier year and show any change in those taxes in the bottom margin of the forms or schedules. Enter the adjustments on this line.

Line 28. If estate taxes or generation-skipping transfer taxes apply to the accumulation distribution, reduce the partial tax proportionately for those taxes. See section 667(b)(6) for the computation.

Individuals. Include the amount from this line on line 56, Form 1040. Write "ADT" to the left of the line 56 entry space.

Trusts and Decedents' Estates. Include the amount on line 1b, Schedule G, Form 1041.

Other Filers. Add the result to the total tax liability before credits on your income tax return for the year of the accumulation distribution. Attach this form to that return.

Paperwork Reduction Act Notice. We ask for the information on this form to carry out the Internal Revenue laws of the United States. You are required to give us the information. We need it to ensure that you are complying with these laws and to allow us to figure and collect the right amount of tax.

You are not required to provide the information requested on a form that is subject to the Paperwork Reduction Act unless the form displays a valid OMB control number. Books or records relating to a form or its instructions must be retained as long as their contents may become material in the administration of any Internal Revenue law. Generally, tax returns and return information are confidential, as required by section 6103.

The time needed to complete and file this form will vary depending on individual circumstances. The estimated average time is:

Recordkeeping	1 hr., 12 min.
Learning about the law or the form	16 min.
Preparing the form	1 hr., 27 min.
Copying, assembling, and sending the form to the IRS	20 min.

If you have comments concerning the accuracy of these time estimates or suggestions for making this form simpler, we would be happy to hear from you. See the instructions of the tax return with which this form is filed.

Department of the Treasury

TD F 90-22.1

SUPERSEDES ALL PREVIOUS EDITIONS

REPORT OF FOREIGN BANK AND FINANCIAL ACCOUNTS

Do **NOT** file with your Federal Tax Return

FinCEN

OMB No. 1505-0063

1

1 Filing for Calendar Year Y Y Y Y

2 Type of Filer a ☐ Individual b ☐ Partnership c ☐ Corporation d ☐ Fiduciary

3 Taxpayer Identification Number

Part I Filer Information

4 Last Name or Organization Name | 5 First Name | 6 Middle Initial

7 Address (Number, Street, and Apt. or Suite No.) | 8 Date of Birth M M D D Y Y Y Y

9 City | 10 State | 11 Zip/Postal Code | 12 Country | 13 Title (Not necessary if reporting a personal account)

14 Are these account jointly owned? a ☐ Yes b ☐ No | 15 Number of joint owners | 16 Taxpayer Identification Number of joint owner (if known)

17 Last Name or Organization Name | 18 First Name | 19 Middle Initial

Part II Information on Financial Accounts

20 Number of Foreign Financial Accounts in which a financial interest is held

21 Type of account a ☐ Bank b ☐ Securities c ☐ Other ______________________

22 Maximum value of account
a ☐ Under $10,000 c ☐ $100,000 to $1,000,000
b ☐ $10,000 to $99,999 d ☐ Over $1,000,000

23 Account Number or other designation

24 Name of Financial Institution with which account is held | 25 Country in which account is held

26 Does the filer have a financial interest in this account? a ☐ Yes b ☐ No If no, complete boxes 27-35.

27 Last Name or Organization Name of Account Owner

28 First Name | 29 Middle Initial | 30 Taxpayer Identification Number

31 Address (Number, Street, and Apt. or Suite No.) | 32 City

33 State | 34 Zip/Postal Code | 35 Country

36 Signature | 37 Date M M D D Y Y Y Y

This form should be used to report a financial interest in, signature authority, or other authority over one or more financial accounts in foreign countries, as required by the Department of the Treasury Regulations (31 CFR 103). No report is required if the aggregate value of the accounts did not exceed $10,000. **SEE INSTRUCTIONS FOR DEFINITION.** File this form with:

U.S. Department of the Treasury, P.O. Box 32621, Detroit, MI 48232-0621.

PRIVACY ACT NOTIFICATION

Pursuant to the requirements of Public Law 93-579 (Privacy Act of 1974), notice is hereby given that the authority to collect information on TD F 90-22.1in accordance with 5 USC 552a(e) is Public Law 91-508; 31 USC 5314; 5 USC 301; 31 CFR 103.

The principal purpose for collecting the information is to assure maintenance of reports where such reports or records have a high degree of usefulness in criminal, tax, or regulatory investigations or proceedings. The information collected may be provided to those officers and employees of any constituent unit of the Department of the Treasury who have a need for the records in the performance of their duties. The records may be referred to any other department or agency of the United States upon the request of the head of such department or agency for use in a criminal, tax, or regulatory investigation or proceeding.

Disclosure of this information is mandatory. Civil and criminal penalties, including certain circumstances a fine of not more than $500,000 and imprisonment of not more than five years, are provided for failure to file a report, supply information, and for filing a false or fraudulent report.

Disclosure of the Social Security number is mandatory. The authority to collect is 31 CFR 103. The Social Security number will be used as a means to identify the individual who files the report.

Continuation Page

Form TD F 90-22.1

This side can be copied as many times as necessary in order to provide information on all accounts.

1 Filing for Calendar Year	3 Taxpayer Identification Number	4 Filer Last Name or Business Name	Page Number
Y Y Y Y			OF

2 Type of Filer	21 Type of Account	22 Maximum Value of Account
a ☐ Individual c ☐ Corporation b ☐ Partnership d ☐ Fiduciary	a ☐ Bank c ☐ Other b ☐ Securities	a ☐ Under $10,000 c ☐ $100,000 to $1,000,000 b ☐ $10,000 to $99,999 d ☐ Over $1,000,000

23 Account Number or other designation	24 Name of Financial Institution with which account is held

25 Country in which account is held	26 Does the filer have a financial interest in this account? a ☐ Yes b ☐ No If no, complete boxes 27-35.	27 Last Name or Organization Name of Account Owner

28 First Name	29 Middle Initial	30 Taxpayer Identification Number	31 Address (Number, Street, and Apt. or Suite No.)

32 City	33 State	34 Zip/Postal Code	35 Country

2 Type of Filer	21 Type of Account	22 Maximum Value of Account
a ☐ Individual c ☐ Corporation b ☐ Partnership d ☐ Fiduciary	a ☐ Bank c ☐ Other b ☐ Securities	a ☐ Under $10,000 c ☐ $100,000 to $1,000,000 b ☐ $10,000 to $99,999 d ☐ Over $1,000,000

23 Account Number or other designation	24 Name of Financial Institution with which account is held

25 Country in which account is held	26 Does the filer have a financial interest in this account? a ☐ Yes b ☐ No If no, complete boxes 27-35.	27 Last Name or Organization Name of Account Owner

28 First Name	29 Middle Initial	30 Taxpayer Identification Number	31 Address (Number, Street, and Apt. or Suite No.)

32 City	33 State	34 Zip/Postal Code	35 Country

2 Type of Filer	21 Type of Account	22 Maximum Value of Account
a ☐ Individual c ☐ Corporation b ☐ Partnership d ☐ Fiduciary	a ☐ Bank c ☐ Other b ☐ Securities	a ☐ Under $10,000 c ☐ $100,000 to $1,000,000 b ☐ $10,000 to $99,999 d ☐ Over $1,000,000

23 Account Number or other designation	24 Name of Financial Institution with which account is held

25 Country in which account is held	26 Does the filer have a financial interest in this account? a ☐ Yes b ☐ No If no, complete boxes 27-35.	27 Last Name or Organization Name of Account Owner

28 First Name	29 Middle Initial	30 Taxpayer Identification Number	31 Address (Number, Street, and Apt. or Suite No.)

32 City	33 State	34 Zip/Postal Code	35 Country

This form should be used to report a financial interest in, signature authority, or other authority over one or more financial accounts in foreign countries, as required by the Department of the Treasury Regulations (31 CFR 103). No report is required if the aggregate value of the accounts did not exceed $10,000. **SEE INSTRUCTIONS FOR DEFINITION.** File this form with:

U.S. Department of the Treasury, P.O. Box 32621, Detroit, MI 48232-0621.

Paperwork Reduction Act. The estimated average burden associated with this collection of information is 10 minutes per respondent or recordkeeper, depending on individual circumstances. Comments regarding the accuracy of this burden estimate, and suggestions for reducing the burden should be directed to the Department of the Treasury, Financial Crimes Enforcement Network, Suite 200, 2070 Chain Bridge Road, Vienna VA 22182-2536.

INSTRUCTIONS

General Instructions

Who Must File this Report Each United States person, who has a financial interest in or signature authority, or other authority over any financial accounts, including bank, securities, or other types of financial accounts in a foreign country, if the aggregate value of these financial accounts exceeds $10,000 at any time during the calendar year, must report that relationship each calendar year by filing TD F 90-22.1 with the Department of the Treasury on or before June 30, of the succeeding year.

Exceptions

An officer or employee of a bank which is subject to the supervision of the Comptroller of the Currency, the Board of Governors of the Federal Reserve System, the Office of Thrift Supervision, or the Federal Deposit Insurance Corporation need not report that he has signature or other authority over a foreign bank, securities or other financial account maintained by the bank, if the officer or employee has NO personal financial interest in the account.

An officer or employee of a domestic corporation whose equity securities are listed upon national securities exchanges or which has assets exceeding $10 million and 500 or more shareholders of record need not file such a report concerning the other signature authority over a foreign financial account of the corporation, if he has NO personal financial interest in the account and he has been advised in writing by the chief financial officer of the corporation that the corporation has filed a current report, which includes that account.

Report any financial account (except a military banking facility as defined in these instructions) that is located in a foreign country, even if it is held at an affiliate of a United States bank or other financial institution. Do not report any account maintained with a branch, agency, or other office of a foreign bank of other institution that is located in the United States, Guam, Puerto Rico, and the Virgin Islands.

General Definitions

United States Person The term "United States person" means (1) a citizen or resident of the United States, (2) a domestic partnership, (3) a domestic corporation, or (4) a domestic estate or trust.

Financial Account Generally includes any bank, securities, securities derivatives or other financial instruments accounts. Such accounts generally also encompass any accounts in which the assets are held in a commingled fund, and the account owner holds an equity interest in the fund. The term also means any savings, demand, checking, deposit, time deposit, or any other account maintained with a financial institution or other person engaged in the business of a financial institution.

Account in a Foreign Country A "foreign country" includes all geographical areas located outside the United States, Guam, Puerto Rico, and the Virgin Islands.

Financial Interest A financial interest in a bank, securities, or other financial account in a foreign country means an interest described in either of the following two paragraphs:

(1) A United States person has a financial interest in each account for which such person is the owner of record or has legal title, whether the account is maintained for his or her own benefit or for the benefit of others including non-United States persons. It an account is maintained in the name of two persons jointly, or if several persons each own a partial interest in an account, each of those United States persons has a financial interest in that account.

(2) A United States person has a financial interest in each bank, securities, or other financial account in a foreign country for which the owner of record or holder of legal title is: (a) a person acting as an agent, nominee, attorney, or in some other capacity on behalf of the U.S. person; (b) a corporation in which the United States person owns directly or indirectly more than 50 percent of the total value of shares of stock; (c) a partnership in which the United States person owns an interest in more than 50 percent of the profits (distributive share of income); or (d) a trust in which the United States person either has a present beneficial interest in more than 50 percent of the assets or from which such person receives more than 50 percent of the current income.

Signature or Other Authority Over an Account A person has signature authority over an account if such person can control the disposition of money or other property in it by delivery of a document containing his or here signature (or his or her signature and that of one or more other persons) to the bank or other person with whom the account is maintained.

Other authority exists in a person who can exercise comparable power over an account by direct communication to the bank or other person with whom the account is maintained, either orally or by some other means.

Military Banking Facility Do not consider as an account in a foreign country, an account in an institution known as a "United States military banking facility" (or "United States military finance facility") operated by a United States financial institution designated by the United States Government to serve U.S. Government installations abroad, even if the United States military banking facility is located in a foreign country.

Filing Information

When and Where to File -This report must be filed on or before June 30 each calendar year with the Department of the Treasury, Post Office Box 32621, Detroit, MI 48232-0621, or it may be hand carried to any local office of the Internal Revenue Service for forwarding to the Department of the Treasury, Detroit, MI.

EXPLANATIONS FOR SPECIFIC ITEMS

Consolidated Reporting

A corporation which owns directly or indirectly more than 50 percent interest in one or more other entities will be permitted to file a consolidated report on TD F 90-22.1, on behalf of itself and such other entities provided that a listing of them is made part of the consolidated report. Such reports should be signed by an authorized official of the parent corporation.

If the group of entities covered by a consolidated report has a financial interest in 25 or more foreign financial accounts, the reporting corporation need only note that fact on the form in Item 20. It will, however, be required to provide detailed information concerning each account when so requested by the Secretary or his delegate.

Item 14

If the filer owns the account jointly with any other party, then yes should be marked.

Item 15

If the filer holds this account with only one (1) other party, and all accounts listed are held jointly with that party, then complete items 16, 17, 18 and 19. Otherwise, leave these items blank.

Item 20

If the filer holds a financial interest in more than 25 foreign financial accounts, indicate the number in this box and do not complete any further items in Part II.

Any person who lists more than 25 foreign financial accounts in item 20 must when requested by the Department of the Treasury provide all the information called for in Part II.

Item 22
Account Valuation

For item 22, the maximum value of an account is the largest amount of currency and non-monetary assets that appear on any quarterly or more frequent account statement issued for the applicable year. If periodic account statements are not so issued, the maximum account asset value is the largest amount of currency and non-monetary assets in the account at any time during the year. Convert foreign currency by using the official exchange rate at the end of the year. In valuing currency of a country that uses multiple exchange rates, use the rate which would apply if the currency in the account were converted into United States dollars at the close of the calendar year.

The value of stock, other securities or other non-monetary assets in an account reported on TD F 90-22.1 is the fair market value at the end of the calendar year, or if withdrawn from the account, at the time of the withdrawal.

For purposes of item 22, if you had a financial interest in more than one account, each account is to be valued separately in accordance with the foregoing two paragraphs. If you had a financial interest in one or more but fewer than 25 accounts, and you are unable to determine whether the maximum value of these accounts exceeded $10,000 at any time during the year, complete Part II or III for each of these accounts.

Item 26

United States Persons with Authority Over but No Financial Interest In an Account - Except as provided in the following paragraph, you must state the name, address, and identifying number of each owner of an account over which you had authority, but if you complete items 27-35 for more than one account of the same owner, you need identify the owner only once. If you complete items 27-35 for one or more accounts in which no United States person had a financial interest, you may state on the first line of this item, in lieu of supplying information about the owner, "No U.S. person had any financial interest in the foreign accounts." This statement must be based upon the actual belief of the person filing this form after he or she has taken reasonable-measures to endure its correctness.

If you complete Part II for accounts owned by a domestic corporation and its domestic and/or foreign subsidiaries, you may treat them as one owner and write in the space provided, the name of the parent corporation, followed by "and related entities," and the identifying number and address of the parent corporation.

Item 36

Signature

This report must be signed by the person named in Part I. If the report is being filed on behalf of a partnership, corporation, or fiduciary, it must be signed by an authorized individual.

Penalties

For criminal penalties for failure to file a report, supply information, and for filing a false or fraudulent report see 31 U.S.C. 5322(a), 31 U.S.C. 5322(b), and 18 U.S.C. 1001.